THE POLITICS OF THE COMMUNICATIONS
REVOLUTION IN WESTERN EUROPE

The Politics of the Communications Revolution in Western Europe

Edited by
KENNETH DYSON
and
PETER HUMPHREYS

FRANK CASS

First published in 1986 in Great Britain by
FRANK CASS AND COMPANY LIMITED
Gainsborough House, Gainsborough Road,
London E11 1RS, England

and in the United States of America by
FRANK CASS AND COMPANY LIMITED
c/o Biblio Distribution Center
81 Adams Drive, P.O. Box 327, Totowa, NJ 07511

Copyright © 1986 Frank Cass & Co. Ltd.

British Library Cataloguing in Publication Data
The Politics of the communications
 revolution in Western Europe.
 1. Telecommunications—Political aspects—
 Europe
 I. Dyson, Kenneth H.F.   II. Humphreys, Peter
 384'.094   HE8084

ISBN 0-7146-3284-8

This group of studies first appeared in a Special Issue on 'The politics of the communications revolution in Western Europe' of *West European Politics*, Vol. 9, No. 4, October 1986, published by Frank Cass & Co. Ltd.

All rights reserved. No part of this publication may be reproduced, stored in a retrieval system or transmitted in any form or by any means, electronic, mechanical, photocopying, recording or otherwise, without the prior permission of Frank Cass and Company Limited.

Printed in Great Britain by

Printing by Adlard & Son Ltd, Dorking, Surrey

CONTENTS

Notes on the Contributors	vi
Editors' Preface	viii
Introduction	1
West European States and the Communications Revolution *Kenneth Dyson*	10
Divergent Paths: Political Strategies for Telecommunications in Britain, France and West Germany *Kevin Morgan and Douglas Webber*	56
Policy, Politics and the Communications Revolution in Sweden *Jeremy Richardson*	80
Policies for New Media in Western Europe: Deregulation of Broadcasting and Multi-media Diversification *Kenneth Dyson and Peter Humphreys*	98
Law, Politics and the New Media: Trends in Broadcasting Regulation *Wolfgang Hoffmann-Riem*	125
European Collaboration in Computing and Telecommunications: A Policy Approach *Claire Shearman*	147
Legitimating the Communications Revolution: Governments, Parties and Trade Unions in Britain, France and West Germany *Peter Humphreys*	163
Policing the Communications Revolution: A Case Study of Data Protection Legislation *Colin Mellors and David Pollitt*	195
Abstracts	212
Appendix 1: Glossary	216
Appendix 2: Tables	221
Index	225

Notes on Contributors

Kenneth Dyson is Professor of European Studies at the University of Bradford, Chairman of its Postgraduate School of Languages and European Studies, and a founder member and past chairman of the Association for the Study of German Politics. He is author of *Party, State and Bureaucracy in West Germany* (1977), *The State Tradition in Western Europe* (1981), *Industrial Crisis* (with S. Wilks, 1983), *European Detente* (1986) and *Policy, Politics and New Media in Western Europe* (1987), as well as of numerous articles and contributions to books on comparative public policy and the history of political ideas and institutions. At present he heads an ESRC research project on satellite and cable broadcasting regulation in Western Europe.

Wolfgang Hoffmann-Riem is Director of the Hans-Bredow Institute for Radio and Television and Professor of Public Law at the University of Hamburg. He has written extensively on West German and American media policies and served as an adviser on new media policies in West Germany.

Peter Humphreys is Research Officer on an ESRC research project on satellite and cable broadcasting regulation in Western Europe, based in the School of European Studies at the University of Bradford. He has written a number of articles on new media policies in Britain, France and West Germany and is co-editor (with Kenneth Dyson) of *Policy, Politics and New Media in Western Europe* (1987).

Colin Mellors is Senior Lecturer in the School of European Studies at the University of Bradford. He has written extensively on local government (notably *Promoting Local Authorities in the European Community*, 1986), legislatures (notably *The British MP*), coalition politics and public policy.

Kevin Morgan is a Research Fellow at the University of Sussex. He has written a number of articles on state policy with respect to regional development and advanced technology-based industries. In collaboration with Andrew Sayer he is the author of *Microcircuits of Capital: 'Sunrise' Industry and Uneven Development* (1986).

David Pollitt is a journalist based in Manchester and has written on privacy and data protection.

Jeremy Richardson is Professor of Politics at the University of Strathclyde. He has written extensively on public policy, notably *Policy Styles in Western Europe* (1983) and (with Jordan) *Governing Under Pressure* (1981).

Claire Shearman is a Research Officer on the ESRC Competitiveness project in the School of Management and Organisational Sciences at the University of Lancaster. She has published several articles and papers on European collaboration in advanced technologies.

Douglas Webber is a Research Fellow in the School of Social Sciences at the University of Sussex. He has written numerous articles on various aspects of West European politics, including West European Social Democracy, the SPD, and the politics of employment policy and relations between the state and organised business interests in the Federal Republic of Germany.

Editors' Preface

Western Europe's web of communications is undergoing complex and profound changes under the impact of new technologies (notably satellite, cable and computers), ideological change and pressures from new fast expanding international markets. In the process industrial and cultural interests are converging and colliding; boundaries between traditionally distinct sectors are being eroded; national frontiers are of decreasing relevance; and traditional cultural identities are threatened. The consequence is that communications have become of major political significance, and a whole range of new policy initiatives have emerged in Western Europe.

This volume provides a collection of empirical studies of the politics of the 'communications revolution' in those West European states that have powerful and influential broadcasting and telecommunications industries. Its principal aim is to examine the relative impact on public policies in these two areas of ideology and politics, on the one hand, and technology and markets, on the other.

The study has two major, overlapping aspects. First, the authors address a set of key policy issues raised by the communications revolution – deregulation, European collaboration, multimedia diversification, legitimation and civil liberties. How have West European governments tackled these issues? To what extent is there convergence or divergence in their political and policy responses? What lessons for policy can be drawn from analysing West European responses to these policy issues?

The second aspect concerns the character of the policy processes associated with the communications revolution and their political context. What factors have shaped the political agenda of broadcasting and telecommunications in Western Europe? What has been the impact of political ideologies and government policies? What changes have taken place in power relationships in broadcasting and telecommunications policy sectors? Who are the main actors; what are their motivations? Do domestic policy-makers simply ratify 'necessary' changes imposed by international markets? These are the sorts of questions with which this volume is concerned.

Introduction

In the early 1980s a series of dramatic events brought home to West Europeans the power and potential of 'the communications revolution'. At first glance these events seem to bear little relationship to each other. In his now famous 'Star Wars' speech of March 1983 President Ronald Reagan articulated a radically new vision of national security. A ballistic missile defence system was to be provided by laser battle stations located on 'killer' satellites and by anti-satellite weapons. The Strategic Defence Initiative (SDI) opened up a major new conflict in the Atlantic Alliance.[1] In November 1984 just over half of British Telecom was sold to private investors for almost £4 billion in the world's largest stock market flotation. Investors were enticed by a picture of BT as the flagship for Britain's information technology. As a consequence of this privatisation measure, Britain emerged – alongside the United States – as a communications policy model for Western Europe. Deregulation and privatisation of BT, in the wake of deregulation and the divestiture of American Telephone and Telegraph (AT and T) in the United States, seemed to indicate that an Anglo-American axis was forming in communications policy with major implications for the rest of Western Europe.[2] The 'Live Aid' concert in July 1985 offered an altogether different concept. Concert performers and audiences around the world were linked together by satellites in a new kind of 'live' international effort for famine relief. For a few brief hours a 'one world' inspired by altruism flickered to life. In November 1985 President François Mitterrand caused a major political storm in France when, after secret negotiations, he suddenly announced that he had decided to allocate channel capacity on France's forthcoming direct broadcasting satellite (DBS) to Silvio Berlusconi, the Italian private television magnate, and to Robert Maxwell, the British newspaper proprietor.[3] Meanwhile, Berlusconi along with Jérôme Seydoux, a close friend of Mitterrand, was enabled to launch his proposed channel as France's first national 'off-air' private television service. A major part of the rationale for this action was to impede the ambitions of Rupert Murdoch's London-based News International in the field of private commercial satellite broadcasting. By September 1985 Murdoch's Sky Channel, which provided an advertising-financed general entertainment service, was already available by satellite to more than four million 'cabled' homes in Western Europe and growing rapidly. Then in April 1986 the new centre-right government in France reversed this 'socialist' policy in the so-called 'sale of the century' when it announced the intention of putting out to tender the three DBS channels in July (as well as one state-owned channel, the two privately-owned national channels allocated by Mitterrand – that is the Berlusconi/Seydoux channel and a music channel – and some local stations).

The connecting thread among these otherwise disparate events was that they provided visible evidence of a revolution in the making, a revolution with dramatic and various potentials. Invisibly, at least to the general public, the communications revolution had been gathering pace over two decades and more. Between 1958 and 1984 some 2000 satellites had been placed in orbit for military purposes, some two-thirds of all satellites launched.[4] They had been joined by general communications satellites for telephone, radio and television communications, by weather satellites, by navigation satellites and by earth-mapping satellites. In 1963 the United States had launched the first geostationary satellite. By being in orbit some 36000 km above the equator – in geostationary orbit – these satellites move at the same velocity as the earth. Hence they appear to hover above a fixed point on the globe's surface and can provide continuous communications. By 1984 there were some 120 satellites in this geostationary orbit; about 80 of these were commercial communications satellites. National participation in, and share of, this orbit emerged as a new indicator of power. The United States accounted for 47, the Soviet Union 30, Intelsat 17, the European Space Agency (ESA) 6, Japan 6, and Britain, France, Italy and France/Germany (joint) one each. With an annual growth rate of 18 per cent in geostationary satellites the International Telecommunications Union (ITU), a technical agency of the United Nations, was confronted with a major threat of overcrowding and problems of allocation, not least when the commercial scramble to take advantage of DBS (direct broadcasting by satellite) begins. Significant change was taking place in the capacity of individual satellites as well as in their number. Thus when Intelsat I (Early Bird), the world's first commercial communications satellite, was launched in 1965 its capacity was 240 telephone circuits. Intelsat 5 in 1980 had capacity for some 12,000 telephone circuits and double the capacity for television transmission.

Satellites were just one dimension of the international communications revolution. By the 1980s digital switching equipment and optic fibre cable were being installed and promising many more channels and greater speed and efficiency of transmission. Also, they enhanced the capabilities of the telecommunications system in the form initially of new audiovisual services (telematics), marrying computing with telecommunications, and ultimately of an integrated services digital network (ISDN), through which telephony, telematics, radio and television could be delivered in a single 'broadband' communications system.[5] Massive investment was required in telecommunications networks in order to create the infrastructure for this new 'wired society'; and huge markets were opening up for those who could provide the new equipment and services. There were, in turn, enormous implications for the structure of employment, work, urban living, transport, cultural production and family life. The outcome would be more than just new products and services. Increased productivity and higher employment and growth throughout the economy seemed possible.[6] The 'third industrial revolution' appeared to be beginning; an opportunity to 'escape the crisis' seemed available.

Though the basic new communications technologies and services are described in a separate glossary (see page 216), it makes some sense to outline the major developments at this stage as basic background. Telecommunications has been developing away from the traditional telephony services towards audiovisual communications, with new 'broadband' cable and satellite technologies carrying data and visual images as well as voice. The first indicators of this development could be found in the growth of 'local area networks' (LANs) for fast and efficient transmission of data, including electronic mail, from terminal to terminal in office blocks; of 'value-added networks' (VANs), in which the operator 'adds value' to information in the form of such new services as electronic mail, financial information and transactions, 'cashless' shopping, 'cashless' banking, travel reservations and microcomputing services on the telecommunications network; and, as a form of VAN, of the videotex systems operated by national telecommunications authorities (Prestel in Britain, Teletel in France and *Bildschirmtext* in West Germany). Videotex enables consumers to consult computer data bases for various services using the telephone line and the television screen. A confusion of public and private videotex/VANs systems has emerged in Western Europe. Sometimes private systems are incorporated into the public videotex system (as 'closed user groups'); other times they are organised separately by leasing lines from the PTT (the national telecommunications authority), whether by the users themselves (such corporate giants as IBM and British Leyland) or by 'information providers' (like Reuters). Public videotex developed most strikingly in France where, by the beginning of 1986, some one million Minitel terminals offered access to over 1,000 information services. On the other hand, the overall VANs market seemed to have developed more vigorously in Britain where, in addition to Prestel, some 700 VANs had been licensed since the Telecommunications Act of 1981.

The eventual aim of the European PTTs was an ISDN. By using large bandwidth cable and electronic switching it becomes possible to transmit signals digitally (voice and date being represented by discrete pulses of electricity or light and transmitted using clever timing routines) rather than in analogue fashion (frequency modulation). Much more information can be passed with greater efficiency and without interference, thus enabling the integration of voice with data and pictures and of a large range of audio-visual communications (including cable television) in a single digitalised network. At that stage the 'electronic cottage' and the 'electronic office' with their LANs can be linked into a national and indeed international electronic highways system.

Greater choice in communications was also becoming apparent as broadcasting evolved under the impact of cable and satellite.[7] By 1986 multichannel cable systems, albeit using old-fashioned cable, were available throughout most of Belgium and the Netherlands and expanding fast in West Germany where the Bundespost was implementing a huge copper-coaxial cable programme. Satellite programmes in increasing number were being fed into European cable systems from communications satellites, programmes like Sky Channel and Music Box from London, RTL Plus, SAT 1 and 3 SAT in German, TV5 in French and Europa TV. Attempts to develop local community programming and open access programming in some cable systems pointed towards a future of 'narrowcasting' that catered for specialised audiences rather than the 'mass' audiences of traditional broadcasting.[8] Eventually the new broadcasting services as well as telecommunications would be incorporated into the 'wired society'.

The communications revolution had its prophets too. In the early 1970s Daniel Bell had identified the 'decisive role of science and technology in transforming the industrial structure'.[9] The emerging 'post-industrial society' was fuelled by the myriad applications from a single major theoretical breakthrough in physics – the integrated circuit. Decline of employment in manufacturing industries – such as textiles, steel and automobiles – and expanding employment in the services – such as business services – were the most visible manifestations of this transformation. Perhaps of greater significance was a deeper process of cultural change. Max Weber had identified 'the depersonalisation of the world' as the central consequence of the ascendancy of scientific rationalism in the modern world: bureaucratic organisation both symbolised and gave practical expression to this phenomenon.[10] Bell argued that science and technology were now making possible a 'repersonalisation of the world'. People's awareness and concerns were being widened as the information age speeded up and enriched the global flow of messages; new priority was attached to personal relations and the acquisition of social skills and intelligence, reflected in a flowering of voluntary associations in social affairs and of 'citizen action groups'. In a similarly optimistic vein Tom Stonier looked forward to an open democracy of data and knowledge processing based on individuals sharing knowledge.[11] By using 'convivial' computer systems linked into networks they could amplify both their own powers and skills and their sense of community. A new 'era of communications' was dawning. These writers had in common the urge to identify the logical structure of a society based on the micro-electronics revolution and an optimism about the capabilities for 'constructive' adaptation by societies and individuals.

In his best-seller *The Third Wave* (1980) Alvin Toffler identified the central political conflict of the age as that between the 'old' politics, based on a loyalty to the values of traditional industrial society, and the 'new' politics with its celebration of individual choice and variety of work organisation and consumption, participation, 'self-help' and 'issue politics'.[12] Toffler spoke of a revolutionary change from an old and dying industrial civilisation that rested on high-volume, standardised mass production and consumption and that had at its centre the impersonally organised (bureaucratic) factory, office and trade union and the 'mass' media. The new civilisation with its greater flexibility and diversity had begun to emerge first and most clearly in the United States which was thus functioning as the world's laboratory. Its technological base was in the electronics revolution associated with computers and integrated circuits; its basic resource was information; and its key symbols were data banks, data-processing equipment, audio-visual communications (like electronic mail, telebanking, videoconferencing), the multi-purpose terminal or work station, cable and satellite broadcasters and 'the information worker'. 'Intelligent' buildings were required to house the 'electronic office' and the 'electronic cottage', two more key symbols of the new civilisation. The combination of sophisticated terminals with interactive (two-way) communications via 'broadband' cable and satellite promised in turn to transform the world of work. Ever larger numbers of people would work 'flexi-time' and part-time and be organised in 'networks' rather than formal hierarchies. In short, the trend was towards 'demassification' of society.[13]

This volume is not centrally concerned with such visions of the 'information age' or the 'wired society', with its attendant expectations of a more decentralised, flexibly organised and participatory society. In the first place, optimism of this kind about the social, economic and political implications of 'post-industrial society' is curiously cavalier in its depiction of a single benign driving force. The transition to 'post-industrial society' involves tremendously high social costs, with the benefits being concentrated in a small privileged core workforce in the new high technology industries and the 'rejuvenated' industries and much of the gain in increased leisure made possible by higher productivity being enforced in the form of structural unemployment rather than chosen.[14] In short, leisure – a presumed 'good' of 'post-industrial society' – is losing rather than gaining status. Large corporations are also unlikely to relinquish power so easily to a new breed of scientist-entrepreneurs. They have an interest in ensuring that technology is used in ways that augment rather than weaken their power. Historically, the exploitation of technology has been shaped by prevailing patterns of institutional power. This work underlines the extent to which reforms of telecommunications policy have tended to reflect the political interests and pressures of large corporate users, with the principle of universal service and national networks – which, in the past, have benefited domestic consumers and small businesses, the potential standard bearers of the 'electronic cottage' – being the main casualties (Dyson); and the extent to which new media and broadcasting policies have facilitated the emergence of larger and more diversified multimedia giants in Western Europe (Dyson and Humphreys). History reveals also how in the past 'homeworking' has been associated with exploitation of 'sweated', unorganised labour. Who will protect 'the electronic cottage'? The coming of 'post-industrial society' is showing once again that the costs of technological change are borne by the large disadvantaged groups that lack the necessary skills to cope. These costs can be mitigated to the extent that societies invest heavily in education and training in order to ensure that individuals can continue to add greater value per capita than machines. Here, Richardson's contribution on Sweden is instructive. There is also little sign of the flowering of a new democracy of data and knowledge sharing. Public policy has done relatively little to promote access and exchange, as Mellors and Pollit indicate. The development of computer systems, including videotex, has emphasised 'password-protected' privacy. Information has become a commodity that is owned and, therefore, whose supply must be controlled. Behind reforms to extend and expedite copyright to cover intellectual property and data protection legislation stand powerful commercial pressures to protect the rewards of innovation and to ensure a strong share in fast-growing international information markets. According to the Information Technology Advisory Panel (ITAP), Britain is in the 'information business'.[15] The information business requires its entrepreneurs. Correspondingly, in Britain and elsewhere in Western Europe the communications revolution has been chiefly defined in corporate and executive terms.

Secondly, the reality of 'post-industrial society' as it unfolds is very messy. There is less comforting reassurance from empirical work that studies this mess closely (in the manner of this volume) than from work that identifies the logical structure of 'post-industrial society'. This volume indicates that the most visible characteristic of the communications revolution, in its early stages at least, was the enhanced role for multinational conglomerates like American Telephone and Telegraph (AT and T), International Business Machines (IBM), Rupert Murdoch's News Corporation, Robert Maxwell's British Printing and Communications Corporation (BPCC), Reuters, Citicorp and Merrill Lynch. By contrast, the 'electronic cottage' was slow to emerge outside specialised high-skill sectors like computer software. The main changes in the world of work were much more 'part-time' work and more short-term contracts. A second major visible characteristic of the communications revolution was trade-union defensiveness in the face of more assertive managements that legitimated 'overdue' and sometimes 'imposed' change by reference to new market and technological conditions. The consequences included job losses and new inter-union rivalries as some unions were downgraded (e.g. the print unions) and others upgraded (e.g. the electricians and the telecommunications workers). Accordingly, political adjustment to the communications revolution was provoking a painful and sometimes bitter experience in Western Europe. As Humphreys emphasises, legitimation of the communications revolution was a difficult process and in Western Europe was associated with some surprising developments. As far as audiovisual communications was concerned, the managements of the multimedia conglomerates and of the international news agencies were the pacesetters (Dyson; Dyson and Humphreys). New small entrants into broadcasting and electronic information services were important as catalysts for strategic change and for new diversification strategies in the large corporations. If revolution was taking place in policies and markets, evolution was more characteristic at the corporate level. With all the complex and rapid changes in West European communications markets and policies there were in fact few new household names at the corporate level. Stimulation of an active and thriving sector of independent programme producers, new information providers and new electronic publishers would require a substantial redirection of public policy.

* * *

This volume provides a series of studies of a process of radical and fundamental change in Western Europe, summed up perhaps over-dramatically in the term 'communications revolution'. Essentially it is concerned with how the communications revolution has developed in different West European states under the impacts of technology and ideology. It does not seek to study the new technologies themselves (see glossary) or processes of commercial innovation and impacts on employment, as the engineer or economist respectively would do. The questions and the approaches are those of the political scientist. At the centre of attention are the perceptions, strategies and relations of the main actors: how are these to be explained and what are their implications for the future progress of the communications revolution? What are the central features of the new political debate about the communications revolution in Western Europe? What is the nature of the power relations in policy-making and implementation; what patterns of state action and pluralistic bargaining are emerging, and with what consequences? To what extent is there a convergence or divergence of communications policies in Western Europe? With these questions in mind the volume provides a comparative political analysis of a set of key policy issues — legitimation, civil liberties, deregulation, European collaboration and multimedia diversification — and seeks to draw some lessons for future policy. In the interests of sheer manageability and length it was decided to omit the military sector (though Dyson's contribution contains relevant background).

Bearing in mind the speed of change and the very broad impact of the communications revolution, and the fact that this is a relatively new field of political science investigation, at least as far as Western Europe is concerned, the authors have been given considerable scope to develop their own interests and approaches within this general editorial framework. Somewhat boldly, the authors were encouraged to undertake a comparative analysis and move out of the relatively safe haven of country-specific studies. The result is not, and could not be, a comprehensive view of the communications revolution in every West European state. Authors were asked to identify and concentrate on those states where communications policy developments were particularly significant, not least for other West European states. The overall concern was to indicate the political and policy aspects that are of common interest and to allow the contrasts of experience in Western Europe to be revealed. An exception to this general approach was made in the case of Sweden. Sweden is of unusual interest for three reasons: it is a pole of technological strength in West European telecommunications; it falls outside the European Community which provides the main framework of the other authors; and, in contrast to the Anglo-American models of communications that have become so influential in Western Europe, it is characterised by Social Democratic ascendancy and a powerful trade-union movement. Sweden is an interesting alternative model for study.

The 'new technologies' and even 'information technology' (IT) are extremely loose concepts that embrace an enormous range of activities. Although 'communications revolution' is also a general concept, it is more delimited than IT. It is given meaning and focus by the specific technologies and services that underpin it and by the way that it is reshaping the traditional boundaries between telecommunications, broadcasting and computing. The communications revolution and IT share a common source in the shock waves emanating from the diffusion of continuing advances in micro-electronics: and they can be seen as the mutually supportive elements of the 'coming information age'. Computing and the microprocessor have expanded the range of communications services and made them more intelligent (telematics); while modern communications equipment (notably cable, satellite and digital switching) has in turn made it possible to transmit the huge amounts of information that can be rapidly processed by modern computers. In this process of technological 'boundary blurring' communications and IT have become increasingly difficult to distinguish. Though this interdependence, as technologies and actors converge and collide, must not be lost from view, it makes sense to provide a more specific focus by looking at the impact of changes in micro-electronics and computing on the traditional industries of telecommunications and broadcasting with their continuingly powerful identities. Hence the study is not about support programmes for microelectronics, industrial robotics, factory and office automation, or IT skill-training programmes. The volume investigates the transformation of the traditional sectors of telecommunications and broadcasting in terms of both the new services that they offer (like 'value-added' and data services including videotex, and cable and satellite television) and the processes of production that they use (like the transition from electromechanical to digital switching). Telecommunications and broadcasting also merit special attention as two of the very few areas of electronics where Western Europe has been able to compete well with the United States and Japan. As both technologies and services are being radically transformed, this competitive position is being rapidly eroded.

Perhaps the most striking feature of the communications revolution is the erosion of traditional boundaries. One dimension of this process is the erosion of the boundaries between telecommunications, broadcasting and the wider IT industry, a phenomenon reflected as we shall see in the diversification strategies of corporate giants and the success of small new entrants in new market niches. Another key dimension is that communications technologies like satellite and 'broadband' cable take less account of national frontiers. In this sense even 'the biggest' West European states seem small states now. As the contents reveal, ideas of regulatory sovereignty are under assault and have received some powerful blows. Cultural identities are in a new flux as communications services gravitate towards the Anglo-American axis, with not least implications for the status and relevance of particular European languages, and as some national élites seek to reassert cultural identity. At another, perhaps more mundane, yet still significant level individual European markets are far too small for telecommunications manufacturers to recoup the heavy and mounting costs of research and development in the new technologies. The market barrier of closed national procurement policies is compounded by absence of common standards in broadcasting and telecommunications. Hence both the realities of emerging communications patterns (symbolised by Rupert Murdoch's Sky Channel) and the requirements of economies of scale and market access give a new saliency to European collaboration, as Shearman shows. In yet another major sense the communications revolution is eroding boundaries within the economy, nationally and internationally. The availability of faster, more efficient and more comprehensive communications is closely linked to major changes in the structure of other industries, notably banking and financial services, consequent on the 'globalisation' of international competition (see Dyson). Large corporations like General Electric and Merrill Lynch are taking charge of their own communications rather than relying on the traditional telecommunication authorities. Corporate customers throughout the economy have become a major spur to the communications revolution, indicating the extent to which it is 'demand-led' and not just 'technology-driven'.

This process of 'boundary erosion' represents a major challenge to the traditional actors in broadcasting and telecommunications, principally the PTTs and the public-service broadcasters. What have been the respective influences of domestic ideological and political factors, on the one hand,

and technology and markets, on the other, on the development of public policy towards these actors? Is there political convergence or divergence in policies towards the communications revolution? The answers to these questions will vary with the nature of the particular activities being investigated, with the ideological and political character of the countries studied and with the kind of approach adopted by the analyst. 'Boundary erosion' has more deeply affected some activities than others, and ideological and political factors have differed in the countries covered (as Morgan and Webber stress). At the same time, technology and markets are having a profound effect on government's capacity to regulate communications, not least in broadcasting (see Hoffmann-Riem). The answers that are provided in this volume can be at best only tentative and provisional. As the first contribution indicates, they are likely to be contested as long as there is a problem of adjudication among the approaches that are used to tackle these questions. The fundamental and primary issue is how to interpret the communications revolution.

NOTES

1. For further analysis see e.g. W. Durch (ed.), *National Interests and the Military Use of Space* (Cambridge, MA.: Ballinger, 1984); H. Brauch (ed.), *From 'Star Wars' to Strategic Defence Initiative: European Perceptions and Assessments* (London: Macmillan, 1986).
2. See e.g. D. Evans, *Breaking Up Bell* (New York: North Holland, 1983); and K. Newman, *The Selling of British Telecom* (London: Holt, Rinehart & Winston, 1986).
3. See the chapter by Dyson and Humphreys in this volume.
4. W. Durch, *op. cit.*
5. See e.g. I. de Sola Pool, *Forecasting the Telephone* (New Jersey: Ablex, 1982); H. Dordick, et al, *The Emerging Network Marketplace* (New Jersey: Ablex, 1981); J. Salvaggio, *Telecommunications* (London: Longman, 1983); C. Sterling, *Electronic Media* (New York: Praeger, 1984).
6. See e.g. M. Moss, *Telecommunications and Productivity* (New York: Addison Wesley, 1981).
7. J. Howkins, *New Technologies, New Policies* (London: BFI, 1982).
8. T. Hollins, *Beyond Broadcasting: Into the Cable Age* (London: BFI, 1984).
9. D. Bell, *The Coming of Post-Industrial Society* (New York: Basic Books, 1973).
10. On Weber see e.g. M. Albrow, *Bureaucracy* (London: Pall Mall, 1970), and H. Gerth and C. Mills (eds.), *From Max Weber* (New York: Oxford University Press, 1972).
11. T. Stonier, *The Wealth of Information* (London: Methuen, 1983).
12. A. Toffler, *The Third Wave* (New York: W. Morrow, 1980).
13. For similar scenarios see Dordick, *op. cit.*; W. Dizard, *The Coming Information Age* (London: Longman, 1982); and Stonier, *op. cit.*
14. On the social costs of modernisation see K. Dyson and S. Wilks (eds.) *Industrial Crisis* (Oxford: Blackwell, 1983) especially Chapter 2 and conclusion.
15. The British Cabinet Office's ITAP report 'Making a Business of Information' appeared in 1983.

West European States and the Communications Revolution

Kenneth Dyson

The argument expressed here is that the responses of West European governments to the communications revolution seem to display little consistency at the level of either ideology or policy, for instance towards deregulation or European collaboration. At the same time, behind the articulation of rhetoric and doctrine – the displays of 'symbolic politics' that often serve to disguise a sense of political unease – a common and less heroic process of relearning the arts of statecraft is underway. Communications policies, and the theories underlying them, are not being analysed and assessed in their own right as technical issues by governments. They are being accepted or rejected or changed as instruments of a fundamental political strategy – to regain a governing competence and to maintain ideological and electoral credibility. The following is not concerned with the arguments of economists and engineers about the respective merits and demerits of deregulation, privatisation, European collaboration, or joint ventures and licensing deals with the Americans and the Japanese. Its focus is upon the behaviour and motivations of West European governments.

West European states are under great and mounting pressures to abandon traditional policy assumptions and commitments that are proving uncomfortable to defend in telecommunications and broadcasting. In contrasting ways, and at different rates, they are learning to work within the powerful new constraints on communications policies imposed by new technologies, international markets and turbulent interest politics. This learning involves governments in the search for political formulas that will enable them to reconstruct a relative autonomy of the state in the face of these new international and domestic pressures. They are attempting to do so on terms that are compatible, or can in some way be reconciled, with their own ideological dispositions. The search is far from completed, and various ideas – of deregulation, privatisation, 'national champions', European collaboration – co-exist in a conflicting and ill-digested manner. Indeed, very few politicians comprehend fully what is happening; understanding the communications revolution seems like 'trying to get your hands around a piece of jelly'. Yet underneath the baroque complexity and muddle the common theme of a search to restore ideological credibility and governing competence can be discerned. It reflects itself, as we shall see, in the way governments are learning to play a new type of brokerage politics in communications.

THE STATE AND THE COMMUNICATIONS REVOLUTION: BASIC TRENDS

An analysis of the changing role of the state in the communications revolution must be grounded in an appreciation of the five main trends that are conditioning that role. These trends indicate how and why West European governments have come to see communications as 'a strategic resource', crucial to the future power potential of their states and hence a suitable matter for 'high politics'. They show also the mounting threat to the traditional freedom of maneouvre of these states in communications policy and the challenge to 'statecraft' and considerable confusion that followed. Those trends are making individual governments much more sensitive to each other's actions in communications policy and eroding the prospects of an independent national policy.

First, governments and politicians have been taken by surprise as communications have been affected by a 'shock wave' of technological changes on many fronts. Advances in micro-electronics and the convergence of computing and communications stand at the heart of these changes as the main driving force, with the development of semiconductors after 1965 from small-scale integration to very large-scale integrated chips (VLSI) in the 1980s being matched by the advent of satellites and optic fibre cable. The hugely expanded data-processing powers of computers are being harnessed to extend the capabilites of the telecommunications and broadcasting systems and to create a new electronic data base industry.[1] Thus digital switching equipment and transmission lines, combined with multipurpose work stations, carrying voice, data and even video are making possible new audiovisual services (telematics) like electronic mail, facsimile, interactive videotext and videoconferencing. Speedier and higher quality transmission of these 'value-added' services on the same telephone line becomes possible. Meanwhile, choice and audio-visual performance are being enhanced in broadcasting by video-cassette recorders (VCRs), satellites, copper-coaxial and optic fibre cable, new transmission standards including C-MAC and high-definition television, digital television and radio equipment ('intelligent' radio and television sets) and electronic news-gathering technology. In these ways the traditionally separate, closed sectors of telecommunications and broadcasting are 'converging' with computing. As they rely on common technologies, like optic-fibre cable, satellites, and digital radio signals, and on computers for expanding their range of services (e.g. broadcast teletext, radio data system, interactive videotext and other data services), telecommunications and broadcasting converge with each other. The consequence has been a vast array of new opportunities for users and suppliers of telecommunications and broadcasting equipment and services, not least for 'information providers' and carriers. Consequently, throughout Western Europe at roughly the same time technological, industrial and commercial lobbies emerged to press the urgent economic need to invest heavily in the new communications infrastructure as the basis for the 'third industrial revolution'.[2] In this way Western Europe could 'escape from the crisis'. It could also, in the words of Ithiel de Sola Pool, invest in a 'technology of freedom'.[3] The initial naivety of West European governments in the face of this technological and economic 'hype' was reflected in the exaggerated political expectations linked to the British government's acceptance of the

Information Technology Advisory Panel's (ITAP) report called Cable Systems, the French cable plan, and the Bundespost Minister's plan to cable West Germany in the interests of a broadcasting revolution – all in 1982.[4]

Secondly, the communications revolution was not simply 'technology-driven'. The continuing political pressures on West European states were to be understood in terms of 'demand-pull' as well as 'technology-push'. Efficient and rapid management of information had become a vital competitive tool in a widening range of industries as well as an essential underpinning for contemporary defence strategies. In addition to changing social habits, associated with demands for 'home-based' leisure, strategic requirements, the needs of new fast-moving global financial markets and the demands of multinational conglomerates compelled a continuing political attention to the economic, military and cultural significance of the communications revolution. Military demands for a 'hardened' communications system were at the forefront in propelling technological change (e.g. optic fibres), while the priority attached to military communications had always acted as a constraint on the development of communications for civilian usage. Radio frequency needs of the military were part of the rationale for the shortage of frequencies that had been traditionally used to justify close governmental regulation of telecommunictions and broadcasting. The first satellites were for military purposes; direct broadcasting satellites (DBS) came three decades later.[5] Improved space technologies from the 1950s onwards, including the greater payload capacity of satellite launchers and more powerful and heavy multifunctional satellites with sophisticated sensors and microprocessors, offered the military better reconnaissance (including high-resolution photography, electronic intelligence gathering, and ocean observation), surveillance (notably for ballistic missile early warning), navigation, military C^3 (command, control and communications) and even the prospect, announced by President Reagan in his famous 'star wars' speech of March 1983, of a defensive shield against ballistic missiles provided by 'killer' satellites armed with laser technology (the Strategic Defence Initiative or SDI). At the same time, greater demands on the efficiency, accuracy and speed of communications were made by NATO strategies like, from the 1960s, 'flexible response' with its idea of a graduated and controlled escalation in the use of nuclear weapons and, from the 1980s, 'Follow-on Forces Attack' (FOFA) with its idea of 'deep strike' at the enemy's rear echelons using 'smart' high technology systems. By the 1980s the combination of space with terrestrial communications, using sophisticated sensors and microprocessors, suggested a global electronic intelligence and warfare revolution. This global web, and FOFA in particular, was based on the automation of C^3 linked to real-time surveillance and target acquisition (creating a 'transparency revolution' in warfare) and to electronic warfare capabilities. Yet, at a more mundane and embarrassing level, NATO continued to need improved battlefield communications systems and a 'friend-or-foe' identification system if its existing strategies were not to disintegrate into muddle. More ominously, reliance on this emerging complex global communications system was creating new military vulnerability – to breakdown, incompetence, electronic countermeasures and sabotage – as well as the potential for more rapid escalation of alerts and an incentive for 'first-strike' capability.[6] Though military demands for its continuing refinement were an ever more powerful factor in the communications revolution, their significance can be over-stated, even in the case of the Reagan administration with its priority to 'making America strong'.[7] Deregulation and divestiture of AT and T is a case-study of the Department of Justice's anti-trust activity bypassing the Department of Defence whose influence on telecommunications reorganisation was marginal.

Communications technologies emerged as a competitive weapon, most powerfully in financial markets which by the 1980s were undergoing frenetic economic and technological change. Here the quality, performance and reliability of technology had become critical to market success. The commercial needs of financial institutions and dealers for fast, accurate and comprehensive information were greatly increased by the deregulation and internationalisation of financial markets after 1971. In the process, impressive commercial opportunities for real-time price information were created for news agencies like Reuters and Dow Jones and 'high-tech' financial conglomerates like Citicorp and Merrill Lynch. The application of new communications technologies and services made information available at the speed and in the quantity to ensure the growth and functioning of financial markets operating on a global scale and communicating and dealing electronically.[8] Providers of electronic financial services and the rapidly growing international financial conglomerates pressed in turn for more open entry into the West European securities markets; while the big jobbing and broking firms in European financial centres saw integration with large conglomerates as their only hope of competing in the world securities industry. The consequence was a series of stock exchange revolutions with dramatic changes in ownership and competitive practice, for instance as commercial banks moved more forcefully into investment banking, bought stockbrokers and jobbers, and sought government bond dealerships and stock exchange seats in London, New York and Tokyo. These revolutions combined deregulation with high-technology growth, putting financial institutions at the centre of the communications revolution. Financial information became the driving force of the electronic data base industry.[9]

More generally, multinational corporations were always seeking to speed up and improve their internal data communications and co-ordination. They accounted for well over half of international information flows by 1985. In Britain data traffic was rising by 30 per cent per annum (voice traffic by 8 per cent), with most of that occurring in private networks.[10] For services like electronic mail, facsimile and videoconferencing multinationals developed private communications networks by negotiating with a labyrinth of national and international regulatory authorities like Intelset and leasing lines directly from the traditional carriers. By 1986 these networks were still based on satellite links and on the International Packet Switching Service (IPSS), a specially designed, very cost-effective and fast public transmission service for computer-based information. Multinationals were also a major source of pressure on public telecommunications authorities (PTTs) to collaborate on a new international network of digital communications services, using optic-fibre cable as well as satellites and linking Europe, North America and the Far East (with the US-Europe link scheduled for 1988). At the same time, their main lobby — the International Telecommunications Users Group (INTUG) — fought for a deregulated approach, for developing the new integrated services digital network (ISDN) in a market-driven way (as in the United States) rather than in a PTT-driven way (as in West Germany). Underlining the strength of market forces was the rapid success of Electronic Data System, a subsidiary of General Motors, in building a private international network called EDS-Net to rent to multinationals. The rise of private digital and hybrid analog/digital networks became a new international as well as national phenomenon. In these ways standards have become an international political issue. Generally, however, governments — and the European Economic Community — were slow to react, their policies lagging behind the complex, ill-understood realities of international electronic information. By 1986 GATT had still to inaugurate full discussions of the issues involved in harmonising the flow of information around the globe; the International Telegraph and Telephone Consultative Council (CCITT) had made relatively little headway in the process of setting world-wide standards.

The demands that governments identified and responded to were not just strategic and corporate. Changing social habits were also evident as more individuals transformed their homes into 'electronic castles' in which to enjoy more 'home-based' leisure and greater consumer choice. By 1983 the enormous success of cable television in the United States, of VCRs in Britain and of local 'off-air' radio and television broadcasting in Italy revealed the commercial potential of technologies that could provide more entertainment, notably feature films. This commercial potential was symbolised by Home Box Office in the United States, by the boom in street-corner video rental shops in Britain and by Silvio Berlusconi's new private television empire in Italy.[11] At the same time, costs and public acceptance could remain major constraints. Thus, interactive videotex was invented in Britain in 1971, began as a public service (Prestel) in 1979 and only became really established by 1986, and then with only just over 60,000 subscribers concentrated mainly in 'niche' markets rather than as a mass consumer service.[12]

Thirdly, and following from the first two trends, prospects for a governmental 'strategy' for communications were bedevilled by the sheer complexity of technological change and industrial and cultural lobbying, as well as by the varying problems of structural co-ordination among departments, tiers of government and with the courts. Communications policy in Western Europe had traditionally been characterised by rather discrete, closed and exclusive 'policy communities' in telecommunications and in broadcasting.[13] Now, under the stimulus of deregulation and attacks on monopoly, each began to be crowded and destabilised by new entrants.[14] Publishers like Murdoch, Maxwell and Springer, and such groups as Virgin and Thorn-EMI moved into broadcasting, and electronics, office equipment, computer and banking companies shifted into telecommunications. Examples were provided in the United States by IBM's takeover of Rolm (the PABX manufacturer), IBM's stake in MCI Communications and the General Electric–RCA merger as well as by Citicorp's bid for Quotron. Technological change and the doctrine of 'fair competition' were used by new entrants like MCI Communications in long-distance telecommunications to legitimise legal reforms in telecommunications. Dramatic changes in distribution methods (with video-cassettes, cable and satellite) were making large or scattered audiences accessible to private broadcasting operators; the consequent competition for audiences was changing the economic balance of broadcasting, to the detriment of public broadcasters. Furthermore, in both telecommunications and broadcasting, it became increasingly clear that individual states were no longer able to exercise an effective sovereignty on their own. Satellites were no respecters of national boundaries; hence new national fears about cultural and political values surfaced. There were new and pressing needs for collaboration at the European level: in telecommunication research and development (for advanced digital switching equipment and satellites), in programming for new pan-European satellite channels (e.g. the proposed joint venture by Maxwell, Berlusconi, Kirsch and Seydoux), in common standards for broadcasting transmission and for telecommunications. Problems of domestic policy-making were caught up in further problems of co-ordination with initiatives of the European Commission (like Euronet Diane, RACE and the Green Paper 'Television Without Frontiers' and the subsequent draft directive) and the activities of such diverse European bodies as the European Broadcasting Union (EBU), the Commission of European Posts and Telecommunications Administrations (CEPT), the European Committee for Standardisation (CEN), the Committee for Electrotechnical Standardisation (CENELEC), the European Space Agency and the European Satellite Telecommunications Organisation (Eutelsat) as well as the Council of Europe (notably its 1984 recommendation on *The Use of Satellite Capacity for Television and Sound Radio*).[15] There were in turn problems of co-ordination among these many European bodies, for instance in the development of common technical standards in order to open up and unify European broadcasting and information markets. The pervasive fragmentation and asymmetries of power in 'Europe' provided opportunities for American and Japanese entry, with MCI using Belgium and Portugal as points of entry, AT and T striking major deals in the Netherlands, Italy and Spain, and Murdoch looking to Luxembourg as a base for cross-national satellite television. In the process France and West Germany found themselves progressively encircled by American alliances.

Fourthly, West European states have become locked into the dynamic expansion of potentially huge markets for telecommunictions equipment (digital public switching exchanges, optic-fibre cable, satellites, PABXs and 'intelligent' terminals), broadcasting equipment (satellite receivers, new display technologies, digital television and radio sets), programme production and distribution (computer software, videos, and material for new cable and satellite channels), advertising (with the larger and more specialised audiences provided by cable and satellite broadcasting and by the new competition for advertising from low-cost electronically-produced newspapers and magazines) and electronic information services (including financial markets, home banking and 'cashless' shopping, and electronic mail). Governments cannot afford to ignore the immense economic opportunities for a wide range of domestic industries, including telecommunications authorities, electronics companies, financial institutions, media companies (including the press), advertisers and news agencies. At the same time the new 'information economy' emerged earlier and more rapidly in the large domestic markets of the United States and Japan. A long process of deregulation, culminating in AT and T's divestiture of its Bell System local telephone companies in 1984, had already produced upheaval in American telecommunications.[16] The powerful economic threat was symbolised most powerfully by the diversifications and aggressive international behaviour of AT and T, IBM, Murdoch's News Corporation and Nippon Electric (NEC); by the technological sophistication and ease of automated dealing in the New York Stock Exchange and the aggressive international behaviour of American Citicorp; and by American pressures on NATO to adopt so-called 'emerging technology' (ET) weapons for long-range interdiction, further underlining the 'one-way street' in NATO arms procurement (the imbalance in defence trade stood at around 10:1 for much of the 1970s). Traditional European regulatory polices were threatened in broadcasting as well as in financial markets. The threat to West European public-service broadcasting was cultural and economic, associated with the perception of American 'Coca-Cola' civilisation, with its attendant celebration of commercial values, destroying the supposed 'high standards' and 'excellence' of news, current affairs and drama in European broadcasting. In Italy the explosion of local 'off-air' broadcasting after 1976 revealed the consequences of a proliferation of channels: massive imports and programming of cheap Japanese cartoons and American series, and the inexorable rise of media giants (Berlusconi). Across computing, telecommunications, broadcasting, information services and military procurement the alarm bells were ringing throughout Western Europe, with Philips of the Netherlands and Thomson and the DGT (the telecommunications authority) of France taking the lead in calling for a co-ordinated European initiative. Those who took European initiatives were typically rebuffed for smuggling corporate self-interest behind 'Euro-rhetoric'; in fact the intra-European deals of Philips/Grundig (consumer electronics), Philips/CIT Alcatel (radiotelephones, microwave systems), Philips/Bull (the 'smart card') and Thomson/Telefunken (consumer electronics) were paralleled by the Philips/AT and T alliance in digital switching equipment and the alliances of Thomson with JVC of Japan in VCRs, with Motorola in semiconductors and with General Instruments in optical fibres. As we shall see later, in the context of newly emerging global markets in communications, Europe was just one option and not necessarily the most attractive for West European companies.

Fifthly, in so far as the West European option was taken seriously, the policies of West European states displayed an irreducibly Janus-like character, embodying the tension between the pursuit of European collaboration and national particularism. In a communications revolution that knew few bounds of geography, scale or sector, Europe appeared as a continent of very small countries indeed. It appeared to be losing control and influence over strategic technologies. Accordingly, the economic rationale for European collaboration seemed powerful, notably in telecommunications.[17] With mounting research and development costs and the shortening life of products, for instance in digital switching equipment, fragmented and closed European markets represented a barrier to commercial success. Enormous duplication and waste were occurring in research and development expenditures. In computing, telecommunications and broadcasting diverse regulatory frameworks in Western Europe provided a further barrier; because of their excess or because of their lack of standardisation, or both, they hindered access to markets. ESPRIT, RACE, and the draft directive on a common market for broadcasting, and – outside the EC – the Eureka initiative, all had a common theme: to give the European component in the emerging global communications markets as high a profile as possible. And yet proud and powerful West European states were as keen to ensure that this new European profile would be provided by their own national champions or that European collaboration did not lead to an erosion of domestic technological strengths through partnerships with weaker companies. Thus British Telecom, Siemens, Olivetti and Ericsson gave priority to penetrating the huge North American market; these companies sought a role as national flagships for IT. European communications policies were too little and too late. The development of EC policies for technology collaboration like ESPRIT and RACE was further delayed by the priority given by some European states, notably Britain and West Germany, to budgetary discipline, with subsequent hostility to new spending programmes not least at the EC level. Fragmentation of effort among European agencies combined with national particularism to ensure the triumph of the forces of political inertia at the European level. The European Space Agency was unable to contain the proliferation of national and bilateral initiatives in DBS (direct broadcasting by satellite); from 1984 Eutelsat fought a long but apparently fruitless battle against Luxembourg's plan for a private broadcasting satellite; the EC, the EBU, CEPT and CEN could not offer a comprehensive, timely and adequate response to the broad technological challenges in communications across the continuum of telecommunications, data-processing and audio-visual media, whether in the form of common standards or collaborative programme development; ESPRIT and RACE were slow to materialise, so that, for instance, each country still had its own plan for introducing ISDN as late as 1986; and efforts at European industrial alliances were painfully slow in the face of the extraordinary scale and speed of change in international markets and indeed took second place to the alliances forged with American and Japanese companies (e.g. Olivetti/AT and T, Olivetti/Toshiba, Spain's Telefonica and AT and T and with Fujitsu, Ericsson with Honeywell and with Digital Equipment, BT with Mitel, Siemens with Toshiba, Corning Glass and GTE, Philips with AT and T).[18] The broad picture is of a fragmented, confused and confusing Western Europe facing complex, new and turbulent communications markets and under pressure to adapt corporate and state strategies; of American or Japanese leads, or prospective leads, in these markets; of considerable disparities of performance within Western Europe, with Sweden as a pole of technological strength in telecommunications (Ericsson), and Britain as a pole of strength in programme production, broadcasting libraries (BBC, Granada and Thames), and financial services; and of many more politicians and industrialists in Western Europe looking at earlier American experience in broadcasting (notably the huge growth of cable television and of Home Box Office, MTV and Ted Turner's WTBS), telecommunications (after the divestiture of AT and T, in particular), and data networks (especially new electronic financial services and the impact of the 'Big Bang' as the New York Stock Exchange was computerised). West European policy debates and policy making have been shaped increasingly by the messages of deregulation and competition (bringing the 'enterprise culture' into communications, *pace* IBM, MCI Communications, Reuters, Citicorp, Murdoch, Maxwell and Berlusconi) and of the need for powerful industrial alliances to exploit economies of scale in research and development, production and marketing (introducing the age of the American electronics and media conglomerates to Europe, *pace* General Electric/RCA, IBM/MCI Communications, Murdoch/Twentieth Century Fox). By attacking the inefficiencies of 'over-regulation' and national monopoly power these messages challenged European public-service traditions in broadcasting and telecommunications. Arguments about 'public goods' and about 'externalities' and the case for non-economic values were put on the defensive or simply ignored. Broadcasting began to be seen, for instance, by the European Commission, as an internationally tradeable service, as an industry, and viewers were redefined as consumers seeking an expansion of choice.

THE ROLE OF THE WEST EUROPEAN STATE

Against the background of these five main trends, what can be said about the role of the West European state in the communications revolution? At first glance, the picture of general trends seems to require two qualifications. First, debate and policy development in Western Europe seems to have taken different forms in different countries. The official intellectual thrust provided by the ITAP report *Cable Systems* (1982) in Britain bears little comparison with the scope and ambition of the Nora/Minc report *The Computerisation of Society* (1978) in France or with the methodical analysis and assessment of the Kommission für den Ausbau des technischen Kommunikationssystems (KtK, 1976) in West Germany.[19] It is interesting also to note that the official intellectual thrust to policy development came earlier in France and West Germany than in Britain. Britain was also striking in having a less vigorous substantive debate about 'new media' or 'audio-visual communications'; indeed the two terms seem strange, 'foreign' or 'theoretical' in British political debate.[20] The debate surrounding the Cable and Broadcasting Act (1984) and the Telecommunications Act (1984) was, as far as the British government was concerned, an aspect of a wider and much more significant debate about 'rolling back the state' by privatisation and encouragement of private-sector investment and by keeping down the Public Sector Borrowing Requirement (helped by selling off state assets like BT). Broadcasting and telecommunications policies were functional appendages to this basic financial and political strategy; they did not themselves become 'strategies', thus transforming the objects and terms of political debate. In large part because the industrial imperative has a long-standing and much more secure place in French and West German political strategies, there was an important public debate: in West Germany about *Neue Medien* (with special party congresses and party resolutions on the issues, with a range of governmental commissions of inquiry from KtK onwards, and with *Land* new media laws and the debate about a

Staatsvertrag for new media in the 1980s), and in France about *communication audiovisuelle* (with the telematics plan of 1978, the law on audiovisual communications of 1982, the cable plan of 1982 and subsequent decrets d'application, and the ideas of Jack Lang, the Culture Minister, to develop France's 'cultural industries').[21] However clumsy such language may seem to a British audience, the striking feature of French and West German debate has been its recognition of the realities of the new international markets.

Secondly, although the communications sector is tied together by the basic technological thrust from micro-electronics and the convergence of computing, telecommunications and broadcasting, the diversity of markets, technological conditions, actors and degree of internationalisation remains striking. Thus, on the one hand, satellite technology has proved a potent force for deregulation in broadcasting and in telecommunications services, eroding the economic and cultural sovereignty of West European states of its substance. On the other hand, the pressures from internationalisation were less immediately powerful in telecommunications switching equipment and in cable and microwave transmission markets; indeed the French cable plan was initially presented as a form of cultural Maginot Line. As in personal computers and VCRs, consumer choice could accelerate change, not least by creating large new software markets. In other sectors, like financial and other information services, large corporate actors could prove to be powerful catalysts for deregulation and internationalisation. *Prima facie*, then, there seems to be a risk of brutal generalisation in offering conclusions about the role of the state in the communications revolution. In a field of such broad-based changes, where the final shape of public policy is still difficult to discern, conclusions are bound to be tentative and provisional.

Among the complexity and change can some order in policy development be identified? Are there common patterns across the particular experiences of West European states? In attempting to interpret the role of the state in the communications revolution from a political science perspective the basic questions relate to the policy processes in Western Europe: who are the chief actors, what are their motivations and relationships, and what are the outcomes of their activities? At this juncture the basic need is to stimulate debate and point to further directions for research by analysing and assessing the different perspectives from which the role of the state in the communications revolution can be interpreted: those of international political economy, of political-science analysis of domestic policy processes, and of politico-legal analysis. Bearing in mind the trends and qualifications noted above, the rest of the chapter investigates three sets of competing theses about the development of communications policies in Western Europe.

Thesis 1: that changes in national communications policies reflect the impact of new turbulent international markets for programme production and distribution, for telecommunications and for computing

This thesis argues that in order to understand the character of new communications policies, and the changing terms of political debate, in Western Europe paramount attention must be given to an examination of the structure and development of international markets. Thus the EC's RACE programme pointed out that the world telecommunications market was worth an estimated £20 billion per annum by 1985; in many industrialised countries, like Britain, telecommunications was already a bigger business than agriculture. For 1985–95 the Commission forecast a telecommunications investment of £90 billion, making it the biggest industry in the EC.[22] Yet prospects looked gloomy. According to an OECD study of 1983, a combination of small national markets with closed, protectionist procurement policies, led to a price differential of 60–100 per cent in telecommunications equipment between Western Europe and the United States.[23] In the major telecommunications market (for digital exchanges), with sales of £7 billion in 1984, the two American companies AT and T and ITT and Canada's Northern Telecom controlled well over half the market, with NEC/Fujitsu in fourth place.[24] In optical fibres Corning Glass of the United States had penetrated Western Europe through a network of joint ventures; while in DBS Hughes Communications and RCA offered lower-cost satellites than West European manufacturers and, by 1986, appeared likely to capture orders in Britain and Ireland. Western Europe could not be complacent simply because it still had two representatives among the top five telecommunications companies in terms of world equipment sales: Siemens (West Germany) at third and Ericsson (Sweden) at fifth were pygmies in comparison with AT and T.

Experience in data-processing and in consumer electronics, particularly colour television sets and VCRs, offered a warning to the West European telecommunications.[25] By 1984 American sales of personal computers accounted for four-fifths of EC sales, Japanese VCR's nine-tenths of EC sales. IBM had 40 per cent of total computer sales in Western Europe, with 65 per cent of the market for mainframe computers. With data processing revenue of $10.6 billion in 1984 in Western Europe, IBM equalled the *combined* turnover of its ten closest competitors. It was well placed to establish its own technology, systems network architecture (SNA), as a *de facto* European standard for interworking of different computer systems and terminals. IBM's power was further entrenched by its employment of some 100,000 Europeans and its annual payment of over $1 billion of taxes within the EC.[26] Phenomenal growth rates were predicted for the electronic information market as a consequence of the increased penetration of microcomputers and as people become more comfortable with screen-based information (in other words, after a consumer learning process). However, even with projected growth rates of 25–30 per cent the European market would stay well behind the exploding American market (which, on one estimate by International Resource Development, would be worth $10 billion per annum in 1990).[27] The United States appears as the Opec of 'on-line' information, thus controlling a basic business asset, not least in investment banking. The balance of trade deficit in electronic information between the United States and Western Europe has been estimated at 10:1 to the former's advantage.[28] Seventy-five per cent of on-line data bases available in Western Europe (for financial information, scientific and technological data, news and current affairs etc.) are American in origin – like Dialog with over 200 databases and Mead Data Control – and take some 40 per cent of market expenditure. In financial and business information

Telerate (the AP Dow Jones Service), Citicorp and IBM/Merrill Lynch are emerging as major American actors in world markets. Citicorp established a joint venture with a publisher McGraw-Hill and in 1986 made a bid for Quotron. IBM and AT and T also entered the fiercely growing computer software market, in which Management Science America (MSA) was the world leader. In this sector at least Western Europe was to enjoy some success. Eight of the top 12 computer software companies operating in Europe were from France; Cap Gemini Sogeti was the European leader in the field.[29]

Perhaps the most dramatic and visible crisis for Europe's communications industries had been in consumer electronics. Heavy pressures for tariffs and quotas had come from Philips, Thomson and Grundig, leading to an EC tariff of 14 per cent on colour television sets, of 8 per cent on VCRs (plus a voluntary import restraint agreement with Japan in 1983) and of 19 per cent on compact disc audio systems. These same European companies engaged in a pattern of defensive mergers in the early 1980s, notably Philips/Grundig and Thomson/Telefunken. More ominous, if less visible, was the lag between Western Europe and the United States and Japan in the production and application of semiconductors, compounded in 1986 by the prospect of US-Japanese agreement on a 'global' system of price monitoring for semiconductor chips. Europe had nothing to compare with Motorola, National Semiconductors and Texas Instruments of the United States or Fujitsu, Hitachi and Toshiba of Japan. Philips was the only European company to make the top ten in world sales in 1985 (at number ten). In 1982 the American and Japanese trade surpluses in semiconductors of $2.45 billion and $1.95 billion respectively contrasted with a Western European deficit of $1.8 billion.[30] European-owned semiconductor manufacturers had a market share in Western Europe of only 36 per cent in 1983. This dismal trade position was complemented by low application. In 1983 per capita consumption of semiconductors varied from just over $50 in the United States to just under $50 in Japan to about $10 in Western Europe. But perhaps the most compelling single statistic was the European Commission's estimate of the EC's balance of trade in IT products: from a surplus in 1975 to a £2.5 billion deficit in 1984.

If the picture of comparative disadvantage was bleak at the computing and telecommunications ends of the communications revolution, the scenario for broadcasting offered no consolation. A proliferation of broadcasting outlets via cable and satellite as well as video and a greater reliance on television advertising to finance these new channels, as seen already in Murdoch's pan-European Sky Channel, seemed to threaten American domination. The EC Commission estimated that by 1990 West European demand for television programmes would grow to 125,000 hours per annum; yet in 1984 the combined production of Britain, France, Italy and West Germany amounted to just 5000 hours.[31] In 1986 Maxwell's service for the French TDF-1 satellite estimated that it would need 6,500 hours per annum; in the first year it planned to make 100 hours of programmes. The new satellite services simply did not have the funds for programming; the £1000–£2000 that Sky Channel was prepared to spend per hour on programming contrasted with the £50,000 spent by ITV and the £40,000 by BBC. The structure of the international distribution of television programmes suggested already a dominance of a few exporting countries, with an apparent one-way flow of American entertainment at the centre of this domination.[33] *Dallas, Dynasty, Kojak* and *Starsky and Hutch* had become symbols of American commercial success in international television. Tapio Varis's study of West European television between 1973 and 1983 revealed that overall 33 per cent of television programming was imported; 44 per cent of that was American, and American programmes accounted for 10 per cent of total transmission time.[34] By contrast, 16 per cent of these imports originated from Britain and only 5–10 per cent from France and West Germany. There were significant differences between small countries which tended to import heavily (Austria 43 per cent, Denmark 46 per cent and Ireland 57 per cent) and Britain (BBC 15 per cent, ITV 14 per cent), France (17 per cent) and West Germany (ARD 13 per cent, ZDF 23 per cent and regional 24 per cent). There were also important flows of programmes within Western Europe, for instance from France to Belgium and from West Germany to Austria. However, the experience of Italy in deregulating traditional 'off-air' broadcasting after 1976 suggested that in the international distribution of television programmes the rest of Western Europe might be about to learn what it is like to become 'a small state' in a world of international media giants. By 1982 Italy had become the world's largest importer of American television programmes, having already become the world's largest importer of Japanese cartoons. The new media, like expansion of the old, would create an explosion of demand for low-cost programmes that could only be supplied by massive imports unless, as French policy-makers envisaged, a large boost was given to the European programme industry. Italy's experience suggested also that an expansion of television outlets could harm rather than aid the domestic cinema industry. With the exception of France American films predominated in the European cinemas.[35] The share of domestic films in national cinema markets fell from 41 per cent to 20 per cent in Britain (1975–80), from 39 per cent to 19 per cent in West Germany (1970–81) and from 60 per cent to 44 per cent in Italy (1970–81). American feature films enjoyed stunning commercial success; responsible for only 5–6 per cent of annual world production and for 32 per cent of total imported films, they took half of world receipts. Meanwhile, annual production of European films for cinema had been declining steadily: between 1973 and 1983 from 180 to 131 films in France, from 80 to 31 in Britain and from 250 to 110 in Italy. Video and cable and satellite channels offered huge new markets in Western Europe for feature films, and the structure of the international markets for film production and distribution suggested urgent cultural policy problems for Western Europe.

Another international market that seemed set to prosper with the communications revolution was advertising. In particular, with expansion of the new media the potential for television advertising in Europe seemed vast. Broadcasting would depend to greater extent for its finance on the sale of airtime to advertisers: and Europe as a whole was less saturated by advertising than the United States and Japan. 'TV adspend' in Europe did not correlate at all with national wealth.[36] Thus in 1983 Britain accounted for 38.9 per cent of Europe's 'TV adspend'; Italy came second with 17.8 per cent. 'TV adspend' per TV home was $82 million in Britain, followed by Finland ($47 million), Italy ($44 million), Ireland ($43 million) and Austria ($40 million). The huge growth potential was concentrated in the French and West German markets and in the possibilities with satellite broadcasting to develop new multinational advertising campaigns. Thus in 1981 'TV adspend' represented 0.30 per cent of GDP in Britain; in the wealthier societies of France and West Germany it absorbed only 0.08 per cent GDP. The basic impediment to the development of the European advertising market was the national legislative restrictions on amounts, styles and subjects of advertising. Commercial pressures against these restrictions mounted in the 1980s, with the advertisers taking the issue of 'freedom of commercial speech' to the European Court of Human Rights. This case centred on France, the world's fourth industrial power and yet ranking only fifteenth in terms of the size of its advertising market. However, beneath, or alongside, the issue of principle rested once again the structure of an international market. The European advertising industry was dominated by American companies like J. Walter Thompson, McCann Erickson and Young and Rubicam. Though France seemed an exception, and the British Saatchi and Saatchi was to mount a major challenge in the 1980s, the American share of its advertising market had grown from 10 per cent to 36 per cent between the late 1960s and the late 1970s. American firms held 30 of the top 50 places in the world advertising industry in 1982: Japan came second with 12, whereas France held only three places and West Germany one.[37]

What conclusions can be drawn about the structure and development of international communications markets? First, they are all changing under the impact of technological development, and they are challenging the assumptions on which West European regulatory policies have traditionally rested. Secondly, American and Japanese corporations are the major agents of change in these international markets. In particular, deregulation in the huge American domestic market has had a major impact on the behaviour of large corporations like AT and T, IBM and Citicorp, and the factors at work in propelling American deregulation are likely to apply in Europe too. Thus changes in communications technologies seemed to have undermined the rationale for government regulation and for traditional monopolies (e.g. based on scarcity of frequencies for 'off-air' broadcasting); they gave an incentive to new actors like MCI and GTE/Sprint to enter the communications field. Also, American business corporations, as major 'consumers' of governmental regulation and users of telecommunications, have lobbied intensively (witness the American Petroleum Institute) to reduce the costs of regulation in order to weather recession and intensifying international competition from the Far East. In other words, part of their corporate strategy for the market has been a political strategy for deregulation. Finally, deregulation has had a cumulative impact across sectors in the United States ('what is good for one sector is good for another'). As far as Europe was concerned, the opening-up of American telecommunications markets to foreign competition proved 'a double-edged sword' as the United States sought reciprocal liberalisation, notably the relaxation of entry standards and certification procedures by West European PTTs. Faced by major import penetration, American equipment makers and trade negotiators put extra pressure on European PTTs to open their markets and on giving top priority to telecommunications in GATT negotiations.

Anti-trust was to be internationalised. Yet with a massive five-fold growth in value of American telecommunications imports between 1978 and 1983 the EC's share dropped from 9.6 per cent to 3.2 per cent; the Far East's share rose from 47.8 per cent to 74.8 per cent.[38] Such an alarming statistic underlined the acute vulnerability of Western Europe in one of its reputedly stronger sectors, telecommunications.

Secondly, communications markets provide evidence of a radical change in the international business environment — from a fixation on national markets to a 'globalisation' of competition in industry after industry. The paradigms for this change are ominously non-European: IBM, AT and T, Nippon Electric (NEC), Citicorp and Murdoch's News Corporation. Some European corporations are already attempting to shift to a global strategy by targeting world market share, notably Olivetti (forming major joint ventures with AT and T in 1983 and with Toshiba in 1985), BT (taking a stake in Mitel of Canada, a leading world supplier of PABXs, and acquiring Dialcom, the electronic mail subsidiary of ITT), Cable and Wireless and Saatchi and Saatchi (which with seven major American acquisitions in 1985 sought to become a global business services company). On the whole, however, European companies are too small and poorly organised to respond to the challenge of a new era of global competition (e.g. CGE of France and Thorn EMI, GEC and Plessey of Britain). What are the nature and the origins of the new global competition? Rising research and development costs and shortening life cycles for IT products place a premium on the ability to seize new marketing opportunities fast, to achieve high-volume production and to generate a large international cash flow to support continuing investment. The gap between an invention and its production and marketing (including by rival companies) has become so short (in telecommunications down from a decade to a year or less) that corporations can no longer afford the luxury of introducing a new product first in one market and then in another. Products must be designed from the outset for a world market (Japanese consumer electronics provide a paradigm here), and markets must be penetrated simultaneously and probably by means of 'strategic alliances' with corporations in other regions of the world in order to secure strong market entry and to spread risk. Kenichi Ohmae has written about the importance of 'triad power': corporations must have a base in each of the three key world markets (Europe, the United States and Japan), thus opening up an affluent market of 600 million people.[39] Absence from one of the legs of the triad leads to inevitable defeat.

Globalisation of competition has three implications for Western Europe. First, what sovereignty over communications can West European states claim when corporations are closely co-ordinating their activities so that international scale can be used as a strategic weapon against competitors and governments? Maxwell's criticisms of the British IBA as a regulator of broadcasting and Murdoch's criticisms of the French Socialist government in 1986 heralded a new dawn in international broadcasting, just as the alliances of AT and T and Corning Glass with numerous European countries underlined the realities of international telecommunications markets. Secondly, who will benefit from these new international strategic alliances? There was clear danger that joint ventures and licensing deals would prove a one-way relationship, with for instance Philips, Olivetti and Telefonica acting as Trojan-horses for AT and T, based on the latter's combination of technological leadership in key areas with managerial competence and its exploitation of joint ventures simply as a means of bypassing national protectionism. The American encouragement to participation by European firms and universities in SDI research posed a further risk to which France's Eureka initiative was a response: that Europe would be drained of its best people and ideas to support American defence research with little reciprocity by the Americans. On the other hand, as Sweden had demonstrated, joint ventures and licensing deals can serve as a valuable means of acquiring skills and expertise, not least in management. Which of the two scenarios predominates will depend ultimately on the negotiating skills and decisions of European corporations.[40] Thirdly, Ohmae has stressed the dangers of forging alliances with corporations that are too close in product or are in the same triad region. In other words, European collaboration can be no more than than one element in a corporation's global strategy. It is likely to be far less important than collaboration with corporations or acquisitions in the other two triad regions. Ericsson, Siemens, Olivetti, Philips, BT, Saatchi and Saatchi and Cap Gemini Sogeti seem to have learnt this lesson. Precisely because European corporations tend to share the same weaknesses, particularly in the commercial application of scientific ideas and similar product ranges, they tend to prefer links with American and Japanese corporations. Why pool weaknesses?

There are four aspects to the relationship between international markets and the development of communications policies in Western Europe. Together they promote an *interactivity* of national communications policies, with typically American actors setting the pace. Boundaries between national systems are being eroded, and a process of 'assimilative repetition' of American deregulatory experience seems under way, pioneered by Britain.

1. The internationalisation of markets is *used* by certain domestic interests as an argument for pressing for overdue adaptation of national policies in the direction of greater flexibility. Deregulation of broadcasting was promoted in these terms by the private cable television industry (led by Rediffusion) and sections of the electronics industry (like Racal) in Britain and by the publishers (notably Springer, Bauer and Burda) in West Germany. Behind the EC Green Paper 'Television Without Frontiers', proposing deregulation particularly of advertising and promoted by the competition directorate of the Commission, stood the European Advertising Tripartite. Big institutional investors sought deregulation of financial markets as a means of breaking the market power of brokers; new automated dealing systems, combined with new participants (banks, insurance companies and overseas firms) in securities markets, made this objective possible. Strong pressure for telecommunications deregulation came from multinational corporations, and especially financial corporations, whose communications costs were huge and for whom information functioned as their central nervous system. The International Telecommunications Users' Group and the Permanent Conference of Chambers of Commerce and Industry of the EC represented their interests in developing their own international communications systems to bypass the national PTTs. Similarly,

the European Computing Services Association (ECSA) campaigned against CEPT, pressing the need to liberate 'the highways for data' in Europe from the stranglehold of national PTTs whose policies of protectionism were impeding the progress of IT in Europe.

In turn, national PTTs began to use efficient foreign competitors as a lever for extracting changes in the domestic telecommunications supply industry, with Sweden as a paradigm of this process (as Richardson's chapter shows). Thus in 1985 BT put commercial pressure on GEC and Plessey, producers of the delayed and costly System X digital exchange, by choosing a second supplier of digital switching equipment (Thorn-Ericsson). After the merger of the telecommunications interests of CGE and Thomson, to which it objected, the French DGT looked for a second foreign supplier too. The West German Bundespost was also prepared to put Siemens under pressure: in 1983 it chose two digital exchanges — Siemens with its own EWS-D and ITT's Standard Elektrik Lorenz (SEL) with the ITT System 12 (Siemens' EWS-A had proved a fiasco in 1979); in 1981 IBM-Deutschland won the coveted contract for the German videotex system (*Bildschirmtext*); and in 1985 IBM and Nixdorf were selected to provide the Bundespost with its own computerised data system. The price of these PTT strategies was to draw domestic telecommunications closer into international markets.

2. Certain actors seek to detach themselves from the influence of domestic regulatory policy by becoming multinationals or even global players. By his attempted involvement in France's DBS satellite (TDF-I) Maxwell could escape British broadcasting regulations, in particular the provisions of the Representation of the Peoples Act relating to broadcasting during British election campaigns. Likewise Murdoch's link with Belgium's Groupe Bruxelles Lambert and Radio Television Luxembourg (RTL) to develop commercial DBS broadcasting was a further warning light for national regulatory authorities which were watching Murdoch's London-based and advertising-financed Sky Channel sweep towards commercial success. Already by a joint venture with RTL (RTL-Plus) the West German media giant Bertelsmann had succeeded in launching a German-language channel outside the jurisdiction of the German *Länder*.

A similar phenomenon can be seen in telecommunications services. In 1984 MCI Communications, linked closely with IBM in 1985, and GTE Sprint challenged AT and T in a price war in the transatlantic telephone market. Whereas BT, Belgium and Portugal welcomed and exploited this development, the French DGT and the West German Bundespost attempted to stand aloof from the new commercial pressures. Yet they found themselves being subjected to tightening encirclement. Perhaps more alarming was the pressure from American companies to bypass traditional public carriers of telecommunications traffic in the Atlantic basin by means of private fibre-optic cable and satellite systems, in particular challenging the effective monopoly of the International Telecommunications Satellite Organisation (Intelsat), in international satellite communications. Intelsat, which was established in 1964, carried about two-thirds of all international telephone traffic (government-owned regional systems carry the rest) and almost all international television broadcasts. In 1983 support was lent by the Reagan administration to the applications from five American companies (including Orion Satellite) to the Federal Communications Commission (FCC) for permission to launch a private-sector international satellite communications system for company use.[41] The consequence was a fierce battle between the American government and Intelsat, which feared that the world would be split apart in a 'mindless sprawl' of uncoordinated systems and that poorer Third World countries would suffer from the consequences of a 'creaming-off' of its more profitable activities. Though the applications were restricted to intra-company video, data and voice transmissions, this sector was the fastest growing and the most profitable. Similarly, the new transatlantic fibre optic cable TAT-8, pioneered by 28 PTTs and due to come into service in 1988, was challenged by a private-sector consortium, Tel-Optik, headed by Britain's Cable and Wireless, and scheduled to operate from 1989.

Far more advanced is the situation in international financial markets. These markets are being radically transformed by the emergence of global multi-billion dollar traders in securities, using computerised trading and operating on the New York, Tokyo and London axis.[42] They will be able to tap directly all the world's largest domestic pools of capital at once, in particular the government bond markets and stock exchanges of the three major centres. Traders like Citicorp and Merrill Lynch and the electronic information services on which they rely, such as, Bridge, Quotron and Reuters, stressed the loss of business that would occur to European financial centres that were 'undeveloped', 'parochial' and 'over-regulated'. Screen systems, like those just mentioned, gave London investors easy access to the New York stock market where by 1985 trading in some leading stocks such as ICI was more active than in London; in turn London had developed an active market in continental European securities. The process of global trading required at least one financial centre in each of the triad regions to open the doors to the new international financial networks like Reuters or Quotron. Their services were extended from transmission of huge volumes of money-market data for dealing rooms to share information and trading in securities by means of automated interactive dealing. Reuters, Bridge and Quotron, along with the international financial conglomerates, emphasised that the amount of data on prices and volumes and the speed and transparency of trading had become key factors in the competitiveness of particular financial centres. Correspondingly, they put pressure on national financial regulatory authorities, like the London Stock Exchange, to restructure their trading system and increase their international competitiveness by a combination of new technology with deregulation (in line with the so-called 'Big Bang' pioneeered by the New York Stock Exchange). Reuters developed an uneasy relationship with stock exchanges; it acted as both a customer for their price collection systems and a rival carrier of information to dealers through its network. More than just highly lucrative business was at stake. As dealing information becomes more fragmented, the problems of supervising markets would grow. The powerful presence of Reuters, as a news agency and financial services group, extended in fact beyond financial markets to broadcasting. In 1985 Reuters increased its stake in Visnews, the London-based international television news agency, with the objective of challenging the EBU. The aim was to establish a private-sector international television news and information exchange for the growing number of private commercial broadcasters (like Murdoch) who were excluded from EBU's daily Eurovision news exchange.

3. The threat of location of investment by multinationals in more deregulated environments promotes a process of competitive deregulation. Deregulation offers the prize of investment and jobs in financial services, telecommunications and broadcasting and increased tax revenue from these sources. In order to achieve these glittering prizes governments are encouraged to view domestic communications policies as 'international gamesmanship' and deregulation as a prime national instrument of international economic policy. Thus deregulation in financial markets grew out of rapid internationalisation, starting in 1971 with the end of the Bretton Woods system of fixed parities; all major currencies began to float and financial markets became more internationalised. Then globalisation and pressures for deregulation developed further with the lifting of exchange controls and more sophisticated telecommunications. As if to underline the significance of these new demands in pushing forward the communications revolution, Reuters' Monitor system began in 1973 to provide electronic screen-delivered financial services. By 1984 33 on-line financial information systems were available in the London market; and in the so-called 'Big Bang' of 1986 the London Stock Exchange planned its own real-time market information service, Stock Exchange Automated Quotations (SEAQ). Meanwhile, Reuters was about to introduce the Instinet electronic trading system to Britain. By 1986 Reuters provided financial data to some 54,000 screens and 6,300 teleprinters world-wide. Throughout West European financial centres there was a fear of becoming increasingly uncompetitive in a world dominated by global American and Japanese traders with superior technology. In London these big global dealers established the International Securities Regulatory Organisation (ISRO) as both a self-policing body and as a lobby for a new regulatory structure. In addition to international pressures the threat of migration of domestic business to more rapidly innovating financial centres like New York and London forced the hand of domestic regulators like the West German Bundesbank. In particular, the move of Eurobond activity to London by the Deutsche Bank and by Paribas and Société Générale caused headaches in Frankfurt and Paris. The European dilemma seemed an unhappy one: either loose valuable financial business or submit to the vagaries of a new global trading system. Britain's Conservative government was determined to secure the City's position in the European Time Zone and thereby generate revenue and jobs. One means was a competitive bidding-down of tax on securities' transactions and lower corporate taxation than in either Japan or the United States. Certainly, the customary privileges and practices of informality, secrecy and 'gentlemanly' self-regulation by traditional élites in the London Stock Exchange and Lloyds had become unviable. The Financial Services Act of 1986, with its refashioned statute-based system of self-regulation, reflected the attempt to inject greater professionalism consistent with the ethos of the large multinational financial conglomerates.[43]

Examples of this process can also be drawn from telecommunications and broadcasting. In telecommunications traffic diversion has become easier as more communications take place between large computer centres which can be shifted from one country to another in search of more favourable telecommunications regulations and tariffs. Thus Belgium and the Netherlands have attempted to woo telecommunications business from a more regulated environment in West Germany. The consequence has been growing pressure on the Bundespost from the Federal Economics Ministry and from Deutsche Telecom, the business users' association, to liberalise its policy on cross-border data flows and reduce high tariffs. Perhaps most strikingly of all, by a policy of low international tariffs BT has persuaded about one-third of American multinationals in Europe, like Bank of America (which closed its Frankfurt centre), to 'hub' their communications networks in Britain. Deregulation in new media policy is also encouraged by the search to attract investment. This process is perhaps most obvious in West Germany where the individual *Länder* are sovereign in cultural and therefore broadcasting policy. SPD *Länder* have been reluctant in principle to encourage private commercial broadcasting, which has been backed by the CDU/CSU and closely related press interests like Springer and Burda. Consequently, the lead in new media legislation has come from CDU *Länder*, and it had proved impossible by 1986 to agree a state treaty to extend traditional 'co-operative' federalism in broadcasting to the new media. Amongst the factors encouraging the SPD *Länder* from 'principled' to 'constructive' opposition were the federal government's use of the incentive of cable investment by the Bundespost to those *Länder* that deregulated broadcasting; and the prospect of a shift of new media investment to CDU/CSU *Länder*. In particular, SPD Hamburg, West Germany's major media centre and a city beset by problems of structural adjustment, feared the rivalry of Munich. The SPD Lord Mayor of Hamburg became the leading advocate in the party of a more realistic new media policy.[44]

The hesitations of domestic policy-makers about this new sort of international gamesmanship were understandable. The concerns of central bankers about the effects of rapid internationalisation and competitive deregulation on financial markets were apparent in the 1985 annual report of the Bank for International Settlements: we are in a 'situation with no historical precedent ... no guide to analysis can be found in past experience'. As the effectiveness of supervision at the national level declined, there were new risks of massive financial imprudence as dealers speculated in nervous markets and exploited weaknesses. Central bankers were uneasy. The blurring of the distinction between banks and other financial institutions was making the process of regulation harder. They noted the greater exposure of the banks to rate-sensitive securities markets and the rapid growth of 'off-balance sheet' business. When combined with the greater mobility of capital, the effect was to inhibit domestic monetary policy and undermine its effectiveness.[45] In addition, newly efficient international financial markets with global actors seemed of little relevance to the big problem of enterprise and job creation in 'unfashionable' declining regions and countries. By attracting banks away from local, regional and even national identities they threatened to exacerbate this problem. In telecommunications the search for low tariffs to encourage international business and 'cream off' highly profitable services was accompanied by much higher charges for local calls, the latter being borne by domestic consumers and small businesses. By 1985 BT's local charges were the highest in Western Europe, a victory for the large corporate users. The West German Bundespost was, by contrast, subject to stronger political and social constraints in pursuing such strategy. Its commitment to the principle of universal service proved more resolute. In broadcasting and new media policy the policy process and legislation itself were in danger of degenerating into a charade of symbolic politics, their function being simply to legitimate changes 'required' by the international economy.

4. The structure and development of international markets creates ideological as well as economic pressures. Thus American economic success in international markets is translated into the 'model' character of American deregulation and American 'enterprise culture', with its emphasis on the pioneering individual, an active venture capital market and ease of market entry and exit for small firms. Earlier, just after 1945, in the heyday of 'the second industrial revolution', the United States had sought to embed into the economic and industrial organisation of occupied Germany a system of competitive oligopoly based on 'decartelisation' and the ideas of 'Fordism' and 'Taylorism'. Germany's role as the most powerful and dynamic European economy was to ensure the spread of the American model of competitive oligopoly throughout Europe. In the 1980s, with 'the third industrial revolution', the earlier American model of 'decartelisation' was replaced by 'deregulation', and the British context of a new neo-liberalism under Margaret Thatcher seemed to offer the new key point of entry and dissemination for American ideas. However, a 'high politics' of 'saving Europe from fascism' by decartelisation was no longer so much in evidence. A 'low politics' of market access predominated in the 1980s.[47]

Nevertheless the rising prestige of the American model of deregulation was not simply to be explained by heavy, mounting and tough lobbying in Europe for an 'open entry' policy in telecommunications and telematics by the likes of the US Department of Commerce, IBM and AT and T and by the appointment of a Coordinator for International Communication and Information Policy in the US Department of State.[48] It represented the more subtle ideological pressure from success. European public policies towards the communications revolution begin to express an American cultural hegemony. Influential converts to the American model – 'Americans in Europe' – could be found as domestic agents of change in the leadership not just of the British Conservative Party but also of the French centre-right alliance (RPR-UDF), the Dutch liberal-conservative VVD and the West German liberal FDP and the centre-right CDU/CSU. In short, the character of international markets played a major part in inducing a changed ideological climate in Western Europe. Further and perhaps surprising support came from the OECD in its economic report on the United States in 1985.[49] It stressed the major macroeconomic effects of sectoral deregulation – lower inflation, productivity gains and more moderate wage settlements. The battle to sustain European sovereignty in communications was serious, and resistance was not without success. It seemed, however, essentially a defensive action whose temporary gains (e.g. quotas on foreign television programming, restrictions on television advertising and on multimedia ownership, conditions imposed by national financial regulatory authorities on the electronic financial information services) seemed unlikely to stand the test of time.

In these four ways international developments are prising open the traditional features of the relations between the state and telecommunications authorities and suppliers and between the state and broadcasting in Western Europe. Their relations are no longer so closed, private and privileged; they are certainly less predictable. These international forces are creating a *convergence* of communications policies. Western Europe seems to be following American experience with a time-lag, and ideological opposition appears doomed to frustration and failure. Thus the French Socialist government and the SPD *Länder* in West Germany had moved to constructive opposition by 1986: the French Socialists had relaxed advertising feature-film restrictions for the new commercial Canal Cinque of Berlusconi and Seydoux and not applied the restrictions on national multimedia diversification promised in Article 80 of the Law on Audiovisual Communications;[50] and the SPD were accepting the idea of a public-private mix in broadcasting and encouraging the public-service broadcasters to compete more aggressively via the new 'Eins Plus' satellite channel.

At the same time no single approach to the international political economy commands general agreement or even opens up the possibility of a consensus amongst those who advocate the primacy of the perspective of the international political economy in interpreting the communications revolution.[51] Nevertheless, despite their major differences, two schools of international political economy — the liberal and the Marxist — share a stress on the subordination of national policy and politics to the international political economy. Ultimately both see a functional logic at work in domestic politics. The liberal approach pictures a private-enterprise, *laissez-faire* and free-trade international economy, in which the fundamental realities are 'rational' producers in a system of economic exchange based on the logic of comparative advantage and the satisfaction of consumer preferences. Against this background continuing close governmental regulation of broadcasting and telecommunications in Western Europe is seen as likely to produce irrational outcomes. Its only justification can be as symbolic politics, the politics of gesture. The Marxist approach pictures an international political economy of dependence and subordination based on exploitation and the neo-colonialist tendencies in world capitalism.[52] Thus the communications revolution provides a case-study of American 'informal empire' with dangerous destabilising consequences, particularly with new global financial trading. The role of West European governments in regulating the process appears as futile, as condemned to legitimate the inevitable.

Both approaches see the story of communications policies in Western Europe as strategies of legitimation and of the symbolic uses of politics to disguise utilitarian calculations of economic interest and the realities of international market power as they view them. These strategies become more elaborate, the more intense is the level of public concern and debate about the character of the communications revolution: and we saw earlier how the level of debate has varied in Western Europe. In Britain legitimation appeared comparatively simple and clear-cut, with the Carter report (1977), the Beesley review (1981) and the Telecommunications Acts (1981 and 1984) leading to a progressive liberalisation of telecommunications, and with the ITAP report (1982), the Hunt report (1982) and the Cable and Broadcasting Act (1984) representing an even more rapid process of deregulation of broadcasting.[53] In France early political opposition to the technocratic telematics plan of 1978, particularly from local press and politicians, suggested the need for a more cautious process of legitimation for the communications revolution. In addition to the continuing role of the DGT's own National Centre for Telecommunications Studies (CNET) in intellectual legitimation by government-backed research, two other aspects of the French approach were distinctive: the co-optation of local authorities into the cable plan as organisers of local cable consortia (the SLECs) and the establishment of the interministerial Mission TV Cable to encourage local authority involvement.[54] The most striking characteristic of West Germany was the succession of eleborate committees of inquiry: from the KtK (1974–76) through the Expertenkommission in Baden-Würtemberg and the Enquetekommission of the Bundestag to the Medienkommission der Länder and the Witte Commission of inquiry into telecommunications.[55] For historical, constitutional and political reasons control of broadcasting was a sensitive issue in West Germany; in so far as the communications revolution affected broadcasting it was, therefore, bound to be controversial. Legitimation requirements were high in West Germany. They were also high at the EC level where the Commission recognised the political sensitivity of cross-national broadcasting when national views on appropriate regulatory conditions, for instance for advertising, varied so widely and when cultural sovereignty could be taken very seriously indeed. Its response was to use a special procedure: to present a Green Paper, 'Television Without Frontiers', as the basis for elaborate discussions with governments, groups and experts before, rather than as usual after, a draft directive had been prepared. In practice few participants, with the exceptions of the advertising industry and the cable and satellite lobbies, welcomed the proposals. Yet the responsible directorate (internal market and industrial affairs, DG3) was unwilling to deviate from its basic principle of tolerance in accepting foreign broadcasts that adhered to certain minimal conditions on advertising and protection of minors. Again, elaborate procedure can be interpreted as a legitimating device.

Powerful industrial interests and concerns about corporate status and power can be discerned behind these legitimating strategies: initially electronics companies and the private cable television lobby, and later BT and the new programme providers, seeking opportunities for diversification in Britain; the DGT, concerned to maintain its new-found status and investment, and the industrial cable lobby CODITEC in France; the Bundespost and the press in West Germany; and the advertisers in the EC.[56] Committees of inquiry and government-backed research could be interpreted as important not so much for their independent impact on communications policy as for their symbolic uses. The sophistication of their development seemed to reflect simply the extent of domestic problems of containing and managing the political conflicts unleashed by the international communications revolution. Such a perspective leads to the prediction that new telecommunications, media and data protection legislation in Western Europe will have symbolic rather than practical values. They seem and indeed seek to restrain commercial actors. In practice they contain neither adequately specified criteria for strong and effective regulation nor sufficiently well-briefed and well-staffed regulatory bodies, with close access to decision makers, to enable effective implementation. Agencies like Oftel and the Cable Authority in Britain appear as cosmetic devices, not even worthwhile 'capturing' by interests; they can be seen as mere spectators.

Thesis 2: that changes in national communications policies reflect the complex interaction of the political ideology of government and the character of the relevant domestic policy sector or sectors

This thesis draws attention to the domestic context of communications policies and has its roots in comparative political science.[57] Domestic policy processes and 'styles' are regarded as distinctive and significant, with particular attention being given to ideas about the role and autonomy of the state and to the degree of monopolisation of interest representation. It is important to consider: who are the actors; what sort of values and beliefs they hold; and what sort of policy 'networks' and power relations exist. Interest focuses on the character of political leadership, the institutional structure of the state and the nature and functioning of 'pressure politics'. This thesis argues for the *diversity* of national (and subnational) policy responses to the communications revolution. It tends to ignore the international political economy or to treat it as 'background'. In so far as international political economy emerges in analysis, the approach is neomercantilist. The international realities are seen as a world of politically self-interested sovereign states facing imperfect competition and a maldistribution of power within the international economy.[58] The consequence is a requirement for government intervention and a close symbiotic relationship between state and econony. Government intervention is potentially rational, and the programmes, structures and functioning of government are of great potential significance.

From a comparative perspective the impact of political ideologies and notions of the state on new communications policies in Western Europe seems clear. In France the twin themes of *étatisme* and (to a lesser extent) *autogestion* (self-management) were reflected in the communications policies of the Socialists after 1981: in the privileged role of the DGT in telematics and the cable plan and more broadly in the *filière électronique*, and in the co-option of local authorities into the cable plan as initiators, negotiators and co-financiers wtih the DGT and as co-managers in the SLECs that were to manage local cable networks. The French Socialists' embrace of the ideology of French national independence was apparent in the emphasis of the Minister of Culture, Jack Lang, on the promotion and protection of the national 'cultural industries' and of a 'Latin audiovisual space'. Mission TV Cable was established to put together a library of French programmes for the new media, plans were announced for tax shelters to encourage more risk capital to be put into film and television production, the SLECs were expected to support the French programme industry with one-third of their revenue, and a maximum quota on foreign programmes (30 per cent) and a minimum quota of local programming were suggested. The equation of national independence with economic modernisation and of economic modernisation with the communications revolution was crucial in another sense. It facilitated an active consensus on audiovisual communications as an economic and industrial requirement for France.

In West Germany policies for the communications revolution revealed the latent tensions at the heart of the ideology of the 'social market economy', with its combination of market competition with public-service values. Though there was a party political consensus on the social market economy, the new Christian Democratic–Liberal federal government after 1982 felt a special responsibility for its more effective application in new technology policies. On the one hand, the monopoly of the Bundespost in provision and management of the telecommunications network was maintained. More sub-contracting work went to private-sector cable firms, and, to stall mounting criticism from within the coalition parties, a committee of inquiry into the telecommunications monopoly was eventually established in 1985. However, the Federal Minister for Posts and Telecommunications, Christian Schwarz-Schilling, indicated that neither privatisation nor network competition Thatcher-style were envisaged. On the other hand, market ideology was asserted in new media policy. CDU *Länder* encouraged new private satellite and cable broadcasting consortia like Sat I and introduced new media laws to ensure their access to a market, while Schwarz-Schilling offered his support in the form of a special huge copper-coaxial cable programme (which also benefited small- and medium-sized firms in line with CDU support for the *Mittelstand*). The SPD used its position in the federal structure to try to block the extension of market ideology to the traditional public-service realm of broadcasting. Indeed the SPD criticised the CDU/CSU for diverting precious resources from the key area of the communications revolution to satisfy its short-term partisan obsession with revolutionising broadcasting. The SPD gave priority to an integrated service digital network (ISDN) based on a new broad-band and extremely expensive optic-fibre cable system. In any case the CDU/CSU retained the commitment to an ISDN managed by the Bundespost.

The central strategy of the British Conservative government after 1979 was to roll back the frontiers of the state. This aim achieved its symbol in reduction of the PSBR and was to be realised in two ways: by cuts in public expenditure and taxes and by privatisation. In particular the themes of privatisation and lower public spending were exhibited in policies for the communications revolution (though, as we have seen, debate about this revolution was rather muted in Britain). Following the recommendations of the ITAP report of 1982 the cable revolution was to be 'entertainment-led' and driven by new private-sector investment. The Cable and Broadcasting Act of 1984 established a Cable Authority to provide a 'light-touch' regulation of the new private cable television operators, with no restrictions on the ability of companies to combine the functions of cable provider, cable operator and cable programmer. This encouragement of private investment in cable by light regulation was not in fact matched either by appropriate tax inducements (in the 1984 budget the *withdrawal* of capital allowances was announced) or by a deregulation of telecommunications so that new cable operators could develop telephony services. Contradiction and muddle plagued also the Telecommunications Act of 1984. Liberalisation of telecommunications was an aim, but increased competition and its effective regulation by Oftel took second place to the aim of privatisation on the best possible terms for the exchequer. The consequence was that reassurance for future shareholders of BT became more important than fostering the maximum competition.[59] Oftel's staffing and powers were weak, and BT secured substantial market power. Yet, whatever the muddle and inconsistencies in implementation, the force of Thatcherism in British communications policies seems very apparent.

The impact of the political ideology of governments would seem to be all the greater when it mobilises powerful traditions within national political culture behind it.[60] Thus Thatcherism draws on a deeply rooted tradition of 'arms' length' government in Britain; French Socialism appealed to *étatisme* and national independence. At the same time new communications policies cannot simply be explained by 'who governs'. Their development reflects also the character of the policy sector or sectors involved and the rapid changes of power relations there. Earlier we saw how traditional policy sectors like telecommunications and broadcasting are being subjected to change, expansion and convergence as a consequence of technological and economic factors. Nevertheless, they continue to be influenced by the inheritance of past policymaking and performance. Reputation and credibility are an important resource of influence. Thus the leading role of the DGT in the French communications revolution drew on its successful modernisation of telecommunications in the 1970s and its subsequent status and prestige. By contrast, in the late 1970s BT had a reputation for outdated equipment, low investment and overmanning.

Domestic policy-making is to be understood, at least in part, by reference to 'who inhabits the policy sector', 'what values are held by these actors' and the extent of solidarity or community that exists in the policy sector. In practice the domestic politics of communications policies in Western Europe reveals little (in fact diminishing) stability and predictability in power relationships. Hence it seems appropriate to think of policy-making in terms of a flux of 'issue networks' – of a model of pluralistic bargaining – rather than of the cohesion and solidarity of one or more 'policy communities'.[61] Cleavages have been striking: witness the conflict between cultural policy and industrial policy perspectives (whether in debate about the EC's Green Paper 'Television Without Frontiers' or in the conflict in France about programming policies for cable between the Ministers of Culture and Communications, Jack Lang and Georges Fillioud, who were concerned to have quotas, and the Ministers for the PTT and of the Interior, Louis Mexendeau and Gaston Defferre, for whom economic viability was central); between rival industrial projects (with in France the DGT promoting its own cable plan and general communications satellites and Télédiffusion de France and the Ministry of Industry promoting the DBS satellite TDF-I); between national and subnational perspectives, with, in France, Defferre and Mexendeau disputing the sharing of costs for the cable plan between the DGT and the local authorities, and, in West Germany, the division of constitutional responsibilities between federation (telecommunications) and *Länder* (broadcasting) aggravating and delaying policy formation, and with new strains between CDU *Länder* and Bavaria as the latter sought satellite capacity to broadcast the regional public-service station Bayrischer Rundfunk nationally as 'the voice of Bavaria' (and of the Bavarian CSU of Franz-Josef Strauss) in competition with the new private channels sponsored by the CDU; and between those who wish to promote the PTT as the national IT champion and those who wish to liberalise telecommunications (with industry ministers in Britain oscillating between these two positions to BT). At most the communications revolution is generating only a very loose 'community' in policy making based on some shared interests. In so broad and fast-changing a field of activities the main impression is of complex, shifting and contending 'networks'.

If the relationship between the ideologies of governments and the character of policy sectors is complex in the development of communications policies, a pattern can be discerned in Western Europe. New governments, whether of right or left, have teased out of particular policy sectors certain interests that have seen an opportunity to advance themselves by identification with the ideology of the government. In Britain certain electronics interests, like Rediffusion, were encouraged by the nature of the Prime Minister's appointments to ITAP (established broadcasting and telecommunications interests were excluded) and its Cable Systems report of 1982, while firms like Cable and Wireless (co-founder and later owner of Mercury, which was licensed in 1981 to operate an alternative network to BT) and Racal (which was licensed to operate a competing cellular radio network to that of BT) responded to the telecommunications challenge and Thorn-EMI to the programming challenge. In the very different context of the victory of the French Socialists in 1981 the DGT and CODITEC marshalled their proposals in a different manner: a bold, national and comprehensive cable plan with a decentralist flavour that would ensure huge industrial orders and sustain the new *grand corps* status of the DGT. In West Germany the Bundespost and allied commercial interests aligned themselves, not least for employment reasons, with Chancellor Kohl's promise to 'unblock cable' in his first declaration of government in 1982. Characteristic of this stage of policy-making for the communications revolution in Western Europe were technological and economic 'hype' and bold heroic strategies. Encouraged by industrial groups, politicians preferred to appear as 'hares' rather than 'tortoises'. The consequences were inflated expectations of technology, markets (notably for cable television and videotex) and employment creation (the immediate and visible impact of digital switching for the telecommunications network and of electronic publishing was sizeable job losses). West European politicians seemed to have been hijacked by powerful lobbies that their own ideological vigour had encouraged. These lobbies might comprise forces mainly within the state, as in France, promising a high degree of autonomy and voluntarism in state action, or forces mainly external to the state, as in Britain.

The subsequent pattern was that heroic strategy – whether positing heroic entrepreneurs, British ITAP-style, or the heroic state, in the manner of the French cable plan – passed to the bureaucratic and group politics of the relevant policy sector or sectors for detailed elaboration and implementation. At this stage the character of the regular policy sector becomes significant for policy development, not least if its structure includes interests at variance with the heroic strategy or even averse to heroism. Specifically, is heroic strategy implemented by those interests that proposed it? In Britain the leading role of ITAP, and its promise of coherent and decisive action, was rapidly dissipated by the inconsistencies and muddle generated by compartmentalised decision-making. There was a failure of 'follow-through' to the all-important details. The pioneer of cable television, Rediffusion, had all but one of its applications for new cable franchises turned down by the Home Office and the Department of Trade and Industry. In 1985 Rediffusion was sold to the publisher, Robert Maxwell. As a consequence of the Department of Trade and Industry's concern to make BT as attractive as possible for privatisation, telecommunications licences for cable operators proved very restrictive. Meanwhile, the withdrawal of capital allowances in the 1984 budget by the Treasury was the very opposite of the benign tax structure that infant industries require in an economy that expects heroism of the private entrepreneur. In the French case a stronger element of continuity was provided by the strategic role accorded to the DGT in the *filière électronique*. Yet the DGT was to find itself beleagured and frustrated. The French Socialist government raided its budget for revenue purposes to support its new policy of *rigueur* after 1983. Also, France reveals another interesting and complicating phenomenon in the development of communications policies – the widening of the policy sector by the government's own actions. The implementation of the cable plan became bound up with the great decentralisation strategy of the Socialists. Initially the DGT saw involvement by local authorities as a useful legitimising device (in the wake of the political problems associated with the telematics plan) and as a means of defraying the heavy costs of the cable plan. In practice, it was frustrated by the difficult and slow process of negotiating with the local authorities and by the more limited technological and programming ambitions of many local authorities.

A further complicating factor was the proliferation of communications policy initiatives. Thus cable television was part of a wider new media and telecommunications picture, and rational implementation of a cable strategy based on entertainment depended on its close co-ordination with policies in these latter areas. In fact, compartmentalism reigned, and these other interests and issues competed successfully for the scarce time of beleaguered and confused governments. In Britain there was a failure of co-ordination between the cable and broadcasting and the telecommunications reforms, a failure attributable not simply to different departmental philosophies in the Home Office and the Department of Industry but to lack of co-ordination within the Department of Industry itself. One statute encouraged an alternative private-sector cable TV network with interactive services; the other sought to reassure future shareholders of the privatised BT that it would remain a powerful force for telecommunications modernisation. The French cable plan was followed by a new fourth 'off-air' pay-television channel Canal Plus, by the rise of DBS to the top of the political agenda with the threat that Luxembourg would launch a private 'Coca-Cola' DBS satellite (an attempt was made to 'buy off' Luxembourg by offering it channels on France's TDF-I), by the recommendation of the Bredin report in 1985 that two new national television channels and some 60 local stations should be established, and, most controversially of all, by President Mitterrand's sudden announcement in November 1985 that a fifth 'off-air' channel, with few advertising restrictions, had been allocated to Berlusconi, the Italian television magnate, and Seydoux and that this channel and another, with participation by Robert Maxwell, would later broadcast from TDF-I. In particular, enthusiasts for cable television had underestimated the unrealised potential of traditional media policy-making; liberalisation of the hertzian airwaves offered a relatively cheap and speedy means of providing greater diversity in broadcasting. Thus, in 1984, a World Administration Radio Conference (WARC) agreement in Geneva released new frequencies for transmission; the *Land* media law of Baden-Würtemberg in 1985 took advantage of this new 20-year plan to encourage local and regional commercial channels. In the words of Jean-François Lacan French communications policy was characterised by '*auto-cannibalisme*'. Different technological, administrative and political logics asserted themselves in policy-making; only 'the logic of the market' remained in abeyance.[62]

Some conclusions may be drawn from a comparative examination of domestic policy processes for the communications revolution.

1. A strength of French communications policy has been the willingness to think strategically and to link the importance of particular policies for modernising communications (like Teletel, France's videotex) to the stimulation of the wider *filière électronique*. The weakness has been the coexistence of several different strategies for the communications revolution, a subsequent lack of coherence and a danger of '*auto-cannibalisme*'. Yet this weakness is in part the product of the very vigour and anxiety that characterises French policies for the communications revolution. Compared with Britain, these policies are rooted in a more critical analysis of international markets; there is stronger evidence of a search for rational and effective implementation at the sub-system level, notably in the DBS venture and in Teletel (whose flexibility and 'loss-leader' services generated many more subscribers than to the older BT Prestel system); and the cooptation of local authorities into the cable policy process, supported by the role of Mission TV Cable, provided an educative function, widening and deepening debate about the communications revolution.[63]

The main thrust of British communications policies has been provided by institutional reforms (notably privatisation of BT) and a finance-led strategy that has sought to encourage non-governmental investment (as in DBS and cable television). This willingness of the British Conservatives to tackle institutional reforms could be contrasted with the apparent conservatism of the French Socialists and the West German Christian Democrats. Perhaps the major achievement was a revitalisation of BT as a consequence of the threat of greater competition. Yet comparison raises some serious questions about

British policies for the communications revolution. Their abstract commitment to privatisation and the market has an appealing rugged simplicity; it seems also naive in its assumption that ownership matters more than market structure and regulatory regime. High-level political will and interest has been invested in simple institutional reforms rather than in the strategic management and development of new communications systems and in a strong regulatory regime. This relative absence of substantive debate about communications policy issues may have been reinforced by the lack of a separate minister for posts and telecommunications as in France and West Germany (France also had a minister of communications). Another aspect of naivety was the failure to ground policy in an analysis of the power structures of international markets; hence the French view of Britain as a Trojan horse for American capitalism in Europe. By 1986 there was open competition for terminal equipment supply, competition between BT and Racal in new national cellular radio networks, exclusion of BT from the new national mobile radio services, competition in value-added services with new government proposals for a liberalisation of the market by omnibus licences for both value-added and data services (a broader definition that further delimited the scope of BT's and Mercury's network monopoly) and interconnection of the BT and Mercury networks on terms very favourable to Mercury. Ominously, and in contrast to the situation in France and West Germany, the impacts of exposure to international markets were not cushioned by preferential public purchasing policies and subcontracting policies with the aim of promoting long-term confidence in the domestic communications industries and of giving a number of indigenous 'lead firms' time to develop. Thus in terminals supply IBM, Digital Equipment and NCR were able to rapidly penetrate the British market and seemed likely to be the major beneficiaries of the nationwide 'cashless shopping' system planned for the late 1980s (EFT-POS, electronic funds transfer at the point of sale). Cellular radio expansion in Britain benefited chiefly Motorola, NEC and Ericsson.

In Britain rational policy-making was little in evidence: witness the inconsistency of aims and subsequent muddle and uncertainty generated by telecommunications reform; the assumption of ITAP that sensible policies could be devised and resources found to develop duplicate networks, BT's own and private cable TV; government's threat to the finances of BBC and ITV (with a small increase of licence fee for BBC accompanied by the Peacock committee of inquiry into the future financing of BBC) when both were being encouraged to shoulder the heavy costs of a British-made DBS satellite without public subsidy (hence the delay of British DBS compared to France and West Germany); and the failure to deliver a tax structure compatible with expectations of private-sector heroism in cable television. Not least, British policy failed to develop an educative role for the state by creating institutional structures through which a public learning process could evolve. Decision-making by Oftel and by the Cable Authority is private; there are not the formal hearings characteristic of the American FCC. Cooptation of local authorities into the French cable plan, allied to the mobilising role of Mission TV Cable, has generated substantial public debate in France. In West Germany the constitutional division of responsibilities in the federal system, combined with the significance of rulings from the Federal Constitutional Court (like the FRAG judgement of 1981), has ensured high visibility for the new media debate.[64]

2. From 1983 onwards communications policies have been subjected to demystification as more modest expectations about the time scale and problems of the communications revolution have taken hold. This process was most apparent in new media policy where, even before 1983, the shaky start of BT's Prestel videotex system and the shake-out in the American cable television industry provided evidence for the sceptics.[65] The financing and marketing problems of new media were subsequently 'revealed' in a series of reports, in Britain from private consultants like CIT Research and in West Germany by a critical report from the Federal Audit Court (*Bundesrechnungshof*) about Bundespost policy. Only the French state, perhaps aided and abetted by 'official' research from the DGT's own CNET, has been able to sustain some degree of myth. In broad terms the policy cycle in new media shifted from heroism through frustrated expectations and a 'new realism' to recrimination as blame was allocated for failures of implementation in new media. The practical lesson is that it is very risky in political and economic terms to employ heroic policy styles in a field like communications; and, conversely, that it is easy to be misled into doing so by the economic and technological 'hype' from special and very professional interests. Heroic technocratic initiatives are not compatible with key features of the communications revolution: the sheer breadth and speed of technological and economic change, the complex convergence and collision of so many 'issue networks', the sensitivity to consumer and corporate choice, consumer resistance to the costs of proliferating communications services, and the reliance on the quality of technological and creative skills available to exploit commercial applications. In particular, timing has proved a critical factor in policy. For instance, ITAP's concept of a Britain wired on the back of an 'entertainment-led' cable television development was launched just as the VCR boom was soaking up demand for entertainment. VCRs have been the definite winner of the 'new media race' in Britain and indeed elsewhere. In Italy the rapid expansion of local 'off-air' broadcasting after 1976 deflected interest away from new media. Meanwhile, while many new media were bogged down in problems of implementation, the Geneva frequency plan of 1984 gave a fresh stimulus to development of 'off-air' broadcasting in Western Europe. In this way the timing of new developments in communications can be decisive for the future pattern of the communications revolution, and, within limits, governments can influence the timing of new developments. Thus the French government attempted to restrain the entry of VCRs on to the French market.

3. West European communications policies have been shaped by three factors since 1983: the shift from a 'high-profile' political strategy to a 'low-profile' set of industrial policies; the shake-out in industry as it was recognised that there would be a long haul to profitability and that significant effects, economic, social and political, from the communications revolution would take a decade and more; and the emergence of new types of conglomerates

and multinational alliances, both of which helped to mitigate risk. Again Western Europe seemed to be following the United States where, for instance, IBM bought into Rolm (PABX manufacture) and MCI Communications (long-distance telecommunications services) and established a joint venture with Merrill Lynch for an electronic financial information and dealing system, Murdoch acquired Twentieth Century Fox and GEC took over RCA with its broadcasting and telecommunications interests. STC's purchase of ICL, Thorn-EMI's of Inmos and Maxwell's of Rediffusion reflected a similar process in Britain. Multi-media conglomerates began to alter the balance of power in domestic policy development. Thus in new media policy in Britain the leading role of cable television operators was displaced by the interests of cable and satellite programmers; liberalisation of the installation of satellite receiving dishes (SMATV) was an important gain for the programmers. These conglomerates also emerged as international actors: Bertelsmann with RTL, Murdoch with Groupe Bruxelles Lambert and Berlusconi and Maxwell with France's TDF-I. Albeit defensively, public broadcasting corporations established an interest in satellite broadcasting: a consortium of Belgian, French and Swiss in the French-language TV5, a consortium of Austrian, Swiss and West German in the German-language 3-SAT, the consortium of West German public broadcasting stations operating the first-channel ARD service (plus a Swiss station) in 'Eins Plus', the association of a West German (ARD), Irish (RTE), Italian (RAI), Dutch (NOS) and Portuguese (RTP) station in Europa-TV under the auspices of EBU, and Britain's ITV – spurred by Granada Television – in a proposed Super Channel offering 'the best of British'. The international activities of media conglomerates were the most visible manifestation of the communications revolution. In practice, however, they were only one aspect of the dynamism for change in regulatory policies emanating from new international markets, notably money markets, and the multinational corporations. The pressures from internationalisation on domestic policy were becoming inexorably more apparent.

4. As states began, slowly and hesitantly, to recognise the need to come to grips with the realities of the international communications revolution, fragmentation and pluralistic bargaining in the domestic policy process emerged as problems rather than just the natural and necessary accompaniments of deregulation. Co-ordination within government and partnership of public and private actors was increasingly seen as essential.[66] Not least, American policymakers and analysts started to count the unintended consequences of their pioneering role in deregulation in terms both of import penetration on the equipment front and of lack of coherence in national policy-making. Fear of a comparative organisational disadvantage in international trade negotiations and pressure to synchronise telecommunications and trade policy affected the American policy agenda, symbolised by the appointment of a Coordinator for International Communication and Information Policy in the Department of State and the shift of initiative from the Department of Justice (as the standard-bearer of anti-trust) to the Department of Commerce.[67] By 1986 West European states were the objects of growing pressure as American trade negotiators sought reciprocal market access. Also, the Japanese model of

concertation and parnership based on interpenetration of state and private sectors achieved a new relevance to the perceived change in conditions. This relevance was not just recognised by American analysts who feared Japan and the Far East; also the idea of European collaboration was strengthened as the threat of foreign competition from both Japan and the United States suggested the advantages of coherence and integration in communications equipment and service policy. In other words, demands for institutional and structural reform were not simply one-dimensional, in the direction of deregulation.

An example of the shift towards the idea of a 'concerted' approach was provided by the report of the British Cabinet Office's Information Technology Advisory Panel (ITAP) *Making a Business of Information* (1983). It spoke of Britain as a potential world leader in the business of selling information and advice (with its computer software, libraries, broadcasting, videotex etc) and estimated that the annual turnover of the 'tradeable information sector' was £15 billion. However, according to the ITAP, Britain stood to lose out if the existing fragmentation of the information industry and of government action remained. In line with one of ITAP's central recommendations the Confederation of Information Communication Industries was established in 1985 to develop coherent policies for the information industries (e.g., on copyright law, export promotion, training, telecommunications). The idea was that it should liaise closely with the Information Technology Minister at the Department of Trade and Industry who was given overall responsibility for the information industry. Even in Thatcherite Britain the need to develop an information trade policy was stimulating a concern for greater co-ordination and partnership.

Thesis 3: that changes in national communications policies reflect a changing relationship between law and politics in Western Europe

This thesis argues that policies for the communications revolution must be understood by exploring the relationship between normative codes, as embodied in statute and regulation, and political structures and dynamics. In one variant the focus is on *continuity* of policies which are to be explained in terms of different national politico-legal traditions in Western Europe; in the other, the stress is on *evolution* towards a new role for the state in social and economic development. As an exercise in politico-legal investigation the thesis emphasises the important role of law in structuring the policy process, for instance in determining who may participate and one what terms and what kind of policy instruments can be used. Thus the British Telecommunications Act of 1984 is important because it does *not* give Oftel the power to license new competition to BT (unlike the situation in the United States) and the Cable and Broadcasting Act is important because (unlike the situation in France) it does *not* allocate a leading role to local authorities in organising and managing new cable television systems. Both are significant again in placing few procedural requirements on Oftel or the Cable Authority in taking their decisions. Formal mechanisms of procedural legitimation appear weak in the British case.

From one perspective the interesting aspect of new communications policies is that they continue to reflect traditional assumptions and views about the relationship of law and society and the proper organisation of the public sphere.[68] These traditions are in turn responsible for *contrasts* in the developments of policy. In Britain one is aware of the tradition of informal and arms's length government, in France of the tensions between technocracy and legalism, and in West Germany of the doctrine of the *Rechtsstaat* and powerful constitutional and administrative courts in providing a strong normative code of policy-making. It is perhaps the foreign rather than German observer who is most struck by the extent to which West Germany has a 'formalised regulatory culture' in telecommunications and broadcasting. Law serves as a standard means of communication and debate about communications' issues, encompasses a broad range of concerns and keeps constitutional principles at the heart of the agenda. Bargaining takes place within and about law with policy actors making a strategic and opportunistic use of it. In this sense German debate about the communications revolution can seem inward-looking, governed by the legacy of Germany's traumatic past rather than by present and emerging international realities.

Against the background of Germany's twentieth-century history, the Federal Constitutional Court's emphasis on *Meinungsvielfalt* (plurality of opinion) in broadcasting has a peculiar political resonance as a requirement for public policies towards new media.[69] In classic judgments of 1961 and 1981 the Court held that all relevant groups in society must be involved in the control of broadcasting and that programmes must reflect a fair balance of opinion.[70] The new media laws of the *Länder* have been drafted on the basis of the Court's distinction between 'internal pluralism' (*Binnenpluralismus*) and 'external pluralism' (*Aussenpluralismus*) in its 1981 FRAG judgment. In the former case, as with the existing public broadcasting corporations, balanced programming is achieved by representation of a plurality of interests in the controlling body of the corporation; in the latter case, by encouragement of a number of distinct groups as broadcasters whose programmes will produce balance overall. Most *Länder* have moved towards 'external pluralism' as the principle on which their new regulatory systems for new media are based, with stronger (e.g. Bavaria) or weaker (e.g. Lower Saxony) public regulatory authorities. Sensing a crisis of regulation in West Germany, the SPD appealed the Lower Saxony new media law to the Federal Constitutional Court in 1984. The hope was that the Court could impose some check on the regulatory drift by reasserting a normative pressure on policy-makers. In other words, in classic German *Rechtsstaat* style, the opposition used resort to law to discipline the government.

An orderly and stable regulatory framework for broadcasting had in any case proved more elusive in post-war France than West Germany. Broadcasting has long been used as a political weapon in the hands of French governments, as an instrument of *raison d'état*. The Socialist majority in 1981 seemed to be associated with a desire to assert 'republican morality' more forcefully in broadcasting. For this reason the High Authority for Audiovisual Communications was created in 1982 to take over many of the functions of government, including top appointments in broadcasting, and to regulate new media.[71] In practice the work and prestige of the High Authority suffered as government continued to bypass it, especially in new media policy (its reservations about the Berlusconi–Seydoux fifth channel were ignored), and as uncertainty persisted about the regulatory framework for new media. Under the Socialists franchising power for new cable systems (SLECs) remained effectively in the hands of the DGT (the telecommunications authority) and for new television channels (like the fourth channel, Canal Plus, and channels five and six or DBS channels) firmly with the Socialist government. The broad outlines of policy contained in the Law on Audiovisual Communications and in the cable plan of 1982 were not followed by the all-important decrees till 1984; then in 1985 the application of these decrees was further amended. In contrast to West Germany, the main basis for French Socialist regulatory policy was provided by the tradition of national independence, reflected in the quotas for foreign and local programming and requirements of support for the domestic programme industry in the 1984 decrees. Here too there was a crisis of regulation by 1985 when a much more flexible position on cable programming was adopted.

There was no comparable crisis of regulation in Britain, and the reason is to be found in traditional assumptions there about the nature of public action. Britain does not have a tradition of coherent public law or a system of constitutional or even administrative courts that are sensitive to fundamental constitutional principles and that enquire into the motives and reasonableness of governmental action. Quite simply, and for historical reasons, there is less conscious and formal concern with problems of legitimation. Both the new institutional structures and the procedures associated with the communications revolution display a striking preference for *ad hoc*-ery, pragmatism and informal methods of government. Thus the Hunt inquiry of 1982 into cable expansion and broadcasting policy, which reported in less than six months, conducted no public hearings and provided no opportunity for a second round of comments from interested and affected parties. In the legislation establishing Oftel and the Cable Authority (the Telecommunications Act 1984 and the Cable and Broadcasting Act 1984) little attempt was made to provide procedures that would ensure fair and accountable decision based on rational analysis and opportunity to comment.[72] The Telecommunications Act did at least contain a Telecommunications Code and provision for 'notice-and-comment' procedures. However, it made extremely limited provision for licensing hearings by Oftel. Public scrutiny was even less in the case of the Cable Authority (for cable television) and the Independent Broadcasting Authority (DBS). Their franchising power was to be exercised secretively and unaccountably, with no reasons required for its decisions, in fact in the manner that the IBA had always behaved in franchising independent television companies. The vagueness of the regulatory criteria of the Cable Authority are clear from its duties to work for a 'progressive increase in the proportion of British programming' and to 'keep in touch' with the performance of each operator (the French government has a commissioner on the board of each SLEC). According to the Act, the Cable Authority is 'to use a light regulatory touch and adopt a reactive rather than proactive style' and to be 'ready to respond to market forces'. In short, the growing regulatory pressures associated with the communications revolution are accentuating traditional

British problems of accountability and of the procedural standards of public decision-making. Certainly Britain's telecommunication reform was not accompanied by anything remotely like the two-year (1985–87), twelve-man committee of inquiry into West German telecommunications, drawn from business, universities and politics (with two leading SPD and CSU politicians, Peter Glotz and Edmund Stoiber) and holding formal hearings. In the British case it is also interesting to note that in a system of adverserial party politics, with a stress on government versus opposition, there is a preference for non-adverserial relations in regulatory policy. A premium is placed on discretion, trust and informality at governmental levels. The policy costs are substantial, not least in the degree of legitimation.

The other politico-legal perspective argues that new communications policies reflect a crisis of formal legal regulation that is associated with an evolutionary change in the relationship between law and society.[73] Underlying the problems of the interventionist state in telecommunications, broadcasting, financial markets and other sectors are sheer complexity, conflict and speed of change. An accelerating speed of technological and economic change and conflicts between the different rationalities of highly specialised but converging policy sectors make precise, detailed and elaborate criteria for regulation and legalistic 'rule-oriented' reasoning neither appropriate nor realistic. They point to the need for new mechanisms for improving political learning under the conditions of turbulence and stress in communications. The problem with much of new communications policy in Western Europe is that it embodies confusion about the proper role of law in such a situation. Yet, though bound up in a legacy of traditional assumptions, Western Europe can be seen as going through a period of experimentation towards a new pattern of flexible and responsive law in the field of communications. As we have seen, this period of political and legal strain is particularly difficult in West Germany where a formalistic 'broadcasting constitution', deeply rooted in the *Rechtsstaat* tradition, faces new changes in the economic basis of broadcasting with cable and satellite technologies and new entrants into the 'broadcasting market'. The forces in the new 'broadcasting market' confront the requirements of the old 'broadcasting constitution'.

While this perspective accepts variations in West European policy responses to the communcations revolution, it argues that it is possible to identify certain trends or common features in their evolution. There was, for instance, growing caution about imposing clear substantive regulatory criteria on technology specification for cable systems (e.g. in Britain and France), on quotas for foreign and local programming (e.g. in France), on advertising, on participation of the press in cable systems (e.g. in France) and on the priority of public-service broadcasting in cable development (e.g. North-Rhine Westphalia). Legal self-restraint is moving into the ascendancy. The process is not so much one of 'deregulation' as of 'regulatory revision'. It involves a challenge to West European states to 're-regulate' by establishing new procedural norms in communications and by designing new institutional structures. Public policy has the opportunity to establish the parameters of decision-making in the field of communications, and that means taking on board such issues as access, 'right of reply', privacy, journalistic freedom, co-determination in industrial relations, public acountability and regional and local decentralisation. The 'new proceduralism' means a more responsive and reflexive law, and its implications still need to be thought through on both left and right. Academic analysis can at least provide pointers to the development of a theory of regulation appropriate to the circumstances of the communications revolution. In essence, the function of the West European state must be to develop 'the external constitution' for telecommunications, broadcasting and new media. Governments can enable and facilitate 'self-regulation' in these fields by defining its organisational and procedural terms (e.g. who participates in decisions, what kind of institutional structures are appropriate, how codes of professional practice are to be enforced); they can encourage a public learning process in communications policy by requiring the participation of affected interests in the regulatory policy process (by proper 'notice-and-comment' procedures and provision for formal hearings) and by the public justification of regulatory policy decisions in the form of a rational policy analysis; and they can seek to promote a greater consistency and integration of policy by requiring mutual consultation between different regulatory authorities (for instance, in Britain between Oftel and the Cable Authority). In general, West European states are shifting, gradually and with difficulty, towards this new kind of regulatory function. Their policy-makers sense the danger that traditional formal regulation of communications will either be ineffective, in which case the law and the state come into disrepute, or too effective, in which case major new industries will suffer in fiercely competitive international markets.

CONCLUSION

The strongest overall impression to emerge from this study of contending perspectives on the communications revolution is of turbulence, domestic and international, and of profound uncertainty, insecurity and confusion in Western Europe. Faced with a subject matter that is so complex and dynamic, with so many *ad hoc* and conflicting activities by governments, it would be surprising if any of the different existing perspectives could capture the full realities of policy-making for the communications revolution. The communications revolution is 'open-textured': and the issues that it raises are contested. At the same time it is an incomplete revolution so that all the evidence is not available for adjudication among the perspectives. Given the scale of the communications revolution, it is scarcely surprising that the development of public policy is taking place at different rates in different fields of policy. In telecommunications, for instance, there is greater resilience and diversity of policy strategies than in broadcasting where a statecraft of 'controlled deregulation' in one country was already proving impossible by the mid 1980s and where, as in France, there was more evidence of *ad hoc* panic actions. Broadcasting policy shows just how little thought West European governments had given to the question of whether deregulation in one country was 'controllable'; in the end they tended to be overwhelmed.[74] Similar ominous signs can be found in telecommunications where major corporate crises are likely to provide the nail in the coffin of traditional policies and generate a further pattern of *ad hoc* panic actions.[75] Adjudication among the perspectives is made no easier by the fact that each has substantial analytical power in terms of the range of phenomena encompassed and in terms of ability to handle major change. It is difficult to ignore or marginalise any one perspective. Each is helpful in that it facilitates a more discriminating analysis of particular phenomena; yet each leaves questions unanswered.

Analysts are likely to be more attracted to a particular perspective the greater is its capacity to accommodate the better features of other perspectives and the more modest, self-reflective and non-exclusive its exponents are. Exponents of the perspective of international political economy must beware of ignoring the specific, including subjective, forces at work in particular situations and of failing to allow for the faculty of political imagination in institution-buidling and procedural reform. In short, the 'arts of statecraft' are lost from view. In their pursuit of greater 'specificity' those who work with the policy process perspective risk ignoring broader structural contexts and evolutionary trends in the relations of law and politics; while in the analysis of normative issues the politico-legal perspective threatens to lose both specificity and structural awareness. These risks may seem best avoided by a flexible and catholic use of perspectives, thereby enriching insight and understanding and advancing empirical analysis. On the other hand, an open-minded outlook must not impede the attempt to identify the 'main bias' in governmental responses to the communications revolution. It is necessary to isolate what is historically more permanent and interesting – namely, governments' problems of policy implementation as they find themselves caught between new external forces and more turbulent domestic politics in communications. The common theme is government's search to re-establish a governing competence along with maintaining its ideological credibility. Government is motivated by threats to the autonomy of state action and consequently its ability to act effectively. Hence the appropriate questions relate to 'statecraft', and the appropriate starting point is the policy process model.

The basic strength of the perspective of statecraft is that it can integrate the main insights of the other approaches considered in this chapter. It is 'big enough' to incorporate the scope and complexity of the phenomena being observed. One strength is that 'statecraft' draws attention to the role of ideology and to issues of identity in communications policy. Ideology and political culture are decisive in influencing the identification of the source of threat to state autonomy and the choice of means to respond. The perspective of statecraft helps us to isolate the specifically political rationale behind policy choices in communications. Deregulation is politically attractive as a way of combating 'overmighty subjects' or 'failed' national champions – typically represented by national telecommunications authorities and suppliers or public-service broadcasters. It embodies a domestic political strategy of 'divide and rule' in communications. Cross-national collaboration or domestic 'concertation' of interests is a way of meeting 'the enemy from without', typically represented by American or Japanese corporations but also perhaps by other European corporations. The fundamental problem is that in tackling one perceived source of threat, the other threat is likely to be magnified. Here we come to one of the dilemmas of statecraft, in the case of communications policy represented by conflicts between deregulation and collaboration. 'Overmighty subjects' are in danger of becoming yet mightier and more complacent with collaboration or concertation. Deregulation is likely to favour 'the enemy from without'. How the dilemma is resolved will be determined by a mixture of the ideology and political calculations of governments and the power relationships in the relevant policy sectors.

A further advantage of the policy process perspective is that it comes perhaps closest (but even then by the back door) to capturing the sense of threat to identity, cultural and personal, in Western Europe from the communications revolution. Outright hostility is less apparent than scepticism and concern about the values to which Western Europe is being committed by the communications revolution. This sense of the high price of the communications revolution underlines the problems of its political legitimation in Western Europe. Even for those, such as London stockbrokers faced by computerised trading, who see the dangers of rejecting or ignoring the new 'information society', and the corresponding need for a high level of technical skills, there is typically an acceptance of the communications revolution as a bleak reality, to be adapted to rather than welcomed. The communications revolution has not proved a left–right issue but an issue of modernity that divided both right and left. Throughout Western Europe parties of the left have sought with varying degrees of resolution and success to link up with the emerging middle class of technicians and professionals by adopting a libertarian image. The process has gone notably far in the Italian Socialist Party (whose leader and Prime Minister Bettino Craxi is a friend of Berlusconi) and in the Swedish Social Democratic Party (during whose governments a strategy of deregulation, joint ventures and licensing deals in telecommunications has been pursued).

It is also apparent in the French Socialist Party (notably among the supporters of Laurent Fabius and Michel Rocard) and in the West German SPD (whose modernising technocrats provided ministers for the Federal Research and Technology Ministry from its creation in 1972 to 1982). The West German SPD and the French Socialists did, however, display more defensiveness in their responses to the communications revolution. At the same time, the nature of that defensiveness was different: for the French Socialists it related to national sovereignty, for West German Social Democrats to social issues. The absence of significant outright opposition to the communications revolution from the French Socialists had much to do with its participation in government, allied to a broad consensus that government's function was to protect national independence and that the communications revolution, involving the domestic electronics and cultural industries, was central to sustaining national independence in the future. Hence in France public debate tended to focus on the economic dimensions of the communications revolution as modernisation policy.

The same political equation did not operate in West Germany where the SPD, ousted from national political power in 1982, faced new strong electoral competition from the Green Party, and where for historical reasons national independence was a less attractive ideology for the SPD. Principled opposition to the communications revolution, specifically to cable and new media, became a major feature of the Greens and many of the SPD left; and leading spokesmen of the German Trade Union Federation (DGB) began to talk of 'an assault on the minds, jobs and bank accounts of employees'. In the process the communications revolution became an issue within the SPD, with pragmatists and modernisers like Peter Glotz (the general secretary) and Klaus von Dohnanyi (Lord Mayor of Hamburg) trying to sustain a strategy of adaptation. The West German left recognised and articulated one of the major prices of the communications revolution — employee solidarity and political identity. Ultimately, however, these cultural anxieties are subordinated to the impact of the government-opposition dimension. A party strategy for government or one in government is likely to accept the 'bleak reality' of the communications revolution; in government the price of disengagement from international markets, and thus modernity, is likely to seem just too high.

The policy process perspective is not just helpful in drawing out the government–opposition dimension, and its relevance to discovering or rediscovering 'the arts of statecraft', and the domestic factors that shape the management of issues of identity in Western Europe. By its careful mapping of the morass of policy networks and of the motives and activities of the actors in those networks, it lends a specificity that encourages and enriches the empirical analysis of the political dynamics of the communications revolution. In particular, it enables us to investigate the political dynamics of government's role. Not least, it is possible to identify the lens of statecraft through which West European governments view technology and economic theory. From the perspective of 'statecraft' government's role in the communications revolution can be seen to develop in stages. At the outset there is bold 'heroic' strategy, typically focusing on cabling for the new 'wired society'. As we have seen, these strategies vary in terms of the ideologies they articulate, the commercial and corporate interests that they reflect and the political calculations that they embody. The next stage begins to emerge as governments pursue a more pragmatic 'trade-off' of interests and seek to 'buy off' dissent with symbolic rewards. Political leaders substitute a more nuanced for assertive behaviour. In other words, governments begin to act as 'brokers'; from the perspective of statecraft, they engage in 'damage control'. They trade off loss of the substance of sovereignty for the prospects of gains in wealth, the calculation being that in this way the effective political power of the state will be better safeguarded. Thus, governments begin to give more serious consideration to regulatory revision, joint ventures and licensing deals and even to the possibility of threatening once cherished 'national champions' with new exposure to the rigours of the international market.[76] Symbolic politics or legitimation strategies are used as an additional political resource in this process of 'trade-offs'. They are not to be understood as simply confirming the passive function of the state in underwriting changes imposed by the international economy. However, governments are not just redefining the resources of power that they can employ. They are learning how to employ them skilfully. The constraint on establishing committees of inquiry or new regulatory authorities as purely symbolic gestures to 'buy-off' dissent is a loss of credibility, and credibility is itself an important bargaining resource. The constraint on importing deregulation and useful management and technological skills is the risk of creating a problem of hegemony with West European states dependent on the United States and Japan. As telecommunications and broadcasting become assimilated into diplomacy and *raison d'état*, the need for caution and pragmatism in playing the role of broker is likely to become even more apparent and to be accepted as the most sophisticated approach. In the complex and interdependent international world of the communications revolution governments become aware also of the opportunities and threats that derive from the ability to exploit linkages across issues and contexts. Linkage politics means that governments are vulnerable. Thus the information needs of new global financial markets can be used by multinationals to force the pace not only in financial deregulation but in telecommunications deregulation. Governments can also use linkage politics as, for instance, when the French government offered valuable channel capacity on its TDF-I satellite to Luxembourg in order to divert that state from the idea of its own private-sector commercial satellite; and when the Belgian government gave Music Box access to its cable systems in return for a Belgian share in its programming.

The shift to brokerage politics is inexorable as governments seek to re-establish relative autonomy for the state. It is a response to the mounting complexity of the issues and interests associated with the communications revolution, to the speed and uncertainties of technological change, to the difficulties of commercial assessment of markets for new communications technologies and services, to intra-governmental competition and conflicts and, not least, to the problems of reconciling the international and domestic dimensions. This new stage in government's role in the communications revolution can be interpreted differently: either as political retreat by West European states as governments take on a passive and defensive role, simply adapting to the *faits accomplis* of new global markets and the technological changes that they mediate; or as political learning as governments adopt a role more appropriate to the complex dynamics of the communications revolution. In the former picture, wholesale retreat is pictured as taking the form of 'deregulation'; in the latter, learning involves a process of 'regulatory revision'.

The capacity for political learning of the West European state is the heart of the matter; only in this way can they master the 'arts of statecraft'. The sheer power of international markets, as represented in the apparent political retreat of West European states, indicates the very limited scope for governments as actors. On the other hand, international constraints and threats underline the importance of developing institutional structures and policies that can facilitate political learning. The open question is just how skilfully will West European governments perform their brokerage role. With its focus on the external environment the perspective of international political economy is not well adapted to tackling questions of political learning and statecraft. At worst it induces an 'all-or-nothing' attitude: retreat either to a utopian activism or to a fatalism remote from the cynicism of governments that are content to act as legitimising agents of the international economy. If there is an urgent need for a political learning process, it is clear that it is incomplete. At this point the policy process perspective — and statecraft — must take on board some of the questions raised by the politico-legal perspective. Unlike the policy process perspective the politico-legal perspective is appropriate for considering the question of the adequacy of political language for coping with the problems of the communications revolution. The final advantage of investigating communications policy from the perspective of 'arts of statecraft' is this focus on processes of political learning and the normative dimension of policy.

One striking feature of the communications revolution in Western Europe is that it has taken place in an intellectual vacuum, without the guidance of a clear and adequate regulatory philosophy. The communications revolution has been a story of political dynamics – from heroism to brokerage in the name of statecraft – and theoretical deficit. Prescriptive 'hard' arguments from technology and markets have displaced or crowded out 'soft' arguments from political philosophy and law. In other words, to the extent that there has been a theoretical debate it has been imbalanced. By taking on board affective symbolic goals and abstract ideals governments can extend the range of political resources available to them in brokerage politics. Only a crude and narrow realist could fail to see the connection between symbolic politics and the brokerage politics of statecraft. Identification with affective symbols enhances the credibility of governments and hence their bargaining power. 'Local identity', 'regional identity', 'European identity' and 'one world' are not only important in their own right; they are useful to governments in helping to forge forms of solidarity appropriate to the new opportunities offered by the communications revolution. Symbolic politics of this kind becomes counterproductive once it loses touch with emerging realities. An example is provided by one-dimensional concerns for European collaboration. Here, limited expectations seem appropriate, reflecting the fact that corporate interests in collaboration are not limited to Western Europe. These interests are increasingly global in character, making the global identity of 'one world' increasingly relevant. The essential point remains: a political language of symbolic politics for the communications revolution is not yet fully developed. When it is, the prospects for new institution building will be much brighter. West European governments will also be more resourceful actors. New bonds of solidarity can be forged by encouragement of local and regional programming, of 'narrowcasting' for special interests including national and ethnic minorities, of pan-European programming and of global media events (on the model of Live Aid). Domestic and EC regulatory policies can also aim at stimulating experimentation and learning, access and participation, accountability and decentralisation. In this way the state comes to play a role of procedural legitimation. It requires the use of rational policy analysis, 'notice-and comment' procedures and formal hearings by regulatory authorities; it builds conscience into corporate structures so that internal representation and control are more effective (e.g. by safeguards for journalistic freedom); and it encourages independent producers and programmers (not just by cultural and fiscal policies but by formal requirements on broadcasting corporations). Then the communications revolution can be given a constitutional framework that recognises yet civilises the power of technology and international markets. The West European state will then attach itself to the argument for change, shed the vain defence of the public-service status quo and motivate by a new vision.

NOTES

1. Generally, see D. Schiller, *Telematics and Government* (New Jersey: Ablex, 1982); J. Martin, *Telecommunications and the Computer* (Englewood-Cliffs: Prentice Hall, 1977); J. Salvaggio, *Telecommunications* (London: Longman, 1983); C. Sterling, *Electronic Media* (New York: Praeger, 1984); B. Wenham (ed.), *The Third Age of Broadcasting* (London: Faber, 1982); T. Hollins, *Beyond Broadcasting: Into the Cable Age* (London: BFI, 1984); J. Howkins, *New Technologies, New Policies* (London: BFI, 1982); G. de Jonquieres and P. Betts, *America's Communication Revolution* (London: Financial Times, 1983); and R. Bruce and J. Cunard, *From Telecommunications to Electronic Services* (Washington D.C.: International Institute of Communications, 1985).
2. For a preliminary survey see K. Dyson, 'The Politics of Cable and Satellite Broadcasting: Some West European Comparisons', *West European Politics*, Vol. 8, No. 2 (1985).
3. I. de Sola Pool, *Forecasting The Telephone*, (New Jersey: Ablex, 1982). For other optimistic scenarios see W. Dizard, *The Coming Information Age* (London: Longman, 1982); R. Ayres, *The Next Industrial Revolution* (Cambridge: Ballinger, 1984); and A. Toffler, *The Third Wave* (New York: W. Morrow, 1980).
4. For an Anglo-French comparison see K. Dyson and P. Humphreys, 'Industrial Policies for the New Media in Britain and France', in C. Farrands (ed.), *Industrial Intervention in Britain and France* (Oxford: Pergamon Press, 1986).
5. For a useful account see W. Durch (ed.), *National Interests and the Military Use of Space* (Cambridge, MA: Ballinger, 1984). On the military context see G. M. Luyken, *Direktempfangbare Rundfunksatelliten* (Frankfurt: Campus, 1985).
6. P. Bracken, *The Command and Control of Nuclear Forces* (New Haven: Yale University Press, 1983).
7. P. Drucker, 'Beyond the Bell Breakup', *Public Interest*, No. 77, Fall 1984.
8. D. Langevoort, 'Information Technology and the Structure of Securities Regulation', *Harvard Law Review*, Vol. 98, No. 4, (1985), pp. 747–804.
9. 'Electronic Financial Services', *Financial Times Survey*, 24 March 1986. Significantly, by 1985 the City of London accounted for some 8 per cent of BT's revenue, with important implications for its investment and pricing policies, as we shall see.
10. This is based on interviews with British Telecom in early 1986. *New Satellite Communications in Western Europe* (London: CIT Research, 1986) argues that the major growth in revenues from satellite services in Western Europe will come from business and institutional customers rather than extra channels of television. News and financial data, private corporate communication networks and other forms of 'closed user groups' will enjoy much faster growth than broadcasting services.
11. On Home Box Office see Hollins, *op. cit.* In 1985 38 per cent of adults in Britain had access to VCRs; in households with children the proportion was 51 per cent. See *Attitudes to Broadcasting in 1985* (London: IBA Research Department, 1986), Tables 19 and 20. By the end of 1983 the three leading private television networks in Italy had three million peak-time viewers more than all three RAI (public-service) channels put together (the total audience was nearly 27.4 million). See D. Sassoon, 'Political and Market Forces in Italian Broadcasting', *West European Politics*, Vol. 8, No. 2 (1985), p. 78.
12. G. Dang Nguyen and E. Arnold, 'Videotex: Much Ado about Nothing', in M. Sharp (ed.), *Europe and the New Technologies* (London: Frances Pinter, 1985). Prestel shifted from a 'common-carrier' approach to a 'managed database philosophy' concentrating on 'vertical markets' such as travel, insurance, agriculture and microcomputing.
13. For the concept of policy communities see J. Richardson (ed.), *Policy Styles in Western Europe* (London: Allen & Unwin, 1982).
14. On the phenomena of 'convergence' and 'collison' as technological boundaries blur see M. Irwin, *Telecommunications America: Markets Without Boundaries* (New York: Quorum Books, 1984).
15. Euronet Diane (Direct Information Access Network for Europe) was a European information service, established in 1980 with a special transmission network providing access to a wide variety of data banks; on RACE (Research for Advanced Communications in Europe) see the chapter by Claire Shearman in this volume. The results of the efforts undertaken under the auspices of the EBU to foster greater co-production and closer collaboration of

public-service broadcasters have included Europa-TV, the first European public-service channel in October 1985 (with European Commission support and involving public broadcasting stations in Ireland, Italy, the Netherlands, Portugal and West Germany); and the European Co-Production Company for TV-Programming (with Second German Television, Antenne 2 of France, Channel 4 of Britain, RAI of Italy as well as SRG of Switzerland and ORF of Austria).

16. S. Tolchin and M. Tolchin, *Dismantling America: The Rush to Deregulate* (New York: Oxford University Press, 1983); J. Tunstall, *Communications Deregulation: USA* (Oxford: Basil Blackwell, 1986); D. Evans, *Breaking Up Bell* (New York: North Holland, 1983); de Jonquieres and Betts, *op. cit.*; and G. Bolling, *AT and T: Aftermath of Antitrust* (Washington: National Defence University, 1983).
17. See notably Arthur D. Little International, *European Telecommunications – Strategic Issues and Opportunities for the Decade Ahead: Final Report to the EC Commission* (Brussels: EC, November 1983).
18. On DBS initiatives see K. Dyson and P. Humphreys, 'Satellite Broadcasting Policies and the Question of Sovereignty in Western Europe', *Journal of Public Policy*, 1986.
19. *The Development of Cable Systems and Services* (London: HMSO, 1982); S. Nora and A. Minc, *Informatisation de la Société* (Paris: Documentation Française, 1978); *KtK: Telekommunikationsbericht mit acht Anlagebanden* (Bonn: Verlag Heger, 1976).
20. These debates can be followed in the two contributions by Dyson and Humphreys mentioned above. On France useful insights can be gathered from A. and M. Mattelart, *International Image Markets* (London: Marion Boyars, 1984).
21. The exhaustive *Sachlichkeit* of West German policymaking is evident in the three-volume report of the *Expertenkommission Neue Medien-EKM Baden-Wurtemberg* (Stuttgart: Kohlhammer, 1981).
22. EC Commission, *Report from the Commission to the Council on Telecommunications* (Brussels: European Commission, Com. 277, 18 May 1984).
23. *Telecommunications: Pressures and Policies for Change* (Paris: OECD, 1983). See also A. D. Little, *World Telecommunications Programme* (Wiesbaden: 1983).
24. G. Dang Nguyen, 'Telecommunications' in M. Sharp (ed.), *op. cit.*, p. 93. Also OECD, *Changing Market Structure in Telecommunications* (North-Holland: Elsevier, 1984), and OECD, *Information, Computer and Communications Policies for the 1980s* (North-Holland: Elsevier, 1984).
25. For figures see E. Arnold, *Competition and Technological Change in the Television Industry* (London: Macmillan, 1985); 'Electronics in Europe', *Financial Times Survey*, 24th June 1985; and generally useful is K. P. Friebe and A. Gerybadze (eds.), *Microelectronics in Western Europe* (Berlin: Erich Schmidt Verlag, 1984).
26. For figures on IBM see 'International Telecommunications', *Financial Times Survey*, 14 January 1985. Also R. Sobel, *IBM: Colossus in Transition* (New York: Bantam Books, 1983).
27. For figures see 'Electronic Information Services', *Financial Times Survey*, 24 March 1986.
28. *The Times*, 7 May 1985, 'Computer Horizons', p. 5. According to *Diane News* (Brussels: EC, July–August 1982) the United States controlled 56 per cent of the world's data banks in 1982, compared with the EC's 26 per cent.
29. OECD, *Software – An Emerging Industry* (Paris: OECD, 1985).
30. *Financial Times*, 1 November 1984, p. 8.
31. EC Commission, *Green Paper for the Establishment of the Common Market for Broadcasting Especially by Satellite and Cable* (Brussels: European Commission, June 1984).
32. Figures based on project interview.
33. See e.g. H. Schiller and C. Nordenstreng (eds.), *National Sovereignty and International Communication* (New York: Ablex, 1981); also H. Schiller, *Mass Communications and American Empire* (New York: Kelley, 1969). For a critical discussion of this literature see M. Tracey, 'The Poisoned Chalice? International Television and the Idea of Dominance', *Daedalus*, Vol. 114, No. 4 (1985).
34. T. Varis, 'The International Flow of Television Programmes', *Journal of Communication*, Winter 1984. For another study see A. Pragnell, *Television in Europe: Quality and Values in a Time of Change* (Manchester: European Institute for the Media, 1985); it shows that the percentage of American programmes in total broadcasting time was notably high in drama (nearly 38.6 per cent) and that nearly half of cinema films shown came from the United States.

35. For figures on Italy and American feature films in the European cinema see A. and M. Mattelart, *op. cit.*.
36. These figures are taken from *The European Advertising and Media Forecast* (London: NTC Publications, 1985), prepared for the European Advertising Tripartite.
37. Mattelart, *op. cit.*, p. 21.
38. For figures see 'Communications: The World Business Market', *Financial Times Survey*, 6 January 1986.
39. K. Ohmae, *Triad Power*, (New York: Free Press, 1985).
40. The case for joint ventures and licensing deals is presented by Margaret Sharp in M. Sharp (ed.), *op. cit*. For a different view on joint Japanese-US ventures see R. Reich and E. Mankin, in *Harvard Business Review*, March–April 1986, reprint 86210. In their view joint ventures have eroded American engineering skills, led to a transfer of learning to Japan and protected higher-paid jobs in Japan.
41. US Department of Commerce, 'A White Paper on New International Satellite Systems', *Department of Commerce*, February 1985. Also L. Knight, 'The Deregulation of International Satellite Communications: US Policy and the INTELSAT Response', *Space Communications and Broadcasting*, Vol. 3 (1985).
42. For useful background see the series 'Banking: The New Frontiers' in *Financial Times*, 2, 7, 9, 11 and 21 April 1986.
43. M. Moran, 'Corporatism Resurrected: Economic Interests and Institutional Change in the City of London', paper to annual conference of the UK Political Studies Association, Nottingham, 1986.
44. For details see Dyson and Humphreys, 'Satellite Broadcasting Policies', *op. cit.*
45. Bank for International Settlements, *Recent Innovations in International Banking* (Basle: Bank for International Settlements, 1986).
46. Based on interviews at BT, 1986.
47. On the domestic sources of the American search for international deregulation see D. Pitt, 'Government and Industry Relations: Key Issues in the US Telecommunications Industry', University of Strathclyde unpublished paper, 1986.
48. *US Objectives in International Telecommunications and Information Policies* (New York: US Council for International Business, 1984).
49. For other relevant reports see OECD, *op. cit.*
50. To such an extent that in April 1986 the French Council of State declared the relaxation of some of these restrictions to be illegal in the case of the concession of the fifth private commercial channel.
51. For general survey see R. Barry Jones (ed.), *Perspectives on Political Economy* (London: Frances Pinter, 1983).
52. See e.g. T. Hopkins and I. Wallerstein (eds.), *World Systems Analysis* (Beverley Hills: Sage, 1982); N. Poulantzas, *State, Power, Socialism* (London: New Left Books, 1978) and J. Habermas, *Legitimation Crisis* (London: HEB, 1976).
53. *Report of the Post Office Review Committee* (Carter Report), (London: HMSO, 1972); *Report of the Inquiry into Cable Expansion and Broadcasting Policy* (Hunt Report), (London: HMSO, 1982).
54. See Dyson and Humphreys, 'Industrial Policies for the New Media in Britain and France', *op. cit.*, for more details.
55. KtK, *op. cit.*, Expertenkommission, *op. cit.*; *Zwischenbericht der Enquete-Kommission Neue Informations- und Kommunikationstechniken* (Bonn: Bundestag, April 1983).
56. See Dyson and Humphreys, *op. cit.*, on CODITEC, the DGT and the British lobbies.
57. See e.g. Richardson, *op. cit.*
58. See e.g. R. Gilpin, *US Power and the Multinational Corporation: The Political Economy of Foreign Direct Investment* (London: Macmillan, 1976); D. P. Calleo and B. Rowland, *America and the World Economy* (Bloomington: Indiana University Press, 1973).
59. J. Vickers and G. Yarrow, *Privatisation and the Natural Monopolies* (London: Public Policy Centre, 1985).
60. On these traditions see K. Dyson, *The State Tradition in Western Europe* (Oxford: Martin Robertson, 1980) and A. Shonfield, *Modern Capitalism* (Oxford: Oxford University Press, 1965).
61. H. Heclo, 'Issue Networks and the Executive Establishment', in A. King (ed.), *The New American Political System* (Washington DC: American Enterprise Institute, 1978).

62. J-F. Lacan, 'L'audiovisual en six salons: la liberté aux portes de l'anarchie', *Le Monde Aujourd'hui*, 10 November 1985, p. 3.
63. On Teletel see Dang Nguyen and Arnold, *op. cit.*, pp. 149–154.
64. On the West German Constitutional Court's role see A. Williams, 'West German Broadcasting in the Eighties – Plus ça change ...?', *ASGP Journal*, No. 7 (1984).
65. G. Wedell and G-M Luyken, *Media in Competition* (Manchester: European Institute for the Media, 1986), see the major impact on broadcasting arriving in the 1990s and VCR as the first major winner in the new media field.
66. See e.g. M. Borrus (ed.), *Microelectronics and International Competition* (University of California Press, 1985); H. Brooks, *Public-Private Partnership* (Cambridge: Ballinger, 1985); and R. Reich, *The Next American Frontier* (Harmondsworth: Penguin, 1983).
67. J. Spero, 'Information: The Policy Void', *Foreign Policy*, No. 48 (1982); also D. Pitt, *op. cit.*
68. On these traditional assumptions see Dyson, *op. cit.*
69. This interpretation of West Germany is emphasised by Williams, *op. cit.*
70. On these judgements see W. Hoffmann-Riem in this volume.
71. See Kuhn, *op. cit.*
72. N. Lewis and I. Harden, 'Privatisation, Deregulation and Constitutionality: Some Anglo-American Comparisons', *Northern Ireland Legal Quarterly*, Vol. 34 (1985).
73. See most notably P. Nonet and P. Selznick, *Law and Society in Transition: Towards Responsive Law* (New York: Harper, 1978) and G. Teubner, 'Substantive and Reflexive Elements in Modern Law', *Law and Society Review*, Vol. 17 (1983).
74. See the various articles by Dyson and Humphreys cited above.
75. On the role of corporate crises in industrial policy-making see K. Dyson and S. Wilks, *Industrial Crisis* (Oxford: Basil Blackwell, 1983).
76. The suitability of the term 'regulatory revision' rather than 'deregulation' is proposed by V. Murray, *Theories of Business–Government Relations* (Toronto: Trans-Canada Press, 1985). See also M. Maxey and R. Kuhn, *Regulatory Reform: New Vision or Old Curse?* (Eastbourne: Praeger, 1985).

Divergent Paths: Political Strategies for Telecommunications in Britain, France and West Germany

Kevin Morgan and Douglas Webber

A spectre is haunting Western Europe in the shape of the growing American and Japanese domination of the strategic information technology (IT) sectors.[1] Telecommunications is the one IT sector in which the position of the European Community (EC) countries has been most favourable. A dozen or so indigenous firms satisfy most of the requirements of the EC market and, taken as a whole, the Community represents 20 per cent of the world telecommunications market. This favourable position contrasts sharply with the situation in micro-electronic components and data-processing equipment, where the EC's position is becoming ever more precarious. The EC countries' traditional strength in the telecommunications sector stems from the fact that this sector is severely partitioned along national lines, a result of chauvinistic national procurement policies and a mosaic of nationally-specific technical standards. In each of the three countries examined here – Britain, France and West Germany – the most distinctive feature of the sector is that a public agency (the PTT), traditionally charged with sole responsibility for the operation and regulation of the network, dominates the market on the demand side, while a small 'ring' of private firms dominate the supply side. With the exception of defence and agriculture, no other sector has been so politicised and so protected.

Once a relatively stable sector in which institutional arrangements went unquestioned, the telecommunications sector faces radical change on three fronts: accelerating technological change; new product markets that are becoming more internationalised; and institutional innovation. Technological advances are well under way in the three basic types of telecommunications equipment. There is the transition from semi-electronic to fully electronic *switching* equipment as a result of the rapid decline in the cost-per-function of digital integrated circuits. Secondly, *transmission* equipment is progressively shifting from conventional (copper) cable towards optical fibre cable, microwave and satellite transmission systems. Thirdly, the range of *terminal* equipment has expanded to accommodate data, text, images as well as basic telephony.

Overall, the range and capacity of equipment attached to the network has steadily increased, with the result that the boundaries between telecommunications, data processing and office equipment are becoming less discernible.[2] The technological advances of the past decade permit existing, 'first generation' services to be upgraded. Also, and more importantly, they signal that a new telecommunications infrastructure is emerging, capable of providing 'second' and 'third' generation services (see Table 1). Converging technologies,

TABLE 1
Three Generations of Telecommunication Services

Generation	Telecommunication System Required	Services	Availability
First	Existing analogue and narrow-band digital telecommunications networks	– Telephony – Telex – Slow-speed data services (up to 9.6 kbps) – Teletex – Videotex	– Traditional or in process of introduction
Second	Digital upgrading of existing telecommunications networks (e.g. ISDN)	– High-speed data services (n. 64 kbps) – Integrated services (digital voice, data, text, facsimile) – Electronic mail – Audio-graphic tele-conferencing	– After introduction of digital switching and digital local loops in basic networks
Third	Broadband transmission and switching for at least 2 Mops channel (e.g. fibre optics, satellite-based, microwave)	– Video-telephone – Video-conferencing – Very-high-speed data communications – Bulk document transmission – Two-way CATV	– Satellite-based system for trial phase – Large-scale fibre-optics system in early conceptual stage

Source: Arthur D. Little, *European Telecommunications – Strategic Issues and Opportunities for the Decade Ahead*, (Brussels, 1983), p. 14

together with the rise of new markets for equipment and services, have fashioned an environment that is radically different from the days when the traditional regulatory regime was framed. Consequently, it is argued that 'we have now reached a point where technical, operational, demand and competitive changes have so dramatically emphasized the limitations of the existing regulatory framework ... that a new look at and approach to regulation becomes a necessity'.[3] Accelerating technological change and the advent of new markets confront all the EC member countries in equal measure. But what is perhaps more striking is the fact that these 'imperatives' have met with quite different political responses in Britain, France and West Germany. Superficially, the greatest divergence seems to be between Britain, which is alone in the EC in pioneering a US-style 'market-driven' strategy, and France, which has nationalised and reorganised its major electronics companies in the hope of creating publicly-owned national champions. This divergence constitutes the starting point of our underlying argument: namely, that technology and markets do not of themselves dictate specific political or institutional arrangements, a point lost on functionalist proponents of 'natural' technological trajectories.[4] However, the chief aim of this chapter is to describe and explain the divergent political strategies for telecommunications in each of the three countries.

BRITAIN: THE NEO-LIBERAL EXPERIMENT

Under the Thatcher government after 1979 Britain's experience in telecommunications is without precedent in Western Europe. In no other country has liberalisation proceeded so far; no other country has broken the state's monopoly of the telecommunications network; and no other country has privatised its national carrier. Liberalisation, which needs to be distinguished from privatisation, formally began in Britain in 1981, when the telecommunications function of the Post Office was hived off and invested in the newly formed British Telecom (BT). Subsequently, the formerly rigid rules governing equipment sales and value-added network services (VANS) have been considerably liberalised. A rival company (Mercury, owned by Cable and Wireless) has been licensed to run a new telecommunications network. Two rival consortia (one led by BT, the other by Racal) have been authorised to operate cellular mobile radio networks. And, in 1984, BT was privatised and subjected to a new regulatory regime in the shape of the Office of Telecommunications (Oftel). In conjunction these changes mean that Britain's regulatory system is among the most liberal in the world. Yet, radical as these changes seem in the European context, the Thatcher government could claim to be acting (in part) upon the neglected recommendations of the 1977 Carter Committee, which called for modest liberalisation in terminal equipment and for the separation of posts and telecommunications.[5] Even so, the government can also claim to have ventured far beyond the cautious Carter proposals by creating the nearest thing to a 'little America' in Europe. However, the British situation still falls far short of the apparent 'free-for-all' in the US.[6]

A number of things have changed since the Labour government refused to act upon the Carter proposals. First and foremost, a radically different political party assumed office in 1979, committed, *inter alia*, to extending the sovereignty of the *private* market. Secondly, as more sophisticated equipment and services became available, especially in the form of private networks, business users became increasingly frustrated and more vocal about their inability to gain access to them quickly enough: and BT showed no apparent intention of introducing new equipment or services other than at its own convenience. Finally, the relationship between BT and its oligopolistic 'club' of suppliers — GEC, Plessey and STC — inspired less confidence as time wore on, especially as regards System X, Britain's family of digital switching systems, which has yet to win a major overseas order. Within this new conjuncture the Thatcher strategy had a number of aims:

- to create a more competitive market and a more dynamic supply industry;
- to boost the economy as a whole by allowing business users to gain quicker access to a more advanced telecommunications infrastructure;
- to use privatisation as a means of reducing the Public Sector Borrowing Requirement, which was inflated by BT because the latter did not have direct access to external financial markets.

Although Britain's basic telecommunications network is still burdened with huge tracts of obsolete equipment, and network modernisation still lags behind France and West Germany, deregulation has undoubtedly induced a spate of new services that are less developed or else unavailable in these continental countries. For example, with some 600 VANS (e.g. electronic mail, videotex networks) licensed in Britain since 1981, more than in the whole of the rest of Western Europe, Britain is set to remain the largest European VANS market for some time. Similarly, cellular radio has already been introduced in Britain, whereas France and West Germany, being more concerned to use indigenous technology, have yet to instal equivalent systems.[7] However, while such services represent very real gains for business users, there are also costs attached to a strategy that puts market-led *demand* before indigenous *supply* capacity. Cellular radio provides a perfect example of this dilemma. Because the Thatcher government set a premium on rapid deployment, the bulk of the technology and the associated equipment had to be imported from the US, Japan and Sweden. Britain, it seems, is more prepared than France and West Germany to bypass indigenous suppliers to gain access to advanced telecommunications.

Furthermore, foreign multinationals now perceive Britain to have the most attractive (i.e. liberal) telecommunications market in Western Europe and many of them, like Mitel, NEC, Northern Telecom and Rolm, have chosen Britain as their chief location in Europe. If this poses formidable problems for indigenous British firms, it is perfectly compatible with the Thatcher government's attempt to promote a *cosmopolitan*, rather than a purely domestic, form of re-industrialisation in Britain.[8]

It is already clear that deregulation is far from being a boon for all the actors in the telecommunications sector. Although BT itself did not foresee the extent of deregulation, particularly as regards network competition and privatisation, it has reacted with an aggression that few thought possible in such a bureaucratised organisation. Having fought in vain against the formation of Mercury, BT appears to have embraced privatisation with alacrity because it allowed management to run BT as a relatively autonomous company rather than as 'part of the economy'. Beginning in 1982, BT's once monolithic structure has been restructured into profit centres, and it has embarked on its self-proclaimed mission to become an international actor in information processing and office automation. To this end it is now far more willing – and able – to forge international alliances and to procure its equipment from suppliers other than GEC, Plessey and STC. Thus far BT's most dramatic decision on this latter front has been to use Thorn Ericsson as the source for up to 20 per cent of its digital exchanges, much to the chagrin of the indigenous System X suppliers. Furthermore, BT is now hastily re-balancing its tariffs to reduce cross-subsidies between profitable business traffic and unprofitable residential services. As a result tariffs for major business users are decreasing. Indeed BT now has the lowest business tariffs in Europe, a strategy designed to entice multinationals into establishing their telecommunications networks in Britain. These changes have been facilitated by privatisation but, so far as BT is concerned, they were actually necessitated by Mercury's strategy of 'creaming-off' business on BT's most profitable trunk and international routes.

As for the other sectoral actors – BT's traditional suppliers and the unions – concerned, the first group has been enraged by threatening *aspects* of deregulation, while the second group is wholly opposed to the *entire* deregulatory programme. The principal supplier firms, GEC, Plessey and STC, had a long history of conflict among themselves before the current conflict between them and government over deregulation. For instance, for the development of System X, described by the Carter Committee as Britain's 'make-or-break' project in telecommunications, the Committee observed that these firms were not a 'natural team'.[9] GEC and Plessey, for example, never fully endorsed STC as a legitimate collaborator in view of the latter's ITT parent. Bitter corporate feuding and protracted delays with System X eventually provoked BT, at the behest of the government, to threaten that some 30 per cent of digital exchange orders would be placed overseas unless a more effective arrangement was forthcoming. In the event, STC was obliged to withdraw from the System X programme in 1982, albeit with exclusive contracts for the older (TXE4/4A) exchanges, and Plessey emerged as principal contractor with GEC as the sub-contractor.[10] On the question of deregulation itself, the opposition from the traditional suppliers revolves around two issues in particular. First, that Britain is *liberalising* its market without reciprocal arrangements elsewhere in Europe. And secondly, that *privatisation* is simply substituting a private monopoly for a public one, and that this provides BT with a greater opportunity to procure from overseas. Oftel judged that the first issue was a legitimate cause for concern, but could only recommend greater political action to promote liberalisation abroad. On the second issue Oftel offered little comfort, declaring that imperfect competition was better than no competition. While Oftel recommended that BT should limit second-sourced digital exchanges to 20 per cent of the market for three years (a suggestion already rejected by BT), it nevertheless approved second sourcing as the only way to make competition a credible threat.[11]

Unsettled and aggrieved, the major suppliers count themselves among the victims of deregulation. They are now subject to a more hostile sectoral regime: BT, for so long a captive purchaser and therefore unable to exercise its latent power, is imposing much tougher procurement policies. For its part the government dismisses the suppliers' grievances as the necessary, if painful, costs of the transition to a more competitive supplier industry. As a response to the deregulatory wave the major suppliers have accelerated their search for corporate partners, in the US and in Europe, so as to strengthen their international position and extend their product range, especially in the computing side of information technology. Because of this more competitive environment, but also because of the perceived need to command greater economies of scale, GEC launched a major take-over bid for Plessey at the end of 1985.

Significantly, GEC has also tried to enlist trade union support in its opposition to BT's new procurement policies. When in 1985 GEC announced 900 redundancies it claimed that these were, in part, a direct consequence of BT's decision to 'go foreign' in the field of digital exchanges. If this was indeed calculated to accentuate 'buy British' demands from its unions so as to pressurise government, it succeeded in the former as conspicuously as it failed in the latter. Nevertheless, job security remains the key issue in trade union opposition to deregulation. BT's workforce, which is still 'over-manned' compared with the French DGT and the German Bundespost, suffered a *net* decline of 17,000 in the three years to 1985 and seems set to fall still further.[12]

Significant redundancies have been experienced too in each of BT's major supplier firms over the past five years. Telecommunications has been gripped by the *jobless* growth tendencies all too evident in other information technology sectors.[13] Deregulation may be hastening the displacement of labour (though this is partly compensated for by additional employment within newly established, foreign firms) but it is neither the only nor the major cause. A more fundamental threat to employment is the transition from electro-mechanical exchanges, which are labour-intensive in both production and maintenance, to digital exchanges which are associated with a numerically smaller, but higher skilled, workforce. Such 'technological' job loss would be difficult to stem without any deregulation. However, having failed to prevent deregulation, the trade unions have now placed their faith in the Labour Party, which is pledged to re-nationalise BT if returned to office. Fully aware of such a threat, the Thatcher government saw 'popular' shareholding as the best deterrent to re-nationalisation. While the Labour Party is still privately anxious on this score, the deterrent is not what it was: within six months of privatisation, BT's shareholders declined from 2.3 million to less than 1.7 million and, of these, private investors account for only 13.7 per cent of BT's total shares.[14] This political prospectus means that the present institutional character of British telecommunications is by no means guaranteed a future.

Within the European context Britain's telecommunications sector has undergone a significant, and so far unique, institutional transformation. Aided and abetted though it was by accelerating technological change and the advent of new markets, both of which compromised the traditional state monopoly, this transformation would not have been accomplished had it not been for resolute political action on the part of the Thatcher government. Even so, we should not exaggerate the extent to which competition now reigns in Britain; nor should we represent the Thatcher government as being hell-bent on promoting competition or as having a unity of purpose. The truth is more prosaic. At every turn the government has been torn in two different, and somewhat contradictory, directions with respect to liberalisation and privatisation. Concerned to ensure that a 'privatised' BT commanded the best possible price, the government retreated from the more radical scenarios of liberalisation canvassed by some of its members. For instance, a proposal to dismember BT — along the lines of the divestiture of AT & T — was considered and abruptly rejected, partly because it might have jeopardised the sale price, and partly because it would have diluted the 'flagship' role of BT *vis-à-vis* the British IT industry, an argument successfully deployed by BT itself.[15] In short, privatisation tempered the government's 'animal spirits' with respect to liberalisation, foreclosing more radical options. Little wonder that the British experiment is said to be inconsistent and contradictory, with the government's allegiance divided between BT's customers and its shareholders.[16]

Notwithstanding the formation of Mercury, BT continues to occupy a formidable position in the British telecommunications sector. It possesses a *de facto* monopoly over the local network up to 1990 and, until then, Mercury will be its sole rival in long-distance and international services. Furthermore, BT has already established a large presence in markets — like large

PABX's — that it did not address before 1983. And BT is already heavily involved in those technologies, like cellular mobile radio and cable television, that will eventually allow users to circumvent the local network. Regulation of BT is already stretching Oftel, whose powers are considerably less than those of the Federal Communication Commission in the US. While it is premature to assess how successful Oftel will be, this much is clear: regulatory policy will have to strike a balance between the government's desire to see BT function as a 'flagship' for the pedestrian IT industry, and the government's other desire to placate critics who believe that BT is now more able to abuse its market power. Time alone will decide how this precarious balance is negotiated.

Finally, it is already apparent that the status of telecommunications in Britain is shifting so that it is less of a *social*, and more of a *business*, service. Deregulation has fashioned a new configuration of winners and losers among suppliers and users. On the *supply* side, as we have seen, BT's traditional suppliers appear to be the major victims, and their inability to exploit the opportunities afforded by liberalisation has been a bitter disappointment to the government. There is clearly an enormous difference between deregulating in a context where one's *indigenous* suppliers are strong (as in the US) as opposed to a context (like Britain) where domestic suppliers are relatively weak. Deregulation, like free trade, favours the strong, and it is no coincidence that many of the world's leading telecommunications firms have selected Britain as their chief European location. On the *user* side, the major beneficiaries of deregulation are large business users like financial institutions and the multinationals. However, small businesses and residential users are now experiencing higher charges so that large business users can enjoy discounts. Britain now has the dubious honour of having some of the highest charges in Western Europe for local calls, and the lowest charges for big business users. This growing inequality among users is causing Oftel a good deal of anxiety; but it could have been foreseen because this is exactly what transpired in the US.[17] Western Europe is now looking closely at the British, rather than at the US, deregulatory experience, because Britain is (or was) institutionally more akin to the continental telecommunications scene. At the moment, these countries seem less willing to cede public control over such a strategic sector as telecommunications. And some, like the FRG, appear far less willing to accept greater social inequality as the price to be paid for 'liberating' telecommunications.

FRANCE: THE SCOPE AND LIMITS OF A STATE-LED STRATEGY

Until recently it seemed that France had embarked on a strategy that was the antithesis of the neo-liberal path being pursued in Britain. The most conspicuous divergence lay in the emphasis that France ascribed to a *state-led* strategy in telecommunications (as well as in computers, semi-conductors and consumer electronics). In 1982 the two largest electronics groups, Compagnie Générale d'Electricité (CGE) and Thomson, were nationalised by the Mitterrand socialist government, and CGCT, the former ITT subsidiary, was added to the publicly-owned list in the following year. Then, in 1982, the *Plan Filière Electronique*, an ambitious five-year plan for the electronics industry, was launched in the hope of using strong sectors (like telecommunications) as a lever for the development of weaker sectors. Later, in 1983, CGE and Thomson initiated an asset swop — sanctioned by the government — with the result that CIT-Alcatel, a subsidiary of CGE, assumed sole responsibility for their merged telecommunications activities, leaving Thomson to specialise in semi-conductors, consumer electronics and military systems. The major rationale for these changes was the desire to provide the leading firms with sufficient *public* investment and economies of scale to enable them to act as national champions at home and abroad. However, without denying the logic behind these events, the fact remains that the telecommunications sector has been forced to contend with the internal upheavals of rationalisation, merger and a bewildering succession of industrial policy shifts, as well as with the external reverberations of deregulation in the US, Japan and Britain.

Before 1985 there was little or no *public* debate about liberalisation in France. Two factors in particular help to explain this state of affairs. Firstly, a bi-partisan commitment to the traditional PTT model effectively removed liberalisation from the political agenda. Secondly, the *Direction Générale des Télécommunications* (DGT) had incurred none of the criticisms that were levelled against the British Post Office in the 1970s. Rather, the DGT had earned itself a prodigious reputation by resolving *la crise du téléphone*. Before the 1970s France had been afflicted by an embarrassing paradox: its grand technological ambitions appeared somewhat ridiculous given that it had one of the lowest telephone densities in the OECD. However, on the basis of a massive and belated public investment programme in the 1970s, the DGT transformed the French telephone network from an embarrassing oddity into one of the most efficient in Europe.[18] At the same time, while Britain and the FRG struggled with digital exchanges in the 1970s. France successfully managed to develop and instal the world's first fully digital exchange. For these reasons the DGT had acquired something of a 'superstar' status in the industry and within the French administration.[19]

While liberalisation was emerging on the British political agenda, the debate in France revolved around the implications of the influential Nora-Minc report (1978), which popularised the notion of 'telematics' (i.e. the convergence of computers and telecommunications). The unequivocal message of this report was that France should establish a position of international comparative advantage in telematics. Furthermore, since France would face a tremendous competitive challenge here from the likes of IBM, the French state authorities were enjoined to make 'unrestrained use of their trump card, which is to decree'. As a result, the pioneering role in this telematics scenario was allotted not to the market, but to the French state.[20] The DGT eagerly embraced these proposals for a major state-led initiative for a number of reasons. In the first place, the DGT saw telematics as an opportunity to accentuate its own authority and also as a means of achieving its objective of becoming an independent state-owned enterprise.[21] Equally important, the DGT had become acutely conscious of the need for its suppliers to exploit new markets once the 1975–80 network expansion programme had peaked and, therefore, telematics seemed an ideal way forward in this respect. What eventually emerged from these pressures was the *Plan Télématique* of 1978, inaugurating bold initiatives in such fields as videotex, teletext and an electronic directory, facsimile, a communications satellite and an experiment in optical fibres (at Biarritz) offering broadband facilities.[22]

With the launch of the telematics programme, the DGT propelled itself into activities that extended well beyond its traditional operations which, until then, had been confined to the telephone network. As if to affirm its new ambitions, the DGT set about establishing a network of majority-owned subsidiaries, established under private law, and therefore outside the conventional restraints of the administration. These subsidiaries were seen as a flexible means of coping with rapidly changing markets and technology.[23] Nevertheless, what the DGT did not sufficiently appreciate was that the telematics project did not lend itself to a state-led strategy in the way that network modernisation in the 1970s so manifestly did. Indeed, the telematics venture was a good deal more precarious because of greater technological and market uncertainties. But, as important, whereas the DGT's remit clearly covered network development, this clarity was not at all obvious with telematics, where the division of labour among the DGT, equipment manufacturers and information vendors was ill-defined and a source of conflict.[24] Furthermore, as a state-led strategy from 'above', it was not entirely surprising that the DGT's telematics programme encountered both market opposition (in the shape of demand constraints in facsimile, videotex and the 'minitel' electronics directory) and political opposition. Towards the end of the Giscard presidency the DGT incurred criticisms, from both left and right, of the authoritarian manner in which programmes were introduced without sufficient parliamentary debate and with too little respect for individual liberty. What best illustrated this authoritarianism was the experience in St. Malo, where inhabitants were provided with free, but *compulsory*, minitels. Overall, and somewhat paradoxically perhaps, the apex of the DGT's power was reached in the late Giscard period, even though it *appeared* to have a greater stature under the Socialists after 1981.

With the advent of the Mitterrand Presidency in 1981 the position of the DGT changed in a number of ways. First, the DGT's director, Théry (a close political associate of Giscard) was replaced by Dondoux and, under his tenure, the DGT began to focus more on its traditional role as a network operator, rather than as a pioneering force in the telematic services. Secondly, in an age of growing austerity, the DGT's profits began to be tapped for general budgetary purposes. Thirdly, the DGT was given responsibility for financing parts of the *filière électronique* which, in effect, amounts to subsidising loss-making firms. And, reflecting the greater responsibilities of the DGT, Cabinet responsibility for the PTT has been transferred to the Industry Ministry.[25] If the formal stature of the DGT appears to have been enhanced since 1981, the fact remains that its autonomy, as measured by its access to and control over funds, has been substantially eroded. However, apart from these changes (and those associated with nationalisation and mergers) the Mitterrand government endorsed most of the pre-existing telematics strategy and, in 1982, initiated a remarkably bold public programme to cable France with optical fibres for the transmission of voice, text and video. This daring, state-led programme is nothing if not a huge gamble because cable TV will have to compete with rival technologies and projects; so much so that a number of established communications lobbies (e.g. press, film, conventional TV networks and satellite) already feel threatened. However, the scale of this state-led cable programme remains unique because most other European and North American countries have proceeded cautiously, allowing the private sector to take the initiative under franchising systems, or else there has been only modest state support.

Despite such grand public ventures the Mitterrand government's faith in state-led growth, in telecommunications as well as in the economy generally, has palpably waned. The austerity plans of 1982 and 1983 signalled the end of the government's early ambition to achieve 'growth-in-one-country'. Balance of payments problems and burgeoning deficits in leading nationalised firms like Thomson, CGCT and Bull, led to a backlash in favour of financial rectitude generally and with respect to the nationalised sector in particular. Thereafter the government became less enamoured of the state ('L'Etat a recontré ses limites: il ne doit pas les dépasser', as Laurent Fabius put it) and instead emphasised the merits of the firm, as in Mitterrand's classic 1984 declaration: 'C'est l'entreprise qui crée la richesse'.[26]

On the telecommunications front, a number of problems and conflicts have emerged that threaten to disturb the status quo. In the case of the DGT, there are three immediate issues. First, there is unease within the organisation (particularly among the *Association des Ingénieurs des Télécommunications* (AIT), the élite corps of engineers who constitute much of the DGT's senior management) over the increasing degree of political intervention. What especially agitates the AIT is the way in which DGT profits are being 'milked' and diverted towards the general budget and the *filière électronique*. As a result, the AIT are in favour of more independence for the DGT. Secondly, the DGT has not resigned itself to its defeat over the formation of the Alcatel–Thomson group, a merger that the DGT fiercely contested because it eliminated competition among major equipment suppliers. Consequently, the DGT is now desperately seeking a second source for digital exchanges. Thirdly, the DGT is having to contend with proposals for deregulation; these range from the more extreme demands of the neo-Gaullist RPR to the milder variants that are being considered, albeit privately, within the DGT itself.[27]

With the exception of Jeumont–Schneider, there appears to be little pressure for change from the DGT's major suppliers. Jeumont–Schneider, one of the few privately-owned firms left in the sector, is critical of the unfair advantages enjoyed by the nationalised groups, especially as regards subsidies. However, Alcatel–Thomson, which now dominates the supply scene, is not enthusiastic about major deregulation, fearing that such a course would jeopardise its close relationship with the DGT and its strategic place in the French market. The formation of the Alcatel–Thomson group was undoubtedly a major political coup for the leaders of CGE and Thomson. They initiated the merger, and, by arguing that it was essential for economies of scale *and* as a means of stemming financial haemorrhage at Thomson, they were able to defeat the DGT by eliciting the support of Fabius, the then Industry Minister.[20] But, quite apart from the problems of merging two groups that until then had been arch rivals, Alcatel–Thomson is now being pressured by tougher DGT pricing policies and by the decline in orders for public network equipment. Against this background, both the government and the DGT insist that the group must rely less on public procurement and more on international markets for its future growth. Corporate alliances are seen as essential if foreign markets are to be effectively penetrated, but 'dans ce contexte, le champion français de l'industrie de télécommunications se retrouve singulièrement isolé'.[29] In keeping with the government's declared goals of promoting reciprocal public purchasing and fostering corporate alliances within Europe, Alcatel–Thomson tried to enter into an accord with Britain. However, BT unceremoniously rejected the French E10 as its second source of digital exchanges because this exchange was old, and because the French group refused to establish production facilities in Britain. CGE's freedom of manoeuvre in alliance building is inevitably circumscribed by its status as a state-owned company. For example, throughout 1985 CGE had intensive negotiations with AT & T; one of the aims was that AT & T would be allowed access to a portion of the French market and, in exchange, AT & T would assist Alcatel–Thomson to market its digital exchange in the US. Although CGE is deeply committed to such an accord, the government seems likely to delay final approval until after the elections because of the risks involved.[30] Should the alliance materialise, it would not only damage Mitterrand's vaunted ambition of promoting a European identity in telecommunications, it would also devalue his earlier criticism of the joint venture between AT & T and Philips of the Netherlands.

A further source of ignominy for the Mitterrand government concerns employment. Back in the euphoric days of 1981 the government was itself responsible for encouraging high, and thus fragile, expectations about potential employment growth in telecommunications. But with the precocious development of telecommunications in the 1970s came over-capacity, a problem that has been accentuated with the merger between Alcatel and Thomson. In fact, employment has been falling since the late 1970s as a result of strong productivity increases and the peaking of network expansion. In this context, from a trade-union perspective, the CFDT sees deregulation as a further threat to employment and is, therefore, totally opposed to deregulation and to any infringement of the DGT's monopoly.[31] Even though a tri-partite study group suggested that product diversification and re-training might help to stem future job loss,[32] major redundancies have been declared at both Alcatel and Thomson, provoking protest marches at Lannion, Brittany. This development reinforces a point made in the British context: that jobs appear to be under siege in telecommunications irrespective of deregulation.

The experience of French telecommunications over the past 15 years illustrates the scope for, as well as the limits of, a state-led strategy. The DGT's successful reputation derives essentially from the 1970s and, even then, it was contingent upon what has been described as 'an exceptional and temporary coincidence of circumstances'. In short, it depended upon a strong political commitment to a huge investment programme, involving public procurement in a protected national market for basic network equipment. This, together with technological de-stabilisation abroad, which *temporarily* weakened major competitors like ITT and Siemens, furnished a context that was highly propitious for a state-led strategy.[33] However, the current decade is not so conducive to such a strategy because both markets and technology are less stable and, crucially, public-sector ordering is a declining proportion of total demand. Furthermore, once deregulation has been established, the consequence is likely to be to circumscribe the scope for state action in telecommunications. Although the French authorities have publicly condemned deregulation in the US and Britain as 'politically motivated disruption', France has already discovered that it cannot totally immunise itself from pressures outside its borders. For example, in response to transatlantic price-cutting, the DGT felt obliged to reduce its tariffs to North America, and it is now contemplating a 're-balancing' of its internal tariffs with a view to increasing local charges. This situation amounts to what the DGT director (Dondoux) has called 'imported' deregulation. Although France has long had a more liberal regime, compared with Britain and the FRG, in the field of subscriber equipment, new services such as VANS are small and continue to be tightly controlled by the DGT. Reluctantly, the DGT is considering deregulation, but it remains cautious and pragmatic. As Dondoux puts it:

> If no problems of hegemony are involved, we are prepared to de-regulate. But if we see that the only consequence of deregulation is to allow the American computer industry to make profits at the expense of the French industry, then we regulate.[34]

In stark contrast to Britain, the DGT is seeking European co-operation in the field of deregulation because it feels that unilateral moves in this direction might degenerate into an 'anarchic process'.[35]

The narrow victory of the neo-Gaullist RPR and the Giscardian UDF at the 1986 parliamentary elections brought with it the possibility of more far-reaching steps towards denationalisation of the major telecommunications firms and deregulation of the telecommunications market. The RPR and UDF won the election on a programme which espoused both these objectives. Certainly, it seemed that the new government would privatise Thomson and CGE. Even leading figures in the Socialist Party, such as Fabius and Rocard, had been expressing support for *limited* denationalisation as a means of relieving the burden on an indebted state of raising the funds needed by the state-owned groups. This indicated the extent to which the *dirigiste* tradition had lost its appeal to the major parties in France. However, it remained to be seen how far the RPR/UDF government would go in *deregulating* telecommunications. Precedent suggested that a government of the French Right, with its much stronger sense of industrial patriotism, would not pursue as radical a policy in this regard as the Thatcher government in Britain.

THE FEDERAL REPUBLIC OF GERMANY: WHY NOT MORE DEREGULATION?

Among the major advanced capitalist states, the FRG stands out as an island of stability in terms of its telecommunications regime.[36] The Deutsche Bundespost (German Post Office) has remained a public *administration*, bound by public-service law and subject in certain respects to the influence of some other government ministries. Postal and telecommunications services remain united within the Bundespost, although some forces would like to see them separated. The Bundespost has not been privatised, and there is no likelihood of this occurring. The provision in the Basic Law which stipulates that the Bundespost must be an 'administration owned by the federation' could be changed only with the support of two-thirds of the Bundestag and would be prevented by the Social Democratic Party (SPD). There has been no substantial opening of the domestic market to foreign telecommunications equipment, although the proportion of the market held by foreign firms was, at 15 per cent in 1980, large compared with other similar West European states. More competition is now allowed in the supply of telecommunications equipment. However, the scope of the monopoly of the Bundespost, which is the sole network operator and supplier of services and some terminal equipment to subscribers, remains broad.[37] Indeed, the present Christian Democratic Union (CDU) Post Minister has been accused of implementing the monopoly more rigorously than any of his predecessors.

The stability of the telecommunications *regime* (that is, the legal and institutional framework within which telecommunications policy is formulated and implemented) should not be confused with the stability of telecommunications *policy* (that is, for example, the concrete stance or measures taken by the Bundespost in respect of new telecommunications services and technologies). Indeed, it will be argued below that the rate at which the Bundespost has expanded the range of telecommunications services and modernised the telecommunications network has helped to contain the pressures for radical reforms of the telecommunications regime. Also, the lack of change in this regime should not be taken to mean that it is uncontroversial. There *is* a deregulation debate in the FRG, and there are significant political forces that would welcome reforms in the telecommunications regime. The most important political response to this debate has been the establishment of a government commission to investigate whether 'new structures can be found for ... the Deutsche Bundespost which make possible a more rapid response to technological, economic and political developments'.[38] However, the absence of major changes in the German telecommunications regime indicates that the forces which more or less support the status quo have so far managed to maintain the upper hand. In the remainder of this section, an attempt is made to account for the hitherto prevailing balance of forces in German telecommunications politics. Such an undertaking requires first a brief look at the way in which telecommunications policy is formulated in the FRG.

A striking feature of the telecommunications policy-making process in the FRG is the extent to which it excludes both the Bundestag and the federal Cabinet. The Bundespost is headed by the Post Minister and his ministry staff and an administrative council, which must approve the Bundespost's budget and all decrees and regulations proposed by the minister. The council's members include five representatives each from the Bundestag and the state governments, seven from the Bundespost staff (six of whom come from the *Deutsche Postgewerkschaft* (DPG, the German Post Office Workers' Union), six from various business organisations and a 'technical expert', who comes invariably from Siemens. The administrative council has not rejected any policy proposals from the minister in recent history, but 'the minister has to take regard of its likely majority opinion'.[39]

The issues that most preoccupy the council are the Bundespost's budget and its charges. In practice much of the telecommunications policy is developed in the interplay of the Post Ministry and its technical branch, on the one hand, and the DPG and the traditional telecommunications equipment-manufacturing industry, on the other. The DPG's voice is most influential on personnel policy issues and that of the industry on technical issues, such as the introduction of new equipment and services. 'All the way up to the Federal Chancellor', there are people who want to avoid a conflict with the DPG, whose influence on the Bundespost is rated by all participants in the policy process as high.[40] Like the DPG, the equipment-manufacturing industry also has close institutionalised and informal links with the Bundespost. These links are mediated partly by the (former) communications technology sub-association of the *Zentralverband der Elektrotechnischen Industrie* (ZVEI, the Central Association of the Electrical Engineering Industry), but bilateral contacts between the Bundespost and the firms themselves predominate. There are reputedly 'six to ten' firms to whom the *Fernmeldetechnisches Zentralamt* (FTZ, the Central Office for Telecommunications Technology) turns to discuss technical issues.[41] The Bundespost's choice of discussion partners among the firms is dictated, according to the board member of one firm, by its perception of their technical prowess.

In the German telecommunications debate, the DPG and the traditional Bundespost suppliers occupy the role of defenders of the existing regime. They are united in wanting to uphold the Bundespost's network monopoly and participation on the terminals equipment market and in opposing any privatisation or unilateral opening up of the German telecommunications market. The reasons for the union's and the firms' stances are, in both cases, fairly clear. The union fears that the privatisation of the Bundespost, and its subordination to stronger competitive pressures, would lead to a decline in employment and a worsening of working conditions. The same considerations account for its opposition to the idea of separating the Bundespost's postal and telecommunications branches (which would lead to a massive rationalisation of the loss-making postal division).

The traditional telecommunications equipment-manufacturers' resistance to any radical changes in the telecommunications status quo is explained by their expectation that such changes would reduce their trade with the Bundespost (or any new network-operators) and with users. For the ten or so small and medium-sized firms that supply the Bundespost with terminals equipment, especially telephones, the maintenance of the Bundespost monopoly and the Bundespost's participation on the terminals market is a matter of existential importance. These firms do not command the financial resources that they would need if the Bundespost were to be banned from the terminals market and they had to erect their own distribution, sales and service networks. They exercised a strong influence on opinion-formation in the ZVEI's communications technology sub-association, which has been the business lobby with the most positive attitude to the existing telecommunications regime.

For the large equipment-manufacturers, such as Siemens, which do have their own distribution and service networks and are not as dependent as the small firms on Bundespost orders, the issue of Bundespost terminals market participation is not as critical. However, they, too, want to maintain the secure domestic market provided by the Bundespost, both of and for itself and as a 'reference market' that can help them to penetrate markets abroad. Furthermore, the firms could probably not expect to negotiate such favourable prices for equipment sold to the Bundespost if it were exposed to greater competition.

Within the federal government, the principal bastion of support for the telecommunications status quo is the Bundespost itself. The Bundespost's position certainly reflects in part the pressures of the DPG and the traditional telecommunications manufacturers. The decline in Bundespost employment that might ensue from greater liberalisation or privatisation or a curbing of its activities on the terminals markets would bring it into serious conflict with the DPG. These measures could also squeeze the traditional suppliers' profits and would very likely drive many of the smaller German firms out of business. Not least, the CDU is sensitive to the needs (and pressure) of small and medium-sized enterprise, a traditional backbone of its support and a strongly organised lobby within the party.

It would be a mistake, however, to interpret the Bundespost's commitment to the existing telecommunications regime as merely reflecting its nearness to the DPG or to the equipment-manufacturing industry. In certain instances, the Bundespost has displayed a capacity to reform itself 'from within'. Thus, the decision, following the débâcle with the EWS-A switching system in the 1970s, to abandon the practice of having just one switching technology was unsuccessfully opposed by the DPG, if not also by some firms, and the degree of competition subsequently introduced in the procurement procedures for electronic switching systems was held by the two suppliers, Siemens and SEL (Standard Elektrik Lorenz, the German subsidiary of ITT), to be excessive. These reforms were championed by the ministry leadership and the ministry's and FTZ's procurement divisions, against internal opposition.

As Dang Nguyen argues, with these innovations the Bundespost began to exercise 'its monopoly buying power rather than Siemens its monopoly selling power'.[42] However, in contrast to these measures, most of the other proposals designed to liberalise telecommunications run directly counter to the Bundespost's institutional self-interest. An institution with extensive monopoly powers is bound to resist its exposure to greater competition and the discipline of the market. This resistance is conditioned partly by the fear that a Bundespost constrained by political obligations could not compete on an equal footing against firms oriented exclusively towards profit-making. So long as the Social–Liberal coalition was in office and the SPD occupied the Post Ministry, such initiatives could be excluded. The SPD could have no interest in implementing measures that would have alienated the DPG and have had – from its point of view – undesirable consequences for employment and income-distribution. Why, however, has the CDU-led federal government hitherto displayed comparatively little zeal to reform the telecommunications regime? After all, did not the CDU Chancellor, Helmut Kohl, pledge to 'roll back the frontiers of the state' in the FRG, and was not the present Post Minister a declared and vocal opponent of the Bundespost monopoly while he was in opposition?

The support of the *majority* of the CDU and CSU for the status quo may be explained in terms of six factors. First, the CDU/CSU is cautious about implementing any measures that might lead to a decline in employment in the Bundespost and the German equipment-manufacturing industry.[44] In view of continuing high unemployment, the implementation of policies that could increase it still further could have adverse electoral consequences.[45] Second, (as seen earlier), it is sensitive to the interests of the small and medium-sized telecommunications equipment-manufacturers. Third, the exposure of the Bundespost to greater competition would compel it to introduce a more cost-oriented structure of charges. In practice, the consequence would be increasing charges for local calls (which cover only 50–60 per cent of costs) and reducing them for trunk calls, thus distributing income from private subscribers (who make proportionately more local calls) to businesses. In a period in which the incomes of wage- and salary-earners and social security beneficiaries are declining or stagnant, these measures, too, could rebound to the CDU/CSU's electoral cost. Christian Democracy needs the support of a relatively large number of lower income-earners in order to be able to form a government. Fifth, as parties of the countryside and the sparsely-populated regions in the FRG, the CDU and the CSU are concerned that liberalising German telecommunications and/or privatising the Bundespost could lead to the abandonment of the principles of *Tarifeinheit* (same charges for services, irrespective of place of residence and cost of providing them) and *Flächenversorgung* (provision of services to all areas of the FRG) and thus to rises in charges and a deterioration in services to areas where important segments of their social bases reside. Sixth, the CDU/CSU's stance on telecommunications policy issues is strongly influenced by their representatives on the Bundespost's administrative council – who may tend more to impose the Bundespost's imprint on the telecommunications policy thinking of the CDU/CSU Parliamentary Party than vice versa.[46] However, the CDU/CSU's telecommunications policies cannot be attributed entirely to its 'ideological colonisation' by the Bundespost. Since 1982 the Post Minister has implemented his cable television policies, for example, against some opposition within the Bundespost.

If all efforts radically to reform the German telecommunications regime have so far failed, the forces pressing for greater (if varying degrees of) liberalisation have, none the less, been growing stronger, encouraged by the international trend towards deregulation. They encompass 'outsider' firms, some industrial and commercial users, some peak and sector organisations of industry and commerce, the FDP (Free Democratic Party), the smaller partner in both the old and new federal coalition governments, the federal Ministries of Economics and of Research and Technology, the European Commission and some foreign governments.

The 'outsider' firms are those that have not been admitted to the extent that they think they ought to have been to the Bundespost's 'suppliers' club'. The foremost of these firms are the computer manufacturers, such as IBM and, above all, Nixdorf, which is the only noteworthy German firm to have proposed privatising the Bundespost. To the 'outsider' firms, the Bundespost is a hindrance to the development of new markets and services. Almost all foreign firms may also be reckoned to the liberalisation camp. Their complaints relate not only to the procurement policies of the Bundespost as such, but also to the high standards imposed for telecommunications equipment by the Bundespost's certification office.

The Bundespost's users in no way form a united lobby for greater liberalisation or privatisation. In so far as the interests of *private* users are represented at all in the political process, this is through the SPD and the CDU/CSU (see above).[47] The positions of industrial and commercial users are represented, in varying degrees of purity, by 'specialist' pressure groups, such as the *Verband der Postbenutzer* (VPB, the Association of Bundespost Users), and peak organisations of business, especially the *Deutscher Industrie- und Handelstag* (DIHT, the German Chamber of Industry and Commerce).[48] Dissatisfaction with the Bundespost and its policies, and therefore pressure for changes in the existing telecommunications regime, are greatest among certain business users, such as news agencies and banks, for which (cheap) data transmission facilities are most important and which require 'tailor-made' telecommunications services. Small- and medium-sized firms, on the other hand, appear to be satisfied with the status quo.

The membership mix of the industrial and commercial peak (and partly, sector) organisations generally prevents them, however, from espousing far-reaching telecommunications reforms. The telecommunications equipment-manufacturers organised in the (former) communications technology sub-association of the ZVEI are none the less almost alone among the business interests in basically supporting the status quo. The ZVEI as a whole does not back the sub-association on the issue of Bundespost terminals market participation, and the *Verband Deutscher Maschinen- und Anlagenbau* (VDMA, the Association of the German Mechanical Engineering Industry), which organises IBM and Nixdorf, also wants more liberal telecommunications policies. Also, the *Bundesverband der Deutschen Industrie* (BDI, the Federation of German Industry), the peak organisation of manufacturing industry, to which both the ZVEI and the VDMA belong, is opposed in principle to Bundespost participation on the terminals market, although not to the network monopoly. More far-reaching demands for telecommunications reforms have come from the DIHT, which organises not only telecommunications manufacturers and other manufacturing firms, but also industrial and commercial firms that use telecommunications services, and retailers of office and computing equipment. The latter see the sale of telecommunications terminals equipment as a potentially lucrative new avenue of business and the Bundespost therefore as a competitor. In the DIHT's view, there should be free competition on terminals equipment markets, and possibly also competition, within limits, in the supply of services and in the network.

The FDP, the Liberal Party, is the only party to have adopted an unequivocal stance in favour of 'more competition' in telecommunications. As an urban party, with its social roots predominantly among upper-level white-collar workers and professional groups, the FDP is not encumbered like the SPD or CDU/CSU by any substantial core clientele among lower income-groups or in the countryside. 'Not a few' people in the FDP support the idea of privatising the Bundespost, although this is not (yet) party policy.[49] The FDP is not in favour of parallel networks, but it advocates competition in the supply of services on the Bundespost network and, in principle, the banning of the Bundespost from the terminals market.

The FDP's main source of leverage on telecommunications policy is provided by its control of the Federal Economics Ministry. In a series of conflicts with the Bundespost, the Economics Ministry has used its veto power over Bundespost charges to resist any moves by the Bundespost to establish a monopoly in new terminals markets and to limit the Bundepost's terminals market participation. The basic stance of the Economics Ministry is that, as long as the Bundespost is a network-operator and controls entry to the market through the imposition of technical norms and product-certification, it should not be able to compete on the terminals market. In the ministry's 'mirror' section for the Post Ministry, competition in the supply of services is advocated and the idea of parallel networks is one that should be 'kept open'. The FDP's control of the ministry is less significant for explaining the ministry's position than the ministry's long-standing philosophy that, 'in so far as it is possible, market processes' should be left to operate 'undisturbed' – and the weight of opinion among the various sectoral and peak business organisations, with which the relevant sections of the ministry, true to its self-conception as a 'service factory for its customers', maintain very close contact.[50]

Within the federal bureaucracy, the Economics Ministry's only ally in pushing for a more liberal telecommunications regime is the Research and Technology Ministry, at whose instigation the government commission on the future of the telecommunications system was established. In the Research and Technology Ministry, the dominant view is that competition not only on the terminals market, but also in the supply of services and in the network would have a galvanising effect on the Bundespost and technological innovation in telecommunications. However, the Research and Technology Ministry is a less valuable ally for the Economics Ministry than the European Commission. On the basis of the Treaty of Rome provisions, the Commission has intervened strongly on the Economics Ministry's side in disputes between the Economics and Post ministries over the limits of the Bundespost's terminals equipment monopoly.

Among the foreign governments pressing for a more liberal telecommunications regime – the other 'external' source of pressure for change – the American has assumed the dominant role, repeating the complaints of American firms about German telecommunications policies (referred to earlier). Hitherto, the Bonn government's only concession to American pressure has been to promise to speed up the decision-making process for the certification of American telecommunications equipment for the German market. Faced as it is with strong protectionist pressures from within Congress to impose import controls on telecommunications equipment from states that have not liberalised their markets according to American wishes, the American administration is sure to intensify its pressure on the German government to open the German market wider to American imports. It certainly cannot be excluded that, provided it is re-elected in 1987, the CDU/CSU/FDP government will make more substantial concessions to American pressure than it has done hitherto.

What is striking in the FRG is not only the comparative stability of the telecommunications regime, but also the comparatively modest nature of the proposals to reform (let alone to transform) it. Privatising the Bundespost (as opposed to some of its existing functions or commercial activities) has hardly been raised as a serious political demand, and there is only very limited support for dismantling the Bundespost's network monopoly. The recommendations of the current government commission on the future of telecommunications will be likely to centre on the form and limits of the Bundespost's participation on the terminals market. While it cannot be ruled out that the commission will make proposals to liberalise the telecommunications regime, these proposals would not be unanimous, thus reducing the likelihood of their being accepted and implemented by the government.

It is important to ask why the pressure for liberalisation from the users' side in Germany has not been very intense – less evidently than in Britain (see above). Arguably, the telecommunications strategies of the Bundespost, the DPG and the dominant equipment-manufacturers (especially Siemens) have limited the growth of dissatisfaction with the telecommunications regime in the FRG and thus deprived neo-liberal philosophies of any potential mass appeal. The Bundespost has, on the whole, introduced new telecommunications technologies and services swiftly. Even the proponents of telecommunications' liberalisation in the peak organisations of business acknowledge that it has a high technical competence and 'provides' for the rapid expansion and for the continuous modernisation of the telecommunications infrastructure.[51] During the 1970s, the proportion of the population with telephones in the FRG more than doubled – not as steep an increase as that achieved in France, but considerably greater than that in Britain. Between 1978 and 1982, various telephone charges were reduced. It is notable that business organisations do not justify their demands for liberalisation by reference to the benefits that this might yield for private users. On the contrary: they acknowledge that the purpose of the telecommunications liberalisation and privatisation measures implemented in the United States and Britain was to 'tailor the national telecommunications systems more strongly than hitherto to the communications needs of business'.[52]

The Bundespost's introduction of new technologies and services has been facilitated by the DPG, which has adopted a basically positive attitude to technological innovation while trying to influence the terms on which it occurs. New services may bring new jobs and new members for the DPG, though this is not the case for all technological innovation. The union's acceptance even of labour-*saving* technological innovation is conditioned by its belief that, if it were to obstruct the introduction of new technologies and services by the Bundespost, then the pressures for liberalisation would become unstoppable, the Bundespost monopoly would be broken, and the technologies that the DPG had prevented the Bundespost from introducing would be introduced by private enterprise under private control.[53]

The dominant equipment-manufacturing firms, first and foremost Siemens, have at the same time preferred not to try to drive their small and medium-sized 'competitors' from the market and achieve a complete stranglehold of domestic equipment supply, but rather have co-operated and carved up the domestic market with them. The small and medium-sized firms themselves constitute an influential lobby in favour of preserving the telecommunications status quo. If they did not exist, and a couple of firms were to attain a total domination of supply, then the government would be exposed to much greater pressure, and would itself be rather more inclined, to open up the German market further and ensure that such firms were faced with competition *from abroad*. Technologically, Siemens does not need to co-operate with firms like TN Telenorma and DeTeWe in manufacturing switching equipment for the Bundespost.[54] Such co-operation is a political necessity, arising from the above consideration and also from the need to avoid coming into conflict with the Federal Cartel Office. Thus, as recently as 1982, the FRG actually had a considerably less oligopolised telecommunications equipment market than France or Britain.[55] Moreover, by adopting a much more innovative telecommunications investment strategy since the fiasco with the EWS-A switching system in the 1970s, Siemens has also given impetus to the Bundespost's modernisation of the telecommunications network.

CONCLUSIONS AND IMPLICATIONS FOR POLICY

The technological revolution in telecommunications has produced quite divergent political responses in France, Britain and the FRG. This fact alone suffices to rebut the notion that technological trends somehow impose themselves irresistibly on public policy. To be sure, none of the states that have been looked at here has opted for a policy of technological 'isolationism', turning its back on new telecommunications technologies. All have sought to stimulate technological innovation, only within the framework of very different telecommunications regimes.

While deregulation is certainly the dominant international trend in telecommunications politics, Britain has gone far further down this road than either France or the FRG. However, it cannot plausibly be argued that deregulation and/or privatisation represent the only possible political response to the 'communications revolution'. Whether they are the best response depends on whose needs are to enjoy primacy in telecommunications policy. Deregulation, like other strategies, has its winners and losers, proponents and opponents. Which brings us to the point: technological change throws up new options and puts new issues on the political agenda, but it does not predetermine political outcomes. The trend towards deregulation reflects changes in the political environment and in the balance of political forces as well as developments in telecommunications technology and markets.

The political forces that have campaigned for and against liberalisation and privatisation measures in the three states have been similar. The trade unions, the parties of the left, the traditional domestic suppliers of the publicly-owned network-operator, the PTTs themselves – they have, by and large, supported the status quo.[56] Some business users, firms wanting to get a foothold in the growing telecommunications equipment markets, the allies of both in the state bureaucracies and business organisations, the parties of economic liberalism, the EEC and foreign governments, first and foremost the Americans – these are the champions of deregulation and privatisation.

The uneven extent of deregulation and privatisation in Britain, France and the FRG seems to be attributable primarily to (1) the degree of dissatisfaction with the performance of the network operator and the traditionally dominant domestic equipment manufacturers and (2) the character of the governing party – of its social bases more than its ideological profile, to the extent that they are separable. Thus, in Britain, there appears to have been *relatively* broad dissatisfaction with the quality and nature of the services provided by BT (even if it was still limited mainly to business circles), and the Conservative government was committed to a programme of radical neo-liberal reforms and unconstrained by the need to pay attention to the interests of the potential 'losers' of deregulation.

In contrast, in the FRG, although the federal government that has been in office since 1982 officially has a neo-liberal economic programme, it is more strongly fettered by the need to take account of the implications of telecommunications deregulation for employment, income-distribution and regional inequalities. At the same time, the Bundespost, the dominant domestic equipment manufacturers (and also organised labour) have pursued telecommunications strategies that have prevented the emergence of much dissatisfaction with the existing telecommunications regime, except among a limited group of business users. Changing *anything* in the existing telecommunications regime is a more difficult project in the FRG than in either France or Britain, given the constraints set by constitutional provisions, by the telecommunications policy-making process (which is not amenable to immediate change), and by institutions such as labour co-determination (which secures labour a voice in the policy process, irrespective of the complexion of the government). Such constraints tend to ensure that changes in the telecommunications regime can only be implemented if they enjoy broadly-based political support. But once they have been implemented, it is then less likely that they will be undone. Hence there is less uncertainty about the future shape of the telecommunications regime in the FRG than in Britain, where it cannot be excluded that a future Labour government will renationalise BT, or in France, where the government of the right will probably denationalise the big telecommunications firms taken into state ownership by the Socialist–Communist government in 1982. The generally greater ideological polarisation in France and Britain, compared with the FRG, manifests itself in conflicts over telecommunications policy as well as in other policy areas.

If there are any 'technological imperatives' at all in telecommunications politics in Western Europe, then they may point in the direction of greater collaboration between firms in the different European states, particularly in research and development, and the creation of a common European market in telecommunications equipment.[57] Thus, the development of a new generation of digital public telephone exchanges is estimated to cost $1 billion. To amortise such investments, a firm's sales would have to reach about $14 billion – a sum that outstrips the prospective market for such exchanges in any one of the EEC member states. It is this 'growing disproportion between the volume of resources required to develop new technologies and the limited size of Western European markets' that lies at the root of the political initiatives being discussed or taken to stimulate greater collaboration between telecommunications firms at the European level and remove obstacles to freer trade in telecommunications equipment within the EEC (RACE, Eureka, European Technology Community, etc.).[58] But will what is 'imperative' as a consequence of technological change prove *politically* possible? Both sets of measures — R and D collaboration, and a common telecommunications market — would have their winners (the strong firms and strong national equipment-manufacturing industries) and losers (the weak firms and weak national equipment-manufacturing industries) and are, therefore, politically contested. The positions that the EEC states adopt on such issues tend to vary not only according to the strength of their domestic equipment-manufacturing industries, but also according to their governments' conceptions of the proper role of the state in these processes and of their relations to the United States. The modest progress that has been achieved on both fronts hitherto (for example, 10 per cent of the PTTs' orders *should* be *open to bids* by firms from other EEC states) suggests that the answer to this question is more likely to be 'no' than 'yes'. Moreover, it may be difficult to implement a common European policy to promote greater collaboration among telecommunications manufacturers in different states against the will of the firms themselves — which frequently prefer American partners.[59]

NOTES

The authors are members of an ESRC-financed government-industry relations project team at the University of Sussex. They wish to thank the other members of the project, Alan Cawson (director), Anne Stevens, Peter Holmes, Geoffrey Shepherd and Susan Cory-Wright for their assistance in the writing and production of this paper.

1. Definitions of IT vary a good deal, but any meaningful definition would have to embrace: integrated circuits, data processing, telecommunications and office equipment.
2. Organisation for Economic Co-operation and Development, *Telecommunications: Pressures and Policies for Change* (Paris, 1983) *passim*.
3. A. D. Little, *European Telecommunications: Strategic Issues and Opportunities for the Decade Ahead, Annex D* (Brussels, 1983), *passim*.
4. For a critique of technological determinism, see Ian Miles, Ken Guy, Howard Rush and John Bessant, *New IT Products and Services — Technological Potential and Push* (Science Policy Research Unit, 1985) p. 5.
5. Charles Carter, *Report of the Post Office Review Committee* Cmnd 6850 (London: HMSO, 1977), p. 66.
6. Michael Borrus, *Telecommunications Development in Comparative Perspective: The New Telecommunications in Europe, Japan and the US*, Report to the Office of Technology Assessment (Washington, 1985), *passim*.
7. Jason Crisp, *Mobile Communications*, Financial Times Survey (London, 1985), p. 1.
8. Kevin Morgan and Andrew Sayer, *Microcircuits of Capital: 'Sunrise' Industry and Uneven Development* (London: Polity Press, forthcoming).
9. Carter, p. 102.
10. Guy de Jonquieres, 'A Crucial Test for System X', *Financial Times* (11 April 1983).
11. Oftel, *British Telecom's Procurement of Digital Exchanges* (London, 1985), para. 14.
12. De Zoete and Bevan, *British Telecom* (London, June 1984) pp. 69–76.
13. Andrew Sayer and Kevin Morgan, 'The Electronics Industry and Regional Development in Britain', in A. Amin and J. Goddard (eds) *Technological Change and Regional Development* (London: Allen & Unwin, 1986).

14. British Telecom, *Annual Report* (London, 1985) p. 3.
15. George Jefferson, 'Why BT Must Have The Freedom to Compete', *Financial Times* (25 January 1984), p. 19.
16. International Institute of Communications, *From Telecommunications to Electronic Services* (London, 1985), *passim.*
17. Borrus, p. 3.
18. Catherine Bertho, *Télégraphes et Téléphones* (Paris: Le Livre de Poche, 1981), p. 484.
19. E. Cohen and M. Bauer, *Les Grandes Manoeuvres Industrielles* (Paris, Belfond, 1985), *passim.*
20. Simon Nora and Alain Minc, *The Computerisation of Society* (Cambridge: MIT Press, 1980), p. 7.
21. Henry Ergas, 'Industrial Policy in France: The Case of Telecommunications', paper presented to seminar on *Industrial Policy and Structural Adjustment*, Naples (April, 1983), p. 18.
22. Godefroy Dang Nguyen, 'Telecommunications: a challenge to the old order' in Margaret Sharp, (ed.), *Europe and the New Technologies* (London: Frances Pinter, 1985), p. 115.
23. A. D. Little, *Telecommunications Regulations Policy in the European Community, USA and Japan* (Bonn, 1983), p. 96.
24. Ergas, p. 22.
25. Ibid, p. 26.
26. Howard Machin and Vincent Wright, 'Economic Policy Under the Mitterrand Presidency' in H. Machin and V. Wright (eds.) *Economic Policy and Policy-Making Under the Mitterrand Presidency 1981–1984*, (London: Frances Pinter, 1985), p. 3.
27. Jeanne Villeneuve, 'PTT: les télécommunications veulent changer d'adresse', *Libération* (27 November 1985).
28. Paul Betts, 'The Struggle to Keep up with the Leaders', *Financial Times* (4 October 1983).
29. Eric Rodhe, 'Alcatel Thomson face à un cercle restreint d'alliés potentiels', *La Tribune de l'Economie* (20 July 1985).
30. Eric Le Boucher, 'Les Risques De L'Accord ATT-CGE', *Le Monde* (16 December 1985).
31. Confédération Française Démocratique du Travail, *Communication De La CFDT*, (Paris, 1985).
32. Group de Stratégie Industrielle, *Report sur les Industries de Telecommunications* (Paris, 1985).
33. Ergas, p. 28.
34. Quoted in Guy de Jonquieres, 'The Future Looks Less Certain', *Financial Times* (1 February 1985).
35. Jacques Dondoux, Address to *Financial Times Conference on World Telecommunications*, (December, 1985).
36. A full, and fully-annotated, analysis of the politics of German telecommunications is contained in Douglas Webber, 'The Politics of Telecommunications De-regulation in the Federal Republic of Germany' (University of Sussex working paper series on government-industry relations, 1986).
37. The Bundespost has a monopoly of simple telephones and competes with private suppliers on four of 10 other terminal equipment markets in the FRG, holding market shares in these markets varying between five and 90 per cent.
38. 'Regierungskommission Fernmeldewesen nahm ihre Arbeit auf', *Zeitschrift für das Post- und Fernmeldewesen*, No. 7 (29 July 1985), p. 35. Significantly, the brief which the government gave the commission said that it was to accept the responsibility of the federation for the postal and telecommunications system laid down in the Basic Law and the basic features of the Bundespost's existing constitution.
39. Herr Emil Bock, deputy chairman of the DPG, interview with Douglas Webber, Frankfurt, 26 November 1985.
40. Quotation from civil servant involved in telecommunications policy-making, in interview with Douglas Webber, Bonn, 16 December 1985.
41. Herr Gerd Wigand, executive board member of TN Telenorma, in interview with Douglas Webber, Frankfurt, 22 November 1985. These firms may be mostly the 'court suppliers' (*Hoflieferanten*) which, in the past, received the lion's share of the Bundespost's telecommunications equipment orders. Rival firms have complained that the technical specifications written into the Bundespost's tender invitations reflected the preferences of their competitors.
42. Dang Nguyen, 'Telecommunications', p. 104.

43. Quotation (freely translated) from the Chancellor's legislative programme announced in the Bundestag in 1983.
44. See the remarks made by the Post Minister, Schwarz-Schilling, at the inaugural meeting of the government commission on the telecommunications system, reported in 'Regierungskommission nahm ihre Arbeit auf', *Zeitschrift für das Post- und Fernmeldewesen*. op. cit., p. 38.
45. One argument used by the Bundespost to defend its participation on the terminals market is that some 30,000 jobs in the Bundespost depend on this. The speed with which the Bundespost is planning to make the transition from electro-mechanical switching has also been influenced by employment considerations.
46. The CDU representative on the administrative council, Pfeffermann, told Douglas Webber, in an interview, Bonn, 16 October 1985, that through his membership of the administrative council, he influenced the telecommunications policy of the CDU/CSU Parliamentary party more than vice versa.
47. In his speech to the government commission (see note 44), the Post Minister drew attention to the 'social component' which he said 'set limits' to the strict cost-orientation of charges.
48. Of all the pressure groups, the VPB, whose modest membership includes all the big German banks and insurance companies, adopts the most radical stance on telecommunications issues, lambasting the 'state monopoly capitalist' practices of the Bundespost and calling for (ideally) its privatisation, the separation of its postal and telecommunications services, liberalisation of the terminal equipments markets, and the admission of competitors to the Bundespost in the supply of services. (Quotation from Wilhelm Hübner, secretary of the VPB, in interview with Douglas Webber, Offenbach, 29 November 1985).
49. Ernst Eggers, chairman of the FDP Commission on the Telecommunications and Postal System. in interview with Douglas Webber, Bonn, 10 October 1985.
50. The description of the Economics Ministry's self-conception as a 'service factory for its customers' was made by the former FDP Economics Minister, Lambsdorff. See *Handelsblatt*, 10/11 February 1984.
51. DIHT, 'Brauchen wir eine neue Fernmeldepolitik?' (Document in possession of the authors, dated July 1985).
52. Ibid., p. 4.
53. Bock, interview with Douglas Webber, op. cit.
54. Wigand, interview with Douglas Webber, op. cit.
55. Cf. ZVEI Fachverband Fernmeldetechnik, *Kommunikationstechnik in der Bundesrepublik Deutschland* (Frankfurt: ZVEI, 1983), p. 60. According to the ZVEI data, the FRG had an average of almost eight suppliers for eight different kinds of telecommunications equipment, compared with five in France and between four and five in Britain.
56. This is not to say, of course, that all these actors share the same position on all issues. The PTTs, for example, generally welcome more competition being introduced among their suppliers.
57. Cf. Dang Nguyen, 'Telecommunications', pp. 108–9.
58. Douglas Webber and Peter Holmes, 'Europe and Technological Innovation', *ESRC Newsletter*, No. 55 (June 1985), p. 18.
59. On the European information and communications technology firms' preference for collaboration and joint ventures with American (and Japanese) firms, see Douglas Webber, Martin Rhodes, Jeremy Moon and J. J. Richardson, 'Information Technology and Economic Recovery: The role of the British, French and West German governments' (unpublished paper, University of Strathclyde, 1985).

Policy, Politics and the Communications Revolution in Sweden

Jeremy Richardson

POLICY-MAKING AND INDUSTRIAL POLICY IN SWEDEN

Ruin has emphasised that Sweden has traditionally been recognised for its anticipatory policy style in which there is also great importance attached to consensus building and conflict avoidance. In his words, '... this has meant an emphasis on trying to direct events rather than letting events dictate policy, on being active and innovative rather than reactive'.[1] Anglo-American observers have been particularly struck by what appeared to be a very rationalistic approach to policy-making and a strong belief in the power of science and objective knowledge as a means of shaping society.[2] Institutional expression of this unusually rationalistic policy style is to be found in two especially important features of the Swedish policy process. First, there has long been a predilection for the use of investigative inquiries to establish facts, define problems and search for possible solutions, often drawing upon foreign experience. Secondly, there is a very long tradition of interest group accommodation and consensus building prior to policy change, through the ever-extending 'remiss' system. A third factor has probably been the stability and continuity of Social Democratic rule — not broken until 1976, after 44 years of Social Democratic government of one kind or another.

These rather favourable images have all been modified in the late 1970s and 1980s. For example, the investigative commissions have gradually become more politicised and increasingly agents of bargaining rather than of objective scientific inquiry. The creation of consensus has proved increasingly elusive. Ruin, in particular, has emphasised that policy-making has become much more difficult in Sweden, as the country has tried to grapple with the problems brought by the world depression and the consequent re-structuring of society that this implies.[3] Many of the seemingly unshakeable aspects of the 'Swedish model' have appeared to crumble in the 1980s. For example, the Labour market has become much more conflict-ridden, exhibiting greater difficulty in reaching and maintaining centralised agreements. The power of the central bargaining organisations — the Swedish Employers' Confederation (SAF) and the Swedish Trade Union Confederation (LO) — has declined, thus weakening two of the main pillars on which consensus in the labour market was constructed. Some observers see the weakening of these institutions as contributing to a potentially serious rise in Sweden's wage costs compared with its main competitors.[4] Despite new problems on the labour market, however, unemployment has remained very low by international standards.[5] Having increased from 1.5 per cent in 1970 to a peak of 4.1 per cent in September 1983, it had taken a downward path to 2.7 per cent by December 1985. Whatever problems have arisen in the Swedish economy, unemployment has not been one of them, when compared with most other Western European countries. (It should, however, be noted that there is a significant degree of 'hidden' unemployment – possibly an extra four per cent – if numbers on special labour market schemes are taken into account.) Sweden's industrial strength has rested upon an ability to market high-quality, technologically advanced products in competitive markets. For example, in 1982, some 60 per cent of the output of the electrical engineering and electronics sectors was exported. Telecommunications equipment represented the largest sub-sector in this grouping with 35,887 employees (out of 82,000) and sales of SEK 12,408 million out of a total sales for the sector of SEK 27,796 million.

Yet on the industrial policy front, Sweden was forced to change its policy in the 1970s in a direction more familiar to British eyes – namely, the subsidisation of ailing and declining industries. Having previously eschewed public ownership, Sweden had to take into public ownership large firms in shipyards, steel and forestry which would have otherwise disappeared. Ironically, this change was effected largely by the non-socialist coalition government that came to power as a result of the historic defeat of the Social Democrats in the 1976 election. The state take-overs were designed to buy time for an otherwise too rapid structural change following the oil crisis of 1973/74. Lundmark's summary of the old industrial policy style bears repeating as a reminder of the extent to which the course of industrial policy changed in response to crisis.

> Despite the political dominance of Social Democratic governments since 1932, the economy remained committed to liberal principles. Tariffs and quotas were minimal. Government found little reason to interfere with market forces, in large part because of rising industrial output and low unemployment. The Social Democrats were able to rely on a sophisticated banking system, centred on the Wallenberg family, to provide a financial infrastructure for growth; and on the high quality of management and technology in a country where engineering and science have long enjoyed social status.[6]

The picture changed rapidly in the 1970s with a big increase in governmental industrial support, particularly 'emergency rescue operations'. Thus what were called 'non-permanent contributions' by government rose very considerably between 1971 and 1979. Until the mid 1970s, industrial aid was designed to achieve modernisation and an efficient labour market. After that time '... a growing proportion of public intervention in industry was accounted for by short-term measures to rescue sectors or enterprises in crisis. These rescue operations involved huge expenditures that no-one could have foreseen'.[7] Lundmark's description of the policy style of this crisis intervention could as easily have been written about Britain, without amendment.

> There was ... no explicit policy and no adequate administrative apparatus within the ministry of industry to cope with the industrial crisis. To a very large extent government had to rely on information and a definition of problems that derived from the 'crisis-ridden' firms themselves ... In other words, government's management of crisis was entirely reactive.[8]

Allen and Yuill have also suggested that the aid to specific firms was 'quite massive',[9] and Meyerson has calculated that company-specific subsidies amounted to approximately SEK 26 billion (= approx. £2.6 billion at January 1986 exchange rates) which was almost equal to the combined total government revenue from corporation taxes and employer payroll fees.[10] During the period 1977–79, subsidies from the non-Socialist governments to particular companies represented 120 per cent of their total payrolls or SEK 280,000 per employee! Henning has also drawn attention to the importance of short-term employment considerations in re-orientating Sweden's industrial policies.[11]

Thus one should be wary of any characterisation of Swedish industrial policy which suggests that it is highly anticipatory and of a different order from other Western European nations. This may have been so, but the crisis from the mid-1970s onwards has shown that Sweden is not quite the ideal model that it was once presumed to be. Even though consensus on R and D policies and the increased importance of science and technology policy exists, there is, according to Wittrock, '... less consensus on what those policies should be'.[12] For example, there is as yet no consensus in Sweden on the need for, and content of, a possible national co-ordinated IT programme. The funding of such a programme is particularly problematic. As yet, the government has not agreed to allocate any new money to a national IT programme. As one interviewee put it, the government has, in the past, '... nursed cripples more frequently than rosy babies'!

Again the well-ordered and routinised policy process appears to be under more stress, with a suggestion from Wittrock that all of the Scandinavian countries have witnessed science and technology policies being subject to increased demands, often of a short-range utilitarian nature, that might well have counter-productive effects'.[13] Wittrock's warning has proved well-founded in at least one respect in Sweden, namely, that the emphasis on encouraging universities to be more 'relevant' may have encouraged an outflow of academic researchers and teachers into the very industries with whom they developed these closer links. There has been a serious decline in academic salaries and a decline in post-graduate work. Swedish industry is now a strong supporter of claims for better academic salaries, and is pressing demands that the universities should concentrate more on basic research. Again, one sees a policy style that 'muddles through' rather than one based upon a rationalistic planning approach to shaping the future.

Sweden's industrial policy is also somewhat familiar in that under a Social Democratic government since 1982, it tried to retreat from the policy shift of the mid-1970s. Thus the government argued that there was a need to decrease subsidies to industry as an important element in reducing the budget deficit and has stated that '... support for ailing industries might be advocated because of short-term advantages but that such measures hamper the necessary structural adjustment and the establishment of an internationally competitve industrial structure'.[14] Social Democratic industrial policy de-emphasised rescue of ailing firms and industries, while trying to maintain support for R & D in the high technology sectors.

Despite some difficult industrial policy problems, however, Sweden has continued to exhibit strengths in the engineering sector and especially in

TABLE 1

INDUSTRIAL SUPPORT 1975/76–1984/85: SHARES FOR ADJUSTMENT/CONTRACTION AS AGAINST GROWTH/RENEWAL

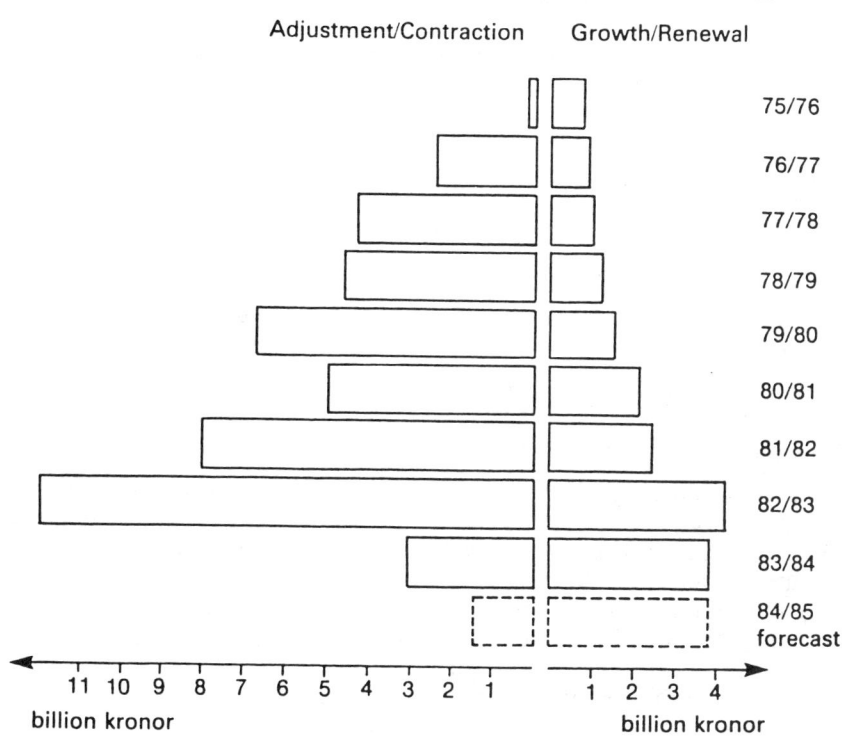

Adjustment/Contraction	Growth/Renewal	Year
		75/76
		76/77
		77/78
		78/79
		79/80
		80/81
		81/82
		82/83
		83/84
		84/85 forecast

billion kronor (11 10 9 8 7 6 5 4 3 2 1) | billion kronor (1 2 3 4)

Adjustment/Contraction = temporary support + sectoral support
Growth/Renewal = support for: R&D, regional development, exports, and small enterprises

Source: Ministry of Industry

telecommunications. This particular sector perhaps best illustrates Sweden's cultural bias in favour of technological change in the context of agreement and consensus on goals. The telecommunications sector has exhibited an enlightened co-operation between the public and private sectors, without resort to protectionist policies. The sector may also illustrate virtues that are not particularly connected with public policies at all, such as a *managerial style* that has been conducive to the avoidance of any technological gap.

Margaret Sharp has suggested that governmental policies may have little impact where there is a significant managerial gap. Thus, she argues, there are two aspects to the technological gap. 'One relates to science and technology proper, the other relates to the commercial application of these ideas and more specifically to business management and production engineering than to basic science'.[15] In her view, Europe lags behind the United States and Japan in the commercialisation and use of new technologies.[16] There are relatively few signs of this problem in Swedish industry as yet. For example, a study conducted by MIT in 1982 suggested that innovative product design and superior performance were especially critical to the success of new, technology-based, firms and that 'larger firms in Sweden play a highly creative role in providing technology, people and especially early markets', for newly formed technology-based firms.[17] Equally, public authorities have been very receptive to the introduction of new technology and have pursued advanced technology purchasing policies. It can be argued that specific and selective interventionist public policies as such have not been that important to Sweden's technological success. One would find it difficult to point to a particular set of interventionist policies, apart from a policy of procuring advanced technology, in telecommunications, for example, in order to explain Sweden's success. This success is more likely to be explained by cultural and organisational factors.

TELECOMMUNICATIONS POLICY IN SWEDEN

Organisational Structure and Behaviour

The telecommunications sector follows the standard pattern of Swedish public administration — a very small central Ministry of Transport and Communications (with a total staff of 85, only two or three of whom deal with telecommunications policy) and a large agency, Televerket (the Swedish Telecommunications Administration). Televerket is a public-service corporation operating on a commercial basis, with responsibility for the development and operation of the telecommunications service.

The responsibilities of Televerket are wide. Thus, as well as the usual national and international telephone service, it provides national telex, teletex, videotex, telefacsimile, mobile telephone and digital radio paging services. It also offers data communication services such as Datel (dial-up service or leased lines in the telephone network) and Datex, a joint Nordic circuit-switched public data network, and Datapak, a packet-switched data network. It also distributes radio and television programmes for the Swedish Broadcasting Corporation. Within Televerket there is a separate department that carries out type approval of equipment to be connected to the network (see below). An appeal system is conducted through the Telecommunications Connection Panel, though there have been no appeals so far.

Televerket was formed in 1853 and, in contrast to what occurred in many other Western European countries, was never linked to the postal service. This early decision may be one of the most important public policy decisions to affect telecommunications in Sweden, as it meant that Televerket was never encumbered by the need to carry a postal service. It has been free to develop the telecommunications system without the need to worry about its effects on postal business. Neither has income from the telephone service been used as a general source of revenue, or substitute tax, by governments. Its special status as a public-service corporation with responsibilities more akin to a business enterprise (i.e. rather different from most Swedish agencies) has also been an important factor in its development.

A change of director general in 1976 gave Televerket a strong push to become rather more market-orientated. Before that date, it might be said to have been dominated by engineers. The new director general, an economist who was formerly Under-Secretary of State in the Department of Industry, seems to have made the organisation more aggressive in developing markets, just as technological developments themselves presented market opportunities. Televerket is best described as having an organisational ideology and culture that emphasises technical innovation and market expansion. It is one of the largest state authorities with over 43,000 employees. Of very special importance in the development of Televerket is the fact that it has its own manufacturing company TELI, formed in 1981 and employing 4,000 people. TELI produces telephones, digital PABXs and crossbar and digital public telephone exchanges (AXE). Approximately 95 per cent of TELI's production is sold to its parent company. TELI is Televerket's largest supplier of telephone exchanges, PABXs and telephone sets.

An unusual feature of Televerket's R & D activity is that in 1970 it formed a joint company with Sweden's main telecommunications manufacturer, L.M. Ericsson. The joint company – Ellemtel Development Company (Ellemtel Ütvecklings AB) – has been responsible for the development of the very successful AXE-system and the new Swedish telephone Diavox. Formed primarily to co-ordinate development efforts in electronic switching techniques, the company has been a successful collaboration between a major purchaser and the major domestic manufacturer of telecommunications equipment. In 1983, technical work ordered by Televerket and Ericsson amounted to SEK 309.7 million, with work concentrated primarily on public telephone exchanges, public data networks and PABXs. For example, the development of a less expensive processor for the AXE-system was completed, making the AXE system economic for small, free-standing telephone exchanges. Also, work continued on the development work for Integrated Service Digital Network (ISDN) and on the development phase of the Nordic Data Network.

There is a broad consensus within the telecommunications policy community in Sweden that Televerket has been an enlightened and progressive telecommunications administration in large part because it is vertically integrated: that is, it has developed its own R & D and manufacturing expertise. Consequently, Televerket has been able to devise a very effective purchasing policy, to the benefit of itself and of L.M. Ericsson. In selling to Televerket, L.M. Ericsson has faced a purchaser with equal expertise and always willing to purchase overseas if necessary. In fact Sweden has been the least protectionist of those Western European countries who have major domestic manufacturing capacity in telecommunications. For example, between 25 and 30 per cent of Televerket's total purchasers are from abroad, and between 15 and 20 per cent of its telecommunications equipment is purchased abroad. At the same time Ericsson has been very successful as an exporter, being the fourth largest manufacturer of telecommunications equipment in the world, behind the two American giants, Western Electric (AT and T) and ITT, and Siemens of West Germany. Indeed it seems reasonable to argue that Ericsson's success is partly due to the fact that it does not have a 'captured' PTT and that its home market is much too small to survive on alone. Thus it is very important to emphasise the technological and managerial strengths of the PTT in trying to explain the development of the telecommunications sector in Sweden.

Equally, one should emphasise the considerable importance of *organisational attributes* in terms of the role of L.M. Ericsson. The telecommunications manufacturing sector is dominated by Ericsson, which has been particularly successful in the field of systems development. Again, a liberal trade policy has allowed Ericsson to be a significant importer through its emphasis on a commercially orientated purchasing policy for components, rather than necessarily favouring Swedish suppliers. The main exceptions to this policy have been where supplies might be unreliable for political reasons (e.g. American trade embargoes) or where buying abroad might present unacceptable risks in terms of the security of design secrets.

Sweden is cited by Sharp as the best European example of a country that has most successfully adjusted to and assimilated new technologies and has bought in skills as required.[18] Ericsson's development and marketing of the AXE system has been especially successful with sales to over 60 countries, compared with virtually no foreign sales to date for the British GEC–Plessey System X. These organisational attributes, as suggested earlier, may be much more important than specifically targeted public policies. The general policy framework – namely an injunction to Televerket to behave commercially, and a non-protectionist public purchasing policy in the context of a very liberal trade policy – may have done much to create 'an environment which encourages innovative decision-making'.[19] As Sharp notes, 'Governments can help create such an environment by pursuing strong competitive policies and eschewing special pleading for protection ...'.[20]

Policy and Technological Developments in Telecommunications

Televerket has to provide basic telecommunications services at uniform prices and with uniform quality throughout the country. It is expected to encourage the maximum interworking with all parties connected to the service, maximum international interworking, and maximum interworking between different generations of equipment. Reflecting a political culture that places strong emphasis on international co-operation, Televerket has developed considerable expertise in the field of international standardisation, with consequent benefits to Ericsson's international activities. Surprisingly (and not always understood in the public debate) Televerket does NOT have a statutory monopoly in providing telecommunication services in Sweden – though in practice this has proved to be a fact, apart from dedicated networks developed by the State Railways and the State Power Authority. There are, however, private networks using circuits leased from Televerket. Third-party sales of services from such networks are not allowed (but see below). Until recently, Televerket had a monopoly of the connection of voice terminals to the network (see below) but not of other terminals such as computers.

Procurement in general is governed by the government's Procurement Ordinance, which specifies that as much of Televerket's purchasing as possible should be subject to open competition. Its performance and economic goals are set by government and Parliament, as each year Televerket submits a three-year plan for approval. For example, the 1984/5 budget set a target of a three per cent real yield on capital and an increase in productivity of five per cent per year. In practice, Televerket's freedom is very considerable. Like all agencies, the theoretical distinction between policy made by government departments and implementation through the agencies is somewhat fictional. Thus, for telecommunications, the 'model' of small ministries determining policy and large agencies administering it is just as misleading as it is for other policy areas. The enormous disparity in size and expertise between Televerket and the Ministry of Transport and Communications suggests that steering and control in this sector is at best superficial. For example, Televerket finances its own working capital and investments and must now borrow on the open capital market – thus giving it even more freedom to behave commercially. Televerket is a relatively successful actor, in policy terms. The process of bargaining with government does, of course, cause long delays and Televerket is sometimes overuled – such as when a small competitor in mobile teleplay, COMVIK, was given approval to connect its network to the public telephone network. Televerket has also had some difficulties over tariff charges (particularly domestic) which have high political salience. In practice, however, governments rarely say no to Televerket's request, although the Social Democratic government after 1982 was perhaps unwilling to move to major tariff reform as fast as Televerket would like.

In terms of the policy-making process in the telecommunications sector, Televerket should be seen as a very powerful actor – so much so that a rather fierce public debate has developed recently, with much media criticism of Televerket. Response to this criticism has been relatively minor but illustrates that the organisation is sensitive to public pressure. For example, experimental Service Advisory Councils will be set up in three telecommunications areas. The following organisations will be invited to nominate a local representative to the Service Councils: LO (Swedish Trade Union Confederation); TCO (Swedish Central Organisation of Salaried Employees); LRF (Federation of Swedish Farmers); KF (Swedish Co-operative Society); Kopmannaforbundet (Swedish Wholesalers' Association); SHIO (Swedish Federation of Crafts and Small-Scale Industries). A comprehensive review of routines and rules for customer contracts is being conducted, with a speedier customer complaints procedure and a more generous replacement policy in the case of faults. There will also be an extension of payment times. Televerket has also begun an analysis of pricing policies in the context of the introduction of new digital techniques which imply a reduced importance for the distance factor in charging. The attempt to resolve this politically difficult issue will be conducted through a commission in the time-honoured Swedish fashion.

Criticisms of alleged inefficiency and excessive power do, however, need to be set in the context of international comparisons. What Swedes complain about, others might envy! For example, domestic telephone charges are the lowest in the world, with company charges being among the lowest in the world. Average total monthly telephone costs for households in Sweden are SK 105 compared with SK 181 for the USA, SK 195 for GB and SK 285 for Japan. Yet this achievement has taken place in a widely dispersed network.

Technological development has been a central feature of the Swedish telecommunications system. For example, by 1987 Sweden will be the first country in the world to have a nation-wide digital telecommunications network. Already Sweden has the highest telephone density in the world, with nearly 8 million telephones for 8.3 million inhabitants. Thus if Televerket is the dominant policy actor, relatively autonomous of government and Parliament, it has at least delivered the goods by international standards, and has assisted the technological advance of the main domestic producer.

To argue that policy formulation (and even more so, implementation) is heavily influenced by Televerket, is not to suggest that policy change does not take place. It is possible to identify a creeping (if unspectacular) process of liberalisation, often on the initiative of Televerket itself and sometimes in the face of reluctance on the part of the Ministry of Transport and Communications. Indeed, this process was envisaged in a Parliamentary Proposition (1980/81:66) which stated that a continuous adjustment of the policies of Televerket with respect to the monopoly and limitations on competition will be necessary in the light of technical developments. For example, since 1982, the rules governing the connection of equipment to the public network have been changed — and, from November 1985, privately owned telephones, telex equipment, and modems with a speed up to 1200 bit/s duplex could be connected, with Televerket's connection monopoly limited to PABXs, high-speed modems and coin box sets.

The number of modems and the rate of growth was very high by international standards. By 1986 the number of network terminations connected to non-voice equipment was rising by 30 per cent per annum, and over 50 per cent of the network capacity additions in some local telephone areas were devoted to non-voice traffic. This rapid embracing of the potential of the communications revolution is possibly a reflection of broadly based cultural values which have lead Sweden to become a 'computer society'. Another example of this cultural trait is the fact that by 1987 Sweden is expected to have the highest use of computer terminals in Europe, with 36 network termination points per 1,000 workers.

Of special note, in comparative terms, is the very positive attitude of the Swedish Trade Union Confederation (LO) towards the introduction of new technology. In general, LO was as concerned with the threat of the *failure* to introduce new technolgoies as it has been with their possible threat to employment levels. Thus LO recognised that Sweden had to adopt the latest technological advances in order to maintain its comparative edge in high-value quality products. The continuity of Social Democracy, referred to earlier, is of some importance in fostering this enlightened attitude by the trade unions. Thus, the state's role has always been to take care of any adverse consequences of structural adjustments caused by technological and other market-led changes. There was, of course, debate about the merits of, say, big computer systems (especially in the public sector) but little evidence that trade unions have actually prevented their introduction.

A further small example of creeping liberalisation was that the testing of equipment for type-approval purposes no longer had to be done in Televerket's own laboratories but could be carried out in other laboratories in Sweden and abroad, meeting certain technical requirements. Formal type-approval is issued by Televerket's Type Approval Office, and is based upon information provided to manufacturers and testing laboratories. Televerket has provided a test report form showing the properties that should be measured and reported for various types of terminals to be connected to the public network. This liberalisation of telephone sets was in part forced upon Televerket by market conditions, as some 10 per cent of new telephones connected to the public system were 'pirate' telephones, not conforming to Swedish standards. (It was legal, after a ruling of the Swedish Market Control Court, to sell such sets, even though it was illegal to connect them.) Thus, there had been a *de facto* liberalisation of the ordinary telephone market, as a result of the sale of these 'pirate' telephones. Televerket's support for a formal liberalisation of telephone sets appears to be an attempt to re-impose some technical standards into the competitive market, as pirate phones have caused significant technical difficulties for their users and for other users of the telephone network. This formal liberalisation is, therefore, somewhat symbolic, and there is no significant demand for the privatisation of Televerket (on the British Telecom model) or for divestiture (on the AT and T model). Televerket has itself to become more competitive in this particular market, in order to defend the interests of its own manufacturing division. This division was scheduled to become a limited company, within Televerket, in July 1986, with the intention of developing export markets – particularly to the rest of Scandinavia and Britain.

Some liberalisation had also taken place in the videotex service, designed to establish an efficient service accessible to all users on equal terms. By using standardised gateways, information from various databases was to be made available, of which Televerket's own Datavision would be just one. The range of charges was designed to be neutral as between different providers of data bases. Against a background of a strong market, Televerket planned to invest SK300 million during the remainder of the 1980s to develop the general videotex service. The service was used by banks, finance companies, travel agencies, and other commercial companies.

A new Radiofrequency Committee was also established to examine appeals against the existing Frequency Management Unit within Televerket, even though the Frequency Management Unit was already independent of Televerket's activities.

Televerket has introduced a number of new services since the early 1980s. For example, in 1983 it introduced a conversion facility enabling communication between telex and teletex terminals; in 1985 it introduced higher speed modems (14,4 kbit/s) on leased digital circuits; in 1984 it introduced leased digital circuits (64 kbit/s and 2Mbit/s) on an experimental basis; in 1984 it signed an agreement to introduce private sub-networks within the public Datapak network, giving banks better management facilities and quality guarantees on their sub-networks; and in 1985 it introduced Minicall, a simple paging system on a regional basis.

CABLE TELEVISION; SATELLITE COMMUNICATIONS; TELEVISION ADVERTISING

Cable Television and other Communications Services

The construction of cable television networks started mainly for the relay of signals from communication satellites. New rules governing cable television came into effect on 1 January 1986 and were based on the recommendations of a commission, the Committee on Mass Media.[21] The recommendations of this committee were based less on questions of cultural policy than on industrial policy considerations, which were in fact given priority.[22] There was a broad consensus '... that Sweden should go in for high tech industrial production. In other words, the development of our electronics industry and national telecommunications infrastructure is seen to be a vital prerequisite to Sweden's entry into the "information society"'.[23] These rules provide for open competition in the construction of cable networks, with at present no compulsory standards. However, there is a voluntary standard agreed by the relevant industry association.

A trial network was established in Lund in 1983; it received television programmes from two British sources and one French source, using the ECS satellite. In 1983/4 the government issued permits for satellite television trials in 20 locations, and 41 localities were given permission to broadcast local programmes. Permits were given to Televerket for 22 networks in addition to those already existing at Lund and Sundsvall.

Currently it is envisaged that Televerket will dominate the market for the large networks. Broadly speaking, two types of cable television permit can be granted:

1. A licence to develop local channels, providing that a local community channel is also established, open to the local community.
2. A licence to rent out a cable channel.

It is thought that the big housing co-operatives, who control enough houses to be able to set up a big network that is commercially viable, may be especially suited to taking out a licence. In practice some 1.5 million houses are controlled by three large housing co-operatives. However, other companies may take out a licence if they want to use the network to distribute their own programmes. Televerket has set up a separate cable television division (KABEL TV).

Televerket has not campaigned for a monopoly, possibly because it feared a public-service obligation. It sought to develop approximately 30 areas of high housing density. By 1986 100,000 households were contracted to receive satellite television programmes by cable (with approximately 250,000 households receiving ordinary cable TV), and a rise to 200,000 was predicted over the next few years. There will be some competition in practice from big housing associations (e.g. in Stockholm) who control enough houses in their own right and can run a network independent of Televerket. However, at the smaller end of the market — say 25,000 homes — there is more likely to be genuine competition. Licensing is under the control of a government-appointed regulatory body — the Cable Committee, consisting of two judges. Public support for the widespread introduction of cable television appeared high. A market survey, returned by between 15 and 20 per cent of households, suggested that 75 per cent of respondents wanted cable television. The structure of the Swedish housing market, together with a high level of interest in foreign television programmes and an ability to understand foreign languages, may well facilitate rapid development of cable television in Sweden.

Other communications services likely to be introduced from the mid 1980s onwards include exploitation of the potential of the network digitalisation programme (40 per cent of investment in the telecommunications network was on digitalisation in 1986). By 1986 there were 300,000 connections to digital PABXs; this figure was expected to rise to between 400,000 and 500,000 by 1987. ISDN services were planned to develop considerably in a two-phase development programme, and it had also been decided to install a digital national long-distance network based upon optic fibres and other transmission technology.

Satellite Communications

Satellite communications policy proved more difficult to manage, in terms of conflict avoidance. Two public agencies were primarily responsible for the policy area — the Swedish Board of Space Activities and the Swedish Space Corporation. The Board was very small, with only ten staff, and was responsible for formulating policy proposals for the government to approve and for the Space Corporation to execute. The Space Corporation was supposed to become profitable eventually.

Sweden's entry into the space sector was perhaps a good example of the use of specific state intervention in order to push industry into a field that it was slow to recognise. The decision was, therefore, an industrial policy decision, on the basis that space technology was an area that Swedish industry could not afford to ignore. The argument was that Sweden had to have a 'national competence' in this area, and that state intervention and funding was necessary for this purpose. The most important function for the Board was, therefore, to promote the development of space technology in Swedish industry and in the Swedish scientific community. It is no surprise that the Board was served by advisory committees designed to integrate both industrial and academic communities into the deliberations of the agency.

One of the main concerns of the Board has been the TELE-X experimental communications satellite, due to be launched by Ariane in 1987. TELE-X was designed to provide high-speed digital data communication for both inter-office links and wide-band services; video communication for outside television broadcasts and other video applications; and direct television and sound broadcasts to home receivers. The project was an example of international co-operation. Other Nordic countries were involved, and it facilitated collaboration between Swedish firms and other European companies more advanced in the field. Aerospatiale of France was responsible for the 'spacecraft' but was assisted by SAAB-Scania of Sweden. Ericsson was assisted in payload design by Thomson-CSF of France. AEG-Telefunken was also involved, as were some Norwegian companies. In terms of industrial policy it has possibly achieved its objective of promoting the collaboration of Swedish companies in a wider European context.

However, the longer-term use of TELE-X after its launch was much more problematic because of the attitude of the PTT – Televerket. An open conflict emerged between Televerket and the Space Corporation over the potential usage of TELE-X. If Televerket's attitude remains unchanged, it is possible that TELE-X will prove to be no more than an expensive experiment. Televerket was doubtful about TELE-X's commercial potential, believing that optic fibres and microwave transmission have better commercial potential. As Hultén notes, Televerket and the Space Corporation have differing organisational interests. Televerket already has existing interests in terrestrial networks and the profitable long-distance traffic generated by heavy users – and is also involved in two other satellite schemes: Eutelsat and Intelsat. In contrast, the Space Corporation has no other interests to protect and may even face competition from private Swedish interests who may enter the satellite market.[24] The next phase of the TELE-X system becoming operational under commercial conditions remained uncertain, with serious reservations from Televerket about the funding of the next satellite, TELE-Y. There is some evidence that an 'industry lobby' was building up, supported by the Ministry of Industry and the Space Corporation, and that a compromise might result in the form of a new joint state and private sector company to develop TELE-Y.

Television Advertising

The question of commercial advertising on radio, television and on cable television presented a difficult political problem although there may be some signs that a new consensus is beginning to emerge. There has been a long-standing policy of no advertising on radio or television based in part on the view that it would present a potential threat to newspapers which depend upon advertising for 60–70 per cent of their revenue.[25] However, two governmental commissions set up in the 1970s (one on video advertising and one on information technology) concluded that advertising on video and on teledata was *not* a threat to the finances of the press.[26] Funding pressures on radio and television have, however, pushed the question of radio and television advertising on to the political agenda from time to time. Advertising and pay television as alternative sources of revenue had their attractions to the broadcasting authorities themselves. For example in January 1985, the governors of Sveriges Radio submitted a proposal to the government for a pay television scheme within the framework of the company (through the formation of a subsiduary combining Sveriges Radio and outside interests). The Board of Governors specified three main conditions:

1 that the new scheme would not affect the existing public broadcasting services;
2 that the scheme would be financed by commercial loans;
3 that the project would be a long-term venture, not a short-term experiment.

The proposal was passed on by the government to a parliamentary *ad hoc* committee, charged with drafting a new contract for Sveriges Radio.[27] Towards the end of 1985, it emerged that an application for the inclusion of advertising on pay television (if pay television is introduced) might be made. The outcome of these proposals was unclear by early 1986.

In practice, the Board of Governors of Sveriges Radio was divided along political lines on such questions as future competition and sources of finance.[28] In 1985 the government commissioned a special study of the possible effects of advertising on television and radio. The issue was politically controversial. Thus the non-Socialist parties favoured allowing advertising on cable television and wanted a very liberal licensing regime, whereas the government was against advertising. In the event the advertising has not been accepted, but (as indicated earlier) a liberal licensing regime was agreed by Parliament. Both the Conservatives and Liberals want a new commercial television channel, but this proposal is opposed by the other three parties in Parliament – which have also rejected the idea of commercial funding of Sveriges Radio.[29] Hultén concludes that the pressures for television advertising are building up, with spokesmen within the Social Democratic Party and the Centre Party now seeing television commercials as a realistic alternative for the existing television channels. These pressures, he suggests '... represent a reaction to what is perceived as an inevitable consequence of the entry of commercial satellite channels into Swedish air space ...'.[30] We may see, therefore, 'technology push' overiding more traditional values which have hitherto supported a strongly anti-commercial view of television. As satellite television – both via cable and eventually using satellite dishes – brings commercial television into Swedish homes (even though advertising directly addressed to Swedish viewers is banned), a consequence may be to force the introduction of advertising on existing channels, especially if accompanied by the pressure of the financing issues referred to earlier.

NORDIC CO-OPERATION

Sweden was active in co-operation with its Nordic neighbours in the communications field, as in other policy areas. For example, TELE-X is a co-operative project between Sweden, Norway and Finland and the satellite will be jointly managed by the three countries. There have, however, been disagreements between the three countries over the financing of this joint venture.[31] In November 1985 the Nordic Ministers of Culture (with the exception of Denmark) agreed to use TELE-X for direct television broadcasting for a period of at least three years, starting in the latter half of 1987. Two channels were to be used: one for news and current affairs, the other for cultural programmes and entertainment. Programmes from the four broadcasting corporations in Finland, Iceland, Norway and Sweden were to be used. However, a proposal, which arose from studies conducted in the 1970s, for several high-powered satellites that would have transmitted direct television channels for an area from Greenland to Finland – called NORDSAT – has not materialised. NORDSAT was an ambitious project in Nordic co-operation, whereby all existing nationwide radio and television channels in the Nordic countries would be distributed to all the Nordic countries.[32] The motivation for the NORDSAT proposals seems to have been idealistic and lacking commercial reality.[33] Televerket does, however, operate a satellite earth station (jointly used by Denmark, Finland and Norway) in the Eutelsat system. Television transmissions started from this station in late 1984.

The five Directors General of the Nordic PTTs meet regularly in Nordtel (Nordic Telecommunication Co-operation). The committee deals with telecommunication problems within the Nordic area, and is concerned with the continued development of the Nordic Data Network (NMT), and the mobile telephone system. It also deals with the reception of television programmes from the communication satellites of Eutelsat and Intelsat, and exchanges information on new telecommunication services such as Datex, paging systems, telex, telefax and Datapak. The Nordic PTTs also co-operate on planning joint facilities for communication with the rest of the world.

A particularly successful example of Nordic co-operation, both in providing a service and in assisting Swedish industry, was the development of the mobile radio service – the most advanced and the largest in the world. Mobile radio proved to be a very rapid growth sector in Scandinavia. For example, Sweden's sales of mobile telephones increased by 82 per cent in 1983/4. The Nordic automatic mobile telephone sysem had 59,000 Swedish subscribers and 175,000 subscribers throughout Scandinavia by the end of May 1985. By 1986 NMT was the world's most successful mobile telephone system with market predictions being exceeded by 100 per cent! This example of Nordic co-operation was of special benefit to Ericsson, (which by 1986 was under contract to supply systems to 16 countries) and to other Nordic suppliers such as AP of Denmark and Mobira of Finland. 'Terminals' for the system were supplied by 11 competing private companies.

CONCLUSION: PROBLEMS AND PROSPECTS

The Swedish record in the communications field is universally recognised. Sweden has embraced the potential of the communications revolution more than any other West European country and appears to epitomise the 'post-industrial' communications society. No doubt there are a number of inter-related reasons for this success. The stock of human capital is high in Sweden, particularly in those areas of direct relevance to the communication revolution, such as electrical engineering. Like West Germany, Sweden has long accorded engineers a high status in society. Sharp (in discussing the case of computer-aided design, CAD) notes that, like Germany, Sweden has 'a general level of skill training ... such that once introduced, it (CAD) was rapidly picked up and adapted to local working conditions'.[34] She also notes that American evidence suggests that there is a shortening lag between basic research and technological application and that: 'This shortening lag puts increasing emphasis on a country's scientific and technological infrastructure, composed of universities, polytechnics and research institutes'.[35] There is also a modernistic *culture* in Sweden rather used to change and innovation and supporting a creative climate for new ideas.

Factors such as the organisational characteristics of the two main actors in the communications sector – Televerket and L.M. Ericsson – have almost certainly been more important determinants of Sweden's success than specific public policies. The public policy framework has been of a type to encourage organisational strengths and open trade rather than to create a protectionist environment which could prove inhibiting in meeting international competition. There has also been encouragement of cross-national links. Thus, in the example of satellite communications cited earlier, industrial policy aims were to bring Swedish firms in close contact with foreign firms that were thought to be more advanced in the field. Equally, the firms themselves have been outward-looking (having little option with such a small home market). For example, Ericsson employs 54 per cent of its staff abroad. Clearly, public purchasing of advanced technology has been important. But it too has been characterised by a high degree of competence on the part of the purchasing agencies (e.g. Televerket or the State Power Authority) and a shared desire between purchaser and supplier to encourage technological innovation.

In general, the industrial policy problems described in the introduction to this article have tended to be absent from the communications sector so far. The big, dominant 'high-tech' firms such as Ericsson, Saab, Volvo, and ASEA have proved to be adaptive to a changing environment. They have remained successful, even in the recession, while specific governmental intervention has been directed at more traditional industries. Like other West European countries, Sweden has introduced policies to encourage the development and use of micro-electronics, for example. However, there is still a strong belief that the most effective role that government can play is to provide and support the basic scientific and educational infrastructure, leaving high technology firms to compete in the open market by drawing upon a supply of well-educated and well-trained manpower. There is a shared view – between government, industry and unions – that Sweden has to have a national competence in key areas of science and technology – which means that industry should be able to turn to academia for fundamental expertise in key areas of knowledge. Moreover, in the 1980s Sweden's government was under pressure to continue the phased withdrawal from 'industrial rescue' and to concentrate on its more traditional role of infrastructure support, enlightened public purchasing, and the creation of an appropriate legislative framework. Most industrialists believed that this framework needs to include some kind of publicly funded IT programme, both as a means of supporting and stimulating qualified technical and scientific education, and as a means of matching what other countries are doing in support of their 'high-tech' sectors.

The future of the communications sector will, however, depend heavily on the continued success of the two main organisational actors. Televerket is developing a decentralised style of management and seems to be set in a direction that will make it even more business- and market-orientated. It has also begun to loosen its collaborative ties with Ericsson, via a negotiated relaxation of the rules governing competition with each other in export markets. Many would argue that the Swedish success in the telecommunications field has rested on the long-standing good relations between Ericsson and Televerket, including a clear definition of respective roles. Televerket's export ambitions may be the early signs of a parting of the ways between Televerket and Ericsson (e.g. on the PABX side) though Televerket will be careful to watch that Ericsson is able to compete in the next generation of advanced digital switching etc. If Ericsson were to fall behind, then Televerket would probably increase its foreign links in order to keep up with market potential.

Ericsson is not without some problems as telecommunications moves into the next phase of closer links with the computer revolution. The company drew up plans to transform itself into a more broadly based company, and took over Datasaab as part of this ambition. Its policy was to become an 'information systems' company. Company sales reflected this shift of direction, but by 1986 profits had not followed – resulting in a reorganisation of the Business Systems Area of the company and the installation of new management in 1984. As the Financial Times observed, there were signs that the giant had stumbled (*Financial Times*, 13 September 1985).

Sweden has also to come to terms with collaborative developments in the European Community. Ericsson is active in developing EEC links – for example, 25 per cent of its 75,000 employees are working for companies located within the EEC. It is also participating on the RACE programme via its subsidiaries in countries such as Italy. In so far as the rest of Europe can get its act together in schemes like ESPRIT and RACE, the consequence could be pressure on Sweden's hitherto successful telecommunications sector. Thus public policy developments outside Sweden may hold the pointers to the future. Should one or two key firms begin to falter, then the difficulties seen in other areas of Swedish industrial policy could yet appear in what has so far been the jewel in the Swedish crown.

Finally, can we draw lessons, in terms of policy design, from the Swedish experience in the communications sector? Sweden has traditionally been a model that foreigners have looked to for solutions. Yet Sweden does not provide a convenient list of specific policy instruments that can work some kind of magic for countries like Britain. Decisions taken many years ago (e.g. the independence of the telephone system from the postal service), the small national market, deeply held cultural values supportive of innovation, change and the use of science and technology to transform society, are all factors not replicable elsewhere. There are, however, three long-term policy instruments that the Swedish case might suggest as worthy of emulation: a liberal trade policy; an emphasis on the fundamental importance of education and training; and a public purchasing policy based on a high level of competence on the part of the purchasing agency and a willingness to purchase overseas if that is where the best technology is to be found. The risks are, of course, high as the broad policy strategy rests on the assumption that Swedish firms can, ultimately, compete. So far this assumption has been tenable. For example, as we have argued, Ericsson is highly competitive in world markets. Similarly, when it was clear that it could no longer rely on the continuation of the high volume of sales to the Swedish power industry, ASEA adapted to the changed situation by developing robots for both home and export markets. If it is found that Swedish industry cannot compete in the future (because of problems of small size or because of externally determined market conditions), then, no doubt, more interventionist policies will emerge.

NOTES

This article is part of a wider project on new technology policies in Western Europe funded by the Leverhulme Trust. The author wishes to acknowledge the assistance of the Swedish Institute and the many officials who agreed to be interviewed.

1. Olof Ruin, 'Sweden in the 1970s: Policy-making Becomes More Difficult', in J. J. Richardson, *Policy Styles in Western Europe* (London: Allen & Unwin, 1982), p. 141.
2. For example see Thomas J. Anton, 'Policy-Making and Political Culture in Sweden', *Scandinavian Political Studies*, IV (1969), pp. 88–102, and Richard F. Tomasson, *Sweden: Prototype of Modern Society* (New York: Random House, 1978).
3. Ruin 1982, pp. 141–67.
4. Per-Martin Meyerson, *Eurosclerosis – The Case of Sweden* (Stockholm, Federation of Swedish Industries, 1985), p. 105.
5. See D. Webber, 'Social Democracy and the Re-emergence of Mass Unemployment in Western Europe', in William E. Patterson and Alastair H. Thomas (eds.), *The Future of Social Democracy* (London: Oxford University Press, 1986), pp. 19–57.
6. Kjell Lundmark, 'Welfare State and Employment Policy: Sweden', in Kenneth Dyson and Stephen Wilks, (eds.), *Industrial Crisis* (Oxford: Martin Robertson, 1983), p. 220.
7. Lundmark, p. 239.
8. Lundmark, p. 241.
9. Kevin Allen and Douglas Yuill, *Government Support to Industry in Sweden. An International Comparison*, (Stockholm: Ministry of Industry, Ds 1 1984:6), p. 62.
10. Meyerson, pp. 61–2.
11. See Roger Henning 'Industrial Policy or Employment Policy? Sweden's Response to Unemployment', in Jeremy Richardson and Roger Henning, *Unemployment: Policy Responses of Western Democracies*, (London: Sage, 1984), pp. 193–216.
12. Bjorn Wittrock, 'Science Policy and the Challenge to the Welfare State', *West European Politics*, Vol. 3, No. 1 (October 1980), p. 359.
13. Wittrock, p. 359.
14. *The Swedish Budget 1985–6* (Stockholm, 1985).
15. Margaret Sharp (ed.), *Europe and the New Technologies* (London: Frances Pinter, 1985), p. 291.
16. Ibid.
17. *Technology and Industrial Innovation in Sweden. A Study of New Technology-Based Firms* (Cambridge, MA: MIT, 1982), p. 7.
18. Sharp, p. 292.
19. Ibid.
20. Sharp, p. 293.
21. S.O.U. 1984: 65 (Via Satellite och Kabel).
22. Olof Hultén, 'Current Developments in the Electronic Media in Sweden', *Media in Transition* (Gothenburg: Nordicom-Sweden, 1986), p. 12.
23. Hultén, p. 12.
24. Hultén, p. 16.
25. Karl Erik Gustafsson, Media Structure and Media Development', *Media in Transition*, p. 76.
26. Ibid., pp. 76–77.
27. Hultén, p. 9.
28. Hultén, p. 18.
29. Ibid.
30. Hultén, pp. 18–19.
31. Hultén, p. 15.
32. See *Nordic Radio and Television via Satellite*, (Nordic Council of Ministers, NUA 1979: 4E), p. 11.
33. Hultén, p. 17.
34. Sharp, p. 281.
35. Sharp, p. 280.

Policies for New Media in Western Europe: Deregulation of Broadcasting and Multimedia Diversification

Kenneth Dyson and Peter Humphreys

During the next two decades the new communications technologies will have a dramatic effect on audio-visual communications in Western Europe, and importantly on broadcasting which is being subsumed in the wider communications revolution. At the focus of these developments stands the television screen which is being transformed into a multipurpose 'visual display unit'. It will be able to carry more television services as well as an expanding range of 'value-added' and data services including 'teleshopping', 'telebanking', 'electronic mail' and information and transaction services for specialised groups (travel agents, estate agents, farmers, financial dealers). New information services can be distributed 'off-air' by broadcasting authorities (as teletext like ITV's Oracle and BBC's Ceefax in Britain or a data transmission service for business subscription like BBC's Datacast launched in 1985) or via the telephone line by telecommunications authorities (as interactive videotex like BT's Prestel, the DGT's *Télétel* or the Bundespost's *Bildschirmtext*). Together these services constitute the 'new media' and begin by using spare capacity on the existing television signal or telephone line. It is the ultimate ambition of West European telecommunications authorities (PTTs) to provide all these services on a single integrated services digital network (ISDN). Already such new means of audio-visual communications as video-cassette recorders, broadband cable and satellite are making larger and previously scattered audiences available to private operators. The consequence is major new competition in West European media markets, not least for 'traditional' network television and for the press. This potential for expansion of media markets leads to a new political interest in the 'culture industries', a point that was emphasised repeatedly between 1981 and 1986 by the French Socialist Minister of Culture, Jack Lang. The implications for Western Europe are far-reaching because the audiovisual media, and broadcasting in particular, are central for the communication of cultural and political values as well as of information. How have West European governments responded to the challenge of 'the new age of broadcasting'?

Like telecommunications, with which it is converging through cable and satellite, and which was the subject of Morgan and Webber's contribution, broadcasting is characterised by growing pressures for deregulation and trends towards internationalisation. As a consequence, the West European state is faced with a new challenge to its traditional regulatory sovereignty in cultural as well as industrial affairs. Public-service monopolies in broadcasting and telecommunications are being exposed to competition as new actors seek to enter the communications market. One major result has been a developing pattern of multimedia diversification that poses a dilemma for public policy in Western Europe. On the one hand, this pattern reinforces the tendency towards new national and international concentrations of private capital in the communications market — with implications for cultural diversity. On the other hand, multimedia conglomerates appear as 'national champions', able to conquer new international communications markets. The active diversification of the press and the electronics industry, accompanied by the erosion of the barriers between traditionally distinct sectors of communications, has become a central characteristic of the communications revolution in Western Europe.

A host of new problems has arisen with the multiplication of new means of programme distribution: cable, satellite and video-cassette. In a time of rapidly rising costs, the production of European programmes will hardly match the rising demands of new media markets for low-cost programmes. At the same time, there will be increasing competition for pan-European advertising markets. The traditional values of European public-service broadcasting are also placed in question. For instance, will impartial investigative news reporting and documentaries and quality drama survive the new commercial pressures? The competition for advertising and, above all, for viewers promises to become increasingly fierce at international, national and sub-national levels. Against this background West European markets seem dangerously exposed. By the mid-1980s Japan had already acquired a dominant world position in the field of audiovisual equipment (television sets and video-cassette recorders) and seemed about to saturate new markets for satellite reception equipment and high-definition television. The United States had the world's most powerful programme production industry. It was actively searching for an expanded overseas market and was able to market low-cost programmes like *Dallas* and *Dynasty* having already achieved profitability in a huge domestic market. More generally, both the United States and Japan were keen to consolidate their lead in the field of the new information and communications technologies. Thus the challenge for Western Europe was at once industrial and cultural, as much concerned with international competitiveness as with cultural identity.

National strategies for communications industries have to take into consideration these pressures from international competition in both hardware (equipment) and software (programme) sectors, as well as the tendencies towards multinational operation and the formation of new multimedia conglomerates. More generally, the technological convergence between broadcasting, telecommunications and computing, the dynamic relations of electronics and new audio-visual media, and the emergence of new communications markets are encouraging governments to identify the strategic importance of communications and, in the process, to redefine their whole conception of communications. A whole series of new ideas contend: communication, including broadcasting, is identified as 'an industry'; 'interactivity' (two-way communication) and 'narrowcasting' (serving specialised, dispersed or very local audiences) are seen as making possible a transition from 'mass' to 'social' communication and a 'new image of broadcasting'. The most immediate and significant political development was, however, pressures for deregulation. In some West European countries, such as Britain, these pressures met with the ready compliance, even the encouragement, of governments; in others, such as France, they asserted themselves regardless of government policy and established practices.

In responding to the challenge of the communications revolution West European governments operate in a complex field of forces. The new technologies and services provide an economic opportunity for powerful industrial actors and would-be new entrants into new and expanding markets. They emerge as powerful lobbies for a changed pattern of governmental policies that will encourage new communications and media services by grants, tax concessions and an appropriate regulatory framework. National telecommunications authorities, electronics companies, information providers (like news agencies), large corporate users of telecommunications services and advertisers form parts of this phalanx of different industrial interests. At the same time actors whose interests are as much cultural as industrial ('the culture industries') are drawn into the debate. The role of public broadcasters, the film industry, the press and publishers is defensive in the first instance. They are responding to pressures emanating from other powerful industrial interests. The 'culture industries' may not, however, be content to seek protection from governments through tight regulations, like quotas on foreign programmes and on advertising. Their approach can be commercially aggressive, seeking by means of multimedia diversification to establish a commanding presence in otherwise threatening new activities. The situation of governments is further complicated by conflicting interests within the industrial lobby and within the cultural lobby (e.g. between telecommunications authorities, seeking to maintain a public-service monopoly, and electronics companies and information providers; and between public broadcasters and the press); by inter- and intra-departmental conflicts within government itself; and by the way in which multimedia diversification is breaking down the barriers between such traditionally distinct sectors as electronics, broadcasting and the press.

This proliferation of interrelated actors, and the fluidity of interest politics, is stimulated and complicated further by the powerful trend towards internationalisation and its implications for public policy. The multiplication of new means of television programme distribution — the new electronic media — offers enormous commercial opportunities for programme producers and distributors and competition for rich new advertising markets. These competitive pressures are unleashed, as we have seen, on a dangerously exposed West European market. Furthermore, it has become apparent very quickly that multimedia diversification is itself an international phenomenon. Rupert Murdoch's News International has come to represent the American challenge in Europe. The international challenge of multimedia giants is, at the same time, internal to Europe: Robert Maxwell in Britain, Silvio Berlusconi in Italy and Springer in West Germany. Some actors, like Bertelsmann, the huge West German multimedia multinational, prefer foreign links, in this case with RTL in Luxembourg, rather than launching home-based operations. Certain West European countries, notably Britain and Luxembourg, seem to be acting, in the view of at least one powerful neighbour, France, as Trojan horses for the Americans in this internationalisation of media. In reality, therefore, West European governments are denied the simplicity of a clear European/American conflict over cultural and industrial policy. They also have to face up to the dilemma of whether certain multimedia conglomerates should be supported as potential 'national champions', able to conquer world markets, or should be restrained in the interests of cultural diversity.

In facing this complex challenge to the traditional regulatory sovereignty of the state in cultural affairs, West European governments have further been denied the strength of ideological solidarity. Concern about cultural identity ranges, between countries and governments, from strong cultural nationalism to the outright embrace of greater freedom in international communications. In the field of political ideas West European governments represent a complex mosaic of conservative, neo-liberal, Christian Democratic and Social Democratic orientations; correspondingly, attitudes to public-service broadcasting and such issues as advertising have varied considerably, within as well as among governments. Public policy has also had a national/subnational dimension, for instance in West Germany, introducing further ideological as well as regional complications.[1]

This analysis outlines the complex evolution of policies for broadcasting against the background of the communications revolution in Western Europe. The story is one of the absence of the predicatability that is provided by a stable, well-ordered 'policy community', of the kind that in the past characterised the distinct sectors of telecommunications and broadcasting. No attempt is made to examine regulatory policies *per se*, as in the contribution by Hoffmann-Riem. Instead the main aim is to investigate the policy processes involved in regulatory revision and to explore the interaction of different policy sectors, notably telecommunications and broadcasting. The themes of deregulation in broadcasting and multimedia diversification are central.

DEREGULATORY TRENDS IN WESTERN EUROPE: THE STATE'S RESPONSE TO THE NEW MEDIA

Initially, government policies towards the new media in Western Europe seem to have been primarily a response to pressures from telecommunications authorities, from powerful industrial lobbies and their administrative supporters, and from influential reports that embodied their interest. In Britain stimulus came from the Information Technology Advisory Panel, which had been established by Margaret Thatcher's Conservative government to explore the future role of information technology in Britain's economic development. The ITAP worked directly through the Cabinet Office and was thus in a privileged position to shape government policy. Significantly, ITAP's members represented exclusively the interests of the British computer, electronic and cable industries, all of which could be presumed to benefit from a government initiative to develop cable systems. Broadcasting was not represented. Though cable systems existed already in Britain, they used old-fashioned technology and had been originally developed for the sole purpose of relaying public-service broadcasting to areas of poor 'off-air' reception. In the early 1980s the growing interest in information technology spurred a wholly new excitement about modern cable's promised interactive capacity. This excitement was not lost on the Cable Television Association whose members faced the problem of ageing and (with improvements in 'off-air' reception) increasingly unattractive cable systems. In early 1982, ITAP produced an influential report, *Cable Systems*.[2] It announced that '... the main role of cable systems eventually will be the delivery of many information, financial and other services to the home, and the joining of businesses and homes by high-capacity data links'.[3] Rapid development of high-technology cable systems now presented interesting opportunities for the previously fairly discrete sectors of telecommunications, computing, and electronics – in addition to an expansion of the 'broadcasting' market. According to the ITAP Report, there were '... powerful economic and industrial arguments for encouraging the growth of cable systems in the United Kingdom' and '... for British industry a late decision (was) the same as a negative decision'.[4] Seeing the opportunity presented by the Thatcher government's ideological commitment to the 'free market' and an 'enterprise culture', the ITAP Report recommended that private investment should be attracted by the introduction of as much freedom as possible for entrepreneurs to develop a wide range of new cable services within the framework of *light regulation*.

The Thatcher government responded to this message with enthusiasm by seeking to encourage an 'entertainment-led cable revolution'. The advanced communications infrastructure of the future *information economy* – the wired society – would be developed by liberating the forces of private entrepreneurship from state regulation. The government's sole but crucial role was to formulate the appropriately deregulated legal environment. In the short term, the prime attention of cable systems would remain new television entertainment services; consequently, the regulatory regime for cable television would be liberalised to complement the government's existing plans for a liberalisation of telecommunications services. The government's responses were, first, a summary consideration of the impact that this expansion of cable would have on the established broadcasting system by the *Hunt Inquiry*;[5] followed by a package of legislative deregulation culminating in the *Cable and Broadcasting Act 1984*.[6] The resulting regulatory provisions established a *Cable Authority*, empowered to issue franchises to cable operators and given the role of only reactive and 'light-touch' regulation. Significantly, no obstacles were placed on the vertical integration of the basic functions of cable supplier, cable operator and programme supplier. Consortia combining these functions were encouraged without any concern for the development of local *information-retailing monopolies*. In this way, the government opened the door to actors seeking to diversify their activities in the field of communications. In other words, in Britain the process of multimedia diversification was given free rein by government policy.

Another striking feature of the development of new media policy in Britain was the failure to follow through ITAP's vision of 'a wired society' to the all-important details. The 1984 budget announced the withdrawal of capital allowances, thereby reversing the economic calculations of new entrants into cable and undermining the new 'heroic' entrepreneur upon whom the success of the cable plan depended. The consequence was in fact to encourage dominance of the new cable sector by large multinational corporations that could weather the harsher climate. Thus Rediffusion, the largest traditional cable operator, was sold to Robert Maxwell. Developments in telecommunications policy and broadcasting policy were also not clearly coordinated, in spite of the fact that cable systems embodied the convergence of the two policy sectors. Deregulation of each was the subject of different legislation in 1984; cable television operators were to find their conditions of operation under the Telecommunications Act less advantageous than they had originally expected.[7] The option of integration of telephonic services with the newly franchised cable television systems was not pursued. Videotex, which was invented in Britain in 1971 and subsequently developed by British Telecom as a world pioneer, was not integrated into the new vision. It remained part of BT's basic network service. British Telecom was itself an actor under pressure from the Thatcher government. Information providers were given scope to seek licences to develop their own 'value-added networks' or VANs, separate from the videotex system. Its network monopoly was broken both when Mercury was licensed as a telecommunications carrier in 1982 and by the new cable systems, and its privatisation was secured in 1985. In other words, Britain appeared to be undergoing an *uncoordinated deregulation*: deregulation was pursued but with few signs of sustained central direction and control.[8]

In France, the *Nora/Minc Report* – *the Computerisation of Society*, presented to Giscard d'Estaing's government in 1976 and published in 1978, played a similar role to the *ITAP Report*.[9] Significantly, though, it did not have the same structure of private-sector economic interests behind it. The *Nora/Minc Report* signalled the crucial importance of information technologies for the economic future of France. It sensitised policy-makers to the technological convergence of telecommunications and computing and the consequent opportunities for advanced electronics and the audiovisual media. As a result of this report, the Giscard d'Estaing government developed a *Programme Télématique* to develop videotex, electronic telephone directories and experimental fibre-optic services. This programme gave the *Direction Générale des Télécommunications* (the telecommunications wing of the PTT) a prestigious programme to follow the modernisation of the French telephone system. However, President Giscard d'Estaing blocked experimentation with cable systems by decree in 1977 – for reasons of media policy – so that by the end of his *septennat* there were far less (old-fashioned) cable systems in France than even in Britain. By contrast, the French Socialists, who came to power after the election of President François Mitterrand in 1981, were dedicated to a grand transformation of the traditional broadcasting system, and they developed a growing awareness of the communications revolution.

As in the British case, industrial lobbying activity heightened in anticipation of the new government's policy. The *Groupement des Industries Électroniques* (GIEL), composed of ten large *syndicats* or associations of the electronics industry, established a commission, the *Commission de Diffusion de la Télévision par réseaux Câblés* (CODITEC) as the corporate voice of the industrial lobby to urge decisive action upon the public authorities. CODITEC stressed the necessity for France to be competitive in the developing new hardware and software markets for audiovisual media; the cabling of the country in the most modern fibre-optic technology would provide a domestic market and a secure base from which to 'attack' foreign markets. The 'missed opportunity' of the Giscard d'Estaing years (1974–81) could be turned to advantage if France were to adopt immediately this technology in a boldly comprehensive manner. CODITEC painted highly over-optimistic scenarios of the size of the cable market, the number of jobs that would be created and the costs of a major cable programme. Moreover, CODITEC presented its arguments in a manner designed to appeal to the ambition and ideology of the French Socialists – in particular, their emphasis on industrial and cultural independence. Unlike the British case, but entirely in conformity with French tradition, industry called upon the state to develop *plans de croissance* and to supply industry with generous contracts. Another point of significant contrast with the British case was that the French electronics industry stressed its sole interest in manufacturing networks and components. The programming of new services would be the affair of other national and regional actors; here the press would play an important role. In this way, the industrialists sought to pre-empt the coalescence of any oppositional interests; for the initial reaction of the local and regional press to videotex had been negative, though subsequently they displayed positive interest.[10]

In France, again in contrast to Britain, the national telecommunications authority, the DGT, amounted to a rather more influential cable lobby than even the industrialists. The DGT's influence reflected the increased social and political status and prestige of its technocrats, who could now claim a *grand corps* status on a par with the *corps des mines* and the *corps des ponts et chaussées*. Now it sought to transform itself from an administrator of traditional telephony into a modern commercial purveyor of the many new audiovisual communications services. Responsibility for a national cable plan would ensure its continued prestige, legitimise its huge investment requirements, secure employment, and assure its monopoly of future communications services. It came as no surprise when in November 1982 it was announced that the government had accepted the *Plan Câble*, presented to cabinet by Louis Mexandeau, the PTT Minister, and that a highly ambitious, state-led, national fibre-optic cable programme would be launched.[11]

Socialist audiovisual policy in France aimed at a *controlled deregulation*. The Reform Law on Audiovisual Communication of July 1982 was designed to 'liberate' the audiovisual media from the state's traditional grip and to establish an enabling legislative framework for 'mixed-economy' initiatives.[12] This approach was reflected in the role the state (the DGT) would play in supplying and owning future cable networks and in the public-private character of the future cable-operating bodies, the *Sociétés Locales d'Expoitation Commercielle* (SLECs), which were given precise definition by a subsequent *statut*. The *collectivités locales* would establish the SLECs and then participate in them alongside private capital. Yet a key article of the July Law (Article 80) was explicitly designed to discourage the formation of American-style private, commercial national networks and, implicitly, to frustrate the multimedia ambitions of the right-wing publisher Robert Hersant.[13] It prevented the involvement of new commercial interests in more than one SLEC. In other words, it impeded explicitly the process of multimedia diversification.

At this stage of development, the French Socialist government seemed keen to limit the development of new national television channels to the introduction of Canal Plus. This fourth channel was launched in 1984 as a private commercial 'pay-television' venture; yet the state retained a strong measure of control through its operating company Havas, the state-controlled advertising concern. Political control was reinforced by the close relations between its managing director, André Rousselet, and President Mitterrand.

By late 1985 the French government no longer accepted the merits of such a restrictive approach and began to consider how to dispense with Article 80 of the 1982 Law; it had come to be seen as a retrograde measure that discouraged private investment and the necessary growth and restructuring of French capacity for audiovisual production. By this time, French Socialist regulatory policy was characterised by retreat, or, if one prefers, a process of learning, on other fronts as well. Originally, the French Socialists had intended to introduce strict measures in order to protect and promote French culture and French cultural production: quotas on the amount of foreign programming, minimum quotas for local programming and levies on the cable operators to be paid into special support funds for French audiovisual production. However, by early 1985 it had become equally clear that the government's *volonté de souplesse* extended also to these provisions. Although they were not abandoned, their application was to be characterised by a new *flexibility*. In practice, it seemed likely that they would become *options* rather than *strictures*, certainly during the start-up phase of cable systems. In the final analysis, cultural policy-makers found themselves increasingly prey to pressures from industrial and commercial lobbies and their political and ministerial allies: namely, the DGT/industrial nexus, championed by the ministries of the PTT and industry and concerned with international competitiveness, and from the many local public and private interests that would form the SLECs, championed by the ministry of the interior and decentralisation. In order to promote the rapid and profitable development of the new audiovisual media, cultural considerations would have to be sacrificed to economic expediency. Economic expediency seemed to call for a liberal regulatory regime to allow demand to develop freely and to attract investment. Therefore, in respect of the development of both new private national networks and programming policy more generally, French Socialist policies for *controlled deregulation* became prone to revision. Ironically Mitterrand himself was none the less to become a casualty of Socialist legislation; in April 1986 the Conseil d'État, the French administrative court, was to cancel a key part of his concession of a fifth national channel to Berlusconi and Seydoux by banning it from showing feature films (for the law encouraged French material, not foreign films and American series).[14]

The West German case represents a hybrid of the British and French cases. On the one hand, there has been no deregulation of telecommunications *à l'anglaise*; the pattern of state-financed, public-service cabling by the national telecommunications authority, the *Bundespost*, resembles much more closely the French case. On the other hand, there have been direct political attempts to deregulate media policy as much as possible so as to encourage private entrepreneurial activity. In the West German case there has also been much more political controversy about the new media than in either Britain or France.[15]

Policy developments were complicated by the division of competences between the constituent states of West Germany's federal system, the *Länder*, which were constitutionally responsible for broadcasting policy, and the federation, the *Bund*, which was responsible for telecommunications policy. During the 1970s a loose coalition of interests of the Christian Democratic parties (CDU/CSU), the newspaper publishers, a section of the electronics industry and the *Bundespost* (the West German PTT) sought the development of a cable programme. This coalition was opposed by Helmut Schmidt's Social Democrat government in Bonn (although the SPD's coalition partners, the Free Democrats, were also pro-cable). While the Social Democrats were in office in Bonn (1969–82) and in control of national telecommunications policy, they were able to block a national cable programme. Nevertheless, in 1974 the Social Democrats had established a commission to inform policy for the new information and communications technologies. Unlike its British and French counterparts, this commission, the *Kommission für den Ausbau des technischen Kommunikationssystems* (KtK) was cautious about cable's promise and suggested that cable technology should be tested in a number of pilot projects before any major programme was launched.[16] The subsequent establishment of the pilot projects made only tortuous progress as Social Democrat-controlled *Länder* resorted to delaying tactics. Nevertheless, while 'blocking' cable television, the Social Democrats developed future-oriented 'modernisation policies' to test and introduce incrementally both videotex (called *Bildschirmtext* in German) and also fibre-optic services (the BIGFON projects). At the same time the major part of telecommunications investment was directed into modernising (digitalising) the national telephone system. However, this situation changed radically in 1982 when the Christian Democratic parties (CDU/CSU) formed a new federal government in coalition with the Free Democrats (FDP).

Federal responsibility for telecommunications policy was now fully exploited to favour the Christian Democratic parties' media policy. This policy had two main components. It aimed at breaking the traditional public-services monopoly of broadcasting and introducing a politically more sympathetic segment of private commercial enterprise. Prominent media specialists, close to the CDU, and CDU/CSU 'media politicians' (*Medienpolitiker*) had been arguing that anti-CDU bias in the public service broadcasting system was a key factor in the CDU/CSU's federal election defeats in 1972, 1976 and 1980. The second component was the CDU's commitment to *Mittelstandspolitik*: the new government was seeking programmes that would benefit small- and medium-sized enterprises. With these twin aims in mind, an ambitious and costly programme was launched to cable the country as fast as possible. The urgency was reflected in the choice of traditional copper-coaxial technology, which has very limited interactive capacity – a point that drew criticism from the Social Democrats and sections of big industry. Now, the promise of federal telecommunications investment was used to prise *Land* concessions in media policy. In the Christian Democrat-controlled *Länder* new media legislation was immediately prepared to enable the introduction of commercial television.

As Hoffmann-Riem indicates, this legislation amounted to an effective deregulation. Subsequently, the combination of this new political situation with the economic realities of inter-*Länder* competition for telecommunications and media investment compelled most Social Democrat-controlled *Länder* (led by Hamburg, West Germany's major media centre) to reconsider their outright opposition to deregulation and even prepare a measure of deregulation themselves.[17] *Land* governments were, after all, concerned with industrial policy as well as with cultural policy, and 'competitive' industrial policy proved as powerful a force at this level as at the national level. At the same time, influential pragmatists within the SPD, grouped around the party's general secretary Peter Glotz, managed to bring about a reorientation of party policy at the national level; international as well as national developments seemed to call for a less 'conservative' communications strategy.

Further pressures towards deregulation of audiovisual communication in Western Europe have arisen from the combination of cable technology with satellite technology. First, ordinary communications satellites − of the Intelsat or Eutelsat type − presented new entrepreneurs with the means of access to the expanding West European cable market. The size of this market was already considerable due to the high density of traditional cable systems in the Low Countries. Now the promised expansion of cable systems in the larger West European countries brought the prospect of an easily accessible pan-European market of potentially huge dimensions. Theoretically at least, restrictive national regulatory policies could still be imposed upon new cable systems by means of 'policing' the cable-headends − namely, the point where satellite programmes are fed into national cable systems. In France, where, as seen, the French Socialists aimed at a controlled deregulation to protect French culture, and just as importantly also to protect the French cultural industries from international competition, the *Plan Câble* achieved an added initial attraction as a potential *Maginot line* in communications policy.

In the medium- and long-term deregulatory pressures will be reinforced still further by the appearance of Direct Broadcasting by Satellite (DBS). DBS satellites represent a new generation of *high-powered* satellite, the signals from which can be picked up directly by consumers by means of relatively small household dish antennae (measuring as little as 90cm in diameter). Direct broadcast transmissions will be no respector of national (or sub-national) frontiers. Hence, the pan-European market will become even more accessible, and effective regulation will become more difficult to achieve by nation states acting independently.[18]

In Western Europe, DBS development, like new cable systems, seems to have been stimulated originally by industrial policy considerations. National aerospace suppliers emphasised the economic benefits of maintaining expertise in modern satellite construction (and in the French case also launch capacity); national electronics suppliers sought to benefit from new requirements for ancillary transmission and reception equipment; and national telecommunications carriers stressed the importance of being able to manage modern satellite communications Government reports, like the *ITAP Report* and the *Nora/Minc Report*, encouraged the interest of governments. For example, the *Nora/Minc Report* suggested that intended as the pivot of communications, the essential link in the development of network systems, and aimed at facilitating the increase in overlapping transmissions, satellites are at the heart of telematics. Eliminated from the satellite race, the European nations would lose an element of sovereignty with regard to NASA, which handles the launching, and with regard to the firms that specialise in managing them, especially IBM. By contrast, if they were capable of launching them, building them, and managing them, the same nations would be in a position of power.[19]

Britain, France and West Germany all became eager to seize the initiative for themselves; in turn, a wave of national particularism was unleashed that was uncontainable within the boundaries of general space collaboration through the European Space Agency (ESA). At the end of 1979 the French and the West German governments announced a joint project for the launching of DBS satellites. This venture was to cement an industrial alliance that dated back to their joint development of the Symphonie communications satellite (within ESA). In April 1980 the two governments duly signed an agreement on technical and industrial co-operation in the field of DBS satellites. The first step was to be the construction of two satellites – TDF 1 (French) and TV SAT (West German) – which would be placed in geostationary orbit by the French Ariane rocket and managed by the respective national authorities, *Télédiffusion de France* and the *Bundespost*. The aim was to secure long-term cooperation in the hope of capturing a large share of a world market for satellites that was held to be highly promising. The principal industrial beneficiaries of the programme were West German and French 'national champions': the electronics firms, AEG–Telefunken and Thomson–CSF, and the aerospace companies, Messerschmidt Boelkow Blohm (MBB) and SNIAS (Aérospatiale). This Franco-German initiative was taken purely for reasons of technology and industrial policy, on the one hand, and of perceptions of a developing international market for communications hardware, on the other. Governments in both countries took an active role in initiating and in financing the project.

The (ill-fated) British DBS project, too, resulted from 'industrial policy' considerations, reinforced by the recommendations of the *ITAP Report*. The original intention was that a British DBS satellite should be constructed by an industrial consortium, again of 'national champions' – British Aerospace, GEC-Marconi and British Telecom, to be called United Satellites Limited (UNISAT). In the British case, the government had made clear from the start that its role would not include the financing of the project. Nevertheless, the government intervened actively to find commercial backers – originally the BBC alone, subsequently a 'club of twenty-one' involving the BBC, ITV and a number of other private companies, including the leading electronics firm, Thorn EMI, and media interests, S. Pearson (publisher of the FT), Granada TV Rentals and the Virgin group. Also, the government orchestrated the subsequent series of negotiations between these would-be commercial operators and the manufacturers. In the end, the project collapsed in the face of insurmountable disagreements, notably about financial viability, and sheer complexity. Nevertheless, at the outset, Britain's commitment to launching its own DBS initiative appeared to be enthusiastic.

The subsequent scramble of particularist DBS plans reflected individual national ambitions: Italy, the Nordic countries, Switzerland and Luxembourg all unveiled rival plans (while the ESA too proceeded with its own). In particular, Luxembourg played a very special role in the development of national policies in Western Europe for the age of space broadcasting. This special role derives from the geographic and linguistic advantages of this tiny country, coupled with the central importance that broadcasting by RTL (Radio Télévision Luxembourgeoise) had assumed for its national economy both as a strong export service and as a major contributor to government revenues. The 'footprint' of a Luxembourg satellite would cover large areas of France and West Germany, both countries with which Luxembourg shares common languages. 'Overspill' from a Luxembourg satellite would, therefore, open up relatively captive and potentially very lucrative national advertising markets in these larger countries to penetration by their tiny neighbour. Therefore, when Luxembourg indicated its determination to develop its own DBS satellite, called LUX SAT, alarm bells started ringing in both France and West Germany.

In West Germany the consequence was to reinforce the pressures towards deregulation, which had been set in motion already by the coalition of political and economic interests in that country. In late 1982 the huge West German publishing multinational Bertelsmann announced that it would take a 40 per cent share with the *Compagnie Luxembourgeoise de Télédiffusion* (CLT), the holding company for RTL, in a new commercial German-language television channel, RTL-Plus, to be broadcast eventually by satellite from Luxembourg. RTL-Plus began service in 1984. This development spurred other large West German publishing interests to speed up preparations for a new private commercial television channel (SAT 1), to be broadcast initially by means of general communications satellite, thus linking with the country's growing network of cable systems, but ultimately to occupy a channel on TV SAT (political factors willing). It was also a stimulus to the West German Social Democrats' policy reorientation towards adaptation and qualified acceptance of deregulation. It was becoming clear that West German capital (and jobs) could flow abroad (as well as into Christian Democrat-controlled *Länder*) to co-operate with foreign capital under conditions of less rigorous regulation, in order to 'cream off' the West German advertising market. Such a possibility was alarming to Social Democrat pragmatists, who were concerned about the country's economic competitiveness and the future of 'Model Germany' (*Modelldeutschland*) and who also realised by now that full-blown commercial broadcasting had become inevitable as a result of both national and international developments. Repeatedly, during 1984 and 1985, negotiations between Christian Democrat and Social Democrat *Ministerpräsidenten* (heads of *Land* governments) appeared to be close to producing a *Staatsvertrag* (interstate treaty between the *Länder*) for regulation of the new media, only to fall at the last hurdle — an indication of the complications of federalism in the West German case. Nevertheless, by the end of 1985, even the strongly 'dissenting' SPD-controlled *Land* of Hesse had agreed in principle with all other *Länder* about a considerable measure of deregulation.

In France, too, perceptions of the threat from Luxembourg reinforced pressures towards deregulation. Subsequent developments were largely involuntary and characterised by a remarkable complexity. Above all else, and more than anyone else, the French Socialists have expressed concern about the menace facing Western Europe from 'coca-cola' satellites. The alarm caused by LUX SAT became a near panic when it appeared that an American company, Coronet, might be encouraged by the Luxembourg authorities to back the commercial exploitation of yet another satellite, called GDL, by a new company. Later, in October 1985 the *Société Européenne de Satellites* (SES) bought a medium-powered American RCA satellite. For the French Socialists, Luxembourg (alongside Britain) seemed poised to become a bridgehead for a penetration of the continent by American commercial programmes purveying American culture.

At first the French Socialists had seemed to be undecided about whether to pursue the DBS initiative of the preceding Giscard d'Estaing regime. Both the *Plan Câble* and *Canal Plus* had been given higher priority; and DBS policy had encountered opposition from the protagonists of these initiatives within both the government and the administration. Moreover, the initial reflex reaction of many Socialists had been to adopt a negative view of a technology that promised to destabilise national sovereignties in broadcasting affairs. Finally, the influential DGT had developed a prototype, called Télécom 1, for a new and possibly more commercially attractive generation of communications satellites that promised to have their own DBS facility. The resulting 'battle of technocrats', aligning the DGT against TDF (responsible for TDF 1), had placed another question mark beside the future of the French DBS initiative. However, like the West German Social Democrats, the French Socialists came quickly to realise their relative powerlessness against international developments. In face of the Luxembourg threat, they decided that their only choice was 'to play the game or be left on the sideline'.

By the time the new Coronet menace materialised to confirm their fears of an escalation of an American 'coca-cola' offensive on Western Europe, the French Socialist government had already begun extremely complicated manoeuvres to pre-empt the Luxembourg threat. The French government considered committing itself to developing TDF 1 as a broadcasting *force de dissuasion*. Pressure was exerted upon Luxembourg to renounce the development of its own satellite. In exchange, channel capacity on TDF 1 was to be made available to CLT. This pressure was applied through the indirect, but very considerable influence on CLT that the French government enjoyed. The state-controlled French advertising and multimedia giant, *Havas*, was a major shareholder in RTL. Negotiations between France and Luxembourg were complex, and uncertainty and tension was exacerbated by the GDL affair and by a series of policy reversals engineered first by Mitterrand himself, to the anger of many in the Socialist government, and then by Jacques Chirac, Prime Minister of the centre-right government elected in March 1986.

Initially it seemed that the affair would be resolved along the lines painstakingly sought by the French government. During 1985, a new and more conciliatory head of government in Luxembourg, Jacques Santer of the centrist Christian-Social Party, announced that CLT participation in TDF 1 would

POLICIES FOR NEW MEDIA IN WESTERN EUROPE 111

proceed and that no Luxembourg-based satellite would broadcast French- or German-language programmes financed by advertising. In return, the 'settlement' suggested that CLT would obtain two channels on TDF 1 and enjoy a monopoly of advertising on the French satellite. In turn, the French government formally announced its firm commitment to the continued development of TDF 1, and its determination to follow it up with a second back-up satellite to carry the programme into a fully operational stage.

This result would have represented at best a compromise solution, since CLT would have gained privileged access to the French market. In return, though, the French would have benefited from a 'solution' that minimised the threat of 'coca-cola' broadcasting and part-solved the problem of turning their DBS initiative into a commercial success. However, at the end of 1985 it became clear that President Mitterrand had conducted and concluded secret negotiations to allocate a new fifth national channel in France to a Franco-Italian group, involving the Italian multimedia giant, Silvio Berlusconi, allied with two friends of Mitterrand, Jérôme Seydoux and Christophe Riboud, who were not unsympathetic to the Socialists. This channel, and another associated with Robert Maxwell, the British publisher, were later to operate from TDF 1. Since Berlusconi had played a major role in the rampant commercialisation and Americanisation of the Italian audio-visual system, this latest policy reversal seemed to mark a 'rout' rather than a mere 'retreat' for French cultural policy-makers. The net result of this complex affair was that, while the Luxembourg threat had a positive outcome for the fate of the French DBS initiative, the elaborately engineered strategy to defuse Luxembourg's own DBS initiatives seemed to have been subsequently abandoned by Mitterrand. In 1986 the new centre-right government of Jacques Chirac was to complicate the story further by cancelling the two TDF 1 agreements, reopening negotiations with Luxembourg and putting the TDF 1 channels out to tender, thereby inviting bids from Murdoch, CLT and Hersant.

These pressures towards a *de facto* deregulation in France were given even greater encouragement by the decision, again originally inspired by Mitterrand himself, to allow the fifth channel to broadcast 'off-air' in the first instance. This initiative followed announcements by Mitterrand in early 1985 that he was considering the authorisation of local 'off-air' television. Subsequently, a government-commissioned inquiry, into the further liberalisation of the hertzian air-waves, produced the *Bredin Report*.[20] The report suggested that around 60 local television stations and two additional national channels were feasible. With this additional initiative in the wake of the *Bredin Report* the field of French Socialist audio-visual communications policy was becoming distinctly 'overcrowded' (even 'anarchic').

Mitterrand's choices appear to have been determined above all else by political expediency. One main aim seemed to have become to produce electoral popularity for the Socialists in the run-up to the National Assembly elections of 1986. With the prospect of defeat looming, another important aim was to ensure that France retained a 'socialist' broadcasting presence of sorts after these elections. Above all, Mitterrand's intervention in the DBS affair was dictated by *raison d'état*. It seemed better to accommodate Maxwell and Berlusconi, who was after all a friend of Italy's Socialist Prime Minister

Bettino Craxi, than to leave the way open to Murdoch and Hersant. Murdoch was seeking a role in the future Luxembourg DBS channels by alliance with CLT, and in September 1985 his News International reached agreement with a large shareholder of CLT, the Belgian Groupe Bruxelles Lambert, to establish Media International with the aim of developing joint strategies for the European television market. Hersant seemed almost certain to become involved after the centre-right won the National Assembly elections. In other words, Mitterrand's decisions were at least partially pre-emptive in their aims. They could, in part at least, be legitimated by reference to a concept dear to the heart of the Minister of Culture, Jack Lang: the idea of a 'Latin audio-visual space' in opposition to that of Anglo-Saxon cultural domination. Nevertheless, many Socialists felt that this optimism was misplaced (especially as the Right was promising to rescind the Berlusconi contract anyway). Many feared that, in fact, Berlusconi would use the channel to import an even more ugly combination of 'spaghetti-coca-cola television' into France than anything that might come from Luxembourg.

Thus, despite all the initial concern of the French Socialists to control developments in order to protect the national interest in economic and cultural independence, deregulatory pressures proved inexorable. More than anything else, these pressures were actually intensified by the sheer scope of the new communications initiatives taken by Socialist government. The major problem was that the French Socialists had not developed a single coherent strategy for communications; rather, they had stumbled into a situation where, for reasons outlined above, they were actually pursuing several different strategies. Each had a logic of its own. The irony was that in spite of heroic attempts to introduce controlled and imaginative change, the French Socialists' liberalisation seemed to be heading for a *de facto* deregulation and broadcasting anarchy. The promised multiplication of broadcasting channels would clearly exceed the capacity of the French culture industries to respond to the demand for programmes thus created. The consequence was the creation of a void that could only be filled by recourse to foreign programmes and outside broadcasters. Moreover, the proliferation of initiatives was leading towards internally-generated competition between them, meaning that regulatory controls would threaten certain, or even all, of them with non-viability. In view of this developing situation, cultural policy aims were abandoned (and regulatory policies softened) before the centre-right returned to power in 1986. One French observer characterised the developing situation under the Socialists as resembling *autocannibalisme*; anarchy was resulting from the pursuit of too many mutually contradictory options, without any respect for what the market or regulatory policy could bear.[21]

Seemingly inexorable deregulatory pressures characterised also developments in other West European countries. In Belgium and the Netherlands media policy became increasingly conflict-ridden as a result of new media developments both at home and abroad. Since the mid-1960s cable systems had expanded at an exceedingly fast rate in both countries. In the 1960s the density of cable systems was 'low' (15–20 per cent), but by 1983 nearly 70 per cent of Dutch households and nearly 90 per cent of Belgian were cabled. In both countries this rapid cable development had been stimulated by the twin attractions of improved reception and of importing programmes from neighbouring countries. Unlike in Britain and France, in neither Belgium nor the Netherlands was cable development the result of telecommunications policy; nearly all the cable systems in the Low Countries employed traditional copper-coaxial cable. The common pattern of regulation was that the PTTs remained responsible for licensing cable systems and the hardware, while software − cable programming − was the responsibility of the respective Ministries of Culture (in Belgium, there is one for each of the two linguistic communities). Traditionally, cable services supplied a diet of both national and imported public-service programmes.

The development of *point-to-point* satellite television − the link-up of cable systems to communications satellite channels − has already had an impact on this traditional pattern. The promise of DBS services brought the prospect of an even greater impact. Consequently, there were growing pressures in both Belgium and the Netherlands for a 'liberation' of broadcasting from state control. The Liberal and, with more reservations, the Christian Democratic Parties led the crusade in favour of commercial interests, motivated in no small measure by fears that, unless domestic deregulation was introduced, only foreign interests would benefit from the new 'open-sky' situation in broadcasting. Moreover, new awareness of the telecommunications policy dimensions of cable reinforced these pressures, in similar ways to the cases already examined. Deregulation in the Netherlands with the Media Policy Note of 1983 meant effectively that the state relinquished much of its traditional control over programming. Consequently, the Netherlands' biggest publishing house VNU and the Belgian publishers Dupuis were quick to display an interest in the newly available Dutch satellite pay-TV. In August 1985 the Belgian holding company Groupe Bruxelles Lambert acquired a 51 per cent controlling interest in Dupuis, thus bringing it within the orbit of CLT; in the next month Groupe Bruxelles Lambert was to establish Media International in partnership with Murdoch's News International. Groupe Bruxelles Lambert was in turn closely linked by shareholdings with the American bank Drexell, which had important customers in American media (such as Lorimar, the producer of *Dallas* and *Falcoln Crest*, and Oak industries, one of the largest cable firms). The activities of Groupe Bruxelles Lambert suggested that Belgian financiers and banks were beginning to play a key role in strengthening Euro-American links in new private television markets.[22] In Belgium, the state continued to 'regulate' domestic programming. Yet, it is legitimate to question the effectiveness of this regulation in view of the existing degree of *de facto* openness of the Belgian communications market and financial system.

Italy is commonly held up as an example of 'savage' or 'anarchic' deregulation. In France especially, the 'Italian example' had been considered to be an illustration of the need for only *controlled deregulation*. In 1976 a judgment of the Italian Constitutional Court declared the public-service monopoly of broadcasting to be unconstitutional, other than at the national level. This judgment followed closely upon, and generally negated, a government reform law of 1975 (Law 103) that had reaffirmed the principle of the public-service monopoly and given RAI−TV a new statute. Already, this law had made allowance for exceptions in the case of future cable television development and programmes originating in the European Community. However, following the ruling of the Constitutional Court, which amounted to a wholesale deregulation, there was an explosion of private commercial television initiatives. In 1976, there were around 80 stations, and by 1982 there were 1,500, of which 450 were broadcasting regularly. One hundred and fifty stations, of which 100 very quickly came to be controlled by three large private commercial networks (Canale Cinque, Italia Uno and Rette Quatro), drew advertising revenues that greatly exceeded those of the RAI. Fierce competition between them led to a massive reliance on cheap imports of American series and films and Japanese cartoons. According to one French source, '... in 1980, Italy was already the principal world importer of Japanese television programmes; two years later, it added the title of principal world importer of American programmes to this honour; and the 21,000 television programmes imported during 1982 was an increase of 100 per cent over 1981 and 400 per cent over 1980.'[23] Constrained by public-service commitments, RAI could respond only modestly to this competition; it had to draw half of its programmes from Italian producers and limit its advertising to five per cent of transmission time. Nevertheless, RAI attempted to match the competition by adopting the opposition's tactics as much as possible. For instance, in 1982 it signed an agreement for the supply of programmes with the American company, NBC, confirming the process of Americanisation of the Italian audio-visual market. In 1982 Canale Cinque had bought the Italian option for the complete output of the American television company CBS. A further consequence of this 'savage deregulation' was the weakening of the Italian television production industry and the near collapse of the Italian cinema, which, before deregulation, had been one of the most successful in Europe — indeed which had resisted the competition represented by television more successfully than any other. In Italy, massive deregulation occurred without the encouragement represented by the new media!

MULTIMEDIA DIVERSIFICATION IN WESTERN EUROPE: THE NEW ACTORS IN AUDIO-VISUAL COMMUNICATIONS

In Western Europe a common feature associated with these developments in regulation has been the leading role of existing private commercial media interests, mainly newspaper and magazine publishers and, in the British case, the consumer electronics industry, and, in the Belgian case, the financial holding companies. They sought to occupy the space that has been opened by deregulation for new entrepreneurial activity in the audio-visual communications market. In fact, such developments in Western Europe follow a familiar pattern. The press in the United States and Japan were the first to diversify their activities into new media. In the United States, Time Inc. created Home Box Office, which became the world's first successful cable distributor. In Japan, the four largest national daily newspapers are associated with the commercial television networks. The purpose of this second section is to examine the pattern of multimedia diversification in Western Europe in greater detail and the response of public-service broadcasters to this competitive challenge.

As we have seen, in Italy deregulation led to an initial explosion of pluralism, followed very quickly by a concentration of ownership. After 1979, three dominant private networks − Rette Quatro, Canale Cinque, and Italia Uno − came to control 80 per cent of advertising revenues. In 1983 Canale Cinque bought up Italia Uno, leaving only two networks. Rette Quatro belonged to the Mondadori publishing, printing, press and advertising group, and Canale Cinque to the Berlusconi real estate, press and insurance group. Then, in 1984, Berlusconi took control of Rette Quatro. As already indicated, this process was accompanied by a growing penetration of foreing (mainly American) programmes, rather than the building up of a national production industry.

Despite its lack of preparation for the communications revolution, the French press also demonstrated a fast-growing interest in diversification. The leading French press baron, Robert Hersant, was initially very cautious about adapting his decentralised network of press interests to the challenge of multimedia diversification. He was effectively compelled to become involved in the local radio explosion in France when Mitterrand announced, in early 1984, that further deregulation would allow local radio to carry advertising. This initiative presented the local and regional press with new competition for local advertising. Hersant was given a further jolt in 1985 by Mitterrand's announcement of a similar expansion of local 'off-air' television. Since early 1985, however reluctantly, Hersant actively prepared to diversify into television, to which end he established the Téleurop (Tve) company. In view of the mutual antagonism between Hersant and the French left, Hersant's preparations were also in anticipation of the return to power of the right in 1986. The French right promised to privatise parts of France's public-service radio and television system. However, the initial stimulus to multi-media diversification was given by the changes of the French Socialists.

Apart from the local radio explosion, the French press was notably active in diversifying into videotex services. Videotex had been developed as a consumer-oriented service in France in a highly voluntarist style. *Minitel* terminals (for *Télétel*, the French Prestel system and for the 'electronic directory ') were literally given away freely as the DGT's rolling videotex programme advanced from region to region. By the end of 1985, the scale of videotex operation in France totally dwarfed Britain's Prestel or West Germany's *Bildschirmtext*. In response, a large number of well-known regional newspapers − for instance, *Courrier Picard, Ouest France* and *La Dépêche du Midi* as well as a few national ones, notably, *Le Soir* and *Libération* − started offering 'telematic newspaper' services.

In general, the French Socialists attempted to control the development of new media in a manner that seems to have given little encouragement to multimedia diversification. Both the *Plan Câble* and the DBS programme originated as industrial policies, and the scale of challenge to the French programme production sector that would inevitably follow was badly underestimated, as the effectiveness of their programme-production promotion measures was grossly overestimated. The *Plan Câble* was accompanied by the establishment of an interministerial *Mission TV Câble* (also known as the 'Mission Schreiner'), among the tasks of which was to stimulate, co-ordinate and assemble programming. Great hopes were placed in the state-run *Institut National de l'Audiovisuel* (INA) and the public-service broadcasting organisations, all of which demonstrated an interest in producing for cable. The French cinema was also expected to fuel the new media. Yet, little new production capacity was actually created. Reflecting the worthy (but idealistic) aims of Socialist cultural policy-makers and decentralisers, especially high hopes seem to have been placed on the role of small local and regional film and video producers. In reality, though, this sector was very poorly equipped to meet the challenge, in general lacking both professional expertise and adequate financial support. Finally, a brave attempt was made by Jack Lang, the Minister of Culture, to promote the 'culture industries'; to this end, he established an institute, the *Institut de financement du cinéma et des industries culturelles* (IFCIC), and created special support funds for programmes (*fonds de soutien à la production audiovisuelle*). By early 1986, however, most of this expenditure had benefited Canal Plus alone.

By preventing the formation of private commercial national networks, Article 80 discouraged a high level of new investment and new entrants into the sector. The French Socialists do not seem to have begun by thinking in terms of aggressively boosting French competitiveness in a new pan-European programming market — by doing their utmost to encourage the growth of economically viable private commercial or 'mixed economy' (private/public) national champions, or by investing much more time, energy and finance in finding a public-service solution. Rather, they adopted at first a much more defensive approach, seeking to regulate for 'cultural protection' and thinking in terms of building a 'Maginot line' of cable against the feared programme invasion. In this respect, both the subsequent progress made by TDF 1 (compared with the disappointments and delays of cable) and the recourse to outside multimedia giants like Berlusconi and Maxwell for the commercialisation of TDF 1 might be seen as a double failure for the French Socialists.

The French Socialists' ambivalence about the extent to which audio-visual communication should become a truly 'liberated' domain was reflected in the continuing measure of state influence. Thus it was thoroughly characteristic of the French Socialists' approach to communications policy that the dominant shareholding in the fourth national channel, Canal Plus, France's first pay-television channel, should have been allocated to Havas, which was by far France's largest multimedia communications enterprise. Quite simply Havas was state-controlled, and the head of Havas, André Rousselet, who became chairman of Canal Plus, was also a former director of President Mitterrand's *cabinet*. Yet, as a further indication of 'retreat' from *controlled deregulation*, by the end of the Socialists' period in office Havas' share of Canal Plus had fallen to only 25 per cent; the channel had been 'quasi-privatised'. The French state was also the principal initiator of France's first satellite television service, TV 5, jointly operated by French, Belgian and Swiss public-service broadcasters. In 1985 this service was supplying (a very modest) three and a half hours per night to European cable systems by means of the Eutelsat 1 communications satellite (ECS 1). TV 5 carried no advertising, its prime purpose was cultural rather than commercial, and it seemed set to transfer to the French DBS satellite when launched. Alongside a proposed cultural channel for

TDF 1 (Canal 1), another initiative with which Mitterrand closely identified himself and for which government financial support was promised, TV 5 reflected at least one minor triumph for the determination of French Socialist policy-makers to control developments in a manner designed to protect and promote French culture.

In contrast to France, Britain rapidly became the staging post for a relatively high degree of international multimedia diversification, behind which lay the undoubted attraction of proximity to the continental European market and the neo-liberal climate of policy in Britain. French apprehensions that Britain, as well as Luxembourg, would become a Trojan horse for the Americans, were confirmed by the progress of Sky Channel. Another special feature of British developments, which resulted directly from the British Conservative government's deregulatory policies, was the sometimes overlapping involvement of commercial interests in the fields of cable construction, cable operation and programme provision.

Since April 1982 Sky Channel has offered a menu of predominantly American (but also British) series, music and movies; priority was given to this type of general entertainment programming. It was financed almost exclusively from advertising revenue; and it reached its audience in the pan-European cable market by means of the Eutelsat 1 communications satellite (ECS 1). Sky Channel was operated by Satellite Television Limited, which was a 90 per cent subsiduary of Rupert Murdoch's News International multimedia group. Murdoch's American links were strengthened when he bought into the Hollywood studio Twentieth Century Fox to supply Sky Channel. In fact, Murdoch has developed a policy of trying to buy into American television interests too – to which end he established a new company, News America Television – in order to strengthen his multinational activities.

Another press giant, Robert Maxwell, bought up Rediffusion's extensive interests in traditional cable television networks in 1984 and aimed at upgrading them according to the new guidelines laid down by the Conservative government's legislation. Maxwell's multimedia ambitions extended also to new modern cable networks. He inherited a franchise awarded in 1983 to Rediffusion Cablevision for a modern cable system in Guildford. In August 1985 the Cable Authority awarded a franchise, for West Surrey and East Hampshire, followed in February 1986 by yet another franchise, for Cardiff and Penarth, to Maxwell's British Cable Services Ltd. In addition, British Cable Services already held 11.4 per cent of shares in Clyde Cablevision, awarded a franchise in 1983. Maxwell has also established a cable programming service, called Mirrorvision, and conducted negotiations with the French in order to gain channel capacity on the French DBS satellite, TDF 1, and, like Murdoch, with the BBC and ITV companies about their huge libraries of television programmes.

Thorn EMI, the British electronics and communications giant, established Swindon Cable Services which gained a franchise in 1983 to operate one of Britain's first new modern cable systems. It also held a 51 per cent share in Coventry Cable Ltd and a 20 per cent share in Ulster Cablevision, similarly awarded franchises in 1983. In addition to its cable operations, Thorn EMI launched several channels to become the major actor in new cable ventures by 1984. It established a music channel, 'Music Box', which was financed by advertising, offered predominantly video clips of pop groups, and was distributed across Europe's cable systems by satellite. Thorn EMI also launched a Children's Channel. Finally, it combined with a number of 'Hollywood majors', namely Columbia, 20th Century Fox and Warner Brothers as well as the British film company, Goldcrest, to offer a movie channel called Premiere. By early 1986, however, Thorn EMI's commitment to the new media seemed to be in doubt, due to a combination of internal financial problems — generated in part by the bold acquisition of Inmos, the chip manufacturer, and the subsequent loss of confidence in the City. The future of Thorn EMI's cable operations seemed uncertain. It sold off its share in Premiere — which was promptly bought by Robert Maxwell — and control of Music Box passed to the Virgin group.

The British public-service broadcasters' ambitions to meet the competitive challenge of DBS suffered serious setbacks, due mainly to the government's contradictory policy; it offered no financial support, while stipulating that the public broadcasters had to 'buy British', namely the UNISAT satellite, which they felt was too expensive. An American satellite was preferred by the consortium. Uncertainty about the future financing of the BBC, with the appointment of the Peacock committee in 1985, also discouraged risk-taking. In 1985 negotiations about the DBS venture collapsed along with the 'club of 21'. Nevertheless, by early 1986 it became clear that 13 of the 15 ITV companies, led by Granada and Thames, still aimed to operate an advertising-based Superchannel. It was to offer a menu of public-service (BBC and ITV) programmes ('the best of British') to a pan-European audience by means of an Intelsat communications satellite. Superchannel was designed as a powerful rival to Sky Channel. Also, in early 1986 the government revitalised the prospect of a British DBS service by renouncing its earlier stipulation that such a service would have to be carried by a British-made satellite. The Independent Broadcasting Authority (IBA), which franchised and regulated the ITV companies, advertised the franchises for three DBS channels in April 1986.

The main actors in the process of multimedia-diversification in West Germany have been the newspaper and magazine publishers. As elsewhere in Western Europe, the greatest involvement is by the well-known giant concerns. As we saw earlier, in late 1982 Bertelsmann joined forces with RTL; subsequently they turned their attention to the West German DBS, TV SAT. Another opportunity for the West German press to supply satellite television services came when, in February 1984, the so-called 'West Beam' of the ECS 1 general communications satellite was allocated to a private consortium, SAT 1, which had been formed by major publishing companies such as Springer, Bauer, Burda and Holzbrinck as well as 165 smaller concerns. The news service was supplied by the Aktuell Presse Fernsehen (APF), a joint venture in which the Springer press held an important share. As with RTL Plus, the ultimate aim of SAT 1 was to transfer as soon as possible to TV SAT, in search of a larger audience. The Ludwigshafen cable 'pilot project', which opened a month earlier, on 1 January 1984, encouraged a number of new privately-owned broadcasting organisations, notably the Programmgesellschaft für Kabel und Satellitenfunk (PKS) and the Erste Private Fernsehgesellschaft

(EPF). Behind both services stood an array of press interests. When the Munich 'pilot project' opened, the Bavarian press held a 20 per cent share in its management company. The *Frankfurter Allgemeine Zeitung*, the conservative quality daily, has also been a very active diversifier; apart from supplying the news service for the PKS, it has diversified into teletext and videotex.

As in Britain, the initial response of the West German public service broadcasters to the new media was generally apprehensive and negative. Subsequently, they became more confident and, encouraged by the new Social Democrat Party tactics, sought to 'take the wind out of the sails' of the private commercial competition. Such a response has two dimensions. First, in 1985 the public-service broadcasters bought a large 'programme package' of American entertainment programmes to prepare for a commercial war with the new media entrepreneurs; secondly, they sought an active role in the new media themselves (an issue that will become increasingly controversial as the date of inter-state renegotiation of the terms of their finances approaches). This situation is complicated by *'Kleinstaaterei'*, the various competitive tactics developed in individual *Länder*. *Second German Television* (*Zweites Deutsches Fernsehen*) became the key actor in a consortium with Austrian and Swiss public-service broadcasters in a German-language satellite programme (3 Sat); in 1986 ARD (the organisation of German public-service broadcasting stations producing the first programme) launched its own satellite programme (Eins Plus) while the Bavarian CSU government sought satellite channel capacity so that *Bayerischer Rundfunk*, the Bavarian public broadcasting station, could broadcast nationwide the voice of Bavaria (and of the CSU).[24] The CDU found itself suddenly on the defensive; SAT 1, which it had sponsored, was being watched by only some 15 per cent of cabled homes and was registering huge losses. It could scarcely stand such competition. Their response was to threaten the public-service broadcasters and the SPD with the prospect of a failure to renegotiate the licence fee in 1988.

CONCLUSIONS: SOME IMPLICATIONS FOR POLICY

At one level differences in the pace and structure of multimedia diversification within Western Europe seem to reflect the character of state action: that is, whether the state forces the pace of development of new media by sustained heavy investment in advanced cable networks, videotex and satellite, as in France and West Germany; whether the state encourages access for private information providers in the videotex system (e.g. by the *Bundespost*'s use of a 'gateway' architecture for *Bildschirmtext* in West Germany and the flexibility of *Télétel* in France) or for private programmers in broadcasting, as in Britain; and whether, when reliance is placed on private-sector investment in cable systems and DBS (as in Britain), tax concessions or subsidies are used to promote the new industry (as did *not* occur in Britain). The state could further influence the developments of new media by its own internal lack of co-ordination: by the confusion caused by a proliferation of initiatives in France, by the failure to co-ordinate budgetary policy (the phasing out of capital allowances with the 1984 budget changed the economics of the new cable industry) and telecommunications policy (restricting the range of activities of new cable operators) with cable television policy in Britain; and by problems of achieving unified action within the West German federal system. If the location of the causes of these failures of co-ordination varied, their consequences did not. Initial euphoria was displaced by widespread disappointment and disillusion about new media. By the end of 1985 only 8.5 per cent of homes in Western Europe were cabled. In Britain early enthusiasts like BET (owner of Rediffusion) and Visionhire pulled out of cable operations, and by 1986 Thorn EMI was indicating a desire to dispose of its cable interests. The BBC, anxious about the implications of the Peacock committee of inquiry into its future financing, lost interest in an expensive DBS venture, in which the government required the use of British satellite technology but refused financial support. In France the 'heroic' *Plan Câble* made a very poor start.

Yet the impact of state action was not so simple and straightforward. Certain large and powerful media interests were able to sustain an involvement in the face of political uncertainties and hurdles. Despite the failure to arrive at a *Staatsvertrag* for new media with consequent commercial uncertainties about access to cable systems in many German states, West German publishers pressed onwards to form the SAT 1 consortium. As BET (Rediffusion) pulled out of cable operations and Thorn EMI pulled out of cable programming (Premiere and Music Box), so Robert Maxwell entered. News International, Carlton Communications, the Virgin group, National Broadcasting Services (NBS Television) and Granada all indicated a continued private commercial interest in satellite broadcasting: notable interest remained in a British DBS service after and despite the collapse of the original UNISAT project in the summer of 1985 (which helps explain the government's U-turn in dropping the 'buy British' stipulation). In early 1986 Sky Channel seemed to be still bullish and confident about reaching break-even point after four years of heavy losses; and the ITV companies were planning to mount their competitive Superchannel. Finally, the perceived promise of satellite television continued to draw interest from continental European investors like Bertelsmann, Berlusconi and Groupe Bruxelles Lambert. The multimedia giants seemed determined to absorb generally high losses (of at least a short-term nature), in order to 'stake out their claims' in the new electronic media.

At another level political strategies proved incapable of effectively contesting pressures from fast-moving and turbulent international markets. Pressures towards convergence of policies seemed powerful, as the experiences of the French Socialist government and the West German SPD at the *Land* level showed. One pressure for convergence was the battle among rival European media centres to attract investment and prestige, notably Hamburg (SPD), Munich, Paris, London, Rome and Luxembourg. The search for media investment induced a competitive pressure to deregulate. Some West European states, like Britain, Ireland, Italy and Luxembourg, were welcoming American capital and culture, providing an internal European base for American media companies. At different rates, and with varying degrees of discomfort, West European governments were discovering that the game of cultural sovereignty was already over in West European broadcasting; they were having to learn to play a new game. In doing so governments sought reliable and powerful partners; thus for Mitterrand better Berlusconi and Maxwell than Murdoch and Groupe Bruxelles Lambert, and better Berlusconi and Maxwell in conjunction with a friendly French capitalist, Seydoux; and for Chirac better Hersant, RTL and Groupe Bruxelles Lambert. Broadcasting had been catapulted by new technology into the realm of diplomacy and *raison d'état*, of secret deals and diplomatic *coups*. An aspect of new media policy in France was the classic diplomatic recognition of necessities, in this case of new economic and technological forces. Faced with the emergence of international multimedia giants, adept themselves at high politics, governments must decide which giants, or potential giants, they will sponsor or accept as national champions. Accordingly, multimedia diversification has rapidly established itself as a common European pattern even when initially discouraged by government. The process of the incorporation of new media into the elevated realm of high diplomacy is not without its risks. There is a very real danger that public policy will ignore the issue of concentration of control over new media in the hands of large and powerful giants and neglect the crucially important role for smaller independent programme producers if cultural pluralism and vitality are to be preserved and extended.

On the other hand, the political and cultural risks associated specifically with the new media can be exaggerated. In the first place, a constraint on the rapid development of new media into a position of political and cultural dominance is provided by the revitalisation of old media. Decisions of the World Administration Radio Conference (WARC) in 1984 made available additional frequencies for civilian usage and provided new stimulus to off-air broadcasting. Italy was already the classic European example of how an explosion of 'off-air' local broadcasting could divert public debate and interest from new media. In France the commitment of the Socialist government to encourage local and regional radio and television, particularly after the *Bredin Report* of 1985, raised questions about the commercial viability of cable television. Quite simply, opportunities in the field of old media are far from exhausted. These opportunities did not, of course, mitigate the danger of a concentration of media control, as the Italian case demonstrated. Secondly, Western Europe is not simply in the iron grip of 'technology-push' in media development. A weakness of public policy across Western Europe has been the tendency, under the pressures of technological and industrial 'hype', to ignore the viewer and the ways in which the interests and choices of viewers are shaped by changing social patterns. Old as well as new media succeed to the extent that they cater for genuinely greater consumer choice. Ultimately success will lie with the media that can provide good-quality and varied programming at low cost and programming that appeals in terms of viewers' experiences. The future of individual media depends on the creativity, market research and efficiency of programme producers rather than on the technology of new media. Accordingly, public policy for the programme production sector becomes a critical ingredient for commercial success of new media. Acceptance of the role of multi-media and multinational corporations must be accompanied by regulatory policies (on programme commissioning policies of broadcasting companies, public and private), by training policies and a combination of tax inducements and subsidies that will stimulate the independent programme production sector.

'Who programmes what' in the media is an important cultural policy issue in Western Europe that requires much more public debate and a more central place on the political agenda. This requirement is established by the proliferation of media initiatives in old as well as new media. As we have seen, the proliferation of means of programme distribution is an invitation to powerful new entrants into the electronic media industry; the consequence is a challenge to existing patterns and practices of broadcasting in Western Europe. A key question for political strategy and public policy in Western Europe is whether and how the state encourages or supports an active role by the public-service broadcasters in the expanding media markets. Public service broadcasters, not least in Britain, have remarkable library resources of programming available for expanding markets; witness the ideas behind the ITV Superchannel and the desire of ITV companies to mobilise a programming participation by BBC. Yet an active role by the public-service broadcasters presupposes a continuing political commitment to allow them a secure and confident future. Moreover, the question arises of the extent to which the public-service broadcasters are to adapt to the new competitive challenge. Entry of public-service broadcasters into too aggressive a commercial role will not be without reservations, regrets and criticism. For many, such an entry will be seen as an abandonment of all that is best in the traditions of 'excellence' and 'standards' in European public-service broadcasting. For others it will represent the best form of defence and some guarantee at least that public-service interests might continue to be strongly represented in the new media environment. More fundamentally, encouragement of a new activism by the public-service broadcasters provides a major new opportunity for a fundamental regulatory revision by governments, embracing public and private broadcasters and establishing a framework of conditions that stimulates greater access, decentralisation and accountability in the media.

Finally, in so far as cultural issues are posed in Western Europe, typically by the French, they have tended to be presented in terms of the spread of American 'coca-cola' civilisation and of the demise of 'European cultural identity' in the face of American cultural imperialism. Such a narrow conceptualisation obscures the question of whether there is or should be any such thing as an autonomous European cultural identity: is identification with such an abstract identity a cloak for particular forms of cultural imperialism *within* Europe? There are after all issues of cultural identity *within* Europe. The problem of American/European conflicts of cultural interests in new media is paralleled by Belgium's problem *vis-à-vis* France and Ireland's problem *vis-à-vis* Britain. Cultural identity has also a sub-national dimension, with for instance the centralisation of media investment and production in London and Paris at the expense of regional centres. With the rapid erosion of the cultural sovereignty of the large European states like Britain, France and West Germany, the earlier experiences of Belgium and Ireland as 'culturally penetrated' small countries may serve as an interesting paradigm. It seems that the spread of the new media means that in Western Europe 'we are all becoming small states now'.

POLICIES FOR NEW MEDIA IN WESTERN EUROPE   123

NOTES

1. See K. Dyson, 'The Politics of Cable and Satellite Broadcasting', *West European Politics*, Vol. 8, No. 2 (1985).
2. Cabinet Office/Information Technology Advisory Panel, *Cable Systems* (London: HMSO, 1982).
3. *Ibid.*, p. 7.
4. *Ibid.*, p. 52.
5. The Hunt Inquiry led to the 'Hunt Report, *Report of the Inquiry into Cable Expansion & Broadcasting Policy* (London: HMSO, Cmnd. 8679, 1982).
6. See the White Paper *Cable Systems and Services* (London: HMSO, Cmnd. 8866, 1983); and *Cable and Broadcasting Act* (London: HMSO, 1984).
7. *Telecommunications Act* (London: HMSO, 1984). Under the terms of this act, broadband cable systems require, in addition to a Cable Authority licence, a licence from the Secretary of State for Trade and Industry. The application to the Cable Authority is accepted as an application to the Department of Trade and Industry for a telecommunications licence. But the statutory procedures in connection with the granting of the latter are quite separate from those associated with the Cable and Broadcasting Act.
8. The authors have analysed the policy failures and inconsistencies of the British cable and satellite programmes in K. Dyson & P. Humphreys, 'The new media in Britain and France — two versions of heroic muddle?', *Rundfunk und Fernsehen*, Vol. 33, No. 3–4, (1985), pp. 362–79.
9. S. Nora and A. Minc, *Informatisation de la Société* (Paris: Documentation Française, 1978); English translation (1980) by The Massachusetts Institute of Technology (MIT Press), 'The Computerisation of Society'. This report reflects the central role of the French technocratic élites — in this case *inspecteurs des finances* — in assessing public policy issues in France.
10. *Rapport sur les réseaux câblés audiovisuels*, GIEL, July 1981; the report is summarised comprehensively in *Vidéo Actualité*, Paris, No. 16 (Oct/Nov. 1981), pp. 106–16.
11. On the transformation of the DGT technocrats' status, see: T. Vedel, 'Les Ingénieurs des Télécommunications', *Culture Technique* No. 12 (1984), pp. 63–79; on the aims of the DGT, see, E. Cherki, État, Administration, Politiques Publiques — Le Programme de Câblage des Villes Françaises', *Bulletin de l'IDATE*, Montpellier, No. 14 (1984); see also, T. Vedel, 'De la Télématique à la Vidéocommunication; Continuités et Ruptures d'une Politique Publique', *Actes des Vèmes Journées Internationales de l'IOMTE*, Montpellier, 1983.
12. See, N. Casile and A. Drhey, *Loi sur la Communication Audiovisuelle*, (Paris: La Documentation Française, 1983). This document contains a very useful analysis of the law.
13. *Ibid.*, pp. 130–2. It cites Georges Fillioud (Minister of Communication), '... En clair, nous ne voulons pas qu'un groupe de presse qui peut, le cas échéant, avoir déjà une position de monopole dans une région couvrant plusieurs départements français, ou bien dans plusieurs régions couvrant plusieurs dizaines de départements français, commande en même temps, dans la même région, dans les mêmes départements, plusieurs réseaux câblés de télévision et une chaine de radiodiffusion sonore.'
14. The authors have described this process, as well as analysed the policy features of the *plan câble* in their *Rundfunk und Fernsehen* article, *op. cit.*; see also, P. Humphreys, 'Cable: the heroic French experiment examined and compared with the British and German examples', *Journal of Area Studies*, No. 12, (1985), pp. 14–19.
15. See chapter on the new media debate in West Germany by P. Humphreys in K. Dyson and P. Humphreys (eds.), *Politics, Policy and the New Media in Western Europe* (London: Frances Pinter, 1986).
16. See, *Bericht der Kommission für den Ausbau des technischen Kommunikationssystems* (KtK), shortened text in *Media Perspektiven*, No. 1 (1976).
17. This spate of new media legislation has been covered thoroughly by the journal *Media Perspektiven*, notably No. 4, 1985.
18. Both the general political science questions raised by satellite broadcasting and a detailed analysis of public-policy for satellite broadcasting are the subject of: K. Dyson and P. Humphreys, 'Satellite Broadcasting Policies and the Question of Sovereignty in Western Europe; a Comparative Analysis', *Journal of Public Policy* (summer 1986).
19. Nora and Minc, *op. cit.* (English translation by MIT), p. 76.

20. *Rapport au Premier Ministre sur les Nouvelles Télévisions Hertziennes*, May 1985 (copy in authors' possession).
21. J. F. Lacan, 'L'audiovisuel en six salons: la liberté aux portes de l'anarchie', *Le Monde Aujourd'hui*, 10–11 March, 1985, p. 111.
22. A. Lange, 'Skizze eines ersten weltweiten Fernseh-Networks', *Media Perspektiven*, No. 2 (1986), pp. 81–9. Lange identifies Albert Frère, a Belgian financier, as the centre of a web of Euro-American financial interests – the so-called 'Galazie Pargesa' – based on the international activities of the Swiss holding company Pargesa (in which Frère had a sizeable holding) and including Groupe Bruxelles-Lambert (where Frere has a major holding), CLT and Drexell. Frère is interpreted as Berlusconi's 'real' European rival.
23. A. Mattelart, X. Delcourt and M. Mattelart, *International Image Markets: In Search of an Alternative Perspective* (London: Comedia Series No. 21, 1984), p. 30; originally published in France as *La Culture contre la Démocratie? L'audiovisuel à l'heure transnationale* (Paris: Éditions La Découverte, 1983).
24. On ARD's initiatives see D. Schwarzkopf, 'Eins Plus und Europa Television', *Media Perspektiven*, No. 2 (1986). On 3-SAT see W. Konrad, 'Ein kulturell akzentuiertes Programm des deutschen Sprechraums; 3-SAT', *Media Perspektiven*, No. 12 (1985), pp. 874–8.

Law, Politics and the New Media: Trends in Broadcasting Regulation

Wolfgang Hoffmann-Riem

The new communications technologies and their applications represent a challenge to the economic structures, political cultures and the legal systems of West European societies. Probably never before in history has a fundamental technological innovation affected so many states almost simultaneously and stimulated structurally comparable responses without any significant discrepancies of time.

In Western industrial states like the United States, Britain, France, Japan or the Federal Republic of Germany, developments in telecommunications are viewed predominantly from the perspective of industrial policy. Export opportunities for national industries are to be exploited. At the same time it is hoped that the harnessing of developments in telecommunications will provide stimuli for the domestic market and boost economic growth. For hardware manufacturers, and also in many respects for software manufacturers, the opportunity of new and fast expanding world markets increases considerably the prospect of profit. At one blow, a world-wide market can be established or opened up. Above all this development will greatly advantage suppliers with a strong market position, while the market will still be large enough to present smaller suppliers with market-niches, to which they will be able to turn their innovative potential. Consequently, developments in telecommunications are characterised by the international dimension and the determinant role of the economic market.

The following analysis will confine itself to the field of broadcasting. In examining the broadcasting market, it is advisable to differentiate between two distinct functions, namely the production of broadcast programmes, on the one hand, and their distribution to the recipient, on the other. Typically, the market for broadcasting software has not been the object of state regulation in most Western countries. In this sector an international market has been able to develop without state- or internationally-ordained limitation or restriction. This situation contrasts with that in the sector of the distribution of broadcast programmes. From the very beginning, the broadcasting systems of most countries have been the object of state regulation. In these countries the distribution of programmes does not result from the free play of the market. National regulation has been the obstacle to the extension of the international communications market, which already exists for the function of production, to this sector of distribution. At the present time, there are intense pressures and strident demands for matching this international 'non-regulation' in the sector of production with the deregulation of arrangements for, and correspondingly the marketing of, programme broadcasting.

Many are hopeful that the deregulation of broadcasting law will have positive repercussions at various levels of the communications market. The field of broadcasting is held to be an expanding market, which promises considerable growth. As well as newspaper publishers and other media concerns, complete strangers to the sector are pressing to enter this new market. At the same time, the hardware manufacturers – for example, in the field of consumer electronics – are anticipating outlets for new products and the creation of new national information markets.

The following analysis will examine the reaction to demands for an 'American-style' deregulation of broadcasting systems, using the Federal Republic of Germany as an example, though similar tendencies can be detected in other West European countries.[1]

THE PARADIGM SHIFT IN BROADCASTING POLICY AND BROADCASTING LAW

The driving force behind current developments is provided by economic interests that are keen to capitalise upon technological innovation. There may be additional goals, for instance the politically motivated desire to break-up traditional public-service broadcasting monopolies – both France and West Germany are obvious cases.[2] Yet such aims remain subordinate, to some extent, to the economic imperative. This predominantly economic foundation of developments has consequences for the manner in which individual states make changes to their broadcasting systems. Here, it is the intention to demonstrate how this primacy of economics is making a special impact on broadcasting regulation. There are indications already that the reaction to interests that seek economic expansion of broadcasting is a paradigm shift in broadcasting policy and broadcasting law.

1. From the Trustee to the Market Model

The various established broadcasting systems in Western states have many different distinguishing characteristics, yet they can all be classified according to their approximation to two contrasting basic models. The first model is the so-called trustee model, according to which broadcasting is legally organised in trusteeship for the whole of society. Broadcasters are obliged to take into account adequately all social interests. Unbalanced and biased programming is not permitted. Broadcasting is not geared primarily towards profit-making. It draws its financial support from licence fees, fixed by the state, or in some cases possibly by (generally supplementary) tax expenditure.

At the opposite pole stands the so-called market model. Broadcasting is financed from the revenues of free enterprise, in particular from advertising income. Its proprietors may strive to realise profit and orientate programming towards the goal of profit-maximation – or towards any other goal that they themselves may choose. Unbalanced and biased programming is not out of the question. There exists no obligation to foster the wider communications-interests of all citizens. Market forces decide which communications-needs are satisfied.

In fact broadcasting reality has for long reflected contrasting mixes of these models. Thus, the market model has been embedded traditionally in some kind of regulatory framework involving, for instance, franchise procedures and programming codes of conduct. A well-ordered minimum of fairness and balance has been imposed upon the free-enterprise broadcasters. In turn, the trustee model can be mingled with elements of free enterprise and market-orientation. In this way many public-service broadcasters benefit from regulatory arrangements that allow them to finance their activities partially from the market, for instance from advertising-revenue.

For broadcasting in the United States the point of reference has always been the market-model. Yet, for a long period, a framework of pronounced state regulation bound broadcasters to respect the common good. In the wake of deregulation – 1981 for radio, 1984 for television – the great majority of regulations will no longer be operative.[3] The express aim of this deregulation is to subordinate broadcasting as far as possible to market forces. By contrast, until recently West European broadcasting systems have not been organised according to the principles of the market model. The state has constantly fulfilled a strict responsibility for regulation of broadcasting. Broadcasters have been subject to commitments as trustees of the public interest, and they have been established in a monopolistic position, or at any rate spared direct economic competition. However, in the course of current changes, the West European broadcasting systems are being opened up more, although not completely, to the market. In particular, there will remain the established public-service broadcasters (e.g. Britain's BBC, Italy's RAI, West Germany's ZDF), which have operated hitherto according to principles of social integration and a wide representation of the diversity of civil society. However, alongside them another sector is being established, which is to operate along free-enterprise lines, although it is generally supposed to remain subject to strict state regulation, at least during the initial phase. This opening to the market model has gone a particularly long way in Italy, where it actually began outside any legal framework.[4] In Britain, private commercial broadcasting has long been oriented towards the profit principle. Nevertheless, Independent Television has also been extensively spared from economic competition and subjected to similar public-service regulation to the BBC. Now, however, a quantitative leap in commercialism and a massive extension of competition is being planned on all sides, particularly in the form of cable and satellite television.[5] In the Federal Republic of Germany the first private commercial broadcasters were allowed to commence operations in 1984, though they remained subject to state regulation.[6] This phase is transitional. A further opening to the market model and dilution of existing trusteeship-commitments can be anticipated.

2. *From a Cultural towards an Economic Legitimation of the Broadcasting System*

This paradigm shift is accompanied by a change in the aims of state regulation of broadcasting. In Western Europe state responsibility for broadcasting has been legitimised until now in terms of the priority given to the political and cultural significance of broadcasting for state and society. This significance has counted, and still counts, as a particularly important reason for the existence of special codes and commitments in the sphere of broadcast communication. Thus broadcasting must fulfil a responsibility of public information, especially to ensure the proper functioning of democracy. Broadcasting has also been assigned a special cultural and educative purpose. Broadcasting organisations are duty-bound to provide for the communications-needs of all sections of the population. Such functions reflect the trusteeship concept of broadcasting.

In so far as broadcasters are now compelled to think in terms of maintaining a competitive hold on the economic market, these traditional duties must be relativised in one of several ways. The aims and objectives can be retained verbally; at the same time, it can be assumed (or claimed) that the economic market is the best of all mechanisms available to meet them. In just such a way, the US Federal Communications Commission (FCC) legitimised its policy of deregulation, which has taken place without any change of the Communications Act and its requirements for the common good (public interest, convenience, necessity). Recent West European legislation too – for example, the new media laws of the *Länder* (states) in the Federal Republic – emphasises the commitments of the trustee model, while assuming that they can also be adequately fulfilled in the market.

Closer examination of US regulation might lead to the observation that orientation towards the public interest has become, to a considerable extent, a rhetorical but empty cliché. It is certainly no longer the cement in a construct of special mechanisms for attaining public interest objectives. This diagnosis can be confirmed by the general absence of regulatory provisions to cover the possibility that the market may fail to function in the desired manner. In the history of state regulation (in particular, that of so-called 'social regulation') this very possibility has been the ultimate rationale.[7] From now on, regulatory authority is dispensed with, without any structural changes having been implemented in the economic market that preclude the risk of its malfunctioning. Those observable structural changes that have taken, and are continuing to take place in both the United States and Western Europe – namely, the provision of more communications vectors than ever before by technological advance and the presence of a greater number of communications actors in a newly competitive relation – cannot be presumed to constitute automatically sufficient guarantees. Already a pronounced general tendency toward imperfect competition can be detected. Intensive processes of multi-media, diagonal concentration are unfolding, involving both press giants and large electronics and telecommunications interests in the new electronic media. Murdoch, Maxwell, W.H. Smith, Reed Publishing and Thorn EMI in Britain are matched by Springer, Bauer and Bertelsmann in the Federal Republic and Berlusconi in Italy. In France, a proliferation of new broadcasting initiatives has brought resort to 'outside' programmers, in the shape of Maxwell and Berlusconi.[8] Generally, larger operators, with huge resources to commit to a long-haul to profitability, seem to be cornering the market effectively. Correspondingly, there can be no guarantees that economic competition will remain functionally effective in the long run. Above all, there can be no certainty, with respect to regulation by the market, that the communications-interests of all sections of the population – for instance, minorities with little economic weight – can be satisfied. The phenomenon, which many observers have detected in the field of so-called social regulation, that market processes are not neutral and are not suited to the fulfilment of all desired values, seems to have been ignored.

Should the development of broadcasting be left to determination by the economic market, its legitimation can only be achieved by a change of its aims. This process can occur through the widespread social acceptance of the subordination of mass communication to inherent economic laws. In this case, any degree of media diversity that might be attained by the market's operation would be deemed to be sufficient. Such a reorientation would raise legal problems. For example, it would not be compatible with West German constitutional law.[9] Nevertheless, it is a conspicuous fact that, in the current West German political and academic debate, more and more voices are pleading the case for the market model to be introduced into the field of broadcasting. It is not always clear whether this change betrays an increased confidence in the ability of the market to attain the (unchanged) goal of media diversity or whether even this goal has now been relativised. Arguably, in many cases there has already been a change of normative aim.

There is much ground for arguing that at the present time in Western Europe a similar change is taking place, to that which has already taken place in the United States. If the market model of broadcasting counted at first as a means toward achieving media diversity, it is increasingly becoming a goal in itself. Economic competition is regarded by many as a sufficient structural principle for the desired broadcasting model. The outstanding and unanswered question is whether, and under which conditions, economic competition assures media competition and a corresponding media diversity.

3. From Freedom of Communication to Freedom of Broadcasting Entrepreneurship

The change of emphasis in the political legitimation of the broadcasting system has repercussions at various levels. One of these levels is the understanding of the fundamental right to freedom of communications. In both the United States and the Federal Republic of Germany there exist express constitutional guarantees of the freedom of communication, including broadcasting freedom (First Amendment of the US Constitution; Article Five of the West German Basic Law). As a principle, freedom of communication has been subsumed historically within the wider concept of the political and cultural freedom of individuals to pursue self-fulfilment and truth. At the same time it has been understood to be a necessary instrument for achieving guarantees of democratic self-regulation.[10] Yet liberal democracies pay tribute to other special basic rights too, such as that of economic freedom (e.g. property rights, rights to choose and practise occupations). In the United States, the commercial basis of the media system led at an early stage to the integration of the principle of economic freedom – within the field of communication – into the protective jurisdiction of the First Amendment. In so far as the spectrum of the media system in general, and the structure of the individual media organisations in particular, are concerned, the proprietor of the broadcasting station is regarded as the principle protégé (or beneficiary of protection) of constitutional guarantees to freedom. Consequently, it is not fundamentally questioned in American constitutional commentary and debate that broadcasting freedom (in analogy with the much prized freedom of the press) embraces the right to deploy one's wealth to communicate one's views. The right to use broadcasting vectors according to such an understanding of free communication, on the one hand, and the property rights of broadcasting entrepreneurs, on the other hand, are thus closely intertwined in the interpretation of the First Amendment and in the application of statutory provisions.

A similar development can now be detected in West German constitutional debate over the new media. Although it has not (yet) been confirmed by the West German Federal Constitutional Court, most protagonists of private commercial broadcasting equate broadcasting freedom with freedom of broadcasting entrepreneurship.[11] The activities of broadcasting entrepreneurs should, according to this argument, be brought as much as possible into line with those of other entrepreneurs. This reasoning aims at a dismantling of the state's special competence to pass specific regulations for the structure of broadcasting.

The transformation of the principle of freedom of communications into the protection of a commercial business is a result of such heuristic efforts. Yet, from a historical point of view, this result could be considered to be surprising. Freedom of communications in Western Europe is rooted in the early liberal tradition of constitutional law, which sought to prevent the state from restricting the content of communication, and which was oriented towards promoting individual self-fulfilment through communication and towards facilitating the quest for truth. From now on, however, the right to communicate and the right to run a commercial business are merged. In principle, this new complex freedom is extended to all media enterprises, including the multi-media concerns and multinational conglomerates. The rise of an economic interpretation of freedom of communications contrasts with the concept of individual self-fulfilment and of citizens' rights to self-government, which has been a key determining influence on the historical definition of freedom of communications in Western Europe.

4. From Freedom of Communications to the Freedom to Supply Services and Establish Businesses

A parallel development can be observed in the European Commission's interpretation of Article Ten of the European Convention on Human Rights: the basic human right to freedom of opinion.[12] In its efforts to establish a 'common market for broadcasting', the Commission cannot rely alone upon drawing support and legitimation from the Treaty of Establishment of the European Economic Community (the Treaty of Rome). This Treaty's authority is primarily limited to economic matters and only in a marginal sense can it be extended to embrace cultural affairs. The basic rights that it contains with respect to the freedom to supply goods and services and to establish businesses are geared towards economic activities and do not incorporate the right to freedom of communications with any legally-defined reference to cultural activities. Therefore, the European Commission has attempted to combine Article Ten of the European Convention on Human Rights with the EEC Treaty in such a manner that the entrepreneurial activities of broadcasters may be covered by a unitary (if complex) basic right. The combination of those freedoms that are provided by the EEC Treaty and those basic rights that are designated by the European Convention on Human Rights applies

> ... also to the freedom, guaranteed under Community law, to supply services within the Community as manifested in the freedom of cross-frontier broadcasting, on the one hand, and to the fundamental right, enshrined in the Convention on Human Rights, to the freedom of expression regardless of frontiers as manifested in the free flow of broadcasts, on the other.[13]

This EEC initiative should be seen against the background of more general endeavours to break-up the existing national structures of broadcasting and to create similar internal market conditions to those that already pertain for the press.[14] They require the transfer of the market model to the field of broadcasting.

By means of this combination of two basic rights, with very different legal qualities, two objectives are to be achieved. Article Ten of the European Convention which protects the free expression and dissemination of communicated messages, but not the economic activity of employing communication for commercial purposes, will be enriched with the additional legal ingredient of freedom to supply services and establish business. Conversely, the predominantly economics-oriented freedoms contained in the EEC Treaty will receive the cultural legal dimension of Article Ten of the European Convention. The designed consequence is to endow the European Commission with a new freedom of manoeuvre within a framework of EC economic liberalism.

However, broadcasting freedom, understood as the freedom to provide services and establish businesses, is not consistent with the traditional West European model of national broadcasting regulation and public-service broadcasting. In the end it may be equated with broadcasting according to the market model. In its Green Paper for the Establishment of the Common Market for Broadcasting Especially by Satellite and Cable, the European Commission has not directly striven towards this goal. Instead it has restricted itself for the moment to the question of the free distribution of broadcast programmes (by advocating, *inter alia*, a lowest common denominator of advertising regulation). It did not treat the issue of freedom to establish businesses in the Green Paper. This reticence can be considered to be of a tactical nature. The overall strategy seems to be aimed at establishing a similar kind of broadcasting market in Western Europe to that which already exists in other economic affairs – and the new media present the opportunity.

Should the European Commission succeed in this design, it would almost certainly mean the end of a West European tradition of broadcasting regulation based more upon cultural than upon economic principles. Such an outcome seems all the more likely when one considers that the concept of trusteeship does not figure at all in those issues for which the European Commission recommends a legal harmonisation. The Green Paper addresses itself to advertising regulation, copyright law, the protection of public order and safety and laws relating to the protection of personal rights; these are areas of regulation which can (or must) be dealt with even in the market model. By contrast, the European Commission formulates no suggestions that trusteeship-commitments might be imposed upon broadcasters – for instance, in order to foster and stimulate the democratic processes of the European Community or European cultural traditions. Such aims – to which the Commission is definitely politically committed – are not, it appears, to be covered in its efforts towards a legal restructuring of broadcasting.

5. *From Primacy of Communicator and Recipient of Information to Primacy of the Entrepreneur*

The eclipse of the political and cultural rights to freedom by the right to economic freedom goes along with a shift in emphasis of state regulation itself. The basic right of freedom of communication protects the communicator and the recipient of information in equal measure. This right has been expressly established by both the US Supreme Court and the West German Federal Constitutional Court. Thus the Federal Constitutional Court reasons that freedom of the media refers to communication as a process; and that protection should be assured for *both* the freedom to express and disseminate opinions *and* the freedom to receive full knowledge about, and to inform oneself by, opinions that have been expressed.[15] The US Supreme Court reached a similar conclusion when it established that '... it is the right of the viewers and listeners, not the right of the broadcasters, which is paramount'.[16] The legitimation and even necessity of state regulation of broadcasting derives, on the one hand, from the impossibility of all citizens becoming broadcasters or gaining access to transmission facilities, and on the other hand, from the dependence of listeners and viewers on the 'information-content' of broadcasting itself. The two Courts emphasise, in addition, the risk of misuse of the medium by governments or by private interests. The broadcasters have to act as fiduciaries or proxies with obligations to present those views which are representative of their communities and which would otherwise, by necessity, be barred from the airwaves. Moreover, the West German Federal Constitutional Court draws attention to the suggestive power, the danger of misuse of the media for the purpose of gaining a one-sided influence on public opinion; the Court considers broadcasting to be a particularly important medium and a significant factor in the process of the formation of public opinion. The risk of one-sided influence gives further grounds for the legitimation of regulation, even in the event of the diminishing (or disappearing) relevance of other traditional justifications – such as the shortage of broadcasting frequencies and the fact that broadcasting makes great demands on financial resources.

In the transition towards the market model this orientation towards wider public interests in communications is threatened with oblivion. The citizen is left with the discretionary role as a potential communicator, who is 'free' to establish himself as a broadcaster. If he is not in a position to do so, the result is not counted as particularly unjust (and in need of change), since in reality this situation applies in other areas of market activity as well. Not all markets are equally accessible. As a recipient (consumer), however, the citizen figures indirectly in the enjoyment of broadcasting freedom. The significance is especially clear in the case of broadcasting financed by advertising revenue. The true partners of the broadcasters are the advertisers, not the recipients (consumers). The communications- or information-interests of the recipients (consumers) in the pure market model are only relevant to the extent that the satisfaction of any particular group of consumers is in the interests of an increase in advertising revenue or the attainment of a favourable relation between programme expenditure and advertising revenue. It has often been demonstrated by media economists that, in this state of affairs, not all consumers' interests are satisfied in the same measure, and that many remain unsatisfied.[17]

This problem of the inadequate satisfaction of communications-interests loses its relevance for law when the legal protection of basic rights is no longer understood in its traditional sense. If broadcasting freedom comes to be conceived of as primarily entrepreneurial freedom, then deficits of any broader character are no longer open to diagnosis and remedy. Such a pattern of thinking is unmistakably evident in some (recent) literature on the subject.[18] The interests of the consumer do still receive some mention: in the premise that the market indirectly satisfies consumer-interests and, moreover, that it still does so, in spite of its many shortcomings, better than any other regulatory instrument.

6. From a Culturally-based to an Economically-based Legal Regulation

A change of emphasis in legal considerations of broadcasting can be generally observed from a primacy of cultural concerns to a primacy of economics. Because of the federal structure of West Germany, the resulting conflict is emerging on a special level as well. In the Federal Republic regulatory competence for cultural affairs — including broadcasting — lies with the eleven *Bundesländer*. The result has been a fragmentation of broadcasting law, which is, in turn, an obstacle to the establishment of a national broadcasting market. In view of the new communications technologies, especially satellite, this state of affairs appears as an anachronism, since it jeopardises the uniformity of regulation that is necessary for expansion of the market.[19]

It is, therefore, no coincidence that many contributions to the literature on the subject consider how the possibility of central (federal) competence might be achieved for the purpose of the establishment of a standardised broadcasting market.[20] The simplest means would seem to be the classification of the subject under economic law, since the federation is already competent to regulate economic affairs. Consequently, there are currently proposals to displace *Land* media-legislation by federal economic legislation.[21] In the process of transition to the market model of broadcasting, this possibility seems imminent. In accordance with the market model state regulation would be limited to safeguarding the beneficient functioning of the market — for instance, in the form of controls over cartels and mergers. Accordingly, the West German *Monopolkommission* (monopoly commission) has suggested that federal anti-trust mechanisms should be extended to the field of broadcasting.[22] Such standardisation of regulatory authority, which anyhow lies in the interest of economic forces, will be inevitably accompanied by other substantive changes, namely a renunciation of legal preoccupations with cultural concerns. The advantages for the broadcasting economy are clear. Fundamentally, in the process of tranfer to the market model of broadcasting, there is a general and readily discernible tendency to dispense with an established body of detailed media law and replace it with a more general body of economic law.

THE SYMBOLIC-RITUAL SIGNIFICANCE OF STATE REGULATION IN THE PERIOD OF TRANSITION FROM THE 'TRUSTEE MODEL' TO THE 'MARKET MODEL'

The transition towards the market model requires a fundamental transformation of the broadcasting system and in particular of the state's influence within it. In the market model, at any rate in its pure form, the demands of the state on programming activity are alien and improper. The state's role is limited to the fulfilment of certain routine functions: for instance, the granting of licences in order to avoid chaos on the airwaves or in cable systems. In addition, the state may apply general regulatory mechanisms for economic affairs, in order to guarantee economic competition or to assure proper economic practice – for example, in the form of copyright laws. At the most, certain precautionary requirements on the substantive content of programmes are made, in order to counter those malpractices and dangers against which the state has anyhow a general obligation to offer protection – for instance, the prevention of pornography or the protection of vulnerable youth. In the wake of deregulation, the US broadcasting system has approached this model to a great extent. By contrast, in Western Europe, undergoing at present an upheaval of its traditional broadcasting systems, this market model has not as yet been realised. Regulations of many and diverse kinds still exist or are being enacted. Of particular evidence in this process are attempts to save elements of the trustee model. In comparison with developments in the United States it is striking that many West Europeans are currently expending great energy on the introduction of regulations and supervisory jurisdictions that have just been dismantled there.[23] This situation seems surprising when American deregulation has been justified by reference to the inadequacy of regulation for the fulfilment of broadcasting's purposes, to its dysfunctional side-effects and to the disproportionately excessive bureaucratic, financial and temporal expenditure that it necessitates. In the United States, it is claimed that regulations impede or frustrate economic competition and therefore contradict (and are inconsistent with) the mode of operation of the market model.

West European confidence in regulatory mechanisms of the kind that have just been abolished in the United States might be justified by the argument that different conditions in Western Europe promise better regulatory outcomes. However, this argument is dubious to the extent that 'regulatory deficits' are ultimately attributable to the fundamental contradiction between state regulation and the mode of operation of the market model of broadcasting. It could be maintained that the prospect of positive regulatory outcomes in Western Europe is in no way any greater than in the American case, but that for political reasons there can be at present no renunciation of legal regulations that give (at least) the semblance of state regulation. Such a semblance might be important in order to deflate political resistance, not only from the established public-service broadcasters but also, and above all, from large sections of the general public. In the Federal Republic at any rate, the introduction of private commercial broadcasting according to the market model – satellite and cable television – is in no way a politically uncontested issue. In many political camps, for example, the Social Democratic Party (SPD), trade unions, the churches and the Green Party, it is either opposed or, at the very least, is provoking demands for guarantees of trusteeship commitments and for the continued existence of the state's regulatory responsibility.

In the Federal Republic resistance flows also from the legal system. As recently as 1981, the Federal Constitutional Court formulated strict standards and requirements for the broadcasting system in face of the advent of the new media. In particular, it stressed that, according to constitutional law, effective guarantees for the fulfilment of trusteeship commitments remain both indisputable and indispendable.[24] Correspondingly, in the Federal Republic this political conflict can also assume the character and form of a legal conflict. In order to win the next battle at the level of constitutional law (it is anticipated that a ruling will be made in 1986) the protagonists of private commercial broadcasting – the Christian Democratic/Christian Social Parties (CDU/CSU) and the Free Democrats (FDP) supported by the powerful newspaper and magazine publishers – have to produce new media laws that guarantee pluralism and diversity. In the choice of regulatory mechanisms the Federal Constitutional Court allows the legislators a certain freedom of manoeuvre. However, the functioning or malfunctioning of the regulatory mechanisms that have now been chosen is not yet empirically verifiable; the new media are still in a developmental phase in the Federal Republic. It is, therefore, possible that, in examining the adequacy of these new regulations, the Constitutional Court might be reserved in its judicial pronouncements. All the same, these regulations must be so designed that they (at least) convey the appearance of adequacy and suitability. The regulatory mechanisms that have now been chosen are being presented to the Federal Constitutional Court as test-cases requiring judgment.[25] If the Court is satisfied with their suitability, the breakthrough of private commercial broadcasting will have been achieved and the economic interests of the commercial broadcasters legally endorsed without any damage to their interests having been incurred. If the Court questions their suitability, the option of stricter regulatory mechanisms remains.

It is possible to conclude that the introduction of private commercial broadcasting with strong elements of the 'market-model' into the Federal Republic is dependent upon accompanying regulatory measures of a symbolic-ritual nature. Similar potential for political conflict and legal dispute exists in other West European countries too. Here similar requirements will follow, varying according to the specifics of each national case. A change of paradigm in broadcasting-policy does not allow for easy classification. Nevertheless, the fact remains that the enlistment of political support and the adoption of measures to deflate protest are always indispensable in managing radical change. To this extent, the question arises of whether the new media laws and regulations can be seen as part of a strategy to gain political support for the paradigm change.

This question can be addressed by means of the concept of the symbolic use of politics, which Murray Edelman has applied from the very beginning to the field of telecommunications.[26] The applicability of this concept does not presuppose that all actors involved in the establishment of a new broadcasting system consciously feel that no concrete and positive regulatory outcomes can possibly be achieved. It should also be stressed that this account makes no claim that members of legislative organs would intentionally employ regulatory mechanisms simply in order to manipulate public opinion. The following analysis is not concerned with intention, but rather with function. At any rate, it is intended to be an indication of the possible symbolic-ritual function of regulations. It questions the enactment of regulations, the effectiveness of which remains open to considerable doubt, especially upon the basis of experience of other broadcasting systems, notably the American.

In the following, for the sake of illustration and without any claim to offer a comprehensive picture, a number of regulatory mechanisms will be examined in order to assess their suitability for the efficient regulation of West European broadcasting. Analysis focuses on those regulations, which seem likely to have primarily symbolic-ritual, support-building effects.

1. The possibilities for Broadcasters to Evade Regulations

If the suggestions of the European Commission that are contained in the Green Paper 'Television without Frontiers' are realised, national governments will still remain empowered to regulate their national broadcasters. On the other hand, the result will effectively mean the disappearance of national regulatory authority *vis-à-vis* the distribution of programmes by outside broadcasters (foreign or otherwise), for instance by means of cable or of satellites. In this way, broadcasters who operate on a European scale will gain the opportunity of establishing their centres of activity in that country (or those countries) where the weakest state regulations have been enacted. They will then be in a position to broadcast their programmes simultaneously in all the countries of the European Community, without being much encumbered by regulations and without being bound to observe the stricter regulations in force in other (target) countries. The European Commission may claim to be respecting the principle of national regulatory authority in the field of broadcasting. However, such a claim is only accurate on the level of legal superficiality. In practice, national regulatory authority in broadcasting affairs will be wide open to erosion – from the point of view of the European Commission, a thoroughly commendable result. The situation thus created can produce a situation in which many states still claim to subject broadcasters to the trustee model, while in reality many programmes that generally escape such regulations will be distributed in their national areas. The beginnings of this state of affairs exist already — without any involvement of the European Commission. Prototypes of the new model are the programmes of SKY channel and RTL Plus. Moreover, the distribution of such programmes has an effect on those broadcasters who stay at home. They have to strive, under new conditions of increased economic and journalistic competition, to absorb the competitive disadvantage from which they suffer in the face of these foreign broadcasters *because* they themselves remain constrained by national regulations. The possibility cannot be excluded that these broadcasters will in turn try as hard as possible to evade national regulations.

A structurally comparable possibility for evading regulations is offered by West German broadcasting law. Individual *Bundesländer* have now enacted new broadcasting regulations consequent upon the advent of the new media; they approximate partially to the market model while also remaining close to the trustee model. Yet nearly all *Bundesländer* permit now the distribution of programmes that are produced by broadcasters from other *Bundesländer* in their cable systems, without subjecting this distribution to the same (possibly stricter) regulatory requirements to which they themselves subject their resident broadcasters. As a result, broadcasters will be increasingly tempted to establish their centres of activity in those *Bundesländer* that demand the least rigorous regulatory requirements for broadcasting. They will then be in a position to distribute freely these programmes to all *Bundesländer*. In this way, the stricter regulations in force in other *Bundesländer* — typically SPD controlled — are threatened with ineffectiveness and circumvention with impunity. Those *Bundesländer* with stricter standards may bedeck themselves politically with regulations to safeguard trusteeship-commitments. However, they are still left with no real possibilities for concretely accomplishing these standards.

2. Flexibility of Norms and the Interests of the Broadcasters

Even if in general broadcasters do not evade regulations by moving their centres of activity, there is still no assurance that regulations will have any significant effectiveness. Broadcasting is a politically sensitive activity. Intrusion of the state and especially censorship contradict the liberal-democratic tradition of basic human rights. Accordingly, broadcasting regulations have to operate as far as possible without such distortions. Furthermore and ideally, regulation must actually preserve the independence of broadcasting *vis-à-vis* the state and other powers. With respect to the technicalities of regulation, it is very difficult to achieve any overall central control over the direction of change in these circumstances. At least in theory, all liberal-democratic states should exercise restraint above all with regard to the possibility of interference in the field of programming. Since responsibility for programming should reside with the broadcasters, confidence must be placed in their journalistic competence and a large measure of leeway must be granted to them in the creation and organisation of programming. In that case, however, the broadcasters are presented with much opportunity to exploit this good faith for the purpose of evading those broadcasting regulations that run counter to their interests.

A further problem ensues. Aims like diversity of broadcasting content, orientation towards the public interest and consideration of the interests of minorities (among others) are not amenable to legal definition in an unambiguously subsumptive manner. Regulation of broadcasting is characterised typically by the vagueness of many of its legal prescriptions and rulings, which allow for various interpretations and applications. Typical too are blanket-clauses, which lay down in a general way a desired aim, but which do not precisely stipulate the means to achieving it. Only exceptionally do aims permit translation into quantitively measurable dimensions. In such cases – for instance, the fixing of percentages for particular types of programme or the setting of quotas for programmes of local or national/supranational (e.g. EC) origin – there remains a certain vagueness over the precise definition of programmes' qualities. What, for example, is public interest programming? How do co-productions and co-financed films and series count? In so far as broadcasters have room for manoeuvre in the process of applying the rules, they can practise a certain degree of evasion if they choose so to do – and, more especially, if they are presented with temptation to do so, as a result of a paradigm-shift in broadcasting policy.

There are hardly any other areas of social regulation, in which regulatory and supervisory bodies work with so few substantive guidelines. This uncertainty can result in cases where the supervisory body actually finds itself prevented from behaving in what it holds to be the correct way. If the supervisory body does not practise any self-limitation on its activity, then broadcasters can and will maintain that regulatory measures amount to censorship or that, at the very least, they have an emasculating effect on programmes, leading to a diminution of diversity and the prevention of a wide and open debate. Of course, independent-mindedness of broadcasters is a powerful check on censorship, but it also opens up avenues for the evasion of regulations. In many instances, broadcasters will succeed in finding public support for *both* these causes.

In practice, regulation can be accomplished most easily if the supervisory body accommodates itself to the broadcasters and provides only for such substantive regulation as appears appropriate to the latter. The consequence is the well-known phenomenon of agency-capture. Clearly, much hinges upon the interests of the broadcasters. Equally clearly, it is a matter of great significance whether these broadcasters see their role primarily in terms of the trustee model – and if they are adequately cushioned from too much competition – or if they operate primarily in terms of the market model.

The US Federal Communications Commission has often gone out of its way to co-operate with broadcasters or with the representatives of their interests – in particular, the National Association of Broadcasters (NAB).[27] An appropriate comment on this process of accommodation has been made by Murray Edelman: '... Administrators are thereby able to avoid the sanctions of politically powerful groups by accepting their premises as valid; while at the same time they justify this behaviour in the verbal formulas provided in the rules'.[28] Examples of such behaviour are easily found.[29] In just such a way, for many years the FCC has taken as a standard for its own activities the self-defined (economic) rules of the broadcasting industry – such as the NAB-Code – and sometimes too it has pressed for an appropriate self-regulation by the NAB.[30] In so far as broadcasters have not carried out their programming duties according to the conceptions of the FCC, the latter has reacted mostly by the policy of raised eyebrows. By contrast, there is no known occasion when the revoking of, or the refusal to renew, a licence has been justified by simple reference to breaches of programming regulations.[31]

Little success, too, greeted the efforts of the FCC when it called upon broadcasters to increase the supply of educational and children's programming. The economic incentives of an advertising-based broadcasting system do little to encourage the provision of specialised programming for children. In a special policy statement the FCC asked the broadcasters to make a 'meaningful effort' to increase the amount of programming for children and air a 'reasonable amount' of programmes for children designed to educate and inform and not simply to entertain.[32] In face of the difficulties of having such demands realised, and in consideration of the opposed interests of the broadcasters, the FCC refrained, however, from imposing mandatory programming rules or quantitative renewal processing guidelines for children's programming. In view of the renunciation of these concrete steps the appeal for more suitable childrens' programmes could not be followed through into practice. If one accepts the (admittedly controversial) analysis of a special task force to evaluate childrens' programmes, this policy of the FCC was a failure.[33]

To the extent that FCC regulations contained quantitive programme guidelines (for instance, for public affairs or local programmes) there is virtually no indication that they have had a lasting influence on the programming practice of the broadcasters. At least the FCC admits that '... the existing programming amounts are largely a reflection of market forces rather than our guidelines'.[34] Evidently, either these guidelines or the level of enforcement (or both) were in tune with the interests of the broadcasters.

There is also much reason to maintain that the Fairness Doctrine, so praised in Western Europe, has not generally achieved its aims.[35] The Fairness Doctrine includes in its general content a dual licensee obligation: first, the broadcasters are expected to devote a reasonable amount of broadcast time to the discussion of controversial issues. Secondly, broadcasters are expected to do so fairly, i.e. to afford reasonable opportunity for the presentation of opposing viewpoints. However, it can be argued with much plausibility that in practice the Fairness Doctrine has actually had more of a counterproductive effect: it seems to have reduced the amount of coverage devoted to controversial matters instead of increasing it. At least, the obligation to present controversial issues has not been enforced in practice. This commitment was called the 'forgotten half' of the Fairness Doctrine.[36] Issue-oriented programming is traditionally supposed as having particularly little economic value: therefore, it is not surprising that a duty, contained in the Fairness Doctrine, to produce such programmes voluntarily has been carried out only to a very limited extent.

In spite of this hardly encouraging experience, the West German legislators in the *Bundesländer* are placing their confidence in a kind of regulatory mechanics (although not in all detailed elements) that the FCC has already dispensed with or, as with the Fairness Doctrine, would prefer to discard. Anchored in recent West German media legislation are programming principles that are similarly general and vague as those formulated in the US Communications Act. Commitments to broadcast programmes of national or European origin are only generally specified: an 'appropriate proportion' is demanded, without any narrower quantification. The American Fairness Doctrine is taken as the model for commitment to balanced programming. In this case, the standard is diluted still further. The programmes (or channel) produced by each new broadcaster do not have to provide an overall balance; rather only all of the new programmes (or channels) in their totality are expected to amount to such a balance. This expectation reflects a faith that more channels, and the very many more programmes made possible by the new media, will introduce a quasi-automatic new pluralism. To this extent, there is even a lack of any definite legal addressee of the commitment. Without legal addressees, however, a commitment is likely to be without consequence; at least it is not easily capable of sanction.

In a very general way, advertisers are forbidden to influence programming. It is not clearly explained, though, how this particular commitment is to be translated into practice, or how broadcasters might be prevented from so organising their programming that it reflects the best interests of the advertising industry (e.g. programming contents adjusted to special commercial messages or with prime time swamped with popular entertainment carrying intensive slots of advertising and more esoteric and informative programmes relegated to the late hours). In so far as can be seen, nowhere have thorough analyses been conducted in order to examine whether there is any prospect that such generally formulated regulations will influence the behaviour of the broadcasters, or whether these regulations are adequate for achieving their professed aims.

The suitability of the kind of regulations contained in this spate of West German legislation by the *Bundesländer* was originally to have been tested within the framework of so-called 'pilot projects' – namely, four cable-television experiments, which were recommended by a government commission in the 1970s, and which were finally organised and opened, after much delay and political disagreement, in the period 1984–85. However, broadcasting with strong elements of the market model has already been introduced in the Federal Republic without waiting for the results of these (tardy) experiments or even without any evidence that such regulation could be effective. It seems that the question of the effectiveness of new regulations was very much a subordinate consideration for the politicians concerned. However, the enactment of new media legislation was admirably suited to giving the appearance of state responsibility and thus to achieving a more easy (and legitimised) introduction of a new segment of broadcasting approximating to the market model.

3. Regulation as a Reflection of the Economic Self-interests of Broadcasters

Even if rules are formulated explicitly and in a manner capable of sanction, they can still remain ineffectual in practice. This outcome is only to be expected if the principles behind the rules are pitched at so low a level that they can be observed anyway by broadcasters pursuing their own narrower interests;

that is to say, if such principles are not likely to be negated, even if the actual legal provisions are dispensed with or fall into neglect. A prototype, in US broadcasting law, was provided by the (unofficial) commercial guidelines designed to prevent an over-commercialisation of broadcasting. The FCC established guidelines that were devoted to the amount of spot-advertising. These rules derived from standards self-imposed by the NAB. Roughly speaking, the television stations were expected to broadcast no more than 16 minutes of advertising per hour. Analysis of the actual behaviour of broadcasters has indicated that the proportion of advertising has remained considerably beneath this threshold. Now the guidelines have been abolished without triggering any appreciable increase in the amount of spot-advertising. Obviously the principle established by the FCC to prevent over-commercialisation had lain within the bounds of the broadcasters' self-interest from the start. FCC regulators claimed the regulations to be effective, even though observance of the principle that they had adopted was presumably not attributable to the existence of regulation. The subsequent deregulation was a thoroughly consistent development.

Despite such findings, the European Commission is proposing to limit advertising by West European broadcasters to 20 per cent of the total daily emission. This limit corresponds to an average of 15 minutes per hour. The proposal of the European Commission tallies with the amount of advertising that is provided for by most of the West German new media laws enacted in the *Bundesländer*. However, the corresponding norms leave it to the broadcasters to decide the precise times of the day in which they will run their advertising. Consequently, they have leeway to exceed considerably 15 minutes per hour, for example during prime-time viewing. Until now West Europeans have not been accustomed, in the same way and to the same degree as in the US, to spot-advertising: in many cases only block-advertising at predefined times and in limited measure has been permitted. Hence most West European broadcasters would probably not want to exceed the 20 per cent threshold for fear of driving away their audience. In other words, the norms allow the broadcasters sufficient room for manoeuvre within bounds that will probably meet with their satisfaction. In all likelihood, the restrictions will not be determinants of the actual behaviour of the broadcasters. The new regulations are, as regard content, a rough reflection of the economic interests of the broadcasters.

4. *The Weakening of Procedures for Legal Action in the Regulatory Process*

It is obvious that not all rules correspond necessarily to the self-interest of broadcasters. In this respect, it is significant whether regulations are actually carried through to implementation. The mere existence of a legal norm does not mean that it will be followed in practice. An important (if not the only) precondition for the observance of regulations is the intensity of enforcement, backed up by the resort to sanctions. Hence, it is especially important to consider the question of legal procedure (*Verfahren*) that follows from breach of regulatory law. Who may plead an offence? How are violations established (recording of broadcasts, etc)? Does punishment lie within the discretion of the supervisory body?

The importance of procedure can also be studied in the practice of the FCC. For instance, the weak application of the Fairness Doctrine can be attributed partly to the high legal hurdles that exist for initiating a case over Fairness. In the United States, the observance of programme regulations increased considerably when not only competitors, but also citizens' groups received the right to participate in legal proceedings over broadcasting issues. Now the FCC is attempting to complement deregulation of material regulatory commitments with a reform of these proceedings. As a consequence of the reform it will become more difficult for complaints to be lodged about alleged violations of regulatory law. In addition to abolition or dilution of material regulatory commitments the possibility of proving a violation of the regulations will be made more difficult (replacing the programme logs by a quarterly issues/programme list requirement: elimination of long-term audits). Moreover, the possibility of proving breaches of commitments will be restricted; for example: an allegation of failure to present amounts of non-entertainment will not be heard.

In view of the importance of legal action for the realisation of regulatory norms, it is striking that the recent West German *Land* laws have only made elementary efforts to prescribe procedures and norms of legal action. Otherwise, it falls to the supervisory bodies themselves to enact subsequent rules of procedure. Thus arises, however, a potential for *de facto* deregulation. Either through the failure to enact suitable rules of procedure or through the subsequent adjustment of such rules, a state of affairs could be reached whereby infringements of certain commitments might be penalised only under the most difficult conditions. The choice not to anchor in law effective procedural safeguards, designed to promote the observance of regulations, can be taken as an indication of the desire to make legal action a flexible last resort. The general public is usually even less aware of the potential to influence developments through procedural safeguards than it is about substantive norms. For the purpose of political legitimation or support-building it suffices therefore to establish general rules.

5. Deployment of Symbols in Order to Strengthen Confidence in the New Model of Broadcasting

In the Federal Republic the transition to the market model of broadcasting means a turning away from the so-called internal-pluralistic model of regulation. According to this model, representatives of diverse social groups – for instance, the churches, the trade unions and the employers' associations – have a say in matters relating to the personnel, financial and programming policies of the broadcasting organisations. Organs of internal-pluralism, in the shape of broadcasting councils, are theoretically the sovereign bodies *within* the various broadcasting organisations and a key characteristic of the West German public-service broadcasting system. However, the right of representatives of such socially-relevant groups to have a say in the organisation of broadcasting contradicts the interests of the new proprietors in determining, alone and according to their own requirements, the operations that they seek to conduct within the market model. Correspondingly, no such right is provided in the new media laws. Instead, elements of internal pluralism are found at a completely different level. Several new media laws provide for an internal-pluralistic composition of *external* supervisory and licensing bodies.

In this case, the label of internal-pluralism is attached to a new but different kind of institution. In public discussion it is maintained by the protagonists of the market model that internal pluralism remains anchored within the new model of broadcasting. They are remarkably silent with respect to the fact that these external supervisory bodies have far fewer competences than the internal-pluralistic organs *within* the traditional broadcasting organisations. On the other hand, certain measures that they are now able to take in the field of programming might even prove to be open to legal interpretation as censorship and therefore unconstitutional — which was certainly not the case for the internal organs. Besides this, the new supervisory bodies are themselves restricted to examination of questions of strict legality (*Rechtmässigkeit*). They cannot take into consideration questions of suitability (*Zweckmässigkeit*) of programming. In this way, an important legitimation for the participation of diverse social interests in broadcasting affairs is lost. A prominent protagonist of the market model has quite rightly said that, in view of the weakness of their competences, these external supervisory bodies can be regarded as 'harmless decoration'.[37]

The adoption of the principle of internal pluralism within a quite different model of broadcasting seems to have primarily a symbolic significance. It suggests to the general public that a tried and tested element of the traditional West German broadcasting system will remain preserved — although care has been taken to ensure that it cannot have much effect.

6. *Intensity of Implementation as An Indication of Regulatory Function*

These remarks should illustrate that within the market model at various levels regulatory mechanisms can and will be provided for, but that they exclude, or at least weaken, conflict between the economic and editorial interests of new broadcasting entrepreneurs and state regulation. It is not appropriate to conclude that there are no new regulatory initiatives that run counter to the economic interests of the new broadcasters and that are opposed by them. Examples of such regulations are measures to prevent media concentration or the ban (in West Germany) on the interruption of programmes with advertising. However, even these regulations can be circumvented. National regulatory measures against media concentration are to a great extent powerless in the face of multinational concentration. Programming can be doctored to suit the requirements of advertising. In the age of transnational broadcasting by satellite both kinds of regulation can be ignored and consequently eroded with ease. Yet it cannot be in doubt that such regulations contradict the interests of the new broadcasting industry and could yet be adopted at the level of supranational regulation (e.g. by the European Community). To this extent, it remains to be seen whether they are applied without exception and whether regulatory norms stay in force in the long run. Should these regulations not be implemented or should they, after the new model of broadcasting has been established, be abolished, then it would be an indication of their symbolic-ritual function of support-building for the paradigm shift from the trustee model to the market model of broadcasting.

CONCLUSION: IMPLICATIONS FOR POLICY

This chapter's concentration on the symbolic-ritual function of regulations should not be misconstrued as an argument that broadcasting regulation has *only* this function. Regulation has also the 'advantage' of preventing an uncontrolled proliferation of broadcasters. Accordingly, it provides existing and would-be broadcasters with a degree of economic and political calculability about the development of broadcasting. Whoever receives a licence during the start-up phase of the new media has, on the basis of state regulations, a good chance of benefiting from a protected existence. Regulations obstruct the entry of new competitors. Taken together with long franchise periods, the law's acceptance of a protected existence for certain broadcasters provides them with a secure environment, far removed from the use of the threat of licence-withdrawal as a sanction for misconduct.

As a consequence, there are grounds for assuming that broadcasting regulation has important functions in the process of transition to the market model. For the fulfilment of these functions, it is a matter of less relevance whether the regulatory measures are suited to safeguarding trusteeship and diversity, values projected in a highly visible political manner. Apparently, it seems far more important that broadcasting regulation permits a politically and economically 'well-ordered' entrance into a new age of broadcasting in accordance with the market model.

Once broadcasting in accordance with the market model has established itself politically in Western Europe, it can be presumed that a second wave of deregulation will follow and that it will involve the elimination of these (symbolic-ritual) rules. Already this stage has been reached in the United States, where previous broadcasting regulations came to be regarded as an obstacle to the further expansion of telecommunications. At the same time the American citizens had become so used to commercial broadcasting that it was possible to dispense with even the appearance of state regulations. At least, Europe has still time.

NOTES

This contribution was translated from the German original by Peter Humphreys.

1. e.g. R. Kuhn (ed.) *The Politics of Broadcasting* (London: Croom Helm, 1985); K. Dyson and P. Humphreys, 'The New Media in Britain and France', *Rundfunk und Fernsehen*, Vol.33, 4 (1985), pp.362–79; W.A. Mahle, *Grossbritannien. Ein Modell für die Bundesrepublik?* (Berlin: Spiess Verlag, 1984).
2. On France see R. Kuhn, 'France: the End of Government Monopoly', in Kuhn (ed.) *op. cit.*; on West-Germany see W. Hoffmann-Riem 'Medienfreiheit und der aussenplurale Rundfunk', *Archiv des öffentlichen Rechts*. Vol.109 (1985), pp.304–68; W. Hoffmann-Riem, 'Tendenzen der Kommerzialisierung im Rundfunksystem', *Rundfunk und Fernsehen*, Vol. 32 (1984), pp.32–50.
3. See FCC, *Report and Order in the Matter of Deregulation of Radio*, 84 F.C.C. 2d 968 (1981); *Report and Order in the Matter of the Revision of Programming and Commercialization*

Policies, Ascertainment Requirements, and Program Log Requirements for Commercial Television Stations, 98 F.C.C. 2d 1076 (1984).
4. On Italy see F. Böckelmann *Italien: Selbstregulierung eines 'freien' Rundfunkmarktes* (Berlin: Spiess Verlag, 1984); W. Meinel, 'Die Rundfunkstruktur in Italien. Ein zur Ruhe gekommener freier Markt?', *Media Perspektiven*, 1985, pp. 401–11.
5. On Britain see R. Collins, 'Broadband Black Death cuts queues. The Information Society and the UK', *Media, Culture and Society*, 1983, pp. 275–96; T. Hollins, *Beyond Broadcasting: Into the Cable Age*. (London, British Film Institute, 1984).
6. On the most recent West German media laws see R. Ricker, *Privatrundfunk-Gesetze im Bundesstaat* (München: C. H. Beck'sche Verlagsbuchhandlung, 1985).
7. For a general discussion see S. Breyer, *Regulation and its Reform* (Cambridge, MA, and London: Harvard University Press, 1982). E. Bardach and R. A. Kagan (eds.), *Social Regulation. Strategies for Reform* (San Fransisco: Institute for Contemporary Studies, 1972).
8. On these developments see e.g. the reports in *Neue Medien* No. 9 (Feb. 1986), pp. 28–31, 96–105.
9. *Entscheidungen des Bundesverfassungsgerichts*, Vol. 57, pp. 295–335, esp. 320, 323.
10. On the historical development compare D. Stammler, *Die Presse als soziale und verfassungsrechtliche Institution* (Berlin: Duncker & Humblot, 1971), pp. 88, 91, 97 *et seq.*; T. J. Emerson, *The System of Freedom of Expression* (New York: Random House, 1970); V. Blasi, 'The Checking Value in the First Amendment Theory', *American Bar Foundation*, Samuel Pool Weaver Constitutional Series, No. 3, pp. 522–649, esp. 529 *et seq.*
11. H. H. Klein, *Die Rundfunkfreiheit*, (München: C. H. Beck'sche Verlagsbuchhandlung, 1978) pp. 41 *et seq.*; J. Wolf, *Medienfreiheit und Medienunternehmen* (Berlin: Duncker & Humblot, 1985).
12. Commission of the European Communities, *Television without Frontiers – Green Paper on the Establishment of the Common Market for Broadcasting, especially by Satellite and Cable*. COM (1984) 300 final, pp. 127 *et seq.*; see also I. Schwartz, 'Rundfunk und EWG-Vertrag', in Schwarze (ed.), *Fernsehen ohne Grenzen*, (Baden-Baden: Nomos Verlagsgesellschaft, 1985), pp. 45, esp. 73 *et seq.*
13. EC Commission, *Television without Frontiers, op. cit.*, p. 128.
14. Compare the Statement of Commissioner R. Narjes, in *Verhandlungen des Europäischen Parlaments* No. 1, 282/234 of 11 March 1982.
15. *Entscheidungen des Bundesverfassungsgerichts*, Vol. 57, p. 319.
16. Red Lion Broadcasting Co v. Federal Communications Commission, 395 U.S. 367, 390 (1969).
17. Classical analyses on media economics are B. M. Owen, *Economics and Freedom of Expression* (Cambridge, MA: Ballinger Publishing Company, 1975); B. M. Owen, J. H. Beebe and W. G. Manning, Jr., *Television Economics* (Lexington, DC: Heath and Company, 1974); R. G. Noll, M. J. Peck and J. J. McGowan, *Economic Aspects of Television Regulation* (Washington DC, The Brookings Institution, 1973). See further B.-P. Lange, *Kommerzielle Ziele und binnenpluralistische Organisation bei Rundfunkveranstaltern* (Frankfurt: Metzner Verlag, 1980); T. F. Baldwin, M. O. Wirth and J. W. Zenaty, 'The Economics of Per-Program Cable Television', *Journal of Broadcasting*, 22 (1978), pp. 143–55.
18. See the books quoted in note 11. See also M. Bullinger, *Kommunikationsfreiheit im Strukturwandel der Telekommunikation* (Baden-Baden: Nomos Verlagsgesellschaft, 1980).
19. Consequently, Switzerland has amended its Constitution and introduced a central legislative power on broadcasting, see Art. 55 bis Bundesverfassung.
20. See M. Bullinger, *Vom Rundfunk zum elektronischen Versandshandel. Rechtliche Aspekte*, in M. Bullinger *et al.*, *Die elektronische Herausforderung* (Freiburg im Breisgau: Rombach Verlag, 1985) pp. 63, 70, 84; M. Bullinger, 'Satellitenfunk im Bundesstaat', in *Archiv für Presserecht* (1985), pp. 1–14, 7 *et seq.*
21. H. Schneider, 'Die Zuständigkeit des Bundes im Rundfunk- und Fernmeldebereich', in *Festschrift für Karl Carstens*, (Köln/Berlin/Bonn/München: Carl Heymanns Verlag, 1985) pp. 817 *et seq.*; K. Lenk, 'Telekommunikationsrecht und Telekommunikationspolitik' in *Computer und Recht* (1985), pp. 107, 110, 111.
22. See Monopolkommission, *Wettbewerbsprobleme bei der Einführung von privatem Hörfunk und Fernsehen* (Baden-Baden: Nomos Verlagsgesellschaft, 1981).
23. W. Hoffmann-Riem, 'Deregulierung als Konsequenz des Marktrundfunks', *Archiv des öffentlichen Rechts*, Vol. 110 (1985), pp. 529–576.

24. *Entscheidungen des Bundesverfassungsgerichts*, Vol. 57, pp. 320 *et seq.*: see further Vol. 12, p. 205; Vol. 31, p. 314.
25. Constitutional lawsuit against the broadcasting law of Lower Saxony (filed by the SPD-Bundestagsfraktion); constitutional lawsuit against the media law of Baden-Württemberg, (filed by the Süddeutscher Rundfunk, the Südwestfunk, and the SPD-Bundestagsfraktion).
26. M. Edelman, *The Licensing of Radio Services in the United States, 1927–1940*. (Urbana: The University of Illinois Press, 1950).
27. See W. Hoffmann-Riem, *Kommerzielles Fernsehen. Rundfunkfreiheit zwischen ökonomischer Nutzung und staatlicher Regelungsverantwortung: Das Beispiel USA* (Baden-Baden: Nomos Verlagsgesellschaft, 1981), pp. 280 *et seq.*
28. M. Edelman, *The Symbolic Uses of Politics* (Urbana, Chicago and London: University of Illinois Press, 1977), p. 48. Compare further T. Streeter, 'Policy Discourse and Broadcast Practice: The FCC, the US Broadcast Networks and the Discourse of the Marketplace', *Media, Culture and Society*, 1981, pp. 242–62, at 255; W. Hoffmann-Riem, 'Fernsehkontrolle als Ritual? – Überlegungen zur staatlichen Kontrolle im amerikanischen Fernsehen', *Juristenzeitung* (1981), pp. 73–82.
29. See E. G. Krasnow, L. D. Longley and H. A. Terry, *The Politics of Broadcast Regulation* (New York: St. Martin's Press, 3rd edn., 1982); B. Cole and M. Oettinger, *Reluctant Regulators, The FCC and the Broadcast Audience* (Reading: Addison-Wesley, 1978); S. J. Simmons, *The Fairness Doctrine and the Media* (Berkeley and Los Angeles: University of California Press, 1978).
30. 'Television Code' of the National Association of Broadcasters. In the meantime it has been abolished.
31. See Cole and Oettinger, op. cit., p. 134 (see also pp. 200 *et seq.*); B. S. Chamberlin, 'Lessons in Regulating Information Flow: The FCC's Weak Track Record in Interpreting the Public Interest Standard', *North Carolina Law Review*, 60 (1982), pp. 1057–1113, at 1067 *et seq.* and also notes 61, 70.
32. See *FCC, Children's Television Report and Policy Statement*, 50 F.C.C. 2d 1 (1974); see also 55 F.C.C. 2d 691 (1975).
33. *FCC, Television Programming for Children: A Report of the Children's Television Task Force*, October 1979 (not published). A short and milder version of it is published in *FCC, Children's Programming*, 75 F.C.C. 2d 138, 142 *et seq.* (1979). Compare further W. Melody, *Children's TV. The Economics of Exploitation* (New Haven and London: Yale University Press, 1973).
34. FCC, *Commercial TV Stations*, 98 F.C.C., 2d 1089.
35. The FCC has criticised the Fairness Doctrine heavily, see *FCC, Report on the Rules and Regulations Concerning the General Fairness Doctrine Obligations of Broadcast Licensees* of August 23, 1985. See also Simmons.
36. R. A. Kurnit, 'Enforcing the obligation to present controversial issues: the forgotten half of the Fairness Doctrine', *Harvard Civil Rights – Civil Liberties Law Review*, (10), 1975, pp. 137–79.
37. M. Bullinger, 'Elektronische Medien als Marktplatz der Meinungen', *Archiv des öffentlichen Rechts*, Vol. 108 (1983), pp. 161–215 at 201.

European Collaboration in Computing and Telecommunications: A Policy Approach

Claire Shearman

The economic crisis or 'technology gap' said to exist as a consequence of the American and Japanese leads in global information technology markets has been a major theme of debate in Western Europe since the mid 1970s. On the European level, and within the communications sector in particular, this debate has involved the question of the relative merits of a policy of technological collaboration. The problems and prospects inherent in such a strategy together with the appropriateness of the various frameworks for action have been largely considered from a technological and/or economic standpoint. This analysis by contrast addresses some of the political implications underlying the debate. It aims to provide a general overview of recent European initiatives in collaboration in two interrelated areas of the communications sector (computing and telecommunications) and to draw from the various experiences some conclusions about the policies and policy processes involved. Analysis focuses on the major factors shaping the political agenda for collaboration − that is, the perceptions of technology in terms of political influence and the complex distribution of power operating within Western Europe between the national governments and the European Economic Community − before going on to explore the relationship between successful policy implementation and the coherence of the groups of policy actors involved. Finally the relative accountability and level of public debate inherent in the policy process is examined together with some of the long-term implications of the policy-making process in general. Such discussions inevitably require some knowledge of the various collaboration initiatives under way, and so the analysis begins with an overview of the main developments in European collaboration.

EUROPEAN COLLABORATION IN COMPUTING AND TELECOMMUNICATIONS:
A GENERAL OVERVIEW

Recent years have seen an increasing patchwork of collaboration agreements in Western Europe, the mode and type of which have varied from the formal to the informal, from those involving governmental to those involving industrial initiatives and from those within, and outside the framework of the European Economic Community (EC). France, for example, has championed the cause of intra-European co-operation by national policy statements and, in particular, the promotion of the Eureka initiative. Collaboration programmes in information technology (ESPRIT) and telecommunications (RACE) have been fostered within the Community by the European Commission, while industry has developed its own initiatives in the form of projects such as the Bull/Siemens/ICL joint research centre in Munich and the formation in 1985 of the European company ES2 to manufacture 'custom-built' chips.

Where collaboration initiatives at the *governmental* level are concerned, France has been foremost among West European governments in explicitly promoting the idea of European co-operation, mounting something of a national crusade for a united European front in the battle for the world's rapidly expanding electronics and information processing markets. Its prescriptions for recovery have focused primarily on public telecommunications where it has called for the formation of strategic European industrial alliances, the liberalisation of procurement policies, the harmonisation of technical standards together with an increase in joint research efforts and public investment.

By early 1986 the response to French initiatives had been modest. Agreement was reached in early 1985 between CIT Alcatel (France), Siemens (West Germany), Italtel (Italy) and Plessey (UK) to co-operate on R&D in public telecommunications. However, the link-up seems unlikely to produce any real commercial benefits before the 1990s at the earliest. In general, French success in establishing small-scale co-operative ventures in specialised fields, such as the accord with Philips (the Netherlands) in radio-telephone and the 'smart' electronic card, has been tempered by the failure of more ambitious ventures such as the government-sponsored bid by the French Thomson group to take over Grundig (West Germany), the envisaged bilateral agreement with West Germany in joint cellular radio systems and the failure of Anglo-French negotiations to reach agreement on R&D collaboration for future generations of switching equipment and reciprocal market access.

Within France itself, governmental emphasis on European co-operation has not prevented the formation of transatlantic industrial alliances, though the scope of such agreements has tended to remain fairly limited. French state-owned companies, including Compagnie Générale d' Electricité (CGE), Bull and Thomson have signed technical co-operation agreements with American partners including Wang, Hewlett-Packard and Xerox. In 1985–86 controversy arose about the proposed alliance between CGE and American Telephone and Telegraph (AT & T) to provide the French telecommunications authority with a second supplier of public telephone switches (in the wake of the merger of the telecommunications interests of CGE and Thomson). Such a move, which would open up the French public telephone switch market to a major foreign supplier, was also designed to help rescue the troubled ITT subsidiary, Compagnie Générale de Constructions Téléphoniques (CGCT). The memorandum of understanding signed by the companies in June 1985 envisaged AT & T/Philips taking over the 16 per cent share of the French public switching market held by CGCT in return for technical and logistical support for Alcatel's (CGE's telephone subsidiary) efforts to market its E10-S digital switch equipment on the US market. AT & T/Philips would, in addition, set up a joint venture with CGE, under Alcatel's leadership, in microwave transmissions. The deal would give the French group second position in this sector in global terms, and thereby boost its expertise in growth areas such as satellite communications. However, there was an increasing, but by no means unified, concern within the Mitterrand administration at the political and industrial implications of allowing the AT & T a foothold in the French public switching market. The consequences were a delay in further negotiations, public expression of reservations by the French Government in

January 1986 about the deal, and an indication of its willingness to consider the rival proposals put forward by Ericsson of Sweden.

A more successful French initiative on the political level has been the pursuit of a European collaboration strategy through the *'Eureka'* forum. Launched in April 1985, this French-inspired proposal was an indirect response to the rallying of American high technology efforts behind the Strategic Defence Initiative (SDI) or 'Star Wars' programme. Though initial responses of other West European governments to Eureka were lukewarm, a vigorous marketing campaign by the French Minister for Research and Technology succeeded in gathering a broad endorsement of the idea within Western Europe. By June 1985, the concept of Eureka had become one of the key themes of the European Community summit meeting in Milan. Supporting the initiative in principle, EC member states agreed to convene a ministerial meeting in Paris. The French agency Cesta outlined five potential areas for Eureka activities – information technology, communications, robotics, biotechnology and new materials. An agreement between the French state-controlled defence and electronics group, Matra, and the Norwegian Norsk Data to co-operate in developing a high-performance scientific computer was formally launched as the first project under the Eureka umbrella. Representatives from 17 European countries (the ten EEC member states, Spain, Portugal, Norway, Switzerland, Austria, Sweden and Finland) together with officials from the European Commission attended the Paris meeting to outline in more detail how the Eureka initiative might support specific areas of high technology. France pledged FFr 1 billion (£82 million) of financial support for the programme, and a further meeting was planned for the autumn in Hanover. Six broad industrial 'forums' – for electronic products, computing products, high-technology systems for homes and offices, advanced manufacturing including robotics and lasers, transportation and biotechnology products – were put forward by the British government with the aim of securing a more market-orientated approach. A consensus was also achieved on the need for state financing. By the end of the Hanover conference, the 18 countries (now including Turkey) and the European Community had formally adopted a Eureka Charter, or declaration of principles, and published a list of multinational projects. The Charter defined Eureka as a forum whereby companies could co-operate across borders, assisted by diminishing national barriers and, ultimately, a genuine common market. Initial areas for projects were to be information technology and telecommunications, as well as lasers, robotics, biotechnology, materials manufacturing, marine technology, environmental protection and transport technologies. A secretariat – its composition, location, functions and status still to be agreed – was to be established to co-ordinate the 'programme'. The ten agreed projects involved companies from 12 countries in areas ranging from personal and high-speed computers to lasers, robotics and flexible manufacturing systems. Those falling into the computing sector covered compact vector computers for high-speed calculations involving Matra (France) and Norsk Data (Norway); the creation of a European standard for personal and educational micro-computers including Olivetti (Italy), Acorn (UK) and Thomson (France); and a European research computer network comprising as yet undefined participants from France, West Germany,

Austria, Finland, Sweden, Switzerland, the Netherlands and the European Commission.

With the exception of French national policy strategy and the development of the Eureka programme, formal collaboration strategies at the European level in computing and telecommunications have emerged largely within the framework of the European Community. Arising out of discussions between the European Commission and Europe's 12 leading IT companies, the European Strategic Programme for Research and Development in Information Technology (ESPRIT) was launched as a pilot programme towards the end of 1982, and then formally adopted by the Council of Ministers in February 1984. Broadly speaking, ESPRIT sought to encourage transnational communications, common technical standards and collaborative approaches to information technology through cross-border collaboration. By confining its attention to research at the 'pre-competitive' stage, the ESPRIT programme aimed to improve European expertise in the basic information technologies. The five sectors covered were advanced micro-electronics, software technology, information and knowledge processing, office systems and computer-integrated manufacture. Overall direction was to be provided by the ESPRIT Management Committee representing EEC Member States, and day-to-day management by the European Commission's IT Task Force. Technical evaluation was to be facilitated by the ESPRIT Advisory Board which comprised members of the professional information technology community who were invited in a personal capacity. Funding was to be provided on 50 per cent basis, and projects were to involve at least two member states. The average number of partners in a project was five, with universities and research institutes participating in about 81 per cent of cases. Leading ESPRIT companies, in terms of total contract value, were Philips (the Netherlands), Siemens (West Germany) and GEC (UK). Partners were to retain equal rights to the results of their research and to choose for themselves how they wished to exploit it. Examples of first-phase projects included work on compound semi-conductor materials and integrated circuits, involving Plessey (UK), Philips (the Netherlands), Siemens (West Germany) and Thomson (France); the development of advanced integrated circuit design aids, involving Siemens (West Germany), Thomson CSF and IMAG (France), ICL, the University of Loughborough and UMIST (UK); and an office systems research work-station for Europe involving Whitechapel Computers Works, Queen Mary's College, London, and the University of Sussex (UK), Olivetti (Italy), Siemens (West Germany), Bull Transac (France) and the Vrije University of Amsterdam (the Netherlands).[1]

EEC activity in the telecommunications sector has, by contrast, progressed more slowly. The European Commission has been actively promoting this policy area since 1983 when it produced six basic action guidelines. These guidelines involved a commitment to the establishment of medium-term and long-term objectives at Community level; the definition and implementation of common activity in R&D; the opening up of the EEC terminals market and the development of a Community solidarity towards outsiders; the common development of the transnational part of the future EEC telecommunications infrastructure; the promotion and infrastructural development of the

Community's least-favoured regions; and the progressive opening of those parts of the Community's communications equipment market dominated by public procurement. A Senior Officials Group (SOGT) was convened at the request of the Council of Ministers to discuss future developments in the telecommunications sector. The result of this consultation process was the development of a Community telecommunications policy along four major lines: namely, the creation and stimulation of a Community-wide market; the balanced extension of telecommunications services throughout the Community; a drive to improve basic technological skills; and the provision of clear indicators about directions for future development.[2]

Within this general policy framework, the European Commission developed the R&D in Advanced Communications-technologies for Europe (RACE) programme. RACE reflected the broad-based consensus among telecommunications authorities and suppliers that the narrowband Integrated Services Digital Network (ISDN), currently evolving in parts of Europe, should be gradually replaced by an Integrated Broadband Communications Network (IBCN).[3] The RACE programme was intended to establish the necessary technological base for the introduction of a Community-wide IBCN infrastructure and services. The definition phase (1985–86) was directed towards the realisation of an IBCN reference model and identification of the relevant R&D, design and pilot work. With regard to IBCN the aim was to develop a consensus on the functional and techno-economic characteristics of the three major elements: namely, the network itself, the terminal environment, and the applications and/or services made possible by their interaction. National telecommunications authorities and suppliers participated in this IBCN definition phase; the companies involved included Plessey, STC and Thorn EMI (UK), CIT Alcatel (France), Siemens (West Germany) and Italtel (Italy). Involvement in individual projects could be quite widespread. GEC Telecommunications (UK), for example, co-ordinated 29 companies from seven countries in a study that was designed to define the basis of technical co-operation in broadband communications customer equipment. R&D work fell broadly within the areas of integrated circuits, opto-electronics, broadband switching and communications software. The first phase of the programme (1987–1992) is intended to develop the technological base for IBCN, to support the formulation of common proposals for specifications and standards and to carry out the necessary pre-competitive developments to provide trial equipment and services for IBCN demonstration. A second phase (1992–1997) is to develop the technological base for enhanced IBCN equipment and services beyond 1995.[4]

Not all EEC-level initiatives in telecommunications are to be found within the RACE programme. ESPRIT contained some R&D work relevant to telecommunications. However, more important perhaps as an additional forum for co-operation is the COST (European Co-operation in the field of Scientific and Technical Research) framework. Although COST is attached to the general machinery of the European Communities, it pursues a greater degree of flexibility and freedom than is normally the case in EC initiatives, both in the range of countries involved and in the nature of the approach to co-operation itself. COST activities are largely devoted to long-term research.

Of particular interest to the telecommunications sector are those activities dealing with digital techniques in local telecommunications networks (COST 202), optical fibre communications systems (COST 208), redundancy reduction techniques for visual telephone signals (COST 211) and the coding and transmission of high-definition television signals (COST 212). These programmes involve a range of EEC and non-EEC countries, and represent an *ad hoc* but nevertheless successful *à la carte* approach to European co-operation.[5]

Other collaborative activities have also been initiated within the framework of the EEC's policy for telecommunications. Examples include a study on the joint development of second-generation mobile telephones, a programme to determine the feasibility of establishing video-communication links between senior government officials within the Community and an analysis of the potential for the development of a high-capacity communications network.

Outside the EEC, the European Telecommunications Standardisation Body (CEPT) provided a further forum for collaboration. Similar in membership to COST, CEPT focused on several activities relating to broadband communications systems. The EVE project (European Videoconferencing Equipment), for example, aimed at a service-orientated evaluation of such systems in terms of human factors, terminal installation, connection with existing networks and operational problems; while the GSLB (Groupe Spécial de Communication à Large Bande) was established to investigate integrated broadband local networks with a view to achieving harmonisation on a European basis.[6]

The field of *standardisation* in information technology has provided an opportunity for Community interests in computing and telecommunications to overlap. Standards are perceived by the European Commission to be of crucial importance to the long-term implementation of some of its major policy objectives such as the establishment of a Community information technology market and the development of a European telecommunications infrastructure. By the early 1980s therefore it was already promoting a variety of activities in the field. Two Working Groups, one on Standards and another on the Standardisation Aspects of Public Procurement, had been established under the umbrella of the Multiannual Data-Processing Programme; efforts towards European standardisation had been co-ordinated within the European Workshop on Informatics and Computing Systems (EWICS) and a computer hardware procurement policy based on the work of the Standards Implementation Committee (SIC) developed. Directive 83/189/EEC laid down the procedure for providing information in the field of technical regulations and standards enabling Member States to exchange information on planned draft standards and the European Commission to conclude agreements with the relevant bodies involved in the preparation of European standards. Community Directives 77/62/EEC and 80/767/EEC concerning public procurement however have only applied to computer equipment since 1981 and still do not cover the telecommunications sector.

The debate on standards within Europe has centred on the relative merits of adopting the 'open standards interconnect' (OSI) model being evolved by the International Standards Organisation (ISO) or adhering to the 'systems network architecture' approach deployed as a *de facto* standard by IBM.

COLLABORATION IN COMPUTING AND TELECOMMUNICATIONS   153

The former provides for the interworking of systems with different architectures while the latter opts for a complete network service within a coherent architectural framework. The decision taken by the ESPRIT Industrial Group, or Round Table, in early 1984 to adopt common interconnection standards provided the necessary incentive for the European Commission to pursue its standardisation objectives further. The Round Table suggestions included the development of a European Information Technology Standards Policy through which the Community would identify the key standards to be adopted, encourage their earliest adoption and embodiment within national public procurement policies, and provide the political guarantee and support for the use of these standards during their formative period. Most importantly, Community policy should involve itself in the definition of standards in advance of new technological development rather than retrospectively in the harmonisation of existing products.

The European Commission presented policy proposals along these lines to the May 1984 Council meeting of the Ministers for Industry, and a Group of Senior Officials for Information Technology Standardisation was established. Current Community policy recognises ISO and CCITT standards and recommendations as the appropriate framework for Community development and the role of the European Commission in co-ordinating and guiding the technical European standardisation organisations CEPT and CEN/CENELEC. Priority areas for development are standards for open communications networks; higher levels of OSI standards; message handling, teletex and document exchange; formal description techniques and programming languages. Additional priorities in the telecommunications sector include integrated service digital networks (ISDN), mobile cellular telephony, telematic terminals and broadband networks.[7] Progress in developing standards at the European level has, however, been inevitably slow given the inherent technical complexities of the task, the vested interests at industrial level, the differing approaches of national telecommunications carriers and the sometimes cumbersome functioning of international bodies.

Meanwhile at the *industrial* level companies began increasingly to take their own steps towards collaboration in the hope that such activities might enable them to strengthen their commercial positions and to expand and diversify into new fields. The nature of this co-operation varied from fairly informal agreements between companies to unite in support of certain technical standards through to joint ventures in research, product development and marketing. Up to 1986 much of the co-operation occurred between companies in the United States and in Western Europe. However, within the computing sector at least there were some notable exceptions. Bilateral agreements negotiated within a wholly European framework included the 1984 Racal (UK) and Norsk Data (Norway) joint venture for computer systems to facilitate the development of artificial intelligence, the 1985 agreement between Thomson (France) and Cambridge Instruments (UK) in the field of high-speed submicron lithography, and the 1986 agreement between Thomson and GEC (UK) for a five-year programme to develop application-specific integrated circuits.

More prestigious was the Bull (France), Siemens (West Germany) and ICL (UK) joint research centre which was established in Munich in 1984 and aimed at the development of new generation computers. Already Philips (the Netherlands) and Siemens had been co-operating in long-lead R&D since 1982. Their collaboration branched out in 1984 with the launching of the so-called 'Mega-project' which — with huge financial support from the West German and Dutch governments — sought to develop and produce a set of new microchips with a much higher storage capacity.

A more unusual approach to European industrial collaboration was the formation of the ES2 microchip venture that was announced in September 1985. Planned as a purely European operation in terms of its sources of finance, senior management, choice of locations and marketing goals, ES2 aimed to employ advanced design and production technology for the cheap and efficient manufacture of small quantities of 'custom' chips. ES2 was incorporated in Luxembourg; its headquarters were in West Germany, its design technology developed within the UK and a production plant built in France.[8]

Although alliances between European companies in the telecommunications sector have been relatively rare, a modest trend had begun to develop by 1986. Two basic problems faced European manufacturers of telecommunications equipment and impeded industrial co-operation. The first was that national restrictions made it difficult for them to sell in each other's markets. The second was that the main strength of most of the leading manufacturers lay in public switching, an overcrowded market with a high degree of duplication between product ranges. Consequently, little complementarity existed between their major businesses.

Despite a number of attempts to promote European industrial collaboration in telecommunications, progress was correspondingly slow. Having for long been encouraged by their governments to think of themselves as 'national champions', leading telecommunications companies were reluctant to make the reciprocal concessions that more than token collaboration required. Nevertheless, some successful agreements were concluded: the alliance in 1984 between CGE (France) and the broadly-based holding company, Société Générale Belgique, to foster hi-tech developments in telecommunications, and the 1985 accord signed by CIT Alcatel (France), Italtel (Italy), Siemens (West Germany) and Plessey (UK) for technical co-operation in new exchanges and transmission techniques. The latter agreement sought to pave the way for joint efforts to build future public telephone switching systems for the 1990s.

Crucially, the major axis of the European telecommunictions sector's industrial alliances remained transatlantic. Both Philips (the Netherlands) and Olivetti (Italy) formed close links with AT & T, while IBM pressed hard to establish ties with West European national telecommunications authorities. West Germany's Siemens were openly dismissive of an 'all-European' strategy in telecommunications manufacturing. Its hopes were pinned on the United States where it conducted negotiations with GTE, the second largest American telephone company, in an attempt to enter the American public exchange market. Similar objectives were pursued by Ericsson (Sweden), Plessey (UK) and CIT Alcatel (France), though with limited success by the mid 1980s.

THE AGENDA OF EUROPEAN COLLABORATION

This general overview indicates that, on the one hand, the range of collaborative initiatives in computing and telecommunications has increased in recent years but that, on the other hand, the level of successful implementation has been relatively confined and modest. Although ESPRIT was slow to be launched and subjected to intergovernmental wrangling, it was the one major policy programme to have achieved any real direction and momentum. For similar programmes in the telecommunications sector success seems less certain. Even if it seems too early for a full evaluation of the RACE initiative, the evidence suggests the existence of a policy group with much less coherence and more fragmented interests than in the case of ESPRIT. Outside formal EEC programmes, the divergence of interests and the problems of policy implementation become even more evident. The French government's initiative in pursuit of European collaboration in telecommunications secured neither adequate backing from other West European governments nor the full support of its own domestic industry. The Eureka programme was overtly political with few tangible results in the form of new projects, while ventures within the COST framework represented *ad hoc* one-off activities for the majority of participants. The major political initiatives — ESPRIT, RACE, Eureka and the French 'European' strategy — shared a certain grandeur of vision that was rarely reflected in bilateral or trilateral arrangements of the kind preferred at the industrial level.

What are the factors shaping the political agenda for European collaboration? Incentives for collaboration have traditionally been explained in terms of the costs, scale or inherent nature of the technological development involved. While these factors are important, they provide little insight into the reasons why European collaboration became an increasingly attractive political option in the 1980s. More pertinent perhaps is the conception of technology in terms of political influence and power. It has been remarked that, for the political scientist, 'technology equals capacity and capacity equals power'.[9] In other words the development and exploitation of technology tends to alter the nature of power relationships, whether social, economic, political or military. Shifts in international economic and political power derive to a large extent from differential access to, and facility with, technological developments. Thus changes in the international balance of political power over the last quarter century can be seen as reflecting a period of unrivalled American superpower, the forging of a firm political axis between France and West Germany, and the slow but inevitable withdrawal of Britain from the sphere of international responsibilities; and these developments can be equated with the relative techno-economic performance of these countries over time.

Such political considerations are inherent in the development of technology, and it can be shown that they have shaped the policy agenda for European collaboration in computing and telecommunications. Communications are increasingly perceived as a strategic sector by politicians and industrialists alike. Not only are the core sectors of information technology — semiconductors, computing and telecommunications — growing exceptionally fast and 'converging'; their pervasive applications also reveal their decisive impact on other sectors of the economy. West European governments of all political hues are, accordingly, paying serious attention to the strategic importance of these new technologies. The belief has taken root that the successful development and exploitation of the opportunities intrinsic to the so-called information technology 'revolution' holds the key to a nation's future growth and prosperity. Accordingly, the maintenance of relative economic, and consequently political, influence of West European states in the international sphere hinges upon their acquisition of significant shares of global communications markets.

Where considerations of national and international perceptions of status and prestige take place within a context of global recession and national budgetary constraints, the notion of European collaboration constitutes an increasingly attractive element of political rhetoric. Attempts by individual West European states to gain a substantial foothold in the global communications markets have been somewhat thwarted by their relative disadvantage in terms of size and resources. At the same time West European governments in general, and France in particular, have experienced a collective sense of threat in response to the steadily increasing penetration of European markets by American multinationals. Though economic actors in principle, such corporations tend in practice to assume a more political role. Consolidation of their presence within Europe ultimately deprives the host nations of some of their political influence. The close links between the communications sector and national defence policies further exacerbates the feeling of European vulnerability. European sensitivity to the potential impact of the behaviour of American multinationals is consequently heightened.

Expression of these political and economic fears has focused on the notion of the 'technology gap' that is perceived to exist between West European countries, on the one hand, and the United States and Japan, on the other. The belief that individually West European states lack the capability to close this so-called 'gap' has been fuelled by the Japanese fifth-generation computer programme and the American Strategic Defence or 'Star Wars' Initiative. Some form of concerted action at the European level has been perceived as necessary if the current technological imbalance with the United States is to be altered. France, in particular, has adhered to this notion; hence its call for a European approach to the development of telecommunications. However, similar themes underlie the rhetoric behind both Eureka and the European Community programmes. The latter continually refer to the 'technology gap' in advocating the appropriateness of the EEC framework for meeting this challenge.[10]

The emergence of the EEC framework as a more successful forum for policy development points to a second theme that underlies the political shaping of the agenda for European collaboration — that is, the complex distribution of power between the national and the Community level. The politics that is inherent in this national/EEC dimension explains not only the delays in the development and ratification of Community policies but also the emergence of the Eureka programme in a determinedly extra-EEC form. Quite simply, the reputation for technological collaboration enjoyed by the European Community had not been particularly striking. While the European Commission pushed for policy development in a number of sectors, perceptions of national interests meant that progress at the level of implementation was rather slow.

Reluctant to formalise their activities within the framework of the Community, member states paid lip-service to the notion of a technology policy at the Community level while leaving the Commission in a position of political impotence. The success of the ESPRIT programme proved a turning point for the role of the Commission. Not only had the Commission developed a more flexible approach to policy initiation and implementation; it had also secured industrial support. With this increased confidence and stature the Commission began to push for a more public profile, exploiting the current interest in collaboration to argue for the Community as the appropriate framework. The response from national governments was not slow to emerge. The French took the initiative in developing the Eureka concept and, with the backing of other West European governments, succeeded in overriding the Commission's bid for the programme's leadership, thus retaining the sphere of political influence firmly outside of the Community forum. In fact the Eureka programme contained a high level of political rhetoric but little that could be called tangible in terms of concrete policy, save that of having removed the political initiative away from the Commission.

The pursuit of collaboration for European political ends generally finds itself at odds with interests at the industrial level where the political profile inherent in collaboration tends to be much less clearly defined. In the fields of computing and telecommunications, for example, the need to share mounting development costs proved an important motivation, as did the race against time to keep up with competitors. Further incentives have included the acquisition of marketing experience and access to new technologies, products and geographical markets. Such aims mean that given the current global distribution of expertise and know-how, the collaborative framework tends to be transatlantic and informal rather than European and formal. Where the interests of political and industrial collaboration manage to coincide, the very process of collaboration within a formal European policy programme tends to engender the kind of delays that industrialists most seek to avoid.

POLICY ACTORS AND THE POLICY-MAKING PROCESS

The successful implementation of a collaborative initiative may well be related to the coherence of the group of policy actors involved. Of the various European collaborative initiatives surveyed above, only the actors involved in the initiation and development of ESPRIT might merit the term 'policy community'.[11] The ESPRIT programme has seen the emergence of a core of key decision-makers comprising representatives from Western Europe's 12 largest computer companies, officials from the European Commission and national civil servants, whose continued contact with each other has developed into and reinforced a relatively closed and 'privatised' world that reflects a consensus on the problems to be addressed and the strategies to be adopted.[12] Formal and informal channels of communication have been established between these key actors and the more peripheral and wider circle of other European companies, universities and research centres involved in the programme. Through frequent meetings and the actual processes of collaboration, the momentum has been reinforced and a certain culture formed that has facilitated developments in other areas such as technical standards. Elsewhere, however, the actors involved in the various European initiatives constitute what might be very loosely termed as 'issue networks' in that their relations are *ad hoc*, informal, fragmented and weak with little real sense of any common identity or objectives.[13]

European collaborative initiatives are more likely to attain long-term success in situations where they have been defined and launched by a strong policy group based on a clear consensus. The speed at which such initiatives gather political momentum, depends on the degree of political acumen of the actors and their 'urgency' as perceived by national governments. Their rate of political progress appears in inverse proportion to the clarity of objectives and the constraints of the forum. Thus Eureka progressed precisely because of its lack of clearly defined objectives and because the framework ensured its participants were free from firm commitments to any rigid policy action. The slow progress of the European Community's ESPRIT and RACE programmes, by contrast, can be explained by reference to the need for the Commission's careful and formal policy development and the inevitable delays caused by the process of the complexities and trade-offs implicit in the processes of Community policy-making.

In all of the European initiatives the policy process leaves little room for public debate. Decisions are made by small groups of industrialists, politicians and civil servants with vested interests; little opportunity is provided to voice the opinions of, for instance, the small company or trade unions. Major policy questions remain undebated. What, for example, are the aims of specific collaborative programmes? Are they designed in the interests of international prestige and the high technology lobby or to meet actual consumer needs and demands? Which should be the industries and areas of technology to receive support? Who within these groups should be the most favoured? What is the appropriate level for action, and what are the policy measures that should be employed?

These are important questions not least because developments in communication technology will affect the nature of work and leisure, the role and definitions of employment and education, and the structure, content and operation of the media and of political control. While some groups in society will undoubtedly benefit from the expansion of the communications sector, many others will suffer disadvantages as traditional services and employment are down-graded and displaced. Yet many of these European collaborative initiatives are concerned with developing the products, services and structures of the future. The assumptions of 'need' embodied in visions of the future European 'information society' are currently in the process of being laid down. In view of their extensive political implications it seems imperative that the wider public should be involved in the debate at both the domestic and the international level. Yet the closed 'club-style' of policy-making inherent in ESPRIT and similar initiatives — by a committee of like-minded people from industry and governments — is becoming an increasingly accepted policy-making model both within the EEC and nationally. Moreover, the normal policy tensions that exist in attempting to achieve a balance between opening up policy debate beyond the so-called 'professionals' and avoiding the debilitating effects of an 'overcrowded' policy community are exacerbated by the actual process of European collaboration. The time-consuming and often relatively bureaucratic tasks involved in carrying out any form of European collaboration are likely to foster an ever more 'closed' approach to decision-making in the interests of greater speed and efficiency in policy development and implementation.

The decision to pursue a policy of European technological collaboration immediately raises two important points for consideration. First and foremost is the question of the most appropriate framework, politically and geographically. The preference of many of those in industry for the transatlantic axis is as much a reflection of Western Europe's weaknesses as of her global competitors' attractions. Both Olivetti and Philips sought European partners before concluding their respective deals with AT & T but found little basis for any real agreement. The lack of complementary products and technology among West European competitors constituted one major problem. Equally important though was the reluctance of European companies to surrender their privileged positions at home. Even where the level of industrial commitment to a European framework is much more overt — as in the Philips and Siemens Mega-project — extra-European agreements have had to be concluded in the course of the project in order to acquire relevant expertise and know-how.[14]

Political concerns about Western Europe's 'technology gap' necessitate the development of some kind of West European cohesion and solidarity. The question then arises as to the most appropriate forum within the West European context. From the European Commission's point of view the advantages and potential of the EEC dimension are clear. Western Europe's weaknesses arise out of its fragmented markets and uncoordinated strategies. The EEC framework offers the potential of a larger market and a unified approach. However, the relative success of ESPRIT may not be easily repeated. Particular factors accounted for that programme's progress. Against a background of increasingly stringent national budgetary constraints, the ability of the European Commission to pre-empt similar initiatives at national level was facilitated by the dissatisfaction of key industrialists at national governmental responses to their demands.[15] Had West European governments proved more amenable, the alliance at Community level may not have turned out to be quite so influential.

Yet the European Community poses a problem in terms of its membership. On the one hand, certain European states and prominent companies such as Ericsson of Sweden fall outside its jurisdiction; on the other hand, increasing tensions are being generated by the Community's expanding membership. With the accession of Spain and Portugal in 1986, regional, industrial and technological disparities between member states plunged the Community into a state of flux with respect to its purpose, direction and general mode of operation. Intergovernmental wrangling over budget and policies continued to increase. As a consequence the EEC did not necessarily seem the most practical framework for European technological collaboration. The EEC did, nevertheless, serve the purpose of articulating and reinforcing the need for an essentially holistic approach to the development of communications in

Western Europe, a view not necessarily shared by alternative collaborative agencies.

The issue of timing is also crucial to any European collaborative policy. It often appears that the decision to collaborate has been taken too late, particularly when it is intended as a response to a 'crisis' that is well under way. Yet, since the pursuit of European collaboration is rarely a long-term governmental strategy, mechanisms to evaluate the most appropriate timing are unlikely to exist, except perhaps in those organisations devoted to collaboration whose policy suggestions are anyway coloured by interests of institutional survival and expansion. Once initiated, however, there is no real evidence to suggest that collaborative programmes enhance the rate of technological development or enable the participants more readily to catch up with their rivals. Indeed, given the level of bureaucracy and inflexibility inherent in most European collaborative programmes, the very opposite may in fact be true. Doubts may also be expressed about the viability of ideas of accelerating technological development in these ways. The nature and complexity of R&D is such that even the best people operating in the most ideal circumstances may only achieve a trickle of results within a given time-period.

POLICY IMPLICATIONS AND CONCLUSIONS

In European collaboration the policy-making process has certain key features – the relative fragmentation and weakness of the policy groupings, the 'closed' nature of decision-making, problems of timing and the question of the appropriate framework. Together they militate against the successful implementation of many of the initiatives, encouraging the reappearance of old ideas in new guises.

This problem of policy implementation has further important implications when one considers that many of the underlying assumptions behind the arguments for European collaboration in communications based on the notion of the 'technology gap' might be wrong. The fragmentation of West European information technology markets arising out of preferential government procurement and the maintenance of strict national telecommunications monopolies has long been cited as the major constraint facing European industries; it denies them the economies of scale available to their American and Japanese counterparts. The problems may, however, lie more in the attitudes of the companies themselves. For example, Western Europe's three 'national-champion' mainframe-computer manufacturers, ICL (UK), Bull (France), and Siemens (West Germany) hold less than two per cent each of the global market, while some of the more entrepreneurial firms such as Olivetti (Italy), Norsk Data (Norway) and Nixdorf (West Germany) have managed to expand with little or no governmental support and in spite of the aforementioned constraints.

Other explanations for the 'technology gap' focus on the relative levels of R&D spending. There is a widespread belief that countries in Western Europe are not carrying out sufficient R&D by comparison with the United States and Japan. Direct comparisons are difficult to achieve given the differences in policy approach of the countries involved, yet what does seem to be at stake is not so much the level of overall West European R&D spending but the *efficacy* of the European innovation effort. Returns on R&D investment are simply too low. The causes lie perhaps in the innovation environment. Market fragmentation may reduce the incentive to innovate; technical infrastructural resources are weak by comparison with the United States and Japan; while fewer people complete the full span of secondary and tertiary education and less money is spent on education and research per capita.[16]

Secondly, the nature of the policy-making process contributes to certain structural changes. One area for concern is the effect on small European firms in the information technology sector. In ESPRIT, for example, they are conspicuously absent from a large number of projects and, despite apparent provisions to the contrary, are gradually being squeezed out of the market. It is the larger interests, including IBM, that ultimately stand to gain. Similarly, it is the well-established companies that are reaping the benefits in the telecommunications programmes, and few opportunities seem to exist for the promotion of new entrants. As a result the 'closed' nature of the decision-making process is inevitably reinforced.

In conclusion, European collaboration in computing and telecommunications at the governmental and EEC level has taken the form of a political process shaped largely by considerations of political influence and prestige within the international arena and arising from differential access to, and facility with, technological development. Within the context of Western Europe the power politics implicit in the relationship between the European Community and its member states have played an important role in the generation of collaborative initiatives at the political level. The long-term success of such programmes and the development of European information technology standards is, however, constrained by the inherent political rivalry between governments, the weakness of the policy groupings involved, and the tensions that result from the conflicting interests implicit in collaboration at the political and industrial levels. The style of policy-making in European collaborative initiatives is predominantly that of the 'club – that is, a committee of like-minded people from industry and governments. This style is increasingly becoming the accepted model for technology policy-making both within the European Community and nationally. The 'closed' nature of this policy forum gives rise to concern not only about the lack of debate over basic and increasingly significant policy questions but also about the long-term implications of the strategies being pursued in the 1980s.

NOTES

1. See, for example, 'Official Documents on the ESPRIT Programme', European Commission, 1984; COM (84) 608 final; and 'ESPRIT Technical Week 1985; Proceedings and Press Releases', European Commission Information Technology and Telecommunications Task Force, Brussels, September 1985. A full list of ESPRIT projects for Year 1 and Year 2 is also available from the same Task Force.
2. See, for example, COM (83) 573 final and COM (84) 277 final.
3. Telephone networks are designed primarily for voice traffic, and their low capacity limits the potential for introducing new services. ISDN, currently being introduced in a number

of countries, allows voice, data, text and video to be carried. The capacity level is still relatively low however. IBC represents a high capacity network which will evolve from and ultimately subsume the present services and network structures of PSTN, IDN, ISDN, Cable TV and mobile communications.

4. See, for example, COM (85) 145 final, and 'Advanced Notice on the Definition Phase of the RACE Programme', European Commission Information Technology and Telecommunications Task Force.
5. 'IBCN Cooperation; R&D Opportunities for the European Community', European Commission Information Technology Task Force Working Document OTR/3,2/3/84, Part One, pp. 14–17.
6. Ibid, pp. 17–19.
7. See, for example, Commission Staff Paper; Standardisation in Information Technology, SEC (84) 796, and the Proposal by the ESPRIT Industry Group to the Commission of the European Communities for Establishing a European Community Information Technology Standards Policy, 18/1/1984.
8. ES2 was conceived by Jean-Luc Grand-Clements (former European Vice-President of Motorola) and established in conjunction with Robert Heikes (former head of National Semiconductor's European operations) and ICL chairperson Robb Wilmott. 'Custom' chips are tailored to the specific needs of individual customers such as the makers of computers and telecommunications equipment. Globally, this market has been dominated by American companies. Interested only in large orders, however, they have been reluctant to supply European electronic equipment manufacturers. The perceived market niche for ES2 therefore, arises out of this mismatch between American supply and European demand.
9. For the quote and the development of the ideas outlined in this paragraph see R. Williams, 'The International Polticial Economy of Technology' in S. Strange (ed.), *International Political Economy*, (London: Allen & Unwin, 1984).
10. For an indication of the current debate on the notion of Europe's 'technology gap' see the 'Can Europe Catch Up?' series of articles, in the *Financial Times*, June 1985.
11. On 'policy communities' see J. Richardson (ed.), *Policy Styles in Western Europe* (London: Allen & Unwin, 1982).
12. The 12 founding members of ESPRIT are all larger companies: GEC, ICL and Plessey from the UK; Thomson CSF, CGE and Bull from France; Siemens, AEG and Nixdorf from West Germany; STET and Olivetti from Italy and Philips from the Netherlands.
13. On 'policy networks' see H. Heclo, 'Issue Networks and the Executive Establishment', in A. King (ed.), *The New American Political System* (Washington, DC: American Enterprise Institute, 1978).
14. The deal, for example, between Siemens and Toshiba (Japan) for a licence on the latter's one-million-bit chip technology.
15. This is particularly evident in the case of the UK Alvey programme where the British government failed to respond to industry's request for 90 per cent government funding and autonomy for the Alvey Directorate itself. Instead a blanket 50 per cent funding arrangement was offered together with a Directorate balancing four separate interests: the Department of Trade and Industry, the Ministry of Defence, the SERC and industry itself. The resulting organisational structure means a greater reflection of governmental interests than is apparent in ESPRIT and a consequent diminishing scope for large-scale industrial interests.
16. For these, and other explanations of the 'technology gap', see the 'Can Europe Catch Up' series of articles, *Financial Times*, June 1985, and Dr Robb Wilmot, 'The Market Perspective', paper presented at the ESPRIT Technical Week, Brussels, September 1985.

Legitimating the Communications Revolution: Governments, Parties and Trade Unions in Britain, France and West Germany

Peter Humphreys

This case study seeks to explore, in a preliminary way, the variations in approach to the communications revolution of key political actors: national and local governments, political oppositions and trade unions. Along with industrial and cultural lobbies, which are examined in other contributions, these actors set the political agenda and thus help shape public attitudes to the communications revolution. So far, little political-science research has focused on their 'agenda-setting' role. Much more academic attention has been directed towards industrial policy variations between countries; and even more energy has been expanded upon the presumed social, economic and cultural effects of the communications revolution, though many of the effects are in the future and remained uncertain by the mid-1980s. Therefore, it seems all the more important, at this stage of developments, to focus more research upon the perceptions and legitimation strategies of political actors who are already staking out the ideological parameters of technological modernisation. In politics perceptions count for much; and policy decisions, the outcomes of which remain necessarily unclear, require legitimation in contemporary politics.

In 1985 an international opinion-research organisation produced a most thought-provoking report: *The Impact of Technological Change in the Industrial Democracies — Public Attitudes toward Information Technology*.[1] The survey revealed considerable variation in public attitudes across a range of Western industrial societies. Of particular interest and surprise was the finding that scepticism about information technology (IT) seemed high in West Germany, a society famed for its pursuit of successful industrial modernisation (*Modelldeutschland*). In fact, the report concluded: '... Germany (was) an exception, notable not only for its negative view of computers and information technology but also for the magnitude of its negativism'. By comparison and perhaps no less surprising, '... Britain was "positive about [information technology's] potential for the future"'. At the same time, the British displayed a degree of ambivalence, suggesting perhaps a rather fatalistic acceptance. Britain had the highest proportion of respondents (almost two-thirds) who believed that IT would worsen unemployment; it had also the highest proportion who felt that industrial modernisation was an urgent necessity, even at the expense of jobs. In West Germany, again surprisingly, an exceptionally high proportion gave priority to job-preservation. The French demonstrated the 'highest positive interest, after the US'. In France, an interesting degree of social consensus was indicated by the fact that the (relatively high) proportion of positive responses varied little between social groups and party political affiliations. The report suggested that French relative 'positiveness' might be explained by the 'dynamic view of information technology held by the government and the French Socialist Party and the positive consensus among opinion formers'. The report also suggested that 'party affiliation in some countries, particularly the SPD (Social Democratic Party) in the Federal Republic of Germany and the Labour Party in Britain, correlates to the belief that information-processing technology creates unemployment'. While the survey indicated that 'resistance to computers and word-processors [was] tempered by the fact that younger people in general [were] more positively inclined toward information technology than older ones', West Germany again proved to be an exception to the rule. West German youth appeared to be more negatively disposed to information technology than the 35–49 age group.

It would certainly be unwise to attach too much weight to a single opinion survey. In any case polls can find it difficult to register the extent to which feelings about technological change may be complex and ambivalent: general concern about job-loss through technological innovation and rationalisation in factories and offices can co-exist with a favourable attitude towards domestic labour-saving and entertainment uses of consumer electronics, like VCRs and home computers. Nevertheless, opinion surveys in West Germany have commonly indicated an increase in scepticism about technological progress in recent years. Given the high political profile achieved by the West German 'new social movements', with the proliferation of 'citizen initiative groups', with the springing up of 'Green' and 'Alternative' groups and with the representation of the Green Party in the Bundestag after March 1983, the consequence has been concern, and even occasional alarm about the prospects for *Modelldeutschland*.

Cross-national differences in attitudes toward information technology reflect many factors. Although cultural attitudes of this kind are very difficult either to measure accurately or to explain, it is a reasonable presumption that public opinion in Western liberal democracies is influenced crucially by certain key actors. Attitudes are shaped by the opinions of elites in national and local governments, political parties and trade unions. Both parties and trade unions face the issue of adapting to and integrating 'new social forces' expressed by the technical intelligentsia, by skilled workers in the white-collar sectors; while ideas of a new 'freedom' (embodied in deregulation; American-style business unionism; new flexibility in work organisation) and a new 'solidarity' (embodied in 'co-determination' or 'participation' in technical change; shorter working week) contend, as parties seek to construct new social coalitions of voters and trade unions of members. In particular, the Atlantic Institute survey's suggestion that national variations might be linked somehow to different approaches adopted by the left deserves serious consideration. In view of the left's traditional concern with the possibly negative effects of capitalist development – unemployment, low wages and other adverse social consequences – West European left-wing parties and trade unions might be expected to be a focus for critical views about the *third industrial revolution*. The communications revolution is bound up not only with the emergence of a new technical intelligentsia but also with the development of 'deskilling and 'low-skill' service employment. These complex changes raise a new problem of how to win the political argument in a more fluid context. This problem bears down especially heavily on the political left and the trade unions as they seek to reconcile their traditional concern for those who carry the costs of major technology-induced economic and social transformation with an openness to 'new social forces'.

Particular attention will, therefore, be given to the question of degrees of acceptance or resistance on the left to information technology and its applications in the media, telecommunications and service sectors. In view of the so-far limited amount of political science work in this field, the author's conclusions must be tentative and provisional and are designed to provoke rather than close debate.

GOVERNMENTS AND OPPOSITIONS: THE LEFT AND MODERNISATION IN BRITAIN, FRANCE AND WEST GERMANY

During the late 1970s and the early 1980s governments in all three countries became increasingly aware of the scale and scope of the communications revolution. To a great extent, their opinions were informed, in turn, by influential reports and commissions. In Britain, elite interest in the new information- and communications-technologies was stimulated by a number of reports from the Advisory Council for Applied Research and Development (ACARD), which had been established in 1976 by the Labour government of James Callaghan. In *Technological Change — Threats and Opportunities for the United Kingdom* (1980) IT was presented as the area with possibly the greatest potential for generating exports and employment.[2] A subsequent report, *Information Technology*, stressed the urgent need for increased commitment to IT development so that Britain might face up to competition not simply from the United States and Japan, but also from France and West Germany.[3] Again, IT was deemed crucial to high employment. It was felt that '... despite some notable achievements, there (was) less awareness in the United Kingdom of (IT's) potential impact' and that the country had '... fallen behind other countries'.[4]

In fact the 1974–79 Labour governments had taken a distinctly pragmatic (and social democratic) approach to the emerging new technologies. They had chosen not to restructure existing industrial and financial structures profoundly, but rather to 'guide' developments through the newly created National Enterprise Board. Nevertheless, by 1978 the NEB '... controlled the largest single part of the software market (Insac), had founded the only mass producer of microprocessors and memories in the UK (Inmos) and had finally laid some foundations for an advanced office equipment industry (Nexos).[5] The NEB had also a considerable share in, although only a limited influence over, ICL, which was still at that time Western Europe's most vigorous and successful computer company. All the signs suggested that Labour was developing a mixed-economy national industrial strategy for the new technologies. However, the approach was too bland in the face of the potent new ideological assault of the 1980s. Britain's pragmatic approach to the 'communications revolution' was soon transformed by the ideological 'heroism' of the Conservative governments of Margaret Thatcher after 1979.

The Thatcher ideology laid great stress on privatisation and economic neo-liberalism — 'rolling back the state' — as well as on modernisation and seizing the opportunities of IT. In 1981 the Thatcher government set up an Information Technology Advisory Panel (ITAP) to report to, and work directly through, the Cabinet Office. It was to examine ways of transforming Britain into a modern and competitive 'information economy'. 1982 was symbolically designated as 'Information Technology Year' — with the aim of increasing the awareness both of the public and of industry about the importance of embracing the new technologies — and Britain's first Minister of State for Information Technology was appointed. The National Enterprise Board was succeeded by the British Technology Group. The previous Labour government's Microelectronics Awareness Programme was adopted and extended. Community training centres in electronics and computing at the local level (so-called 'I Tech' centres) were encouraged and part-funded by the Department of Industry; plans were implemented to introduce microcomputers into every secondary school. In these ways the young were to be widely introduced to computing techniques. In addition, the government became involved in a number of new projects to promote office automation, electronic mail and viewdata. The government also established within the Department of Trade and Industry the so-called 'Alvey Directorate' to supervise an ambitious new collaborative research effort, to be funded on a 50/50 basis by government and industry, which aimed to reverse the decline of Britain's relative share of the domestic IT market and to make British industry more competitive. However, the Conservative government's industrial policies diverged sharply from those of the previous Labour governments. Private initiative and privatisation became the catchword in the micro-electronics, computer and office-automation sectors. Insac and Inmos were privatised successfully; Nexos collapsed before it could even establish itself. Moreover, the 'change in government policy was marked by an avalanche of new measures ... which set out to open up the UK market for information technologies. The most dramatic changes were those planned for broadcasting and telecommunications'.[6]

The radical changes in telecommunications policy have been described above by Morgan and Webber. Of all the new technology sectors, telecommunications was the one that the Labour government had failed to exploit noticeably. Under the Conservatives BT was hived off from the Post Office and then privatised, and the telecommunications sector was opened up to competition. BT was encouraged to accelerate its modernisation programme, notably digitalisation of telephonic switching (System X) — high volume production of which only began in 1984. At the same time, to stimulate domestic production and productivity under the new regulatory regime after the 1984 Telecommunications Act, BT's British suppliers of digital exchanges, GEC and Plessey, were exposed to competition from Ericsson, the Swedish manufacturer — a 'radical' step in the West European context of protected and privileged national telecoms suppliers. Increased support was extended to the optical fibre industry, and BT's optic fibre programme was opened to

LEGITIMATING THE COMMUNICATIONS REVOLUTION 167

competition from Mercury, a new company that was licensed to lay and operate a fibre optic network.

As part of its privatisation BT was 'sold off' to the public as a 'national champion' of the high-technology era in what amounted to a public relations exercise on a grand scale. Huge publicity was given to the extension of 'shareholder democracy', designed in part to prevent renationalisation but also conveying an important ideological message, consistent with the more general theme of the 'UK Ltd'. The Labour Party's objections to selling off a major national asset met with the damaging retort that under a Labour government the British public would remain excluded from a share in the high technology future. After BT's privatisation the British public was then exposed to an advertising campaign to reinforce BT's new *high-tech* public image.

The radical changes in broadcasting were to be part of this wider development. The greatest long-term effects of information technology on the economy were likely to follow from development of new means of transmitting and receiving 'information'. Following the recommendations of a particularly influential report, the ITAP's report *Cable Systems* (1982), policy for the urgent development of cable systems promised to equal the government's 'heroic' approach for telecommunications more generally. The recommendations reflected very clearly the seemingly omnipresent ideology of the Conservative government. Opportunities for new entrants into markets created by technological convergence — of computing, telecommunications and broadcasting — provided the Thatcher government with an ideologically more acceptable alternative to a statist infrastructural policy for the modernisation of communications. Essentially, new, wholly private forms of investment in cable were to be stimulated by a deregulation of government restrictions on cable services. The government was persuaded by the cable lobby and by the ITAP — whose composition reflected exclusively the interests of the British computer and electronics sectors — that, in this way, the promise of profits from new entertainment services (cable television) would stimulate private-sector development of a new infrastructure to carry the value-added new communications services of the future information economy.[7]

The government's cable plans were characterised by a large measure of technological and industrial hype — there was much talk about an entertainment-led 'cable revolution' — and initial optimism was soon to be disappointed. These policy failures and mistakes are documented above by Dyson and Humphreys.[8] For the purposes of this analysis, one especially important feature of government policy should be stressed. In pursuing its 'heroic' policy for the wired society, the government rushed through a radical package of deregulation — which raised issues of fundamental significance both for the future of broadcasting specifically and for the future shape of an information-based society more generally — without encouraging a public debate. This failure was matched by the lamentable deficit of programmatic activity by the opposition parties. Some criticism came from the Labour Party, the public-service broadcasters and the broadcasting unions, the Post Office and Engineering Union (POEU), certain interested academics and the Campaign for Press and Broadcasting Freedom. This limited opposition seemed locked into the 'private versus public-service' dimension of the debate. Notably, debate did not focus on the opportunity cost for society of such massive expenditure. Equally, it failed to consider adequately such closely related issues as the impact of 'homeworking' ('teleworking'), rationalisation of work, cashless banking and shopping and the many other wider effects of the new technologies on the economy and society. Generally, political opposition was surprisingly mute and overshadowed by opposition to the specific institutional reforms involved in privatisation and deregulation of BT. An effort was made by the Greater London Council (GLC) and Sheffield City Council (both controlled by Labour's 'participatory left') to involve a range of voluntary associations and the wider public in the cable debate.[9] This effort was, however, overtaken by the pace of the government's actions, which also indicated that local authorities were not to be given any scope for direct involvement (and realistically for any further interest) in cable development. The consequence of this narrowness of the policy community, the pace and covertness of the policy-process and the muteness of opposition was that the debate about cable in Britain remained conspicuously limited – and the public ill-informed. From a comparison with the French and especially the West German cases, it is reasonably safe to conclude that this relative absence of party political debate about cable seriously impeded and delayed the development of a wider public discussion about, and awareness of, the nature of the communications revolution.

More generally, though, the Conservative government's attempts simultaneously to occupy the high ground of technological modernisation and to stake out the ideological parameters of technological change stimulated responses from the opposition parties. In quick succession during 1985 the Labour Party, the SDP and the Liberal Party produced new policy statements on the new technologies. The lynch-pin of future Labour strategy would be development of a long-term industrial strategy in a corporatist manner. This strategy would be based on the co-involvement of government, firms and unions in industrial policy and in the identification and development of new applications for IT. A National Investment Bank would provide long-term finance, R&D expenditure would be increased, for instance to allow ICL, the British computer firm, to benefit from the kind of state support now being enjoyed by most of its foreign competitors (under the Conservatives, ICL's revenues had fallen behind those of Bull in France, Siemens in West Germany and Olivetti in Italy: see Appendix 2). Telecommunications modernisation would be similarly developed: digital switching (System X), fibre optics, Prestel, all received a favourable mention. A national training strategy ('especially for women') would promote IT education, training and re-training. Public purchasing, public enterprise and a public stake in high technology firms would all play a key role. A glossy consultative document, entitled *Labour and Information Technology* (1985), made clear Labour's unequivocal commitment to seizing a 'great opportunity' (incidentally, within a scenario of European collaboration).[10]

Labour's new approach to new technology and industrial change seemed to resemble the essentially social-democratic alternative adopted by the previous Callaghan government within the framework of a social-contract. The only major change seemed to be greater enthusiasm for modernisation.

Adverse effects of 'the computerisation of society' hardly received a mention. Rather, glowing reference was now being made to the positive application of computer technology to rejuvenate old, and to promote new, industry (on the model of the efforts of the Greater London Enterprise Board and the West Midlands Enterprise Board) and to increase the quality of, and decentralise, public services. Local authority initiatives (Labour ones) in IT were a new and respectable ingredient of overall Labour strategy. It is significant, however, that the GLC's approach (outlined in the *London Industrial Strategy* and in the *Communications Campaign*) contained more radical pointers toward a socialist alternative, laying great stress on post-Keynesian interventions in the production process and also raising important questions about the possible negative effects of the communications revolution.[11]

The SDP's *Focus on the Future − a Strategy for Innovation* (1985) reflected another brand of social-democratic ideology, laying stress on the need for partnership and a rejection of class-based attitudes − a theme it shared with its Liberal allies − in place of a corporatist approach and 'grand plans'. The SDP at least acknowledged widespread public fears that higher unemployment would follow the introduction of new technologies. Yet the SDP rejected such pessimism, arguing that 'improvement in productivity could even help to reverse the current tragic situation'. While attempting to distance itself from the Labour Party's 'socialist' approach, the SDP advocated government intervention, what it called 'leadership and bold initiatives', in view of the 'urgency that cannot wait for the invisible hand of the market place to take effect'. In fact, many of the SDP's proposals were variants of Labour's − for instance, the establishment of a New Technology Enterprise Corporation to provide private and public 'seed-corn' capital and British Innovations plc to supply long-term development finance. This investment bank would initially be both owned and financed by government, but the aim was that it should develop into a unit trust with its shares on sale to the British public. In addition, the SDP promised much greater promotion of R&D, combined with expanded education, training and retraining initiatives (again with positive action policies for women). Great stress was given to fiscal incentives and other financial incentives to promote entrepreneurial activity. However, the unions received only a single mention − the rhetorical, sweeping and seemingly inaccurate cry of 'why do our unions put short-term job preservation above long-term job creation?' Generally, the SDP seemed set to rival the Labour Party's revived Wilsonian enthusiasm for modernisation.[12]

The Liberal Party's document *Progress through Change* (1985), too, embraced the theme of technological modernisation, particularly in information technology. However, the Liberal Party expressed concern that new technologies might lead to a 'new enslavement'; accordingly, it was important that employment and social welfare legislation kept pace with industrial policy. Partnership and consultation, both between government and industry and at company-level and the work-place, were strongly advocated; so too was decentralisation in the administration of new industrial policy.[13]

This brief summary of the opposition parties' policy statements in 1985 demonstrates, above all, a common determination to wrest public identification of technological modernisation away from the Conservative government's policies and Thatcherite ideology. There seemed substantial common ground: for instance, about the need for improved policies for education, training and retraining to bridge the 'skills gap' and cope with dislocations of the labour market; for much wider social partnership and consultation; and for decentralisation.

It was above all in France that these particular ideological themes – modernisation, participation, education and training, and decentralisation – were given the highest possible salience by the Socialist government that was swept to power in the Presidential and Assembly elections of 1981. Immediately upon coming into office, the French Socialists significantly increased government support for information- and communications-technologies. The rationale was at once both economic and cultural; the concern to preserve industrial, political and cultural independence was combined with great optimism about the new technologies' potential for achieving a more communicative *société conviviale*.

In the French case, the Socialists' ideological approach contrasted with the generally pragmatic approach of the previous centre-right Giscardian regime between 1974 and 1981. Like the 1974–79 Labour government in Britain, the Giscard administration had been faced with an incomplete (but growing) awareness of the technological convergence of computing and telecommunications. As in the British case, a sectoral approach had been taken: for instance, to carry very substantial government support for the computer industry into a third phase of the (still patently unsuccessful) *Plan Calcul*; and, with much greater and visible success, in the telecommunications sector, where modernisation of France's once notoriously inadequate telephone system was achieved. Also importantly, a report into *télématique* ('telematics', or the convergence of computing and telecommunications) was commissioned. It led to the publication in 1978 of the well-known 'Nora/Minc Report', *The Computerisation of Society*.[14] Subsequently, the *Programme Télématique* was launched, including pilot projects in videotex and optic fibre cable. Yet by the early 1980s, like Britain, France faced a negative trade balance in most areas of advanced electronics (telephonics excepted).

By means of much increased investment, nationalisations and rationalisation within the electronics and IT sectors and planning contracts, the French Socialists aimed (and to some extent managed) to reverse a decline of French information- and communications-technology.[15] Above all, French Socialist attitudes to the 'communications revolution' had been shaped by the highly influential 'Nora/Minc Report'. This report had carried the message that the 'telematic society' carried both risks and opportunities: foremost among the former the report recalled the alarm at the US lead in high technology voiced a decade earlier by Jacques Servan-Schreiber in *Le Défi Américain* (1967), and expressed profound fears about France's resulting loss of national sovereignty (mainly to IBM); among the latter, and of particular appeal to the French Socialists, was the possibility that, under certain conditions, the wired society offered a 'new model of growth', accelerating the rise of a highly productive society; it raised also possibilities for decentralising and demassifying the political structure and society as a result of 'telematics'.

With respect to industrial policy, the French Socialists sought to develop a global strategy; the 'Nora/Minc Report' had called for a national strategy to meet the challenge of the American domination in computers, satellite systems and telecommunications. They blamed the incoherence and lack of unified purpose behind Giscard d'Estaing's industrial policies for increased import penetration and reliance on American and Japanese technology. In particular, the French Socialists believed that the development of telecommunications, advanced electronics and data-processing should no longer be pursued largely independently of each other. They attempted to develop a 'unified' strategy, based upon the *filière* approach to national industries; a strategy that aimed to discover, integrate and exploit synergies, and reinforce technological, industrial and commercial links between the different areas of advanced electronics, information and communications technologies. Consequently, in July 1982, the *Programme d'action filière électronique* (PAFE) was adopted and given special priority in the ninth Five-Year Plan (1984–88). The PAFE was premised upon a radically new understanding of the interdependence and interrelatedness of different high technology sectors and the opportunities that this *filière* approach presented for internally generated domestic growth and the fostering of domestic production. In the wake of Socialist nationalisations and reorganisations, the state controlled 50 per cent of production in the electronics *filière*. It also controlled 75 per cent of total research and development expenditure, much of which was allocated to telecommunications and advanced electronics.

Above all, the PAFE had a symbolic significance; it gave publicly identifiable meaning and definition to the new government's commitment to attaining strategic national objectives in a wide range of the new information technologies. The message was that France had to reconquer domestic markets and develop an economic strike force in order to attack foreign markets. Other steps were taken that had a symbolic as well as, and in some cases, more than, a practical value. A full-scale national programme was developed with the aim of promoting a technological culture in research organisations and, above all, in public opinion. A series of widely publicised National Research Meetings was staged. Paris began to host extravagant national exhibitions representing all branches of the new information- and communications-technologies. Following the recommendations of the 'Nora/Minc Report', a Ministry of Communications was established (the 'Nora/Minc Report' had suggested the need for a minister with competences and political weight enough to face up to IBM!). In Paris, a Study Centre for Advanced Technical Systems was created and housed in former *Ecole Polytechnique* buildings. At the regional level, *technological culture centres* were to be built all over France. Even after the Socialist return to more pragmatic economic policies of *rigueur* after March 1983 – involving a revision of state investment and R&D targets – priority continued to be given to the theme of *modernisation*. Labour-market dislocations would still be met with appropriate policies for the *formation* (training) and *reconversion* of the workforce; measures for longer holidays and a shortened working week were promised; the programme of *l'informatique à l'école* was the only element of the national education budget to escape *rigueur*. In short, the message of the need for technological modernisation (and industrial restructuring) became even more urgent.

The same 'heroic' approach was evident in the French Socialist approach to 'audio-visual communication'. The reform law of 1982 for 'audio-visual communication' involved more than merely a new definition of broadcasting. It reflected the French Socialists' recognition of the wider economic potential of the 'communications revolution', while at the same time indicating their determination to incorporate technological change into their plans for 'liberating' broadcasting and decentralising information and cultural production. Important initiatives by the French Socialists in the field of 'audio-visual communication' included the *Plan Câble*, which was announced in November 1982. The *Plan Câble* was to be the French answer *par excellence* to the 'wired society' of the future; it was explicitly designed to launch the country into the first division of information societies. The French Socialists perceived the rewiring of the nation as the key to developing an integrated national communications system — a future Integrated Services Digital Network (ISDN) that would carry all the new value-added information services on one support. For the French government it was a *grand projet* and launched with corresponding élan.[16]

The *Plan Câble* also reflected the specific administrative ambitions of the *Direction Générale des Télécommunications* (DGT, the telecommunications wing of the PTT). During the 1970s the investment capacity and prestige of the DGT had grown inordinately due mainly to its role in modernising France's once backward telephone system. Subsequently, it had gained new degrees of virtually autonomous initiative and social and political influence with the launch of the telematics programme at the end of the Giscardian *septennat*. When the French Socialists came into office, the DGT was already the flag-bearer of French communications modernisation. The DGT was, accordingly, given a key role in the *filière électronique* (in effect, though, the DGT became the milch-cow of the *filière* with ultimately adverse consequences for the *Plan Câble*). The telematics programme was stepped up in a highly voluntarist manner that promised to increase still further the DGT's prestige and influence. Minitel terminals (visual display units for the French videotex system) were now distributed free, with a huge 'marketing' and back-up service, in a phased process of mass introduction to the French public. Initially the telematics programme had met with local opposition; now it was 'socialised'. The *Plan Câble* was designed to be the final stage of the telematics revolution. For the DGT, it would open new vistas of commercial activity and assure its future telecommunications monopoly. In turn, the DGT's social prestige helped to glamorise the communications revolution.

Not surprisingly, the French Socialist government's approach to the 'wired society' reflected a very different set of values and interests from those pursued in Britain. The French Socialists saw cable as part of a much grander social and cultural project than the British Conservative government. The *Plan Câble* sprang from an industrial policy logic, but it also promised French Socialists much in the way of *décentralisation* and *participation*. For many French Socialists and Communists the notion of *interactive* communication exceeded any restrictive definition of new telematic commercial services, such as videophone, teleshopping, teleconferencing, data systems and Minitel-type services. With potential applications in the fields of education and training, local employment initiatives, local and regional culture, tourism, healthcare, *'télésurveillance'* (e.g. in old peoples' flats), telematic *journaux de quartier, télévision de proximité* and personal *messagerie* (by no means exhausting the list of 'socially useful purposes'), 'interactivity' offered a means of advancing from 'mass communication' ('one-way' and centralised) towards 'social communication' ('two-way' and decentralised). It was seen as promising more participation, 'communicativeness' and increased social and cultural exchange. Communications modernisation promised to contribute to the development of a 'new citizenship' (Pierre Mauroy), building on the burgeoning new associational life (*vie associative*) at the local level that already marked such a radical break with French tradition. For some Communists, fibre-optic cable even took on the dimensions of *le fibre démocratique*. The novelty of the *Plan Câble* was that it gave an important role to the *collectivités locales* (local authorities). The intervention of local actors, both public and private, was to complement that of the national state. Such local political intervention was ruled out of consideration by the British Conservatives, although it had been sought by certain municipal authorities like the GLC, which shared many of the more 'bold' and 'imaginative' aspirations of the French Socialists.

Consequently, the French Socialists widened considerably the policy community in cable policy. While the policy process itself was thus complicated, this element of *décentralisation* injected greater legitimation into it. In turn, against a background of basic élite consensus, this effort at legitimation was almost certain to have a positive effect on public acceptance of the new communications technologies. The telematics programme was popularised by the DGT's largesse and by well publicised preliminary social experiments or pilot projects (notably at Vélizy). In the case of cable, however, legitimation went one step further. It was supplied by, and popularisation was encouraged by, the *autonomous* actions of local élites, generally politicians (of the right or left) seeking personal prestige, electoral popularity and an *image de marque* as *technopôles* for their municipalities. The battle for communications modernisation was thus carried down very effectively to the local level. Municipalities as diverse as Montpellier (Socialist) in the non-industrial south, and Metz (Centre des Démocrats Sociaux, CDS) and Lille (Socialist) in the de-industrialised north and east, now developed strategies for the post-industrial information society. Strategies varied considerably in detail: for example, between the public-service, 'cable-on-the-rates' strategy of the Communists in the dormitory communes of northern Paris or of Socialists in Montpellier, and the market-oriented 'entertainment-led' approach of pragmatic Socialists in Rennes and of Gaullists in central Paris. Yet, the positive and active basic consensus among élites and opinion-formers about cable's promise could not fail to escape the French *grand public*.

While structural complexity proved, subsequently, to be the 'Achilles heel' of the *Plan Câble*, the *Programme Télématique* made spectacular progress. By early 1986 there was a general popular clamour for *Minitels* from all parts of the country not yet reached by the DGT's 'rolling programme'. It was becoming clear that the huge FFr 46 billion, 12-year project to equip France's 30 million households was likely to be recovered relatively quickly by profits from the increased use of the telephone network (which videotex systems use at present). It was possible to conclude that, despite certain disappointments and delays, the French *grand public* was fast 'learning to love' the 'wired society'.

In West Germany, the background to the debate over the introduction of the new information- and communications-technologies was essentially similar to the British and French examples: namely, increasing doubts about West Germany's economic competitiveness, especially in the high technology 'sunrise' industries; fears of a growing technology gap with the United States and Japan; combined with mounting awareness of the impending 'communications revolution'. Under the initiatives of SPD 'technocrats', the 'social liberal' government (1969–82) commissioned an inquiry, the *Kommission für den Ausbau des technischen Kommunikationssystems* (KtK), to examine the question. The KtK emphasised the urgency of the need to develop modern information- and communications technologies, and stated that the advantages to be gained thereby, in particular increased economic productivity, would outweigh any adverse social costs. The SPD technocrats, influenced by this commission, determined to develop and introduce the new technologies as quickly and efficiently as possible. Subsequently, a 'Programme for Technical Communication' (*Programm Technische Kommunikation* 1978–82) was developed by the Ministry of Research and Technology (established by the SPD) and the Bundespost Ministry. This led to the development of a number of advanced communications systems, like videotex, a super-telex type data network and localised optic-fibre networks; however, the SPD technocrats followed the KtK's recommendation that cable television systems should only be experimented in 'pilot projects'. The KtK was concerned mainly with the lack of evident demand for cable. The SPD technocrats, however, were further constrained by the 'anti-cable television' media policy of their party. Helmut Schmidt himself qualified cable as potentially 'more dangerous than nuclear power', reflecting a certain *Wertkonservatismus* within his party, as well as its easily comprehensible interest in maintaining a balance between the public-service broadcasting sector and the private commercially organised press. During the 1970s a furious debate broke out over cable television between the SPD and the CDU/CSU. The latter parties now sought to exploit the new opportunities provided by a technology promising an abundance of television to introduce a more sympathetic commercial broadcasting sector. This polarisation had a mixed effect. In the short term, it meant that political articulation of the possibilities raised by the 'wired society' quickly came to focus upon issues of the future nature of 'mass communication' (broadcasting). In the longer term, it gave *Kabelpolitik* a visibility on the 'political agenda', ensuring that the wider issues raised by cable technology, such as its effect on business communications, work practices and emloyment, became incorporated into an already polarised debate. In West Germany, at any rate, positive ideas of 'social communication', such as appeared in France, co-existed with negative fears of 'anti-social communication'.

Before the 'social liberal' government, traditionally state support for new technology had been in the form of indirect assistance channelled through an extensive network of government investment incentives to industry. To a great extent, this 'hands-off' approach had reflected the characteristic budgetary restraint of the West German state. Nevertheless, as doubts about West Germany's economic competitiveness mounted during the 1970s, direct funding in the form of selective sectoral policy gained importance with the modernisation policies of the SPD's *aktive Strukturpolitik* or 'active industrial policy'. When, later, the Christian-Liberal coalition (CDU/CSU/FDP) came to power in 1982, generally the SPD's 'active industrial policy' was adopted although renamed 'new research and technology policy oriented towards innovation' (despite their promises of 'mehr Markt, weniger Staat' or 'more market, less state'). In fact, under the new CDU/CSU/FDP coalition in Bonn, Heinz Riesenhuber's Ministry for Research and Technology formulated West Germany's first integrated government programme for Information Technology, which received massive support for its first five years in order to promote micro-electronics, data bank, office automation, audio-visual technologies and telecommunications.[17] The previous initiatives of the SPD 'technocrats' were to be developed, including digitalisation of the telecommunications network, development of a new integrated ultra-high-speed telex- and data- communication network (a kind of 'electronic mail'), introduction of *Bildschirmtext* (the West German Prestel), and the so-called BIGFON development of fibre-optic systems – leading in a series of stages to an Integrated Services Digital Network (ISDN). These developments remained priorities of the *Bundespost* (the West German PTT) under the new Christian-Democrat/Liberal coalition of Helmut Kohl. Continued state support for micro-electronics was promised, for instance, by the 'Megaproject' to produce a 'super chip', with the likelihood of a massive DM 260 million subsidy to the national champion Siemens for its collaboration with Philips of the Netherlands. Only in the sphere of cable policy did direction change radically, under the impact of media policy rather than technology policy considerations. This new direction was reflected in the programme that was launched by Christian Schwarz-Schilling, the new CDU Minister for Post and Telecommunications, to cable the country in tried-and-tested, and arguably outdated, copper-coaxial cable that had only a very limited *interactive* capacity so that commercial broadcasting might be more rapidly introduced. As Morgan and Webber have indicated, plans for institutional reform in telecommunications, notably to curb the *Bundespost*'s monopoly of telecommunications, were not a priority for the new government. Equally strikingly, an ideological debate began within the CDU that skilfully sought to identify the party with the 'third industrial revolution'. Politicians like Lothar Späth, the dynamic CDU *Ministerpräsident* in Baden-Württemberg, and Kurt Biedenkopf, leader of the CDU in North-Rhine-Westphalia, attempted to stake out a claim for the CDU to be 'the party' of 'the third industrial revolution'.

Despite this relative continuity of industrial policies for the new technologies, there has been no absence of critical discussion about technological modernisation in West German society. For much of the period of the Social-Liberal coalition (SPD/FDP), the trade unions were constrained as 'hostages to a friendly government'. Yet, within both the unions and the SPD itself, the left developed an increasingly critical attitude towards technological modernisation, and the SPD-led government in Bonn was constrained increasingly to take this into consideration. Thus Volker Hauff, as Minister for Research and Technology, had a harder time of it carrying the trade unions with him than his predecessors, Horst Ehmke and Hans Matthöfer. Moreover, towards the end of the 1970s 'post-materialist' critiques gained much ground beyond the 'established Left', finding highly vocal expression in 'citizen initiative groups' and in the 'Green' and 'Alternative' movements. Under the Social-Liberal coalition certain key issues had assumed a symbolic significance: the nuclear power debate, the use of computers for social control, electronic surveillance and the cable debate all combined to increase critical reflection about the direction of technological developments. They came to symbolise the failure of the SPD to deliver promises of major social reform in coalition with the Liberals after 1969 and to symbolise the rigidity and unresponsiveness of the 'party state' (*Parteienstaat*), a state of established parties that used such power to consolidate their own positions as office holders. The particular, 'protest-oriented' and 'anti-technocratic' shape and expression of the 'new social movements' in the form of 'citizen initiative groups' and the 'Greens/ Alternatives' seemed to be rooted in special West German circumstances.

Nevertheless, to complement structural policy during the 1970s, the West German Social Democrats had conceived the strategy of a 'socially oriented technology policy'. Although it must be emphasised that this was not related to IT specifically, still less to the new communications technologies, this concept linked 'forced economic and technological modernisation with efforts to include the union movement in the societal shaping of technology and work organisation'.[18] In accordance with the fragmented corporatism or liberal corporatism characteristic of West German industrial organisation with its emphasis on 'social partnership', the strategy recognised the high economic and political integration of West German labour and sought to maintain it and enrol it in the legitimation of innovation. It was, therefore, an early and specific policy approach to new technologies and industrial change that promised to give West Germany under the Social Democrats, alongside (although to a lesser extent than) Sweden, a certain distinction among Western industrialised countries. The strategy of a 'socially oriented technology policy' centred on trade union involvement in the political regulation of research and development within the auspices of the Ministry of Research and Technology (it included the trade-union inspired programme for the 'improvement in the quality of work life'). Its immediate implications for government policy became the subject of much government, trade union and independent research and debate. It seems likely that, as one authority on the subject has suggested:

> ... while the direct effects of the programme [were] fairly modest, the indirect effects [were] considerably greater. Socially oriented technology policy ... spurred much debate in the plant and among the public at large about heretofore largely taboo aspects of developing alternative technology and the social structure of work. Within the unions, too, it ... encouraged a mobilisation that cannot be underestimated and ... intensified union demands for a stronger voice in matters relating to technology and organisation of the work place.[19]

In other words, the moderate hopes and modest aims of reformist circles within the SPD (originally inspired by Chancellor Willy Brandt's slogan 'daring more democracy') for a *socially oriented technology policy* actually stimulated and legitimated more widely a continuing critical assessment of new technologies in general in a way that contrasts with the British and French cases. It seems reasonable to suggest that the SPD's distinctive approach to technological change, itself an attempt to legitimate a modernisation strategy, had the side-effect of legitimating critical discussion of the social, as well as the economic, issues that 'modernisation' raised. At the same time, the advance of micro-electronics during the 1970s became increasingly the main object of trade union concern; leading to a debate about the silicon chip as 'Job-Killer'. In turn, this debate came to inform increasingly the debate about *Kabelpolitik* during the early 1980s.

A decentralised political system too brings both advantages and disadvantages for technological innovation. As in the French case after the decentralisation reforms of 1982/83, it may stimulate initiative, encourage a social learning process and contribute to the legitimation of new policies. Indeed the West German *Länder* have competed vigorously to attract new investment and develop their own strategies for modernisation in the field of media, telecommunications and micro-electronics generally. At the same time decentralisation provides a wider arena for potential conflict. It would seem reasonable to suggest that political resistance to 'modernisation' will be accompanied by a heightened public awareness of the issues or at least greater uncertainty about the appropriate policy responses. In the cases of both cable policy and videotex (*Bildschirmtext*), the combination of federalism and polarisation (that extended beyond the parties) over 'media politics' led to delays and frustration. Unified and centralised policy-making was impeded. The constitutional division of responsibilities between telecommunications (a federal responsibility) and broadcasting (a responsibility of the *Länder*) was an obstacle to the development of a national strategy for communications. At the same time, the surrounding politial debates about the social consequences of new information- and communications-technologies were fought out in many decentralised forums, where the left within the SPD and the 'Greens/Alternatives' were able to articulate alternative views.

Significant divisions within the SPD about technological modernisation, in particular the new communications technologies, appeared at the party's 1984 national conference in Essen. Paradoxically, this conference is better known for the SPD pragmatists' victory over 'media policy', which reoriented the party away from 'fundamental opposition' to the 'new media', namely cable and satellite television, towards an adaptive and 'constructive' approach that accepted the introduction of a commercial broadcasting sector. Yet, this 'victory' was very narrow and there was also a very controversial debate about the general direction of SPD *Technologiepolitik* or 'technology policy', in which the new communications technologies' wider social implications were discussed. Led by Johannes Rau (now the party's *Kanzlerkandidat* or 'chancellor candidate') and Peter Glotz (its general secretary), the party executive argued that West Germany could not renounce modernisation, and the consequent rationalisation, in order to secure and create new jobs. However, numerous resolutions and interventions in the debate were far more negative. From the *Parteibasis* or 'grass roots' there were calls for an 'active confrontation with the (party's) growth- and technology-fetishists'. Concern was expressed about the *Rationalisierungstechnologien* or 'rationalisation technologies' (women delegates were particularly vocal in attacking the 'electronic office'). Subsequently, the SPD executive has attempted to absorb this critical current by developing the themes of a shorter working week, 'humanisation of work', an expansion of *Mitbestimmung* ('co-determination') and 'eco-growth' (also designed to build a new 'concertation' with the unions).[20]

Finally, as Dyson has pointed out earlier, a special feature of the West German political system seems to be the high level of legitimation requirements of policy. The new information- and communications-technologies were the subject of a number of commissions of inquiry: notably, the *Kommission für den Ausbau des technischen Kommunikationsystems* (KtK) in the period 1974–76; the work of the *Expertenkommission: Neue Medien* in Baden-Württemberg; and the Bundestag's *Enquetekommission: Neue Informations- und Kommunikationstechniken*. In addition, videotex, fibre optic cable and cable television were the objects of 'pilot projects' to examine social, as well as technical, effects. Undoubtedly, this process of 'formal' or 'procedural' legitimation contributed to, as well as reflected, the 'politicisation' of the issues raised.[21] In short, negative viewpoints on the communications revolution were expressed more widely in West Germany than in Britain or France.

TRADE UNIONS AND MODERNISATION: THE CHALLENGE OF ADAPTATION

In all three countries, governments have linked introduction of new technologies and management of industrial change to strategies for emerging from the economic crisis. As we have seen, the political arm of the left embraced growth-orientated technological modernisation, often as enthusiastically as the right; in doing so, it concentrated generally on policies for the stimulation of production and application of the new technologies. In West Germany, however, a vocal minority current, finding its expression both within the SPD and in the 'Green' movement/party, developed a more negative critique. The question remains, how has the industrial arm of the left confronted the issues? The new technologies (and the accompanying political 'techno-logic') presented trade union movements with a special challenge; namely, adaptation to a major new transformation of the nature of economic production that promised immediate costs and (uncertain) benefits only in the medium or long term. While governments disposed of an array of instruments for managing – and legitimating – social change, trade union options were limited generally to the sphere of production. Moreover, their own legitimation depended upon their effectiveness in defending the narrow interests of their memberships. Yet, major changes in the sphere of production – deemed crucial by governments and, as seen in other contributions, by industrial, administrative and commercial lobbies for the promotion of economic efficiency – depend crucially upon the development of new perceptions, values and goals in the trade union movement. History would seem to suggest that modernisation brings no automatic propensity for moderation and consensus; the 'communications revolution', especially, threatens to undermine the effectiveness of trade unions and to challenge their legitimacy. Accordingly, trade unions have to consider their future strategies as major autonomous and conscious actors in the wider legitimation of industrial restructuring and modernisation; these strategies are in turn shaped by the framework or partnership or corporatism favoured by the political left.

The communications revolution is likely to have a particularly great impact on 'information workers' in the service sector. Theorists of post-industrial society have disagreed, or expressed uncertainty, about whether the coming of 'post-industrial' society would lead to a new radicalism or passivity, to activism or to new manipulation and exploitation, to the 'good society' or to a technocratic nightmare. Generally, they have stressed, however, the declining significance of the traditional 'working class' and emphasised the growing significance of 'new social forces'.[22] In this analysis, attention is focused on the role of unions that represent new information workers and technicians and on their role as pacemakers of new agenda-setting. Unions that are active in the sectors of telecommunications, the media and the information processing services are especially relevant to the communications revolution: and the interaction of these 'pioneers' of the information society with the wider trade union movement will certainly become increasingly significant.

In examining the question of acceptance of new technology (micro-electronics technology particularly) at the place of work in the early 1980s, a recent comprehensive study of the British case came up with the surprising conclusion that it has been a 'non-problem', with certain exceptions, most notably the craft unions of the newspaper industry in Fleet Street.[23] Technological innovation encountered many obstacles, such as skill-shortages and difficulties in raising finance. Yet 'opposition from trade unions (was alleged to be) twice as common in France and Germany as in Britain'.[24] Trade union behaviour in Britain was 'co-operative'; trade unions took a generally positive attitude to new technology, although they sought to negotiate the protection of their members' interests during its introduction, and also a share of the benefits and a role in decision-making. At the same time the report did not advocate complacency. It suggested that the main reason for this degree of acceptance of new technology was the as yet incremental and limited nature of its introduction in Britain with (so far) only marginal effects on working life.

It seems that this relative acceptance of new technology by British trade unions reflected also the underlying political and economic realities that faced them during the late 1970s and early 1980s – mediated by the inherent structural weaknesses of British trade unionism. In particular, union responses faced serious problems as a consequence of exceptionally high and rising rates of domestic unemployment. In the telecommunications sector, for instance, there had been much evidence of trade union concern – and even militancy – about the levels of unemployment that had already resulted, partly from recession-induced rationalisations, partly from the internationalisation of telecommunications markets with new technology, and partly directly from the introduction of new technology itself. However, in Britain trade union responses in this key sector were characterised mainly by inter-site rivalry and competition for a diminishing number of orders. This rivalry and competition was compounded by a history of trade-union sectionalism. A unified response was inhibited by the multi-unionism of many sites. In addition to a cleavage between blue- and white-collar workers, in many cases unions competed to represent the same category of workers. Even more significantly, the computerisation of work meant that increasingly a new category of 'technical' worker was blurring the distinction between blue- and white-collar activity.[25]

Union strategies in Britain varied considerably. For example, at first the approach of the Post Office Engineering Union (POEU) reflected the received Keynesian wisdom that new investment should be matched by a stimulation of demand. Job losses from investment in new technologies would then be compensated by economic growth. By contrast, the Electrical, Electronic, Telecommunications and Plumbing Trade Union (EETPU) seemed early on to embrace a new wisdom by advocating liberalisation of the telecommunications market and the dismantlement of the Post Office monopoly. The Association of Professional, Executive, Clerical and Computer Staff (APEX) and the Association of Scientific, Technical and Managerial Staffs (ASTMS) followed a 'middle way' and signed the first new technology agreements, thereby hoping to mitigate job losses and secure improved terms. There was, in short, little trade-union co-ordination at the national level.

Responses varied over time and within unions too. For example, the POEU campaigned at first (in 1978) for a 35-hour working week, a measure of control over the introduction of new technology and voluntary retraining. After management steamrollered the introduction of System X exchanges – a technology that had already caused, and promised to cause even more, job-losses – the POEU Broad Left won conference opinion over to a boycott strategy. Yet, such militancy soon seemed to be doomed to early failure. Very quickly aggressiveness gave way to a new defensiveness, in large measure due to a changed political situation.[26]

The TUC's concern about the negative effects of new technologies mounted during the late 1970s; its economic policy texts emphasised the need for a reduced (35-hour) working week in 1977–78, and from 1979 onwards it began to devote considerable attention to new technologies. After the Conservatives' second successive election victory of 1983, the leadership of the Trade Union Congress (TUC) acknowledged the weakness of aggressive responses in the face of a changed political situation by advocating a 'new realism'. Under the Conservatives a new threat had appeared. Both multinationals, for instance IBM, and an increasing number of small 'high tech' electronics companies had been encouraged to bypass trade unions altogether; a new situation appeared of staff associations representing the 'winners' as the 'losers' disappeared from the companies' books to swell the dole queues. At the same time, certain unions seemed ambitious to consolidate their own position by gathering 'winners'. Undoubtedly the most aggressive in this approach was the EETPU, which now began to negotiate novel 'no-strike' deals often with foreign firms. This union seemed increasingly determined to expand within the 'high tech' electronics and telecommunications sectors, often at other unions' expense. By early 1986, the EETPU seemed to have established a measure of independence from TUC policy – for instance, by ignoring agreed guidelines about the introduction of new technology in the printing industry.

The introduction of new technology in the printing sector (electronic typesetting etc) broke down over the objections of craft unions, the National Graphical Association (NGA) and the Society of Graphical and Allied Trades (SOGAT 82) to the advance of workers with new skills, notably members of the EETPU, and to the introduction of non-unionised workers into the sector. These developments were in turn encouraged by entrepreneurs seeking new advantages from technological change. Again the EETPU was prepared to negotiate no-strike deals, even to the extent of incurring general opprobium within the wider trade-union movement.

The telecommunications sector had not been subjected to incremental change. It was a sector of monumental change; so too was the printing sector. The wider impact on the service sector had also not escaped the trade unions' notice. In banking, for example, new technology was being introduced at a particularly fast rate, while the Banking Industrial and Finance Union (BIFU) was even excluded from consultation. By 1985 BIFU was threatening industrial action, such as the refusal to operate automatic cash dispensers, should this exclusion persist. Meanwhile, cashless banking and shopping emerged as a more threatening development. Moreover, by mid-1986 the impending 'Big Bang' in the City led both BIFU and the banks' in-house staff unions to fear that they would be excluded from having a role in a major new growth area of their industry. City employers were arguing that the new business emerging as the result of a combination of deregulation and technological modernisation belonged to areas like merchant banking, which were traditionally non-union, and they were refusing to recognise the unions' role.[27] Therefore, in many diverse sectors there appeared a wholly new degree of threat of 'non-union enclaves' in growth areas of the economy.

At the same time, new documents from white-collar unions reflected general apprehension about the effects of micro-electronics-based systems on the quality of work as well as on employment (deskilling and job-loss) in the 'electronic office'.[28] 'Home-working' by computer programmers and systems analysts – a still very limited phenomenon, and one that so far seemed to affect women more than men – raised further cause for concern. Its emergence had not been characterised by Alvin Toffler's utopian vision of the 'electronic cottage' but rather by low pay, poor working conditions, isolation and stress. It seemed to bring the danger of a return to non-unionised 'sweated labour'.[29] By the 1980s, rather than reflecting optimism over new technology, trade-union responses in Britain were generally more characterised by a growing awareness of the scale and scope of problems that it raised. A major problem was the difficulty of organising resistance effectively on the shop-floor. This new disinclination to industrial militancy is consistent with the findings of the PSI report; again, however, it must be situated within the wider political and economic context.

Increasingly, trade unions seemed to become disposed to react by negotiating a number of new technology agreements; they recognised that such an approach offered the best hope for the minimum defence of their members' interests. In particular, there was a new feeling that the price for 'participation' in decisions over the introduction of new technology would be a new 'responsibility' and the relinquishing of traditional restrictive practices. In this process, trade unions were informed by the TUC's 'new realism', which had itself been partially inspired by technological change, as was clear from the TUC's statement on Employment and Technology, approved by Congress as 'early' as 1979.[30] 'Outdated' attitudes were attacked by Clive Jenkins and Barrie Sherman, both of ASTMS, in their influential book *The Collapse of Work* (1979).[31] Significantly, the new technology agreements were mainly an initiative of white-collar unions, three of which (APEX, ASTMS and NALGO) accounted for the majority of agreements and were concerned with the introduction of computer-based office, administration and communication systems.[32] However, it must be emphasised that the trade-union position remained conditioned by the continuing recession, the weak labour market and the ideological/political climate. The government seemed intent upon excluding the trade unions from its vision of the 'UK Ltd'. By mid-1986 Norman Willis, the TUC general secretary, was writing to the Trade and Industry Secretary to make a formal plea to the government to lift its 'unofficial ban' on union representatives serving on the national committees responsible for high technology.[33] The TUC was taking ever greater pains to dispel the negative image that British unions were opposed to new technologies. Generally they were not; however, the British case remained messy. There was a wide gap, for instance, between the pro-technology opportunism of the EETPU and the continuing hard-line responses of the NGA and the ACTT (The Association of Cinematograph, Television and Allied Technicians).

In France, the level of trade-union organisation has traditionally been much lower than in West Germany and Britain. French trade-unions have long been ideologically fragmented; and trade-union behaviour has been highly ideologically-conditioned. Both the relative weakness of, and political divisions within, the French trade-union movement have inhibited the ability of unions to negotiate practical conditions in the face of overwhelming changes in large sectors of the economy – including the sectors of 'information' and 'communications' workers. Traditionally it had been comparatively easy for employers to disregard French unions; and during the 1970s this situation was exacerbated by the economic crisis and by the increasing sophistication of employers, more and more of whom were introducing 'American-style' management methods that further short-circuited unionism, without polarising industrial relations. It has been suggested that 'this relative weakness has been compounded by the exceptional importance placed on information technology (*informatique, bureautique* and *télématique*) by recent governments'. It can be argued persuasively that French government policy and the dominant presence of the state in the 'information industries' has '... paved the way for French society (including the trade unions) to accept new work processes'.[34]

In France, major trade-union attitudes to technology have been informed by their characteristic ideological preoccupations. For the Confédération Générale du Travail (CGT), it was a 'progressive force, an agent of social transformation'; for the Confédération Française Démocratique du Travail (CFDT), it gave rise to a 'new working-class' of 'radicalised' technicians and white-collar workers. In each case, broad-sweeping Marxist theoretical concerns led to primacy being given to class-based analyses of the role of technology in capitalist society at large. One consequence of this 'transformative' logic was that the material effects of technology on the organisation of work tended to remain of only subordinate interest; another was that '... the need to rely on the state (was) a prominent feature' of union attitudes, completely consistent with the predilection of the French labour movement '... for calling upon Leviathan'.[35] In particular, union strategies placed exaggerated expectations on the use of state power by a left-wing government; the CGT emphasised nationalisations, while the CFDT looked for measures to facilitate 'self-managing socialism' (*socialisme autogestionnaire*) and decentralised industrial democracy. In turn, this reliance on the state, on politics, and on legislation, reflected the weaknesses of trade unionism and the under-institutionalised nature of collective bargaining and industrial relations in France.

However, from the mid-1970s onwards, but particularly after the left's disappointing defeat in the Assembly elections of 1978, together with the effects of recession and accelerating technological change, focus began to shift towards a more pragmatic consideration of 'traditional' trade-union concerns, such as the modernisation of the work process itself, employment and working conditions. The impact of computerisation, in the office sector as well as in manufacturing, had become increasingly a matter of concern throughout the 1970s. The CFDT, with its strong presence in the new high technology and service sectors, was the first to engage in a new debate about automation. In the early 1970s strikes had started to hit the PTT and the service sector – banking and insurance companies – where computerisation was already making great strides. The CGT's main strength lay, by contrast, in the traditional heavy industries, where automation generally lagged behind France's main competitors, and its outlook changed more slowly and much less. Moreover, the CGT's main concerns tended to remain political (hyper-political), reflecting the dominance of 'opposition force' over 'proposition force' arguments within it.[36]

The CFDT's new preoccupation with the impact of technological change, particularly computerisation (*informatique*), on actual working conditions was clearly reflected in a very defensive attitude until the late 1970s; the CFDT was especially disheartened by predictions in the 'Nora/Minc Report' of possibly massive job losses in the service sector.[37] However, there followed a second phase that was characterised by a much more positive attitude. At the end of 1979, Edmond Maire, Secretary General of the CFDT, announced 'nine propositions' of the CFDT on computerisation. They called for a strengthening of the role of the *comité d'entreprise* (works council), increased consultation, more research and experiments on the effects of new technologies, the possibility of recourse to outside experts and the need for more information and training. Interestingly, both the UCC–CFDT (union of engineers, technicians and 'cadres'/managerial staff) and the CFDT–PTT (telecommunications union) played an important role in reshaping attitudes.[38]

The 1982 *lois Auroux* of the Socialist government formulated certain 'new rights of workers' that had been demanded by the CFDT with respect to technological change. The *comité d'entreprise* had now to be widely informed and consulted about the introduction and effects on working conditions of new technologies. In turn one of the Socialists' aims, implicit in these reforms, was to reconcile workers with technological innovations. The technology policy of the CFDT was of particular importance to them because the union was close to the Socialists and was expected to play a significant role in the implementation of their new industrial policies, which stressed the major role of 'strategic new technologies'.[39]

Subsequently, the CFDT has sought to exploit these new changes at the workplace, although it is still generally unclear to what degree it has succeeded. What is clear, however, is that the CFDT has undergone a transformation of attitude to technological change. The CFDT now seeks to influence management decisions over a wide range of issues — not just employment, but also work organisation, skill requirements, and investment — in a pragmatic process of bargaining and formation of counterproposals that represents a departure from its more ideological tradition. This fits into the wider aim of the CFDT to *se resyndicaliser* by seeking to participate more widely and more constructively in the life of the firm. The UCC-CFDT, in particular, seems to be leading the way towards an essentially pragmatic evaluation of the risks *and* opportunities of new technologies.

For the CGT, with its main strength in heavy industry where automation and computerisation had made slower progress (with notable exceptions such as Renault), the change was more gradual.[40] It was also more difficult for the CGT to move beyond regarding new technologies as 'productive forces' in the abstract and heavily ideological sense. Moreover, for the CGT Leviathan remained of enduring importance; much hope had been placed in obtaining a government of the left, in particular in the role of nationalisations. However, 'socialist retreat' and the French Communist Party's (PCF) 'return to the ghetto' compelled the union to distance itself from socialist *modernisation*, seen as an excuse for capitalist rationalisation and attacks on the working class and the labour movement. Under the Socialists, *informatique* remained a 'weapon' deployed against the workers. Moreover, the CGT was unable to adapt, in a similar way to the CFDT, due to its ideological aversion to 'participation' in management decisions. Nevertheless, during the late 1970s the white-collar UGICT (union of engineers, technicians and 'cadres'/managerial staff) played an important role in developing a more pragmatic approach to technological change within the CGT; in particular, it played an important role in sensitising the CGT to the 'communications revolution'. For the CGT, the 'communications revolution' raised, perhaps above all else, the important issue of patterns of media ownership and access.[41]

At the opposite pole, the traditional moderation of the Confédération Française des Travailleurs Chrétiens (CFTC) was reflected in its approach to technological change. As in the case of the CFDT, the 'Nora/Minc Report' combined with considerable disquiet about the new technology in the banking and insurance sectors during the 1970s to produce a catalytic effect in the CFTC. Yet again, the likely impact of technological change on white-collar employment — 'information workers' — seems to have caused particular concern. A leading role in developing a response to technological change was adopted by the UGICA–CFTC (the CFTC's union of engineers, technicians, 'cadres'/managerial staff and associated workers). By the early 1980s the message was clear; there was no point in attacking what was inevitable. At its 42nd Congress at the end of 1984, the CFTC's call was *humaniser les mutations*; resistance to the introduction of new technologies was deemed to be *suicidaire*. Similarly, the CGT-Force Ouvrière (CGT-FO) feared that even worse unemployment would follow failure to innovate, than would be caused by 'computerisation' (*informatisation*). Generally, both the CFTC and the Confédération Générale du Travail-Force Ouvrière (CGT-FO) stressed the themes of *consultation* and *concertation* and emphasised the theme of *reconversion*, to cope with the adverse effects of technological and industrial change.[42]

The Confédération Générale des Cadres (CGC, independent trade union of salaried, 'middle-strata' and 'white-collar' workers) also preached *concertation*. Above all, this union sought to compete with the white-collar federations of the other unions by promoting the narrow hierarchical interests of 'middle strata'. Unlike the UGICT-CGT or the UCC-CFDT, it was more of a professional association than a trade union. However, the CGC had a fast growing influence among the 'middle strata'. Its major contribution to the debate about new technology was a revealing document entitled *La Novotique* (1981), which was so characterised by blatant economic nationalism that this 'white paper' was little more than a self-confessed *plan de bataille* to mobilise opinion for the *indépendance novotique de la France* (*novotique* being a catch-all term for *informatique, bureautique, télématique* and *robotique*).[43]

Interestingly, the role of cable and satellite technologies in the 'communications revolution' produced varying degrees of positive responses from all of the French trade unions. Generally, the cable and satellite revolution produced a consensus that what was most at stake was the economic and cultural *indépendance nationale*. Clearly, this trade union consensus matched the dominant concerns of the government in this field. The CGT-PTT (the CGT federation representing telecommunications workers) was the most enthusiastic about the fibre-optic cabling of France, and the delays and inconsistencies of the *Plan Câble* became the object of its particularly severe criticism. At the same time the CGT opposed the abolition of the state-monopoly in broadcasting and remained the most concerned that the new media might lead to privatisation of 'communication', in particular to an 'Americanisation' of the media and an increased influence of the private press, notably Hersant.[44] Generally, though, trade union responses in France reflected the overwhelming élite consensus that the new media *per se* were to be welcomed. Even the trade union federations that represented workers in the traditional media adopted an attitude of qualified acceptance (which was certainly not the case in West Germany).

In West Germany, for much of the post-war period the Deutscher Gewerkschaftsbund (DGB, the German TU Federation) has adopted a relatively positive attitude to new technologies, although not as a result of any ideological theories; technological modernisation during the long post-war boom has helped to assure the West German worker's comparatively high standard of living and job-security. In turn, the positive or constructive orientation of the trade unions has been central to the extraordinary success of the West German economy. At the same time, though, the West German labour movement was also 'one of the first labour movements to integrate a more *critical* view of general technological developments in their policy making'.[45] As already seen, the SPD had attempted to meet a strong union demand, originally led by IG–Metall, for influencing the direction of technological modernisation by incorporating them into discussions within the Ministry for Research and Technology. Throughout the 1970s this remained the main focus of trade union influence (although the programme for 'humanisation of working conditions' remained the only state-financed development programme in which unions and their members *formally* had a certain say). As the new media debate developed during the 1970s, against the background of industrial crises and growing doubts about West Germany's economic competitiveness, initial trade union responses remained generally limited to concern about the defence, the public-service broadcasting and telecommunications monopolies. By the end of the decade, however, vocal elements within the trade unions were expressing much more general apprehension about the effects of new information- and communications-technologies.

During the 1970s trade union concern over job-loss through rationalisations steadily mounted. The introduction of new technology in the printing sector was, by West German standards, a major problem. The price of attempts to introduce computerised type-setting in the teeth of trade-union opposition was serious industrial action in the winter of 1977–78 by IG Druck und Papier (the print-workers union) – one of the industrial unions that developed a fairly militant position on technological change. However, the strike led to the conclusion of an agreement that included considerable safeguards for jobs and skills.[46]

At the same time the furious debate about cable gave ammunition to the critical current within the West German trade unions. Cable seemed to gain a symbolic significance, simultaneously focusing overarching concerns about its effects on several sectors – broadcasting, telecommunications and the computerisation of the service sector. In 1982 Lothar Zimmermann gave expression to the new mood of apprehension within the DGB by qualifying cable as '... an assault on the mind, bank-account and job' of workers. By now, the trade unions had begun to develop an analysis according to which the new communications services – closely identified with cable – might bring about massive rationalisation of jobs, particularly in the service sector.[47] The DGB became impressed by indications of a growing concern among white collar workers (*Angestellten*), traditionally weakly organised in unions, that their employment would be adversely affected by the new information- and communications-technologies (one DGB survey indicated a rise from 26 per cent in 1974 to 42 per cent in 1981 in the number who evaluated new technologies 'negatively'). From the early 1980s onwards, the DGB mounted a campaign to mobilise these white collar workers.[48]

For the DGB, the new information- and communications-technologies raised the problem of reconciling interests between, on the one hand, large and powerful industrial unions that represented employees who produced and introduced these technologies – organised in IG Metall (the large industrial union representing workers in manufacturing, including electronics goods) and the Deutsche Postgewerkschaft (DPG, the post and telecommunications workers' union) – and the unions that represented employees likely to be directly affected by their applications. These were organised in the IG Druck and Papier, RFFU (the broadcasters' union), HBV (the union of workers in the retail, banking and assurance sectors) and ÖTV (the union of workers in the public sector, transport and insurance sectors). These latter unions expressed considerable alarm at the impact of the new technologies and developed an unusually radical critique. Yet the 'industrial unions', too, found themselves in the position of having to reconcile conflicting interests. IG Metall might expect job-creation to flow from the manufacture of new equipment in consumer electronics and computers; moreover, this might disincline its members to militancy. On the other hand, the introduction of computer-aided manufacturing had already caused widespread job-loss among its workers, leading IG-Metall to take up the issue of technological modernisation early on in the 1970s when the microchip had been widely seen as a 'job-killer'. In fact, IG-Metall had played a leading role in developing the debate about technological modernisation and 'rationalisation', culminating in the 1984 campaign and resulting strike for the 35-hour week. This strike was the longest in German post-war history and lasted seven weeks, a very long time by West German standards. Similarly, the DPG was concerned to maintain the investment capacity of the Bundespost and, above all, to secure future employment after modernisation of the telephone system; so it tacitly supported the construction of new cable systems and the supply of new services like *Bildschirmtext* (the West German videotex system). Yet, the DPG also feared rationalisation; for example, postal services might be revolutionised by 'electronic mail'. Moreover, it opposed any erosion of the Bundespost's telecommunications monopoly that might follow the introduction of new systems and services by the centre-right coalition.[49]

It would be a grave mistake, however, to confuse programmatic statements and occasional symbolic strikes with general trade-union practice. A recent Anglo-German comparative survey of the introduction of new technologies in general office work and banking, as well as in manufacturing, has indicated that West German works councillors (*Betriebsräte*) were as overwhelmingly inclined as British shop stewards to support their companies' resort to new technology in order to promote competitiveness and protect jobs, even at the expense of shedding jobs.[50] Moreover, in September 1985 the DGB held its first national conference devoted exclusively to technology policy – a *technologiepolitische Konferenz*. During the proceedings the DGB executive member responsible for questions about the new technologies, Siegfried Bleicher, rejected the idea that West German unions were *technikfeindlich* and reaffirmed the tradition of positively welcoming technological innovation, while also pointing out that there could be no trade union sympathy for the kind of policies of the ruling conservative-liberal coalition in Bonn (which clearly aimed to reduce trade-union power).[51]

The general conclusion that can be drawn from a cursory comparison of trade-union attitudes is that, under the impact of technological change, Britain and France may be experiencing a recent and quite sudden shift from traditional adversarial approaches towards the more co-operative approach that has to date characterised West German industrial relations. In West Germany trade-union attitudes reflect an unusually radical concern about the new information and communications technologies; and this concern apparently started manifesting itself substantially generally earlier than in Britain and France. Yet, in practice, here too the trend has been towards adaptation and an expansion of issues for collective negotiation. Traditionally smooth bargaining practices may mean that better conditions are negotiated for workers adversely affected by technological change in West Germany than in Britain and France. In Britain, for example, it seems that the new technology agreements that have so far been negotiated are a far cry from the 'model agreements' that were originally envisaged. The 'new realism' should perhaps, therefore, be seen as primarily an admission of the weak position of British trade unions in the prevailing political and economic circumstances of the mid-1980s. Similarly, in France, such *accords* remain exceptional. In West Germany, by contrast, it appears that unions have managed so far to negotiate rather more favourable conditions for technological change. At both national level and at works council level (*Betriebsrat*) many agreements, containing safeguards relating to rationalisation, have been concluded.

As regards the technological change that promised large-scale infrastructural modernisation of communications, namely cable, in all three cases the telecommunications unions were favourable; although there was a substantial difference between the French unions' enthusiasm and the ambiguity of the West Germans. When it came down to more narrow sectional or sectoral interest, any overall perspective that this technology, perhaps above all, might revolutionise the economy in the long-term, remained subordinated to the shorter-term employment benefits that it would bring to a particular section of the workforce. Moreover, in the British, French and West German case, union strategies were aimed at defending the public-service telecommunications monopoly of national carriers (unsuccessfully, as it turned out, in the British case). On the other hand, trade unions concerned with the effects of cable on the media, and on communications- and information-workers more generally, were more hostile in the British and West German cases. Again, this hostility appeared to be more overt in the West German case. In France, however, even these unions adopted a guardedly positive attitude (the CGT being the most guarded).

CONCLUSIONS

Definite conclusions cannot be drawn, and predictions made, about a revolution that is still 'in the making' and against the background of political and industrial systems in flux. Nevertheless, the results of the Atlantic Institute survey no longer appear surprising. It seems that there is a correlation between positive attitudes towards new information- and communications-technologies among the French public and the attitudes promoted by the French Socialist government. In turn, the government's policies have involved a high degree of symbolic support-building measures, as well as crucial institutional innovations that have socialised French society into an attitude of acceptance.

The ideological content of French Socialist policies has stressed the possible benefits of these new technologies, with social and cultural concerns reinforcing industrial policy logic. Nowhere is this characteristic more clear than in the emphasis given to cultural and economic *indépendance nationale* – apparently a theme to which the French public most readily responds. In France there has been little evidence of substantial or enduring resistance to the communications revolution. The wholesale enthusiasm for *modernisation* which characterises the major political force that one might expect to focus on the risks as well as the opportunities of epochal change correlates with a deficit of criticism on the political agenda. An analogous phenomenon is the comparatively high level of support for the 'force de frappe' (nuclear deterrent) and the relative absence of a peace movement in France. Local political élites, too, have been generally enthusiastic modernisers and are themselves incorporated into many policies for structural modernisation. As seen, for various reasons, the trade unions have not generally been an alternative source of resistance. In fact, the promise of 'interactive communication' was actively embraced by both communist local authorities and the CGT. The development of the new technologies in the telecommunications sector led to enthusiastic embrace by the unions concerned. The impact on the media led to no great hostility. Finally, the impact on the service sector of information workers did initially produce defensive attitudes. Growing concern, however, was soon reflected in a trend towards varying degrees of pragmatic and constructive responses. Moreover, the relative weakness of the French trade union movement was a factor of considerable significance.

In Britain public acceptance might also be partially explained by the ideological positivism of all the major party political forces. The implicit suggestion (made by the authors of the Atlantic Institute survey) of a link between Labour Party allegiance and greater negativism towards IT seems oversimplistic and likely to be increasingly so. The British left and centre-left, despite divisions, seem to emulate the French Socialists' approach. In the meantime, symbolic support-building measures for the new technologies have abounded under Margaret Thatcher, perhaps best exemplified in the concept of a high-tech 'UK Ltd'. At the same time sectoral opposition has been marginalised – as in the absent cable-debate. The trade unions have developed an ambivalent attitude that generally does not merit description as 'resistant'. There has been little enthusiasm, but only isolated militancy. In general, trade union responses have reflected the realities of the political and economic circumstances of Thatcherism. They reflect, too, as in the French case, the classical weaknesses of British trade unionism, notably, its sectionalism and rivalries. Militancy has also encountered markedly decreased support from the membership, a feature that has at least partially to be explained by the economic and political climate. At the same time there is growing concern that pragmatic responses must be accompanied by extension of traditional collective bargaining issues. The need for a united response to new issues is also increasingly recognised by trade-union activists.

The West German case has been characterised by a remarkable complexity, deriving from the interaction of ideological factors (party political polarisation over 'new media'; trade union defensiveness; and the development at sub-cultural levels of a left critique of new technologies) with institutional factors (federalism; liberal corporatism; and the importance accorded to 'legitimation processes'). There have been highly visible focuses of resistance to these new technologies, most notably on the 'greening left'. Certain of the programmatic statements of the West German trade unions have also reflected an uncharacteristic alarm. However, these features must be balanced against the actual practice of adaptive behaviour. Generally, the trade unions seem so far to have translated their concern into pragmatic negotiations, which are marked by considerable success in securing defensive safeguards for their members' interests. Nevertheless, the communications revolution has caused an unusually radical impetus within the service-sector unions — HBV and ÖTV — and IG Drupa, which have been faced with the serious and new possibility of massive rationalisations. IG-Metall and the DPG have been ambivalent in their responses to the 'communications revolution', since they represent both 'winners' and 'losers' within their ranks; yet both unions contain a vocal radical minority current. Concerned since the early 1970s about the wider impact of microelectronics on industry, IG-Metall deployed its weight in the German trade union movement to lead the (Europe-wide) fight for a shorter working week in 1984. Of all the telecommunications unions studied, the DPG alone has been uncertain over its approach to cable policy, which is a clear reflection of the symbolic significance that *Kabelpolitik* (cable policy) has assumed in West German politics. In fact, the West German trade union movement was united in fear of the impact of the new technologies on the media, leading towards the creation in 1986 of a new 'media union' (*Mediengewerkschaft*). This particular dimension of the communications revolution also produced a fierce party political polarisation during the 1970s and continued to divide opinion within the SPD in the 1980s. Moreover, it transcended party politics; a visible Christian Democrat current shared the *Wertkonservatismus* (moral conservatism) of many in the SPD.

The Atlantic Institute survey's findings about the exceptional negativism of West German youth *vis-à-vis* the new technologies is consistent with the downright *Technologiefeindlichkeit* of many of the 'youth-faction' within the SPD (the *Jusos*) and of the 'Greens' and 'Alternatives'. Moreover, these elements are largely composed of highly-educated youths, who are well able to articulate complex arguments in support of this position. Many of these highly critical and vocal young people are in occupations where they can have a 'multiplier effect' on opinion (as journalists, academics, teachers, trade union researchers and middle-ranking officials, etc.). In West Germany, academic and journalistic activity has resulted in a prolific output of critical works on the new technologies — a new 'Orwellia'. It is perhaps strange that the optimism of much of the French left about the 'communications revolution' finds its counterpart on the Centre–Right in West Germany, namely the position represented by Lothar Späth, the *Ministerpräsident* of Baden-Württemberg. Späth's vision of a 'high-technology and computer society with a human face' seemed to reflect genuine conviction as well as the fact that the area around Stuttgart was West Germany's 'silicon valley'. Aware of the danger that his party might now be judged to be, in important respects, the more 'conservative' one, Peter Glotz (as General Secretary of the SPD) has battled more and more furiously to identify the SPD with the 'third industrial revolution' and the new technical intelligentsia.

West Germany would seem to present an interesting paradox: namely, that the West European champion *par excellence* of industrial innovation embodies a strong and vocal subcultural hyper-sensitivity to the possible social costs of this success. This ambivalence derives from, and finds its expression in, different forms: the cultural pessimism of the Greens, the moral conservatism (*Wertkonservatismus*) evident among the opposition to even limited commercialisation of the media (transcending purely ideological cleavage and reflected in Helmut Schmidt's opposition to cable as Chancellor), the radical post-Keynsian critique of modernisation on the SPD Left, and the new defensiveness of trade union responses to technological innovation. Part of the explanation may lie in the very nature of the West German political and economic system, which attempts to combine a fundamentally efficiency-orientated economic rationality with an extra high priority to 'social peace' and 'social progress'. Questions of legitimation were, accordingly, taken very seriously; intricate mechanisms for reaching consensus in turn encouraged debate. At the same time the industrial forces drove onwards regardless of the surrounding social debate. However, the traumas seemed to go deeper than this ambiguity, reflecting a deeper acknowledgement that the halcyon years of *Modelldeutschland* may be drawing to a close. The consequence was a process of self-searching doubt about the nature and implications of post-industrial society. Resulting tensions embraced both conservative and progressive impulses and were all the more painful against the background of West Germany's post-war record as the European 'champion' of the 'second industrial revolution' (automobiles, chemicals, electrical engineering). On the threshold of the 'third industrial revolution' (micro-electronics, opto-electronics, space technology) West German supremacy was no longer assured. There was an understandable uncertainty in the face not only of material threats but also of the erosion of a major integrative symbol.

The analysis contained here points to a continuing debate about the future potential of West Germany as Western Europe's senior industrial power and the relationship of politics to that potential. In one scenario, West Germany is experiencing the decline of the imperatives that drove the economic miracle of the early post-war period, and that underpinned subsequent successes. From the perspective of *Modelldeutschland* politics has come to contain dysfunctional elements, symbolised most clearly by the rise of the Greens.

In another scenario, West Germany is undergoing a careful learning process about the nature and implications of the 'third industrial revolution'. There is less of the political boldness (and naivety) of Britain and France: there is less of the absence of criticism found in France, where concern for national independence has led to blind enthusiasm for anything that might prove to be a *technologie de pointe*; and less of the absence of social concern found in Britain, where 'hard' commercial logic has prevailed over 'soft' social responsibility. West German politics displays highly functional elements still. In 1986 the West German economic system continued to perform well, while the established political parties of the left and right were successfully absorbing the 'critical current', on the way to developing efficient features of a post-industrial value system.

NOTES

1. Atlantic Institute for International Affairs, *The Impact of Technological Change in the Industrial Democracies — Public Attitudes Toward Information Technology* (Paris: The Atlantic Institute for International Affairs, 1985), Atlantic Paper No. 58, Edited by R. D. Vine. An international comparative opinion survey, it polled 9000 people in six European countries, the United States and Japan. Interestingly, the poll was sponsored by a group of national and international newspaper and broadcasting media.
2. Advisory Council for Applied Research and Development (A.C.A.R.D.), *Technological Change — Threats and Opportunities for the United Kingdom* (London: HMSO, 1980).
3. A.C.A.R.D., *Information Technology* (London: HMSO, 1980).
4. Ibid., p. 7.
5. I. Benson and J. Lloyd, *New Technology and Industrial Change — The Impact of the Scientific-Technical Revolution on Labour and Industry* (London: Kogan Page, 1983). A very useful analysis of the role of government in assisting, and of unions in adapting to, technological and industrial change in Britain.
6. Ibid., pp. 144–50, quote from p. 148.
7. Cabinet Office/Information Technology Advisory Panel (I.T.A.P.) *Cable Systems* (London: HMSO, 1982).
8. Also see K. Dyson and P. Humphreys, 'The New Media in Britain and France; two versions of heroic muddle', *Rundfunk und Fernsehen*, Vol. 33, 4, 1985, pp. 362–79; and K. Dyson and P. Humphreys, 'Industrial Policies for the New Media in Britain and France' in C. Farrands (ed.), *Industrial Intervention in Britain and France* (London: Pergamon, forthcoming 1986/7).
9. As an indication of these efforts see *Cable — Evidence to GLC/Sheffield City Council Hearings* (London: GLC, 1983), 2 Volumes; and *Cable Working Papers* (prepared for, and obtainable from the GLC).
10. *Labour and Information Technology* (London: The Labour Party, 1985). This consultative document is part of The Labour Party's 'Jobs and Industry Campaign', launched in 1985.
11. The Greater London Council (GLC) *The London Industrial Strategy* (London: GLC, 1985). It contains relevant sections on 'the Cultural Industries', 'IT and Office Work', and 'Information and Communications', including sub-sections on printing, cable technology and homeworking. The 'Communications Campaign' was promoted jointly by a group of British Telecom workers and the GLC, and co-ordinated by the GLC's 'Communications Unit'; it produced a number of documents highly critical of government policy.
12. *Focus on the Future; a Strategy for Innovation* (London: The Social Democrat Party, 1985), Green Paper No. 22.
13. *Progress through Change* (Hebden Bridge: The Liberal Party, 1985). This was a Liberal Party Trade and Industry Panel policy statement.
14. S. Nora and A. Minc, *L'Informatisation de la Société* (Paris: La Documentation Française, 1978).
15. For a detailed and useful analysis of the background and execution of the French Socialists' IT policies see M. Rhodes, 'French Government Subsidies for Information Technology', Paper presented to ECPR Workshop on *The Politics of Industrial Subsidies*, Barcelona, 25–30 March 1985. A monograph is obtainable from the European Consortium of Political Research (ECPR), Essex University.
16. See P. Humphreys, 'Cable: the heroic French experiment examined and compared with the British and German examples', *Journal of Area Studies*, No. 12 (1985), pp. 15–19. See also Dyson and Humphreys, op. cit.
17. Der Bundesminister für Forschung und Technologie, *Informationstechnik; Konzeption der Bundesregierung zur Förderung der Entwicklung der Mikroelektronik, der Informations- und Kommunikationstechniken* (Bonn: BMFT, 1984).
18. F. Naschold, 'Technology Policy in the Federal Republic of Germany' in R. L. Merritt and A. J. Merritt (eds.), *Innovation in the Public Sector* (Beverly Hills/London/New Delhi: Sage Publications, 1985), Chapter 7, pp. 155–64, quote from p. 156.

19. Ibid., p. 162.
20. See P. Oehlke, 'Zur technologiepolitischen Diskussion der SPD auf dem Parteitag 1984 in Essen', *S.P.W. 24* (Zeitschrift für Sozialistische Politik und Wirtschaft), 'Neue Technik – alte Politik?', special issue on the new technologies, September 1984, pp. 299–308.
21. Kommission für den Ausbau des technischen Kommunikationssystems (KtK) *Bericht der KtK*: shortened text in *Media Perspektiven*, No. 1, 1976; Expertenkommission Neue Medien – EKM. Baden-Württemberg, *Abschlussbericht* (Stuttgart: Kohlhammer, 1981), 3 volumes; Enquete-Kommission, 'Neue Informations- und Kommunikationstechniken', *Zwischenbericht* (Bonn: Deutscher Bundestag 9/2442, 9 wahlperiode); See also *Versuch mit Breitbandkabel in der Region Ludwigshafen/Vorderpfalz 1. Zwischenbericht an die Landesregierung Rheinland-Pfalz* (Mainz: Kultusministerium, June 1985).
22. For example see A. Gorz, *Adieux au Prolétariat* (Paris: Editions Galilée, 1980) and A. Gorz, *Les Chemins du Paradis* (Paris: Editions Galilée, 1983), both published in English versions by the Pluto Press; see also, S. Mallet, *The New Working Class* (Nottingham: Spokesman Books, 1975). A. Toffler, *The Third Wave* (London: Pan Books, 1981); R. Williams, *Towards 2000* (Harmondsworth: Penguin, 1983).
23. J. Northcott, M. Fogarty and M. Trevor, *Chips and Jobs – Acceptance of New Technology at Work* (London: Policy Studies Institute, 1985), No. 648, p. 1.
24. Ibid., p. 1.
25. P. Thompson and E. Bannon, *Working the System* (London and Sydney: Pluto Press, 1985). This interesting book explores how the introduction of new technology has affected shop-floor politics; it focuses upon telecommunications, and in particular upon Plessey's Liverpool plants 1970–84.
26. See T. Manwaring, 'The Trade Union Response to New Technology', *Industrial Relations Journal*, Vol. 12, No. 4 (1981), pp. 7–26; see also Thompson and Bannon, op. cit., Chapter 7.
27. H. Hague and D. Lascelles, 'Unions fight for a role after the Big Bang', *Financial Times*, 2 May 1986, p. 19.
28. Association of Professional, Executive, Clerical and Computer Staff (APEX) *Automation and the Office Worker* (APEX, 1980); Association of Scientific, Technical and Managerial Staff (ASTMS) *Technological Change and Collective Bargaining* (ASTMS, 1979); Banking, Insurance and Finance Union (BIFU) *Microtechnology: a Programme for Action* (BIFU, 1980); B.I.F.U. *New Technology in Banking, Insurance and Finance* (BIFU, 1982); National Union of Public Employees (NUPE) *Danger: New Technology at Work* (NUPE, 1982).
29. U. Huws, *The New Homeworkers; New Technology and the changing location of white-collar work* (London: the Low Pay Unit, 1984).
30. Trades Union Congress (TUC), *Employment and Technology* (London: TUC Publications, 1979), a Report by the TUC General Council to the 1979 Congress; see also TUC, *New Technology and Collective Bargaining* (London: TUC Publications, 1981).
31. C. Jenkins and B. Sherman, *The Collapse of Work* (London: Eyre Methuen, 1979).
32. See R. Williams and F. Steward, 'New Technology Agreements: an assessment', *Industrial Relations Journal*, Vol. 16, No. 3 (1985), pp. 58–73.
33. D. Simpson, 'Hitech bodies "should have a union voice"', *The Guardian*, 21 April, 1986, p. 20.
34. Benson and Lloyd, op. cit., p. 181.
35. G. Groux, 'Trade Unionism and Technology' in M. Kesselman (ed.), *The French Workers' Movement* (London: Allen & Unwin, 1984), pp. 132–45.
36. See G. Ross, 'The Perils of Politics: French Unions and the Crisis of the 1970s' in P. Lange, G. Ross and M. Vannicelli, *Unions, Change and Crisis: French and Italian Union Strategy and the Political Economy 1945–80* (London: Allen & Unwin, 1982). On the French 'lag' behind Britain and West Germany in micro-electronics in manufacturing see J. Northcott, P. Rogers, W. Knetsch and B. de Lestapis, *Microelectronics in Industry* (London: Policy Studies Institute, 1985), No. 635.
37. Confédération Générale Démocratique du Travail (C.F.D.T.), *Les Dégâts du Progrès* (Paris: Editions du Seuil, 1977); and C.F.D.T., *Le Tertiaire Eclaté* (Paris: Editions du Seuil, 1979).
38. See UCC–CFDT, (Union Confédérale des Ingénieurs et des Cadres CFDT) *Cadres et Technologies* (Paris: UCC–CFDT, 1985). This document contains a description of the CFDT's changing approach to new technologies, and of the role of the federation of 'cadres' in reorienting attitudes.

39. See J. Auroux, *Les droits des travailleurs* (Paris: La Documentation Française, 1982); see also the statement by the Minister of Labour in *Le Monde*, 6–7 June 1982, p.6 – 'il faut réconcilier les travailleurs avec l'innovation technologique, qui a souvent été ressentie comme une agression' (made during a debate in the National Assembly on the new laws).
40. This is a point made by Groux, op. cit., pp.136–7.
41. UGICT–CGT (L'Union Générale des Ingénieurs, Cadres, Techniciens et Agents de Maîtrise CGT) *Haute Tension sur les Médias*, Special Issue of *Spécial-Options*, the quarterly journal of the UGICT–CGT, September 1985.
42. See *Syndicalisme CFTC*, No. 162, April 1981; see also the various *déclarations des groupes* of the French trade union federations to the *avis* adopted by the *Conseil Économique et Social* on 30 March, 1984, regarding *Informatique et Emploi* (Paris: Journal Officiel, 1984).
43. Confédération Générale des Cadres (CGC) *La Novotique* (Paris: CGC, 1981).
44. UGICT–CGT, *Haute Tension sur les Médias*, op. cit.
45. A. J. Hingel, 'A Promethean Change of Industrial Relations: a Comparative Study of Western European Unions and Technological Developments' in W. Warner (ed.), *Microprocessors, Manpower and Society; a Comparative Cross-National Approach* (Aldershot: Gower, 1984), Chapter 14, pp.255–72, p.256.
46. European Trade Union Institute (ETUI) *Negotiating Technological Change – A Review of Trade Union Approaches to the Introduction of New Technology in Western Europe* (Brussels, E.T.U.I., 1982), p.44. This document contains quite detailed descriptions of the types of technology agreements negotiated in a number of West European countries.
47. DGB- Landesbezirk (LBZ) Rheinland-Pfalz (Hrsg), *Neue Medien – Angriff auf Kopf, Konto und Arbeitsplatz des Arbeitsnehmers* (Mainz, DGB, 1983). Medientag 1982 des DGB in Rheinland-Pfalz, pp.31–33.
48. DGB, *Angestelltenberufe im Wandel: die Zukunft bewältigen; Technik für den Menschen* (Düsseldorf: DGB, 1983).
49. See K. Winckler, 'Gewerkschaften und Neue Technologien – Positionen und Strategien' in H. Holzer and K. Betz, *Totale Bildschirm-Herrschaft? Staat, Kapital, Neue Medien* (Köln; Pahl-Rugenstein Verlag, 1984), pp.157–86; also H. Ebinger, *Neue Medien; Strategien von Staat und Kapital*, (Frankfurt: Nachrichten-Verlags, 1983), pp.68–77.
50. P. Rathkey, W. Fricke and P. Konig, *New Technology and Changes; an Anglo-German Comparison* (Jim Conway Foundation, 1982), cited in J. Northcott, Fogarty and Trevor op. cit., p.11.
51. *Die Quelle*, No.10, 1985, p.517.

Policing the Communications Revolution: A Case-Study of Data Protection Legislation

Colin Mellors and David Pollitt

A central feature of the communications revolution has been the explosive growth of international information markets, allied to the recognition that information is an increasingly valuable and politically strategic commodity. At the heart of this development stands the marriage of growing capabilities for data-processing with cable and satellite transmissions of huge quantities of data at great speed. A central political question emerges: how is the communications revolution to be policed in the interests of privacy for the individual, while allowing the public to enjoy the benefits of participating in this new information age? The most distinctive political response to developments in information and communications technologies has been the enactment of data protection legislation and the creation of data protection agencies.

Since the beginning of the 1970s many countries in Western Europe, as in North America, have introduced data protection measures as a means of easing the introduction of these new technologies into both public and private sectors. It is an area in which international bodies – notably the Council of Europe and the Organisation for Economic Co-operation and Development (OECD) – have played a significant role. Not surprisingly, therefore, cross-national surveys of the legislation in force reveal a remarkable degree of similarity among West European countries. Similarities in legal construction, however, do not necessarily imply that measures are identical in their operation and application. Other factors, such as the political culture, the immediate causes of legislation, the existence of controversial privacy issues and, not least, the perceptions of data protection administrators, are instrumental in determining the effectiveness of legislation. In all cases, the data protection legislation has aimed to reconcile two fundamental objectives: the protection of personal privacy in respect of the recording, storing, transfer and release of personal data, and realisation of the various benefits associated with the development and deployment of new technologies. These latter benefits include access and information-exchange by the public. More significantly, they include considerable administrative and commercial benefits for governments and industry. The latter considerations have been more important than the issue of personal privacy in persuading West European governments to act because of the growing economic contribution that is now made by information-based industries. In Britain, for example, the 1983 report of the Information Technology Advisory Panel (ITAP), *Making a Business of Information*, estimated that the tradable information sector produced an annual turnover in excess of £15 billion per year. Moreover, it was one of the few high-growth areas.

The measures so far introduced fall a long way short of being general information laws that reflect the recent advances in information and communications technologies. In this sense, the responses of governments have been partial, 'adaptive' rather than 'active', coping with immediate requirements rather than attempting to face up to the massive implications of the communications revolution. The issues associated with control of the new information processes have not yet reached the main political agenda of most countries, partly because publics themselves have yet to recognise the full implications of recent technological advances. There have certainly been expressions of concern – both specific (related to such things as census-data collection, population-numbering schemes and machine-readable passports) and general. Nowhere have data protection and information laws really developed into a central political issue. The sheer pace of technological progress in this area means, of course, that any legislation is likely to require frequent modification, and already existing laws are being reviewed and revised. Even so, law and politics in this area lag behind technology. As one expert has argued, 'There is a development towards second-generation information laws in an era of fifth-generation computing'.[1]

THE ORIGINS OF THE CONCERN WITH DATA PROTECTION[2]

The issue of data protection is an adjunct to the public's growing concern with the concept of privacy: a concern which has been heightened by a mistrust of new technologies, the 'Orwellian' syndrome. The difficulties that are associated with making a precise, legally-workable (and socially acceptable) distinction between an individual's *private* and *public* spheres have tended to move the practical, as opposed to the theoretical, basis of the privacy debate towards the concrete issues involved in data protection.[3]

Privacy is a recent concern and was not, for example, explicitly taken up in any early catalogues of basic human rights and liberties. The 'right to be let alone' was not specifically cited before the late nineteenth century largely because it was both assumed and not generally threatened. Privacy itself is not new: it is the concern that we may be losing it that is new. Thus, by the middle of the twentieth century, respect for privacy had been enshrined in the Universal Declaration of Human Rights, the United Nations Covenant on Civil and Political Rights and the European Convention for the Protection of Human Rights and Fundamental Freedoms.

The concept of individual privacy assumes that there are areas of a person's life that he or she may legitimately seek to protect from intrusion by others. A need for private space is visible among many animals,[4] and the Younger Report in Britain even went so far as to suggest that mental stability may be affected if human needs for privacy are not fulfilled.[5] Identification of social and psychological needs for privacy does not, however, help the law-maker. Moreover, the right to seclusion must inevitably be qualified by the responsibilities of being a member of society since, as the Younger Committee concluded, an unqualified right to be let alone would be 'an unrealistic concept, incompatible with the needs of society'.[6] This balance between the individual's right of privacy and wider social needs was also recognised by the Justice Committee: 'There are innumerable examples of where the individual's desire to preserve his privacy has to yield to the greater needs of the community to regulate its affairs for the benefit of all its members'.[7] In any case, the need for personal seclusion is firmly culture-bound, varying between societies, generations, individuals and even within individuals at different times.

Faced with the difficulties of giving legal precision to the concept of privacy, the debate moved towards the specific area of the handling of private information. Thus Westin has argued that privacy is 'the claim of individuals, groups or institutions to determine for themselves when, how and to what extent information about them is communicated to others'.[8] In a similar vein, Miller suggested that the basic attribute of an effective right of privacy is 'the individual's ability to control the circulation of information relating to himself'.[9] It is not surprising that the privacy debate has focused on the specifics of handling personal data since it may be argued that it is the increasing appetite for personal data, and the new technology to exploit these data fully, that has posed the most potent threat to personal privacy.

Both the public and the private sectors have an increasing appetite for personal data, the main difference being that governments can frequently make the surrender of information an obligation, whereas a private organisation often has to persuade the individual to release data, perhaps in return for the services that such an organisation might provide. The welfare state, in particular, has stimulated the government's requirement for personal data, since public provision generally requires proof of social need. Such data may be surrendered by claimants (the sick, unemployed etc.) or be collected as a means of measuring wider social needs (census data, pattern of disease, housing, transport requirements etc.). In most cases the surrender of information causes little difficulty since those who collect the data — whether they are governments, banks, building societies or credit bureaux — enjoy the co-operation of the public. Personal information is divulged to those bodies in return for the benefits and service that are obtained as a result. There are, however, a number of implicit assumptions surrounding the release of this information, in particular that: the information is wholly necessary; the information is accurately recorded; the information is only issued for the required purpose and is neither misused nor divulged, accidentally or deliberately, to other persons; and, sometimes, that information is only retained for so long as is absolutely necessary. It is the fear that such principles are not always observed, and that public or private agencies misuse information collected without the individual's permission, that is at the centre of recent concerns with privacy and data protection.

Rapid developments in information and communications technologies, and their application to the processing and transmission of personal data, are central to the issue of data protection. Invariably, it is the use of computers that has aroused most concern.[10] However, it should be recognised that other facets of the new technology — telecommunication monitoring equipment, surveillance devices, satellites, and broadband cable — can have an equal impact on the handling of personal data. Computers are the main focus of concern for two reasons: the much greater capacity they offer for the storage and transfer of data and the lack of public confidence in how this data is handled.[11] Where data are manually processed, there are some in-built safeguards for personal privacy afforded by the difficulties of combining data collected for different purposes and the sheer volume of data. They deter excessive collection, collation and storage of data over a protracted period. By contrast, automated systems overcome difficulties of storage (almost encouraging the collection of 'peripheral' data on the basis that they might prove useful) and, even more importantly, offer opportunities for the combination of data obtained from separate sources. Transfer of data, between countries as well as systems, is easily achieved. Moreover, by merging previously discrete data, 'new' data are created. J. B. Rule has referred to the 'interactive' quality of combining data supplied to various agencies where 'two bits of information may ... have an effect when combined quite different from the effect of either one alone'.[12] In other words, the essential benefits of automated information systems for the data-processor — speed, capacity, ability to combine and transfer — are the very features that cause concern to data-subjects. There is the additional problem of security. While most stores of sensitive data will include elaborate safeguards designed to prevent unauthorised access and disclosure, breaches of security are not uncommon.

The widespread applicationn of new technology to personal information systems has frequently met with expressions of public disquiet. Sometimes there has been a specific issue to focus public attention — for example, proposals to introduce a central population register. However, even without a specific catalyst, there has been concern. Public concern about the misuse of personal data held on computers has been the fear of what might happen rather than a response to abuses that had actually taken place. An additional factor is the lack of trust in those who have access to automated systems. The basic training required to operate a computer is relatively uncomplicated, and there is often a high mobility of staff. Public trust is not helped by the fact that those operating the systems often have no personal contact with the individuals about whom they process data. It has also been suggested that, being a new profession, they have not yet managed to nurture public confidence.[13] Associations of computer operators still have some way to go before they can expect to enjoy the professional status and, therefore, confidence in their ethical standards on the same level as that generally enjoyed by doctors, lawyers and other professional groups.[14] This is one reason why voluntary codes of conduct have not been seen as a satisfactory substitute for data protection legislation. Surveys reveal the extent of public mistrust. In Britain, for example, at the time of the Data Protection Bill, a survey conducted by the Consumers' Association found that 'three out of every ten people thought that personal information about them *had* been passed on without their knowledge. In the 25–34 age-group, 45 per cent believed this to be the case'.[15]

PRINCIPLES OF DATA PROTECTION: THE ROLE OF INTERNATIONAL AGENCIES

Against this background of concerns data protection legislation has been introduced in many West European countries. There has been considerable agreement about the principles that need to be met in order to ensure that an individual's privacy is not threatened through the misuse of personal data processed by automated systems. Some countries — notably Sweden, the United States and West Germany — were quick to legislate in this field, while others have been slower in their responses. The West German state (*Land*) of Hesse passed the first general law in 1970; Sweden was the first nation to legislate in 1973. Both had strong Social Democratic traditions of government. Two international bodies, the OECD and the Council of Europe, have been especially influential in both formulating standards of protection and, subsequently, encouraging other states to act.

The OECD's interest in the matter stemmed in part from its concern to maximise the commercial benefits of the free flow of personal data.[16] In 1976 a panel of experts drafted a set of principles on data transfers across national frontiers and by 1980 had produced *Guidelines Concerning the Protection of Privacy and Trans-Border Flow of Personal Data*. Significantly, these guidelines were intended to apply to both manual and electronic files. By the mid-1980s, all of the 24 members of OECD, except Ireland, had adopted these guidelines. In 1981, the Council of Europe produced its own guidelines: *The Convention for the Protection of Individuals with Regard to Automatic Processing of Personal Data*, commonly known as the European Convention. Apart from the more limited scope of the Convention, i.e. the exclusion of manual files, the two sets of principles were broadly similar.

OECD Guidelines

i   Collection limitation principle
ii Data quality principle
iii Purpose specification principle
iv Use limitation principle
v   Security safeguards principle
vi Openness principle
vii Individual participation principle
viii Accountability principle

European Convention

i   The information shall be obtained and processed fairly and lawfully;
ii   It shall be held for a specified and legitimate purpose;
iii It shall not be used or disclosed in a way incompatible with those purposes;
iv   It shall be adequate, relevant and not excessive in relation to the specified purposes;
v   It shall be accurate and, where necessary, kept up to date;
vi   It shall be kept in name-linked form for no longer than is necessary for the specified purposes;
vii The data subject shall have access to the information held about him and be entitled to its correction or erasure where the legal provisions safeguarding personal data have not been complied with;
viii Appropriate security measures must be taken against unauthorised access, alteration or dissemination, accidental loss and accidental or unauthorised destruction of data.

There has been one further actor at the international level — the European Community. Both the European Commission and the European Parliament have been involved in the question of data protection for over a decade. In 1973, the Commission recognised the need to safeguard privacy in respect of the handling of personal data and that it would be better to establish common ground-rules at an early stage rather than to have to harmonise conflicting national legislation at a later time. It sought the views of the Parliament in 1974 before drafting a directive, and the Parliament passed two supportive resolutions in 1975 and 1977. The Legal Affairs Committee of the European Parliament has been especially active in this matter and succeeded in having a resolution (Bayer1 Report)[17] unanimously adopted by the Parliament in 1979 and another in March 1982.[18] Despite its earlier intention, the Commission has yet to come forward with any directive and has taken the view that it is better to attempt to persuade member states to ratify the European Convention rather than to produce its own guidelines. By the end of 1985, only two EC member countries (France and West Germany) had in fact ratified the European Convention. A further six (Belgium, Denmark, Greece, Italy, Luxembourg, and United Kingdom) had signed it; the remaining two (Ireland and Netherlands) had still to sign.[19]

THE NATIONAL CONTEXT: PUBLIC PRESSURE OR COMMERCIAL AND ADMINISTRATIVE CONVENIENCE

There has been a mixture of motives behind the enactment of national data protection controls, involving public pressure, administrative convenience and commercial benefit. Although specific proposals to extend and integrate automated personal information systems in the public sector have caused outbreaks of concern, data protection legislation has rarely been the direct result of concerted public pressure. Proposals to introduce a central population register or system of population numbering in Sweden, West Germany, France, Denmark, the Netherlands, Belgium and Luxembourg led to unease, but they were not entirely the cause of legislation.

The linkage between the introduction of data protection controls and proposals for population registration is seen most clearly in West Germany where, in September 1973, the Federal Interior Ministry reintroduced a Data Protection Bill and followed it in October with a Population Registration Bill that provided for the computerisation of the central population register.[20] In the event, the Bundestag delayed the passage of the latter until the Data Protection Bill had been approved.[21] The measure only reached the statute book after both bills had been considered by five parliamentary committees and a mediation committee of the Bundestag and Bundesrat. Even so, considerable opposition to the population registration scheme remained.

In the 1980s the passions of the civil liberties lobby in West Germany have been aroused by the proposal to replace existing identity cards by machine-readable ones. The scheme was initially approved by the Bundesrat in February 1983, but only received final agreement in the Bundestag three years later. Despite considerable objection from data protection experts, trade unionists, lawyers and even the police who foresaw the possibility of widespread abuse, the scheme was to be introduced in April 1987. Notably, the five *Länder* ruled by the Social Democrats have indicated that they will boycott the scheme.

Similar public unease was seen in Sweden in the early 1970s. Sweden was a pioneer in the use of a new generation of computers in government agencies, and as early as 1963 the Swedish Agency for Administrative Development was charged with the co-ordination of computer policies in the various departments of central government. Rumblings of concern came shortly afterwards when, in 1965, the Supreme Administrative Court ruled that punch cards, computer disks and tapes should be regarded as 'documents' in the context of Sweden's long-established freedom of information provisions. Accordingly, the wealth of personal data stored on computer would have to be made available to any inquirers, subject only to the limitations imposed by the 1937 Secrecy Act.[22] By 1969, when plans for population registration by computer were announced, public unease had grown significantly. In April 1972, Parliament suspended the development of the central population register until after the report of a Royal Committee on Publicity and Secrecy. The Committee's recommendations[23] were incorporated in the May 1973 Data Act — the first national legislation of its kind.

As in West Germany, the enactment of data protection controls did not mark the end of public concern with the potential misuse of personal data. A survey conducted early in 1986 — 13 years after the passage of the Data Act — revealed that 67 per cent of Swedes still believed that authorities misuse data held on them. The concern was not only felt by the general public. In January 1986 the director general of the Data Inspectorate, Jan Freese, and most of his inspectorate resigned after several battles with the government about the use of data banks, especially by the police. At about the same time came the revelation that Stockholm University held a secret computer register as part of a sociological research project containing intimate details on approximately 15,000 young Swedes born in 1953.

In both West Germany and Sweden — and also in Denmark — proposals for central population registers coincided with data protection controls. One should not conclude, however, that governments legislated unwillingly or wholly in response to public protest. Often there was a symbiotic relationship between government and public. Administrations were quite content to appear to concede public demands if they thereby facilitated the introduction of new technology. Indeed, in some countries, governments took the initiative — for instance in Luxembourg and, more significantly, France.

When the French government drew up a long-term plan in the mid 1960s to promote the use of computers in public administration and develop the French computer industry (*Plan Calcul*), scant regard was paid to the implications for privacy. There was also no substantial protest. In 1969, the authorities themselves took the initiative by establishing an inquiry into the effects of computers on privacy. Later, when public concern began to emerge, it was limited to small groups worried about specific proposals. In 1970, for example, plans to merge driving records with those on traffic violations and to supply these to insurance companies aroused some opposition. There was further unease in 1974, when the *Safari* project to transfer municipal population registers to central computers linked with a registration number became public. Four years later, concern widened over separate plans to computerise children's health and school records. Both sets of proposals were later scrapped. In fact, the instigation for legislation came as the result of the agreement by the then Prime Minister, Pierre Messmer, to establish a Committee on Data Protection and Liberties. The Data Processing and the Protection of Liberties Act, based largely on the report of this committee, was passed in January 1978. Socialists and Communists opposed the measure, fearing that by smoothing the way for more state computers, the act would strengthen the hand of the state rather than protect civil liberties.[24]

France was quick to recognise the administrative advantages of computerisation of public record systems and, therefore, instigated legislation in anticipation of possible public reactions. Concessions were offered, in the shape of data protection controls, in return for the longer-term benefits of automation. Significantly, in West Germany the introduction of data protection controls coincided with the tightening of vetting procedures for public servants (the so-called *Berufsverbot*) and the imposition of severe anti-terrorist provisions. In both it was believed that the impact of these measures might be softened by the introduction of measures protecting civil liberties in another area. The introduction of data protection legislation in Britain illustrates a further reason for introducing controls: commercial motives.

Unlike most West European countries, Britain has not had a single issue, like population numbering, to galvanise public distrust of new information handling processes. While Britain has not had such a catalyst it has had a much more vocal civil liberties' lobby. There is, interestingly, no continental European equivalent of the National Council for Civil Liberties. Equally, professional groups such as doctors, lawyers and computer experts have been effective through national bodies (British Medical Association, Justice, British Computer Society and National Computing Centre respectively) in focusing attention on the data protection issue.[25]

Pressure for legislation on privacy Britain goes back to 1961, when Lord Mancroft presented a Bill 'to protect a person from any unjustifiable publication relating to his private affairs'. The specific concern with data protection came a few years later. In July 1967, a sub-committee of the Legal Research Committee of the Society of Conservative Lawyers was established to examine the effects of the computer on privacy in Britain. Eighteen months later it reported that existing law was insufficient to deal with the threat and that new controls were needed to cover both computers and manual files.[26] Kenneth Baker introduced a Data Surveillance Bill — which drew on the recommendations of the Conservative lawyers' report — in the House of Commons, in May 1969. Although it applied only to computers, it covered both public and private sectors. The Bill had all-party support, but it failed to get a second reading. Other, similar bills followed, including one by Brian Walden (November 1969) which, although it failed, led to the establishment of a committee (the Younger Committee) to investigate the need to protect against the intrusions by private organisations and individuals.[27] The public sector was excluded, although the guidelines outlined in its report in 1972 were also intended to apply to the public sector.

A decade of delay and procrastination followed. During the debate on the

Younger Report in 1972, the Home Secretary had promised to produce a White Paper on public sector computers.[28] In the event it took over two years and a change of government to produce the White Papers. In the meantime the 1974 Consumer Credit Act had been passed; it was the first measure designed to control personal data handling in the private sector by establishing a licensing system and personal access provisions with regard to data held by credit bureaux. The two White Papers of 1975 contained the first official promise of legislation.[29] A Data Protection Committee (Lindop Committee) was established to formulate precise legislative proposals and reported in December 1978.[30]

Official reaction to the Lindop Report was again one of delay. In January 1979, the Labour Home Secretary said the costs of controls needed further consideration before final proposals could be brought forward. Dismayed by the delay, Sir Norman Lindop warned that the country could suffer commercially if it did not legislate soon, because other countries might refuse to allow information to be handled on British computers.[31] The conflict between these two aspects – the costs of legislation, on the one hand, and the potential commercial penalties of failing to legislate, on the other – came into sharper focus with the election of a Conservative government in May 1979. The Conservatives were keen to reduce the number of *ad hoc* official bodies rather than increase them through new safeguards. At the same time information technology was a sector marked out for development by the Conservatives, and they were obviously wary of the possibility that more and more countries with data protection controls might ban the transfer of information to Britain.

During 1980 the British government received 'a spate of complaints' from private industry about lost contracts because Britain had no data protection legislation. The computer industries and industrial consultancies were particularly harshly affected.[32] However, the government still favoured allowing the Home Office to act as its own watchdog over public-sector computers. As late as September 1981, the Home Office Minister of State was referring to the call for an independent data protection authority as 'fundamentally objectionable'.[33] In July of that year, Lindop, frustrated at the lack of progress, had reconvened the Committee on Data Protection to issue a second report. By January 1982, the government had made a 'U-turn' and came to accept the need for an independent authority. In April it finally published a White Paper, *Data Protection: The Government's Proposals for Legislation*.[34] The proposal fell short of Lindop's recommendations and again warned that there might be a delay in implementing the measure since 'the public sector costs and manpower will have to be contained within existing planned totals, even if this means deferring application of legislation in this area'.[35]

The explanation for the British government finally being prompted into action was to be found in two inter-related factors: influence from abroad and consequent commercial pressures. A failure to observe international guidelines, and especially the European Convention, would have resulted in considerable commercial losses. Indeed as early as 1975, the Swedish Data Inspection Board had halted further processing in Britain on Swedish citizens until Britain imposed more stringent rules.[36] Although Britain had signed the European Convention in May 1981 – an indication of intent – full ratification required legislative action. The 1982 White Paper noted that 'without legislation, firms operating in the United Kingdom may be at a disadvantage compared with those based in countries which have data protection legislation'. Similarly, the Home Office Minister of State later conceded that the legislation 'goes far enough to allow us to ratify the European Convention which is important in itself ... a great number of jobs are at stake'.[37] Labour's spokesman, Roy Hattersley, put it more bluntly: 'There is only one principal purpose and that is to ensure that a new age of technology ... is not handicapped by the refusal of our European partners to provide technological information to Britain because there is no protection here at all'.[38] This view was later shared by Labour's new shadow Home Secretary during the passage of the Data Protection Bill: 'The principle of the Bill is not to protect the privacy of the subject. It is about trade and about money'.[39]

It had taken just a decade from the publication of the Younger Report to the eventual decision to introduce data protection legislation. In December 1980, the Select Committee on Home Affairs had criticised the government for its 'dilatory and complacent' attitude towards a number of reports. Two of the reports cited were those of Younger and Lindop. The attitude persisted until it became clear that complacency would incur commercial and financial losses. Civil liberties groups maintained the pressure for legislation throughout this period, although, unlike in several other European countries, they were denied the opportunity to use a single issue to focus public attention towards the more general subject of privacy and data protection. Instead it was left to professional and commercial lobbies – notably the British Computer Society, the British Medical Association and information technology industries – to bring the final pressures to bear. It was the need to protect Britain's position at the 'crossroads of the international data highway' and to exploit the full commercial potential of the new information technologies, rather than a reaction to public fears about privacy that caused the government to act. As the Home Secretary admitted when introducing the first Data Protection Bill, it was intended to 'safeguard the increasing number of concerns that depend on the free international interchange of computerised data and so safeguard the many jobs that exist in that area'.[40]

The first Data Protection Bill was introduced in December 1982. It fell with the dissolution of Parliament in May 1983. A revised Bill, with only minor modifications, was published shortly afterwards, received the royal assent in July 1984, and was to become fully operational over a period of two years. Britain joined Austria, Denmark, France, Iceland, Luxembourg, Norway, Sweden, West Germany, Canada and the United States in enacting data protection controls. By 1986 a number of other states were in the process of putting their proposals on to the statute book.

DATA PROTECTION IN OPERATION

Although there are distinctive characteristics about the way in which countries have implemented data protection legislation, partly as a result of the need to

POLICING THE COMMUNICATIONS REVOLUTION 205

conform to a specific constitutional settings, similarities among provisions far outweigh the differences.[41] There is universal agreement, for example, that the provisions should apply to both public and private sectors, although there is less agreement about whether they should take in both automatically and manually processed data. The former is, of course, the focus of most controls. However, of the 13 countries with legislation in force by 1986, nine allow the extension of these provisions (at least in some circumstances) to cover manual files. Of the eight countries that are in the process of introducing controls, four intend to include manual data. In principle, of course, if the object of the legislation is to protect personal privacy, then the distinction between 'automated' and 'manual' is artificial. In practice, also, the distinction can be blurred, and there is evidence to suggest that some of the most sensitive stores of data remain on manual files.[42] The difficulty of including all data stores, irrespective of their type, is the implication for the volume of work of data protection agencies. In Britain, it was estimated that the new act would produce 300,000 registrations; extending it to manual files would have increased this figure to many millions.

There is one further issue about the scope of provisions: the question of files assembled by police and security services. Not surprisingly, most legislation is careful to exclude so-called 'security' files from the purview of data protection agencies. A vivid illustration is the British law, under which all that is required to make data wholly exempt from the provisions of the Act is the certification of a minister that national security is involved. Such a statement is deemed to be 'conclusive evidence of the fact'.[43] By contrast, while the West German Federal Data Act exempts stores concerned with state security and crime, details of their type and purpose must still be kept in a special register.

All the legislation enacted, as well as the proposals in those countries that have yet to legislate, allow subjects access to file-data and the right to modification in cases of inaccuracy. Most legislation also allows legal claims to be made in respect of damages occurring as a result of inaccurate data. One crucial difference between West European systems relates to the powers of regulatory agencies. In some countries like France, Sweden and Britain regulatory agencies have the power to license or register the data operator, and the withdrawal of such a licence is a major sanction. By contrast, the West German Commissary is strictly advisory and does not actually license stores. On the other hand, it might be argued that by being freed from the massive paperwork involved in a licensing system, the West German agency has much more time to 'conduct independent investigations and audits of information practices'.[44] It does not seem to have been inhibited by a lack of licensing power.

Regulation necessarily incurs cost, both in the establishment of a data protection agency and, more significantly, to those who are required to adhere to the controls. Initial estimates of enforcing data protection measures in Britain put the administrative costs of the Registrar and his staff at up to £3 million in 1986 with some of this being recovered by registration (£22) and other fees. The direct costs of access provisions are difficult to calculate until the level of demand has been established; other European countries have found that it has taken some time before demand for access has built up. The costs to government departments of developing hardware and software systems that comply with the act were calculated in 1982 at £5.5 million during the two year phasing-in period. An access rate of 0.1 per cent was estimated to cost £1 million per year. A further £9—£11 million was expected to be incurred by local authorities and other public bodies in implementing the Act, with annual running costs of £13 million. No reliable estimate of costs has been made for the private sector, although one major corporation has claimed to be spending £500,000 in complying with the Act.

After nearly a decade of European experience of data protection, it is possible to identify the factors that appear to determine the effectiveness of controls. In this context 'effectiveness' is taken to mean the protection of personal liberties and promotion of accountability of both public and private operators. A more pragmatic view of 'effectiveness' would be that of helping governments pursue the commercial and administrative benefits of new technologies while minimising public protest.

The nature and the scope of the legislation are obvious factors that affect the operation of data protection controls. Outside Europe, for example, control is weakened by the absence of a proper data protection agency at federal level in the United States. However, as important as the letter of the law is its spirit, and it is useful to consider both the intentions of the legislators and the political climate in which the measure was formulated. For the most part, legislation has been enacted in order to facilitate new technologies rather than in response to significant public pressure. The intention of legislators has been to forestall opposition rather than respond to it. While the issue of privacy may have been a salient consideration among certain sections of society (like politicians of the left and trade unionists) and over particular issues (e.g. population-numbering schemes and, more generally, the collection of census-data), uppermost in the mind of legislators were the administrative and economic benefits of applying new technology to appropriate sectors. It is significant that in Britain the Department of Trade and Industry, rather than the Home Office, has shown most interest in data protection. The explanation is, of course, their concern, along with other OECD countries, to promote transborder data flows.[45]

Few countries have experienced a sustained high level of public interest in data protection measures, despite widespread distrust in the handling of personal information. Privacy is usually regarded as a general issue; data protection measures are seen as specific and, it has to be said, often rather complicated. This fact inevitably weakens the application of controls, since all depend to some extent on the public enforcing their rights. Almost all data protection registrars have commented on the low level of applications for access to personal files. Clearly the greater the level of public concern about data protection, the more data protection agencies are likely to feel under pressure to exercise maximum control. Similarly, the higher the number of requests for access to data stores, the more likely data-users are to be scrupulous in their compliance with the legislation. European experiences in this regard suggest: demand takes time to build up; it is related to the controversy of issues and the prevalent political climate; and it is, to some extent, culture-bound. On this basis, it is perhaps to be expected that the new data protection agency in Britain will come under relatively little public pressure unless, or until, a specific and controversial issue arises.

One factor that can increase the awareness of the general public is a vigorous individual at the head of the data protection agency. Many of the successes of data protection agencies in Sweden and West Germany in alerting the wider public to important issues can be attributed to the high-profile and firmly independent approaches taken by key personnel in those two countries. Both Jan Freese and Hans Peter Bull were uninhibited in taking strong stands, particularly with respect to the police and security services. The careers of both raise a second issue, that of political independence and security of tenure. Freese resigned early in 1986, as was noted earlier; Bull was denied a second term of office by the newly-elected CDU/FDP government when his first term came to an end in 1983. There is perhaps a parallel with the role of ombudsmen which exist in many countries. Like ombudsmen, data protection commissioners have put their own style on the operation of the appropriate legislation.[46] They can, however, only go as far as the legislation and the political climate allow.

DATA PROTECTION AND THE COMMUNICATIONS REVOLUTION

The question of information law must figure in any discussion of the politics of the communications revolution, partly because it is one of the main areas that brings together the often discrete disciplines of law, politics, sociology and information technology. There is nothing essentially novel about the issue of privacy; indeed, aspects of 'information' law already find expression in legal codes dealing with such matters as trespass, nuisance, negligence, defamation, breach of confidence, contract and copyright. What has changed is the advent of a new technology that makes it so much easier to gather, store, use and sometimes misuse personal information. Through the use of new technology, both the state and private organisations have vastly superior information-gathering and processing capabilities.

Although the peaks of public distrust have occurred when governments have attempted to make use of these new automated processes in respect of census and personal identification schemes, the gravest fears have been expressed about the use of new technologies by police and security services. These fears have not been allayed by the creation of data protection agencies. All the legislation introduced since the early 1970s allows exemptions in respect of security matters, and it is notable that the police and security forces have been resourceful in exploiting these exemptions to the full. Clashes between data protection agencies and the police and security services have been quite common, especially in West Germany where the police authorities hold computer records on eight million citizens – one in five of all adults. Even apparently routine data can attract interest, and, for example, the Office for the Protection of the Constitution which vets public service employees has access to the computerised lending files of university and public libraries as one of its investigative sources. The increase of terrorism and civil disobedience has brought added reasons for the collection of information for intelligence purposes. It is understandable that the state will wish to make every use of new information technology in its battle against terrorism; it is equally understandable that there will be concern that governments should not sacrifice liberal democratic values in their struggles to uphold liberal democracy.

Despite these fears, data protection has never become a major political issue, nor has it really found a prominent place on the agenda of political parties. This situation is in stark contrast to the related issue of freedom of information or open government. Rather, it has come to prominence when a particular controversy (e.g. the 1983 census in West Germany) has brought it firmly into the political arena. Governments, in fact, have been anxious to prevent political conflict over the issue 'at a time when the economic system is increasingly dependent on information and communication technology'.[47] Data protection controls have therefore often been introduced as a means of avoiding conflict and smoothing the implementation of new technology. The commercial and economic imperative of this approach has been strengthened by the increasing dependence of many West European economies on information-based industries. The ITAP report 'Making a Business of Information', for example, stressed that the UK has all the requirements to be a world leader in the post-industrial business of selling information and advice. It was therefore essential that governments avoided any hurdles in the way of this potential development. Information has become a raw material for many new enterprises, and governments have not been slow to recognise the need to avoid the sanctions that could be applied if their countries fail to conform to international guidelines. Now that the European Convention has been ratified by five member countries – West Germany, France, Sweden, Norway and Spain – it has become legally binding and therefore even more important that countries comply with its provisions for commercial reasons.[48] For similar reasons, the United States has recently been persuading American-based multinational firms and banks to adopt voluntarily the OECD guidelines in respect of their data practices in order not to risk the loss of overseas business. Approximately 180 major corporations have agreed to do so.

Like any legislation in a rapidly changing field, data protection controls need frequent modification. Sweden amended its Data Act in 1979, and a complex process of revision is now under way in West Germany. One of the difficulties facing legislators is the vast growth in micro-computers. In the 1970s the main fear focused on the extensive centralisation brought about by automation. By the 1980s there was the added difficulty of attempting to control the mass of small information systems that were beginning to take their place in every office and home. These systems will be much more difficult to locate and identify and therefore the basis of the policing system that is incorporated in present legislation – the individual's right of access – will become less easy to operate. The revolution in data-processing and telecommunications – home computers, cable, 'value-added' services like videotext, facsimile machines – has transformed the home from a relatively opaque place of refuge into a focal point for the instantaneous reception and communication of information.[49] It may take time for it to be appreciated that the technology that brings communications into the home also has the potential to transmit information out. Any technological advance has social costs, and some observers did warn in the 1970s that the introduction of data protection measures could result in relaxed public vigilance by taking the issue out of the public eye. James Rule recognised that the 'seductive appeal' of new technology could easily lead to the public becoming dependent upon its ensuing benefits before the real dangers became apparent.[50]

Existing controls over the processing of data should be seen as a first political and legal response to some of the issues raised by the application of new information and communications technologies. How far they will remain effective and relevant will depend in part on the extent of public sensitivity about the subject and in part on the future direction of developments in information-processing systems. From the perspective of information law, current data protection controls represent a partial, and almost certainly temporary, approach. They represent merely the first generation of measures that will be required to legitimise the continuing application of the inevitable advances in information and communications technologies. Recent modifications to existing controls, notably in Sweden, suggest that the next generation of data protection measures will concentrate on the 'purpose' of data collection and processing. Like new media legislation, the first generation of data protection law heralded the arrival of new technology; the next generation will need to respond to its widespread deployment and use. As Britain is now finding, the first generation of legislation is a cumbersome attempt to balance the protection of privacy with the need to make best use of new technologies. Critics of the British Act argue that, while it fails to do the former, its inclusion of even the most mundane automated records results in an unnecessary burden for all those who process even routine and innocuous data. As the use of micro systems in the office and home become still more commonplace and individuals become increasingly involved and committed to a new information-based society, the impracticability of the approach will become transparent. The Swedish solution has been to adopt a much more relaxed approach to routine data which allows it to concentrate instead on more sensitive areas.

It was a coincidence that the deadline for registration under the British Act occurred at approximately the same time that the British government announced its intention to introduce controls in another area of information law to keep pace with technological developments – the overhaul of intellectual property rights.[51] There are some interesting parallels, notably the fact that both make significant economic contributions (copyright accounts for 2.6 per cent of Britain's GNP); both require legislation to strike the balance between the protection of privacy or of the rewards for authors and creators and access to data and creative ideas in order to make fullest use of new technology; both have been affected by international conventions; and both have suffered from official delay and procrastination.

Although data protection controls attempt to strike a balance between individual rights and economic necessities, their evolution is explained much more by reference to the needs of bureaucracies and commerce than to meeting the demands of a concerned public. There is evidence of public unease, but the prime motive of legislators has been to minimise political conflict in order to maximise the exploitation of new technologies: in other words to 'control' the political agenda of the communications revolution.

Information has become a key commodity in post-industrial economies; controlling the balance between social costs and public benefits that result from new information and communication technologies will remain a significant part of the new political agenda.

NOTES

1. H. Burkert, 'Public Administration of Information Conflicts: An Attempt at a Functional Evaluation of Information Law', paper presented to ECPR Workshop on Confidentiality, Privacy and Data Protection, Barcelona, March 1985, p. 10.
2. This section draws upon C. Mellors and D. Pollitt, 'The Data Protection Bill', *Political Quarterly* (July 1984).
3. There has grown an extensive body of literature on the subject. See D. Flaherty (ed.), *Privacy and Data Protection: An International Bibliography* (London: Mansell, 1984).
4. See A. F. Westin, *Privacy and Freedom* (London: Bodley Head, 1967), pp. 8–11 and J. Jacob, *Data Banks, The Computer, Privacy and the Law* (London: NCCL, undated), p. 2.
5. Report of Committee on Privacy, Cmnd. 5102 (London: HMSO, 1972), para 109. See also R. Ingham, 'Privacy and Psychology', and C. Bryant, 'Privacy, Privatisation and Self-Determination', both in J. B. Young (ed.), *Privacy* (London: Wiley, 1978).
6. Ibid., para 63.
7. *Justice, Privacy and the Law*, (London: Stevens and Sons, 1970), p. 4.
8. Westin, op. cit., p. 7.
9. A. R. Miller *The Assault on Privacy* (Ann Arbor: University of Michigan Press, 1971), p. 25.
10. See for example, Jacob, op. cit.; P. Sieghart *Privacy and Computers* (London: Latimer New Dimension, 1976); M. Warner and M. Stone, *The Data Bank Society* (London: Allen & Unwin, 1970); A. R. Miller, 'Personal Privacy in the Computer Age', *Michigan Law Review*, 67.
11. See, for example, Louis Harris and A. Westin, *The Dimensions of Privacy: A National Opinion Research Survey of Attitudes Towards Privacy* (New York: Garland, 1981), and N. Vidmar and D. Flaherty, 'Concern for Personal Privacy in an Information Age', *Journal of Communication* (forthcoming).
12. J. B. Rule, *Private Lives and Public Surveillance* (London: Allen Lane, 1973), p. 309.
13. Miller, op. cit., pp. 256–7.
14. The British Computer Society is closest to being a full professional body. It was founded in 1957 and has a membership of approximately 23,000. There are similar associations in West Germany, France, Italy, Denmark and the Netherlands.
15. Consumers' Association Press Release, 27 January 1984. See also references cited in Note 11 above.
16. See 'Policy Issues in Data Protection and Privacy', *OECD Informatics Studies 10*, 1976.
17. Official Journal of European Communities C 140/1979.
18. Official Journal of European Communities C 87/1982.
19. See Debates of European Parliament: 2–326/68 15 July 1985 and 2–332/195–6 (14 November 1985).
20. *Bundestag-Drucks* 7/1027 (September 1973) and 7/1059 (October 1973).
21. *Bundesrat-Drucks* 422/76.
22. G. B. F. Niblett, 'Digital Information and the Privacy Problem', *OECD Informatics Studies 2*, (Paris: OECD, 1971), pp. 42–3.
23. See *Data and Privacy* (Stockholm: SOU:47, 1972).
24. See, for example, 'Exposé des Motifs' in the private member's bill presented by Lucien Villa, National Assembly, 1976–77, 2nd Ordinary Session *No 3092*, pp. 2–3.
25. See, for example, Justice, *Privacy and the Law* (London: Stevens and Sons, 1970); L. Ellis (ed.), *Privacy and the Computer – Steps to Practicality* (London: British Computer Society, 1972); and B. C. Rowe (ed.), *Privacy, Computers and You*, (Manchester: National Computing Centre, 1972).
26. *Computers and Freedom* (London: Conservative Research Department, 1968).
27. Cmnd. 5012 op. cit.

28. In 1969 the Civil Service Department had announced that it would try to create conditions for the easy transfer of data between departments.
29. 'Computers and Privacy' *Cmnd. 6353* (London: HMSO, 1975) and 'Computers: Safeguards for Privacy *Cmnd. 6354* (London: HMSO, 1975).
30. Report of Committee on Data Protection *Cmnd. 7341* (London: HMSO, 1978).
31. *Guardian* 25 January, 1979.
32. *Guardian* 26 September 1980.
33. *Guardian* 16 September 1981.
34. *Cmnd. 8539* (London: HMSO, 1982).
35. Ibid., para 23.
36. *New Scientist*, 13 January 1977.
37. BBC Radio, *World This Weekend*, 10 April 1983.
38. Ibid.
39. (Gerald Kaufman) *House of Commons Debates*, 30 January 1984.
40. *House of Common Debates*, 11 April 1983.
41. A useful comparison is available in 'The Problem of Data Protection in Europe' (Luxembourg: European Parliament Directorate General for Research, 13 August 1984).
42. The Austrian Commissioner has estimated that 80 per cent of complaints concern manual files.
43. Data Protection Act 27(2).
44. See D.H. Flaherty, 'Limiting Governmental Surveillance and Promoting Bureaucratic Accountability: The Role of Data Protection Agencies in Western Societies', paper presented to ECPR Workshop on Confidentiality, Privacy and Data Protection, Barcelona, March 1985.
45. See OECD, *Synthesis Report on the Application of Guidelines Governing the Protection of Privacy and Transborder Flow of Personal Data* (DST1/ICCP/83.17).
46. F. Stacey, *Ombudsmen Compared* (Oxford: Clarendon Press, 1978).
47. Burkert, op. cit., p.9.
48. In addition it has been signed by Austria, Belgium, Denmark, Greece, Iceland, Italy, Luxembourg, Portugal, Turkey and United Kingdom.
49. See, e.g., H. Maisl and A. Vitalis, 'Les libertés enjeu d'une société informatisée', *Les Libertés* (362/4), pp. 471–482.
50. Rule, op. cit., p.358.
51. *Intellectual Property and Innovation* (London: HMSO, 1986, Cmnd. 9712).

ABSTRACTS

West European States and the Communications Revolution
Kenneth Dyson

The author looks at the major trends in the field of communications affecting West European states. He then surveys the main established approaches that can be used to interpret the political and policy responses of their governments to these trends. Particular attention is given to international markets, their structure and development; to the character of domestic policy processes; and to the changing relationship of law and politics in communications. It is suggested that the central feature of the politics of the communications revolution is the process of political learning by governments about their future role. The 'arts of statecraft' are being relearned as autonomy of action in communications is being threatened. Some reflections on the development of governments' role in communications are offered.

Divergent Paths: Political Strategies for Telecommunications in Britain, France and West Germany
Kevin Morgan and Douglas Webber

This analysis identifies the significant differences in the nature of political responses to the 'communications revolution' in Britain, France and the Federal Republic of Germany. This 'revolution', it is argued, may put new issues on the political agenda, but how these are resolved depends heavily on the character of the governing party.

Policy, Politics and the Communications Revolution in Sweden
Jeremy Richardson

Sweden's favourable image of rationality and objectivity in policy-making began to change in the 1970s as its industrial policy had to deal with economic crisis in certain sectors, such as steel and shipbuilding. The communications sector – particularly telecommunications – has so far avoided the need for any crisis measures and has continued to epitomise the Swedish commitment to advanced technology. The success of this particular industrial sector rests more on cultural values, an effective system of education and training, and a liberal trade policy eschewing protectionist measures, than it does on specific interventionist policies designed to benefit the Swedish telecommunication industry. Some tensions are developing, however, over such issues as the use of satellite communications and the objectives of the PTT. There is also growing concern that the hitherto admired system of education and training may be failing to meet the current and expected skill requirements of the communications sector.

Policies for New Media in Western Europe: Deregulation of Broadcasting and Multimedia Diversification
Kenneth Dyson and Peter Humphreys

The authors examine the effects of the communications revolution on broadcasting and new media in Western Europe, notably in Britain, France, West Germany, Luxembourg, the Low Countries and Italy. They detect seemingly inexorable pressures towards deregulation as governments are faced by the constraints of a new internationalisation of audiovisual communication. Even brave attempts at controlled deregulation have buckled as national policies seem to 'converge' under the pressures of international competition and competitive pressures to deregulate. In this situation there arises a new expansion of multimedia diversification in Western Europe, notably by giant publishing interests, and a new openness to an 'American cultural invasion'. The authors analyse these developments and consider the policy implications of these phenomena.

Law, Politics and New Media: Trends in Broadcasting Regulation
Wolfgang Hoffmann-Riem

The author examines the impact of the communications revolution on the Western European traditions of national regulation of broadcasting. Using the Federal Republic of Germany as a case study, he suggests that the 'West European' response to demands for an 'American-style' deregulation of broadcasting will be to comply. In this process, predominantly economic forces are already gaining sway over traditional cultural concerns, leading to a paradigm shift in broadcasting policy and broadcasting law from the public service principle towards a new commercialism. It is contended, too, that regulatory policies in Western Europe have a symbolic-ritual function of making this transition appear to be more acceptable.

European Collaboration in Computing and Telecommunications: A Policy Approach
Claire Shearman

Europe's so-called 'technology gap' has been a major theme of debate in Western Europe since the mid 1970s and raised the issue of the relative merits of technological collaboration as a policy instrument. This study addresses some of the political implications underlying the debate. It provides a general overview of recent European initiatives in computing and telecommunications – including the European Community's ESPRIT and RACE programmes, French governmental initiatives in support of European collaboration, the Eureka programme and developments in evolving a European Information Technology Standards policy – and draws from the various experiences some conclusions about the policies and policy processes involved. Analysis focuses on the major elements shaping the political agenda for collaboration, the policy actors involved and the nature of the policy-making process and the long-term implications of these factors. It is argued that European collaboration in computing and telecommunications has taken the form of a political process shaped largely by consideration of political influence and prestige within the international arena and arising from differential access to, and facility with, technological development. The long-term success of such programmes is constrained by the inherent political rivalry between governments, the weakness of the policy groupings involved, and the tensions that result from the conflicting interests implicit in collaboration at the political and industrial levels.

Legitimating the Communications Revolution: Governments, Parties and Trade Unions in Britain, France and West Germany
Peter Humphreys

This contribution explores the nature of the political agenda and of political responses to the 'communications revolution' in three major West European societies. It examines in detail the development of different perceptions and ideological responses of governments, parties and trade unions. The author suggests that the communications revolution raises particularly important issues and problems of legitimation for the European left. In the West German case, acceptance of the new communications technologies has proved surprisingly troublesome. At the same time, this account highlights the relative absence of critical views and debate that, for various reasons, has characterised Britain and France.

Policing the Communications Revolution: A Case-Study of Data Protection Legislation
Colin Mellors and David Pollitt

The advent of new information and communications technologies has brought not only significant social and commercial benefits but also increasing concern about the effect on personal privacy and, specifically, about the possible misuse of data that are held on computers. Although the level of public concern has never been such as to bring the issue of data protection on to the main political agenda, particular fears have been expressed about such issues as population-numbering and the use of census data. At the back of these fears was a lack of confidence in those who control electronic information-processing systems. West European governments have been anxious to exploit the bureaucratic and commercial benefits of new technologies; accordingly, they have introduced data protection measures as a means of legitimising new technology and avoiding public resistance to the application of new information systems. As the economic significance of information-based industries has grown, the importance of meeting international guidelines on data protection has similarly increased.

The nature of the controls does not vary greatly between West European countries, although their effectiveness is conditioned by the specific circumstances and the characteristics of the national setting. In general, technology appears to have out-paced law and politics in this field, and the West European legislation now in force is undergoing a process of revision.

APPENDIX I: GLOSSARY

Analogue: information can be stored and transmitted via analogue signals (frequency modulations) or digitally (in streams of numerals). Analogue form is slower, less versatile and more prone to interference than digital form. See *digital*.

Bandwidth: a measure of transmission capacity in communications. Full colour television pictures require wide bandwidth; much less is needed for voice communications. See *cable*.

Broadcasting 'Off-Air': the process of transmitting information (generally TV or radio programmes) to the public over the radio (hertzian) airwaves. By definition, it is a form of 'mass communication' only. See *narrowcasting*.

Cable: is one of three means of transmission in telecommunications (microwaves and satellites are the other two). This form of communications by wire is provided by three types of cable which vary in *bandwidth*. The greater the bandwidth of cable, the more information it can carry simultaneously and the more complex that information can be (e.g. video as well as audio signals). Multi-pair copper cable has been traditionally used for television reception; it has a narrow bandwidth with four to six channels. Copper-coaxial cable and fibre-optic cable offer *broad-band* (high-capacity communications). Cable's development proceeds in the following phases: making broadcast signals available in areas of poor 'off-air' reception; making distant stations available thereby increasing the number of channels received; making new types of local, 'telematic' and pay-TV channel available (including *narrowcasting*); and integrating television services with *interactive* services.

Cable Television: a telecommunications system that delivers TV channels and by wire (cable) to a subscriber's TV receiver. New developments in cable technology mean that modern cable systems can carry other services such as 'home shopping', 'home banking', data transmission and telephone.

CCITT (Comité Consultatif International Télégraphique et Téléphonique): the International Telegraph and Telephone Consultative Committee is the committee, through which the ITU regulates telecommunications standards. It is essentially consultative with no legal jurisdiction over its members. Nevertheless, CCITT standards are generally accepted throughout the world. They cover the transmission of data in many forms via telex, telephone and other public data networks.

Cellular Radio: uses the airwaves more efficiently than traditional radio telephone technology for the purpose of mobile communication. A country is divided into a honeycomb of small cells around low-powered transmitters/receivers. Mobile subscribers are connected to other cells or the main telephone network by means of cables linking the local transmitters/receivers to a computer-controlled exchange. Microprocessor technology is at the heart of the technique. The largest service in operation is the Nordic Mobile Telephone system which spans Sweden, Norway, Denmark and Finland and had by 1985 over 150,000 subscribers.

CEPT (Conférence Européenne des Administrations de Postes et Télécommunications): the European Conference of Postal and Telecommunications Administrations is the European branch of the ITU, organising 26 member administrations. Its basic aim is technical standardisation, in order to 'harmonise and improve the administrative and technical services' of its members. It is essentially a consultative organ with no legal jurisdiction over its members.

Closed User Group: an arrangement giving designated users exclusive access to part of a videotex data base.

APPENDIX I: GLOSSARY 217

Computer Programme: a set of instructions fed into a computer enabling it to handle data which are also fed into it (see *software*).

Copper Coaxial Cable: has a higher bandwidth and thus larger capacity than traditional cable technology. It uses a copper conductor and amplifiers or repeaters at intervals to boost the signal. This technology can offer up to between 30 and 50 channels but typically has limited *interactive* capacity compared optic-fibre cable.

Digital: information can be stored or transmitted in digital (as a series of distinct pulses) or analogue (as a signal fluctuating in intensity) form. In digital form the information consists of a series of separate characters that usually have only two possible states (e.g. 'on' or 'off', 1 or 0, etc.). Information stored or transmitted digitally is resistant to interference, can cope with much more information and can integrate voice with data and pictures. Digital signals can be more easily stored and manipulated.

Digital Television Sets: produce better-quality television pictures and allow the viewer to 'play' with the image on the screen, e.g. 'freezing' the picture or displaying several different signals simultaneously ('windowing').

Direct Broadcasting Satellite: (DBS) a geostationary satellite which picks up broadcast signals from an earth station and then retransmits them back to earth. The signal is powerful enough for it to be received direct (by the consumer) by means of a domestic dish aerial fixed to the roof (or in the garden) measuring as little as 90cm in diameter.

Display technologies: liquid crystal display technologies replace cathode ray technology as television receivers and enable small television sets and flat screens for 'wall-hanging' to be made.

Electronic Mail: a service which combines teletex and facsimile; subscribers are provided with 'electronic mail boxes'. An example is British Telecom's Telecom Gold.

Electronic Switching: effectively replaces electro-mechanical systems of telecommunications switching by computer control. The British 'System X' is an example.

European Broadcasting Union (EBU): was established in 1950 and has 40 members (mainly West European public broadcasting organisations) in 33 states. It is perhaps best known for its daily Eurovision news exchanges. EBU has three main activities — programming (including programme exchange and co-production), legal (e.g. copyright issues) and technical (e.g. transmission standards). Under its auspices a number of West European public broadcasting stations experimented with a joint European television programme (Eurikon), eventually launched on satellite as Europa-TV in 1985.

European Space Agency: is an organisation founded in 1975. It reflects the ambition of European states to develop an independent space technology programme, including satellites and launchers. It produces the Ariane launcher (mainly a French product), and the ECS and Olympus satellites. It has 11 members, but is heavily reliant on finance from its larger members, notably France and West Germany (and to a lesser extent also Britain and Italy).

Eutelsat (European Telecommunications Satellite Consortium): is an association of 26 European PTTs, established in 1982 to provide satellite services in Europe. It manages the OTS/ECS satellites (Orbital Test Satellite/European Communications Satellite), allocating available transponders.

Facsimile: a service that enables documents to be copied and transmitted from one location to another at great speed via the telephone network, thus bypassing the postal services.

Filière: describes a web of relationships and interdependency between industrial actors in and among sectors; typically it involves a flow of goods and is based on a strong technological relationship (e.g. *filière électronique*). Analysis of these chains of relationship is aimed at providing a basis for rational government intervention aimed at 'strategic' points in the *filière*. It had a strong influence on French industrial policy under the Socialists.

Footprint: (of a Direct Broadcasting Satellite): Geographical area over which a satellite signal can be received.

Frequencies: radio waves are one form of electro-magnetic waves, which consist of electric and magnetic vibrations and were discovered by Herz. They carry radio signals and are described in terms of wavelength (with radio waves being the longest) and frequency (the number of waves passing a given point in a given time).

Gateway: in videotex, an arrangement providing access to a third party computer.

Geostationary Orbit: if placed in orbit 36,000 km above the earth, a satellite's speed matches the earth's rotation and hence its position relative to the earth's surface remains constant.

Hardware: A general term to describe the electronic or mechanical components of a communications system: e.g. satellite, computer terminal, TV set, etc.

High Definition Television: developed by NHK, the main Japanese broadcasting organisation offers high picture quality by using 1,125 lines (as opposed to the 625 lines now in use for colour television and earlier 405 for black-and-white) and 60 fields (picture repetitions) per second to reduce screen flicker. The main competitor is the British IBA's *C-MAC*, which seeks a more evolutionary approach using fewer lines (625) but achieving much sharper picture quality by keeping colour and brightness separate. *Extended C-MAC* will permit cinema screens in the home.

Home Banking/Telebanking: term used to refer to the ability to call up information about one's bank account, transfer money from one account to another, pay bills, etc., from one's home terminal by means of an interactive videotex or cable system.

Home Shopping/Teleshopping: terms used to refer to the ability to order goods, make transactions, etc., from the home by means of an interactive videotex or cable system.

Information Provider: an organisation that supplies the information stored on the computer of a public videotex or private 'value-added' or data service, e.g. banks, news agencies, mail order firms, travel agencies.

Integrated Circuits: complete electronic circuits on tiny chips of semi-conductor (silicon). They make possible the microminiaturisation of electronic equipment.

Intelsat (International Telecommunications Satellite Organisation: is an international organisation with over 100 member states. It is under the overall direction of a board of governors representing these states, but in fact its technical and operational functions are supplied by COMSAT (the American Communications Satellite Corporation). It manages the Intelsat communications satellites, and is responsible for running the majority of the world's communications satellites.

Interactive: a term to describe 'two-way' communication or a 'two-way communication system' that permits transmission as well as reception of messages. An interactive facility on a cable or videotex system can be used for a wide range of purposes: including home shopping, home banking, automated dealing in securities etc.

International Telecommunications Union (ITU): an international body under the auspices of the United Nations that is responsible for the allocation of radio frequencies. It has been traditionally dominated by technical experts and engineers. In recent years politicians have increasingly recognised the ITU's strategic importance. Consequently its work is becoming more and more 'political'. See also *WARC*.

ISDN (Integrated Services Digital Network): ultimately this system will transform telecommunications into 'videocommunications'. By means of a combination of digital signals and new cable systems, much more information will be transmitted,

APPENDIX I: GLOSSARY

at greater speed and efficiency, on a single system; this will permit the integration of voice with data and graphics, e.g. cable television, high-speed facsimile transmission, videophone.

Microprocessor: silicon chips that are themselves miniature computers, combing the different functions of a computer – memory, control unit etc. They can be incorporated in all types of equipment, revolutionising telecommunications and broadcasting.

Microwave: very short wavelength radio waves which are used for high capacity terrestrial point-to-point links.

Modem: is a modulating/demodulating device used to process electronic signals for transmission: for example, a telephone modem translates signals from a home computer for transmission over a telephone line to another computer. These devices allow a remote terminal to be used when connected to the computer over the normal telephone system.

Narrowcasting: term used to refer to the aiming of programmes at specialised interest groups. It involves a step beyond 'broadcasting', where programmes have to contain a mass appeal, and is facilitated by broadband cable systems.

Online: direct contact between one computer and another; or between a terminal and a computer.

Optical-fibre cable: a 'vanguard technology' (*technologie de pointe*), this type of cable is more modern and complex, but also much more costly at present than copper-coaxial cable. It has a high 'interactive' capability. It use light pulses to transmit a large amount of information through micro-thin glass or plastic fibres. It provides a very wide bandwidth with much less signal loss (with distance) and distortion than copper-coaxial cable.

Overall (of a Direct Broadcasting Satellite's signal): signals from DBS satellites may cover parts or all of countries, other than the country to which the WARC conference allocated a particular channel.

PABX (Private Automatic Branch Exchange): modern digital PABXs can switch computer data, telex messages, and even facsimile as easily as voice conversations. The PABX lies at the heart of any modern office system.

PTTs: the term traditionally refers to the authorities that have sole responsibility for the operation and regulation of the telecommunications network.

Satellites: to an extent replace and to an extent augment terrestrial technologies like cable and microwave relay systems. Located in space, they receive and transmit signals across huge distances and can be used for international or domestic communication. There are different types: general communications satellites (like the Intelsat and ECS satellites), weather, earth-mapping, scientific research, navigation, military reconnaissance and surveillance, and *direct broadcasting (DBS)* satellites. The European Communication Satellites have been launched by the European Space Agency and are managed by Eutelsat. Like the Intelsat satellites they handle broadcasting as well as telecommunications transmission. Broadcasting from these satellites requires large receiving dishes and is typically suited to the programming of cable television systems. DBS (direct broadcasting by satellite) e.g. France's TDF-1 has a more powerful signal that can be picked up by a much smaller dish. Many satellites are in *geostationary orbit*.

Semi conductor: a material, such as silicon or germanium, which can be arranged as an insulation or a conductor of electricity, dependent upon the direction of an externally applied current.

Silicon chip: a wafer-fragment of pure silicon, only a few milimetres square, upon which an 'integrated circuit' is printed. See *integrated circuit, microprocessor* and *semiconductor*.

Software: information and instructions that have been specially designed to provide the user with something useful when combined with a particular item of hardware, e.g. videotape, tv programme, computer programme etc.

Switching equipment: opens up a circuit for a subscriber when he/she requires it. See *electronic switching*.

Teleconferencing/Videoconferencing: two or more people can be brought together by videophone for a conference. This facility can be supported by other 'interactive' services, e.g. facsimile.

Telematics: refers to an extension of services beyond voice to data and video communications; telematics has been made possible by the microprocessor which enables terminals to become 'intelligent'. It signifies the totality of techniques involving the 'marriage' of telecommunications and computing.

Teletex: a service resembling Telex (but much quicker and more versatile) in which messages can be transmitted via word processors.

Teletext: information (text and very simple static graphics) displayed on the television screen, which is transmitted on the back of the broadcast TV signal. Only a limited number of pages (frames) can be broadcast per TV channel. The system is not interactive. Examples are Antiope in France and the BBC's Ceefax or the ITV's Oracle in Britain.

Terminal: a term used to refer to an item of hardware that allows information to be displayed (usually on a screen) and allows information input (usually by a keyboard).

Value-Added Network services (VANs). combine communications and the power of computers to provide a wide variety of information and transaction services, e.g. electronic mail, videotex services, reservation and billing services.

Video-Cassette Recorder: plays back video-tapes on which are recorded video (or vision) signals as well as audio (or sound) signals. When the original electronic signals are reproduced, they can be transmitted as a television picture.

Videophone: permits 'audiovisual' (sound plus sight) telephony by means of 'intelligent' terminals and broadband cable links. At present, it is being tested in Western Europe, notably by the French at Biarritz.

Videotex or *Viewdata*: a term used to refer to a communications system that makes computer-based information available on a visual display unit or TV screen. It uses the telephone lines or a cable network to connect the screen to the computer. Information is called up by the user by means of a keyboard.

Visual Display Unit (VDU): a screen attached to a computer or word processor by means of which the user can see the information that is being fed into/called up on the system.

WARC: World Administrative Radio Conferences: they allocate radio/satellite frequencies and orbital positions. The WARC are convened by the ITU. At WARC 71 (in 1971) the first allocation of frequency bands to the broadcasting satellite service were made. At WARC 77 (in 1977) a complex international plan for satellite broadcasting was drawn up, which will be valid until at least 1994 and possibly into the next century.

Word Processor: a specialist function of a computer which processes information, manipulates texts, etc.

APPENDIX 2: TABLES

1. WORLD'S TOP TEN SEMICONDUCTOR SALES (1985 forecast)

Rank (brackets 1984 rank)	Company	Headquarters	Sales ($bn)
1. (2)	NEC	Japan	1,950
2. (1)	Texas Instruments	US	1,815
3. (4)	Hitachi	Japan	1,750
4. (3)	Motorola	US	1,650
5. (5)	Toshiba	Japan	1,370
6. (8)	Fujitsu	Japan	950
7. (7)	Intel	US	900
8. (6)	National Semiconductor	US	890
9. (10)	Matsushita	Japan	870
10. (9)	Philips	The Netherlands	850

Source: Integrated Circuit Engineering.

2. EUROPEAN SEMICONDUCTOR CONSUMPTION (1984)

		Percentage
A) By Region	West Germany	27.1
	Britain and Ireland	25.8
	France	14.4
	Italy	10
	Scandinavia	8.2
	Benelux	6.3
	Rest of Europe	8.2
B) By End Use	Telecommunications	23.5
	Industry	22.4
	Consumer	20.3
	Computer	20.2
	Govt/Military	9
	Automotive	4.6

Source: Dataquest.

3. WORLD'S TOP TEN COMPUTER MANUFACTURERS (1984)

Rank	Company	Headquarters	Computer Revenue ($bn)
1.	IBM	US	44.3
2.	Digital Equipment Corp.	US	6.2
3.	Burroughs	US	4.5
4.	Control Data	US	3.7
5.	NCR	US	3.7
6.	Fujitsu	Japan	3.5
7.	Sperry	US	3.4
8.	Hewlett-Packard	US	3.4
9.	NEC	Japan	2.8
10.	Siemens	West Germany	2.8

Source: Datamation.

4. DATA PROCESSING REVENUES IN WESTERN EUROPE (1983)

	Company	$m
1.	IBM (US)	10,634
2.	Bull (France)	1,537
3.	Siemens (West Germany)	1,380
4.	Olivetti (Italy)	1,160
5.	Digital Equipment (US)	1,053
6.	ICL (UK)	984
7.	Nixdorf (West Germany)	926
8.	Burroughs (US)	860
9.	NCR (US)	841
10.	Hewlett-Packard (US)	775

Source: IDC Europe.

5. WORLD'S TOP TEN TELECOMMUNICATIONS EQUIPMENT MANUFACTURERS (1983)

Rank	Company	Headquarters	Sales ($bn)
1.	AT & T	US	11.16
2.	ITT	US	4.86
3.	Siemens	West Germany	4.49
4.	L. M. Ericsson	Sweden	3.16
5.	Alcatel-Thomson	France	2.74
6.	Northern Telecom	Canada	2.66
7.	NEC	Japan	2.41
8.	GTE	US	2.38
9.	Motorola	US	2.31
10.	IBM (excluding Rohm)	US	1.73

Source: Arthur D. Little.

6. WORLD LEADERS IN DIGITAL SWITCHING EXCHANGES (1984)

With annual world sales of £7 bn, this market accounted for one-third of all telecommunications equipment sales.

Supplier	Market Share ($)	Lines Ordered	Export Markets
AT & T (US)	2 bn	3m	3
Northern Telecom (Canada)	1.4 bn	13m	29
ITT (US)	1.5 bn	11m	20
NEC/Fujitsu (Japan)	1.5 bn	12m	35
Siemens (West Germany)	1.1 bn	6m	22
Ericsson (Sweden)	850m	11m	61
Alcatel Thomson (France)	800m	20m	30
Plessey (Britain)	300m	1.5m	2
GEC (Britain)	260m	1.5m	2

Source: Financial Times.

7. R & D COST OF DIGITAL SWITCHING SYSTEMS ($ bn by 1983/4)

System	$ bn
System X (GEC/Plessey/BT)	1.4
E10 and E12 (CIT-Alcatel)	1.0
System 12 (ITT)	1.0
ESS-5 (Western Electric)	.75
DMS (Northern Telecom)	.7
EWS-D (Siemens)	.7
AXE (Ericsson)	.5

Source: M. Sharp, *Europe and the New Technologies*, p. 108.

APPENDIX II: TABLES

8. EUROPEAN PTT COMMITMENT (1983)

PTT	Telematics Commitment	Liberalisation Possibility	Regulations	Protectionist Attitude	Foreign Penetration
Belgium	3	4	3	0	10
France	10	0	10	10	2
Italy	3	3	9	9	9
Netherlands	2	5	8	7	8
Spain	10	3	9	9	9
Sweden	5	0	7	5	8
UK	8	10	5	5	8
W. Germany	2	5	10	10	3

Commitment on a scale of 0 – 10
(0 = no commitment, 10 = high commitment)

Source: The Yankee Group, *Report on European Telecommunications*, Vol. 8 (1983).

9. EUROPEAN TV ADVERTISING EXPENDITURE (1983)

	Total Expenditure $m	TV Share %
West Germany	4,757	15.6
Britain	4,295	31
France	1,960	19
Netherlands	1,419	5.1
Italy	1,294	45
Spain	962	30.9
Belgium (transmitted from Luxembourg)	413	11.3
Sweden	356	0.0
Denmark	232	0.0
Greece	86	47.6
Ireland	75	38
Portugal	32	60

Source: Advertising Age Focus.

10. CABLE PENETRATION IN WESTERN EUROPE

Country	Households (in millions)	TV Households (in millions)	Cabled Households (in %)
1. Belgium/Luxembourg	3.3	3.2	81.1
2. Netherlands	5.0	4.9	54
3. Switzerland	2.4	2.3	47
4. Ireland	0.9	0.8	25
5. Norway	1.5	1.4	14
6. Denmark	2.2	2.0	10
7. Austria	2.75	2.6	9
8. Finland	1.7	1.6	6
9. Britain	21.1	20.6	6
10. Sweden	3.3	3.2	5
11. West Germany	25.1	24.5	4
12. France	19.4	18.0	2
13. Greece	2.85	2.7	–
14. Italy	18.5	17.6	–
15. Portugal	3.0	2.7	–
16. Spain	10.5	9.9	–
17. the rest of Europe	0.5	0.5	–
Figures for comparison USA		83.9	41.2
Japan		30.0	13.0

Source: CIT Research 1984.

11. MAIN SATELLITE BROADCASTING CHANNELS IN WESTERN EUROPE (DECEMBER 1985)

Satellite	Station	Language	Material
ECS 1	RAI	Italian	National 1 programme
	3 SAT	German	Films and news
	EUROPA (from 1987/8 on the Olympus satellite)	Eng/Dutch	General interest
	TV5	French	Best of French TV
	CATALAN NEWS	Catalan	News feed daily
	EBNET	Various	Religious channel
	WORLDNET	English	US Information Agency
	SKY	English	General and also stereo
	TELECLUB	German	Films
	FILMNET	Eng/Dutch	Films
	WPN	Eng/French	Documentary
	SAT 1	German	Films, News
	VOA	English	Pop music and news (audio)
	MUSIC BOX	English	Pop Video Channel
INTELSAT F 10 (27.5° W)	* PREMIERE	English	Films
	CHILDREN'S CH	English	Children's programmes
	SCREEN SPORT	English	Many different sports
	* MIRRORVISION	English	Films
	CNN	English	USA 24h NEWS
	EINS PLUS (from March 1986)	German	General
INTELSAT VA (18° W)	BBC	English	Very rare. News feeds
GORIZONT (11° W)	USSR	Russian	Rare. Prog. 1 tests
ECS 2	NORWAY	Norse	C-MAC system
	EBU	Various	News feeds and sport
	EBU	Various	News feeds and sport

* In March 1986 Robert Maxwell announced the closure of Mirrorvision and became controlling partner in Premiere.

Source: *Electronics and Wireless World*

Index

ACARD (Advisory Council for Applied Research & Development) 165
Acorn, 149
ACTT (Association of Cinematograph, Television and Allied Technicians), 182
Advertisers (see advertising), 100, 140
Advertising (markets, industry, lobby, etc.), 15, 22–3, 25, 32, 92–3, 99, 100, 101, 109, 111, 115, 116, 117, 118, 126, 127, 131, 132, 140, 141, 143
AEG-Telefunken, 16, 21, 91, 108
Aerospatiale, 108
Agency for Administrative Development (Swedish), 201
Aktive Strukturpolitik, 175
Alcatel-Thomson, 63–7
Alternatives (West German movement), 164, 176, 177, 190
Alvey Directorate, 166
Anti-terrorist provisions (West Germany), 202
APEX (Association of Professional, Executive, Clerical and Computer Staff), 180, 182
ARD, 22, 41, 119
Ariane, 108
Article 80 (French audiovisual reform law), 104–5, 116
Association des Ingénieurs des Télécommunications (AIT), 65
ASTMS (Association of Scientific, Technical and Managerial Staffs), 180, 182
AT & T (American Telephone and Telegraph), 1, 6, 13, 15, 16, 17, 20, 21, 23, 24, 25, 26, 66, 85, 148, 154, 159
Atlantic Institute survey, 164–5, 188–90
'Audio-visual communication', 98–122, 172, 175
'Auroux Laws' (*Lois Auroux*), 183
Austria (Austrian), 22, 149, 150, 204
Aussenpluralismus, 43

Baden-Württemberg (West German *Land*), 38, 175, 178, 190
Baker, Kenneth, 202
Bank for International Settlements, 29
Banking (see Cashless Banking and Telebanking), 181, 183, 184, 187
Basic Law, the (West Germany), 129
Bauer, 25, 118
Bayerl Report, 200
Bayrischer Rundfunk, 36
BBC, 17, 21, 22, 39, 108, 118, 120, 122, 127

BDI (*Bundesverband der Deutschen Industrie*), 72
Beesley review, 32
Belgium (Belgian), 3, 15, 26, 29, 50, 107, 112, 113, 114, 116, 122, 154, 200
Bell, Daniel, 3–4
Berlusconi, Silvio, 1, 14, 15, 16, 18, 31, 38, 41, 44, 48, 100, 105, 111, 112, 115, 116, 120, 121, 128
Bertelsmann, 26, 41, 100, 109, 118, 120, 128
Berufsverbot (W German), 202
Betriebsrat (Works council), 187–8
Biedenkopf, Kurt, 175
BIFU (Banking Industrial and Finance Union), 181
BIGFON, 106, 175
Big Bang (in the City), 181
Bildschirmtext, 3, 26, 98, 106, 115, 119, 175, 177
Binnenpluralismus, 43, 142
Bleicher, Siegfried, 187
Brandt, Willy, 176
Bredin Report, 38, 111, 121
Britain (British), 1, 2, 3, 11, 14, 17, 18, 22, 23, 25, 27, 28, 30, 32, 34–5, 36–7, 38–9, 42, 43, 44–5, 57, 58–62, 74, 75–6, 99, 100, 101–3, 105, 106, 108, 109, 110, 113, 114, 117–18, 119, 120, 122, 125, 127, 128, 148, 149, 150, 151, 153, 154, 155, 163–94, 196, 198, 200, 202, 203, 204, 205, 208, 209, 212, 213, 214
British Aerospace, 108
British Computer Society, 202, 204
British Innovations plc, 169
British Leyland, 3
British Medical Association, 202, 204
British Technology Group, 166
Broadband (see cable), 151, 153, 197
Broadband switching, 153
Broadcasting, 98–124, 125–46, 166, 167, 172, 174, 175, 177, 185, 186, 213
Broadcasting markets, 21–2
Broadcasting regulation, 98–124, 125–46, 213
BT (British Telecom), 1, 17, 18, 24, 25, 26, 29, 30, 32, 35, 36, 37, 38, 39, 42, 48–62, 66, 76, 98, 103, 108, 166, 167, 168
Bull, 16, 65, 147, 148, 153, 160, 168
Bull, Hans Peter, 207
Bundespost (West German), 3, 12, 26, 29, 30, 32, 34, 36, 40, 60, 67–75, 98, 105, 106, 108, 119, 174, 175
Bundesrat (West German), 200

Bundestag (West German), 200
Burda 25, 29, 118, 128

Cable (cable television, cable systems, cable services, cable debate etc.), 2, 3, 11, 13, 20, 27, 34, 56, 98–125, 125–46, 167, 168, 170–78, 185–90, 195, 197, 208
Cable Authority, 33, 34, 39, 42, 44, 102, 117
Cable and Broadcasting Act (1984), 18, 32, 34–5, 42, 44, 102
Cable plan, French (see *Plan Câble*)
Cable Television Association, 102
Cable & Wireless, 24, 27, 36, 58
Callaghan, James, 165, 168
Cambridge Instruments, 153
Campaign for Press and Broadcasting Freedom, 167
Canada (Canadian), 204
Canal Plus, 38, 44, 105, 110, 116
Canale Cinque, 114, 115
Cap Gemeni Sogati, 21, 25
Carlton Communications, 120
Carter report, 32, 58
Cashless banking, 168, 181
Cashless shopping, 168, 181
CBS, 114
CCITT, standards, 153
CDS (*Centre des Démocrates Sociaux*), 173
CDU/CSU (West German Christian Democrat/Social Parties, Government etc.), 29, 30, 34, 36, 70–3, 106, 109, 119, 135, 174, 175, 190, 207
Ceefax (BBC), 98
Cellular radio, 39, 58, 59, 62, 94, 148
CEN (European Committee for Standardisation), 15, 17, 153
CENELEC (Committee for Electrotechnical Standardisation), 15, 153
Census (census data, etc.), 196, 197, 206, 207, 208
CEPT (Commission of European Posts and Telecommunications Administrations), 15, 17, 26, 152, 153
Cesta (Paris-based study centre for advanced technical systems), 149, 171
CFDT (*Confédération Française Démocratique du Travail*), 66, 182, 183, 184
CFDT-PTT (French Telecommunications Workers' Union, see CFDT), 183
CFTC (*Confédération Française des Travailleurs Chrétiens*), 184, 185
CGE, 24, 26, 62–7, 148, 154
CGT (*Confédération Générale du Travail*), 182, 183, 184, 188, 189
CGT-*Force Ouvrière*, 185
CGT-PTT (French Telecommunications Workers' Union, see CGT), 185

CGC (*Confédération Générale des Cadres*), 185
CGCT (*Compagnie Générale de Constructions Téléphoniques*), 62–7, 148
Chirac, Jacques, 110, 111, 121
Christian Democrat (general), 101
Christian Democrat (Low Countries), 113
Christian-Liberal Coalition (see CDU/CSU/FDP), 175, 187
Churches (West German), 135, 142
Cinema, 22, 114, 116
CIT-Alcatel, 16, 62–7, 148, 151, 154
Citicorp, 6, 13, 14, 16, 18, 21, 23, 24, 27
Civil liberties, 195–211
CLT (*Compagnie Luxembourgeoise de Télédiffusion*), 109–13
'Club of Twenty-One', 108, 118
C-MAC, 11
CNET, 32, 40
'Coca-Cola' (satellites, broadcasting, etc.), 110, 111, 112, 122
Codes of conduct (television programming), 127
CODITEC (*Commission de Diffusion de la Télévision par Réseaux Câblés*), 32, 36, 103, 104
Collaboration (see European collaboration)
Collectivités Locales, 104, 173
Columbia, 118
Comité d'entreprise (works council), 183
Commercial broadcasting, issues concerning, 98–124, 125–46
Committee on Data Protection and Liberties (French), 202
Communications Act (United States), 128, 140
'Communications Campaign' (GLC), 169
Communists (French), 172, 173, 184, 189, 202
Compact discs, 21
Computer-aided manufacturing, 187
Computers (Computer, Computing), 2, 4, 7, 11, 20–1, 99, 101, 102, 103, 147–62, 163–94, 195–211, 213–14
Computers, personal, 20, 149, 208
Computer registers/records (see population registering), 195–211
Computer register, Stockholm, 201
Computer software, 21
Computerisation (of society, work, public-record systems, etc.), 103, 169, 170, 180, 183, 184, 186, 200, 202
Conservative (British Conservative Government, Party, etc.), 34–5, 58, 76, 101, 117, 166–9, 172, 173, 180, 203
Conservative (General), 101
Constitutional Court (Italian), 113
Constitutional Court (West German, see Federal Constitutional Court)

INDEX   227

Consultation (*Consultation*), 169, 170, 185
Consumers' Association (Britain), 198
Consumer Credit Act (1974, Britain), 203
Consumer electronics, 21, 24, 126
'Convergence' (of technologies, policies, etc.), 103, 155, 170
Copper-coaxial (see cable), 3, 11, 34, 106, 113
Copyright law, 132, 134
Corning Glass, 17, 20, 24
Coronet, 110
Corporatist (Corporatism), 168, 169, 176, 179, 190
COST (European Co-operation in the field of Scientific & Technical Research), 151, 152, 155
Council of Europe, 15, 195, 199
Council of Ministers (EC), 150, 151, 153
Craxi, Bettino, 112
'Custom-built chips', 147, 154

Data Act (Sweden), 201, 208
Datacast (BBC), 98
Data Inspectorate (Sweden), 201, 208
Data-processing (see Computing)
Data Processing & Protection of Liberties Act (France), 202
Data protection agencies, 195, 198–200, 205–7
Data Protection Bill/Act (Britain), 198, 204, 205
Data Protection Bill/Act (W German), 200, 205
Data protection commissioners, 207
Data Protection Committee (Lindop Committee, Britain), 203
Data protection legislation, 5, 195–211, 214–15
Data protection registrars, 205, 206
Data Surveillance Bill (Britain), 202
DBS (Direct Broadcasting Satellite), 1, 2, 17, 20, 36, 38, 39, 44, 107–22
Decentralisation, 116, 169, 170, 172, 173, 177
Defence (policies, strategies), 12–13, 16, 156
Defferre, Gaston, 35
Denmark (Danish), 200, 201, 204
Deregulation, 16, 18, 19, 23, 25–31, 41–2, 47–8, 49–50, 56–79, 98–124, 125–46, 164, 167, 168, 181, 213
Deskilling, 164, 158, 181
de Sola Pool, Ithiel, 11
DGB (*Deutscher Gewerkschaftsbund*), 49, 185, 186, 187
DGT (*Direction Générale des Télé-communications*), 16, 26, 32, 33, 35, 36, 37, 40, 44, 60, 62–7, 98, 103, 104, 105, 110, 115, 172, 173

Dialcom, 24
Digital switches (Digitalisation, see Switching), 2, 3, 7, 8, 11, 15, 16, 17, 19, 20, 26, 39, 56, 58, 60, 61, 66, 76, 85, 106, 148, 152, 168, 179
DIHT (*Deutscher Industrie- und Handesltag*), 72
Dohnanyi, Klaus von, 49
Dondoux, 64, 67
Dow Jones, 13, 21
DPG (*Deutsche Postgewerkschaft*, West German Telecommunications Workers' Union), 68–9, 70, 74, 187, 190
DTI (Department of Trade and Industry, Britain), 166, 206
Dupuis, 113

EBU (European Broadcasting Union), 15, 17, 28, 41, 52 n. 15
Economic crisis, strategies for emerging from, 178
Edelmann, Murray, 136, 138
EEC Treaty (see Treaty of Rome)
EETPU (Electrical, Electronic, Tele-communications and Plumbing Trade Union), 180, 181, 182
Eins Plus, 31, 41
Electronic mail, 3, 4, 11, 13, 15, 98, 166, 187
'Electronic Cottage', 181
'Electronic Office' (see Electronic Cottage and Homeworking), 178, 181
Electronics (industry, markets, sector etc., see *Filière Electronique*), 99, 100, 101, 102, 103, 104, 106, 108, 114, 117, 128, 148, 149, 163–94
Electronic telephone directories, 103, 115
Enquetekommission: Neue Informations- und Kommunikationstechniken, 178
Ericsson, 17, 20, 25, 26, 39, 59, 80–97, 166
ESA (European Space Agency), 2, 15, 17, 108, 109
ES 2 (microchip manufacture), 147, 154
ESPRIT (European Strategic Programme for Research and Development in Information Technologies), 17, 96, 147, 150, 151, 153, 155, 157, 158, 159, 161, 213
Essen party conference (SPD), 177
Eureka, 17, 25, 77, 147, 149, 150, 155, 156, 157, 158, 213
Europa TV, 3, 4, 53 n. 15
European Collaboration, 16–17, 18, 25, 47–8, 51, 147–62, 168, 213–14
European Commission, 130, 131, 132, 136, 137, 141, 147, 149, 150, 152, 153, 156, 157, 158, 159, 200

European Community (EC), 7, 14, 15, 17, 18, 20, 21, 24, 25, 32, 56, 73, 76, 77, 96, 114, 136, 147–62, 200, 214–14
European Computing Services Association, 26
European Convention (Data protection), 199, 200, 203, 204, 208
European Convention for the Protection of Human Rights and Fundamental Freedoms, 130, 131, 196
European IT standards policy, suggestions for, 153
European Parliament, 200
Eutelsat, 15, 17, 107, 116, 117
Expertenkommission: Neue Medien, 178
EVE project (European videoconferencing equipment), 152
EWICS (European Workshop on Informatics & Computing Systems), 152

Fabius, Laurent, 48, 65, 67
Facsimile, 11, 13, 208
Fairness Doctrine (United States), 139, 140, 142
FDP (West German Free Democratic Party), 71, 72–3, 106, 135, 174, 176, 207
Federal Audit Court, West German, 40
Federal Communications Commission (FCC), US, 27, 39, 62, 128, 138, 139, 141, 142
Federal Constitutional Court, West German, 40, 43, 129, 130, 131, 135
Federal system (West German), problems associated with, 106, 120, 177, 190
Fernmeldetechnisches Zentralamt, 69
Fibre-Optic(s) (cable, networks, systems, etc.), 2, 11, 13, 20, 27, 34, 56, 103, 104, 106, 151–2, 167, 168, 170, 173, 174, 185
Fifth generation computers, 156, 196
Fillioud, Georges, 35
Financial services, electronic, 8, 12, 13, 15, 17, 18, 19, 20–1, 27, 28, 98, 102
Finland (Finnish), 109, 149, 150
Filière (Filière Électronique), 171, 172
First Amendment (US Constitution), 129, 130
Force de frappe, 189
France (French), 1, 2, 3, 12, 15, 18–19, 22, 23, 25, 26, 27, 30, 31, 32, 33–4, 36–8, 43–4, 48, 50, 57, 59, 62–7, 75–6, 100, 103–5, 106, 107, 108, 109, 110, 111, 112, 113, 114, 115, 116, 117, 119, 120, 121, 122, 125, 126, 128, 148, 149, 150, 151, 153, 154, 155, 156, 157, 160, 163–94, 200, 201, 204, 205, 208
Franchise (procedures etc.), 126
Frankfurter Allgemeine Zeitung, 119
'Freedom of Communication', 129, 130, 131, 132, 133

Freese, Jan, 201, 207
French Socialist (government, Party etc.), 48, 103, 104, 105, 107, 110, 111, 112, 115, 116, 117, 120, 121, 170, 171, 172, 173, 189, 202
Fujitsu, 17, 20, 21

GATT, 14, 23
Gaullists, 173
GDL (satellite), 110
GEC (GEC Marconi), 24, 26, 58–62, 108, 150, 151, 153, 166
General Electric, 8, 14, 18, 41
General Instruments, 16
General Motors, 14
Geostationary orbit, 2
Germany, West (West German), 2, 3, 12, 14, 15, 18–19, 22, 23, 25, 26, 28, 29, 30, 31, 32, 34, 36, 43, 45, 48, 59, 62, 67–77, 100, 101, 105–7, 108, 109, 118–19, 120, 122, 125–46, 148, 149, 150, 151, 153, 154, 155, 160, 163–94, 199, 200, 201, 202, 204, 205, 207, 208
GIEL (*Groupement des Industries Électroniques*), 103
Giscard d'Estaing, President, 63–4, 103, 104, 110, 170, 171, 172
GLC (Greater London Council), 168, 169
GLEB (Greater London Enterprise Board), 169
'Globalisation', 8, 24–5, 27, 125
Glotz, Peter, 45, 49, 107, 177, 190
Goldcrest, 118
Granada TV, 17, 41, 108, 118, 120
Greece (Greek), 200
Green Paper for the Establishment of the Common Market for Broadcasting Especially by Satellite and Cable (EC Commission), 131, 136
Green Party, West German, 48–9, 135, 164, 176, 177, 178, 190, 191
Groupe Bruxelles Lambert, 26, 41, 112, 113, 120, 121
Grundig, 16, 21, 148
GSLB (*Groupe Spécial de Communication à Large Bande*), 152
GTE, 17, 23, 26, 154

Hamburg, 29, 49, 107, 120
Hauff, Volker, 175–6
Havas, 105, 110, 116
HBV (West German Retail, Banking and Assurance Workers' Union), 187, 190
Hersant, Robert, 104, 111, 112, 115, 121, 185
Hesse (West German *Land*), 109, 199
Hewlett-Packard, 148
High Authority (*Haute Autorité*), 43–4

INDEX   229

High-definition television, 11, 99, 152
Hitachi, 21
Holtzbrinck, 118
Home Box Office, 14, 17, 114
Home Office (British), 203, 204, 206
Homeworking (see Teleworking), 169, 181
Honeywell, 17
House of Commons (British), 202
Hughes Communications, 20
'Humanisation of work' (programme/West Germany), 178, 186
Hunt Inquiry (Hunt Report), 32, 44, 102

IBA, 24, 44, 118
IBCN (Integrated Broadband Communications Network, European), 151
IBM (International Business Machines), 3, 6, 14, 16, 18, 20, 21, 23, 24, 26, 39, 41, 63, 71, 108, 152, 154, 161, 170, 171, 180
Iceland (Icelandic), 204
ICL, 41, 147, 150, 153, 160, 165, 168
IG-Drupa (Druck und Papier, West German Printworkers' Union), 186, 187, 190
IG-Metall (West German Manufacturing Workers' Union), 186, 187, 190
IMAG, 150
Independent programme producers, 121
Information providers, 100, 103, 119
Information services, 3, 8, 15, 19, 20–1, 53 n.28, 98, 102
'Information workers' (in the service sector), 178–92
Inmos, 118, 165, 166
Insac, 165, 166
Institut National de l'Audiovisuel (INA), 166
Integrated circuits, 150, 151, 153
Intelsat, 2, 13, 26–7, 107, 118
Interactive (communication, services etc.), 98, 99, 101, 106, 172, 173, 175, 189, 198
Interior Ministry (West German), 200
Internal pluralism (see *Binnenpluralismus*)
International political economy, 19–33
International Telecommunications Users Group (INTUG), 14, 25
International Telegraph and Telephone Consultative Council (CCITT), 14
IPSS (International Packet Switching Service), 13
ISDN (Integrated Services Digital Network), 2, 3, 14, 17, 34, 85, 98, 151, 153, 172, 175
IT (Information Technology), 99, 101, 103, 147–62, 163–94, 195–211
Italy (Italian), 2, 14, 15, 16, 22, 40, 48, 52 n.11, 109, 111, 113, 114, 115, 120, 121, 127, 128, 148, 149, 151, 154, 160, 168, 200
Italia Uno, 114–15

ITAP (Information Technology Advisory Panel), 5, 12, 18, 32, 34, 36, 37, 39, 40, 42, 101, 102, 103, 107, 108, 166, 167, 195, 208
Information Technology Year, 166
IT Task Force (European Commission), 150
I-Tech Centres, 166
Ireland (Irish), 22, 120, 122, 199, 200
ISO (International Standards Organisation), 152, 153
Italtel, 148, 151, 154
ITT, 20, 26, 60, 62, 66, 70, 85
ITU (International Telecommunications Union), 2
ITV, 21, 22, 39, 41, 108, 118, 120, 122, 127

Japan (Japanese), 2, 15, 16, 17, 21, 22, 24, 42, 56, 99, 114, 125, 156, 160, 161, 171, 174
Jenkins, Clive, 182
Jeumont-Schneider, 65
Job-loss (see Unemployment)
Joint research (see Research)
Joint Ventures (see European Collaboration), 147–62
Jusos, 190
Justice (British lawyers' group), 202
Justice Committee, 197
JVC, 16

Kohl, Helmut, 175
KTK (*Kommission für den Ausbau des technischen Kommunikationssystems*), 18, 32, 106, 174, 178

Labour (government, Party etc.), 164, 165, 166, 167, 168, 169, 189
Lang, Jack, 19, 33, 35, 98, 112, 116
Law on Audiovisual Communications (1982), French (see Reform Law, etc.)
Legal claims (in respect of damages relating to data), 205
Liberal Party (British), 168, 169
Liberal parties (Low Countries), 113
Lille, 173
Lindop Committee (Britain), 203
Lindop Report, 203, 204
Lindop, Sir Norman, 203
'Live Aid', 1, 51
LO (Swedish Trade Union Federation), 80, 88
Local area networks (LANs), 3
London Industrial Strategy (GLC), 169
Low Countries, 107, 113, 213
Luxembourg, 15, 17, 38, 50, 100, 109–12, 117, 120, 154, 200, 201, 204, 213
LUX SAT, 109

Machine-readable passports/identity cards, 196, 200
Maire, Edmond, 183
Management Services America, 21
Mancroft, Lord, 202
'Market model of broadcasting', 125–46
Matra, 149
Maxwell, Robert, 1, 6, 14, 15, 18, 21, 24, 26, 37, 38, 41, 100, 103, 111, 116, 117, 118, 120, 121, 128
MCI Communications, 14, 15, 18, 23, 26, 41
Media Policy Note 1983 (Netherlands), 113
Media union (West Germany), creation of, 190
'Mega-project', 154, 159, 175
Meinungsvielfalt, 43
Messerschmidt Boelkow Blohm (MBB), 108
Messmer, Pierre, 202
Mercury, 36, 39, 58–62, 103, 167
Merrill Lynch, 6, 8, 13, 21, 27, 41
Metz, 173
Mexandeau, Louis, 35, 104
Microcomputers, 149, 166, 208
Microelectronics Awareness Programme, 166
Micro-electronics, 150, 166, 175, 177, 179, 181, 191
Microprocessors, 165
Minister of Communication (France), 171
Minister of Culture (France), 98, 112, 116
Ministries of Culture (Low Countries), 113
Minister of State for Information Technology (British), 166
Minitel, 3, 115, 172, 173
Mirrorvision, 117
Mission TV Câble ('Mission Schreiner'), 32, 33–4, 38, 39, 115
Mitbestimmung, 178
Mitel, 17, 24, 59,
Mittelstandspolitik, 106
Mitterrand, President François, 1, 38 64–5, 103, 105, 110, 111, 112, 115, 116, 117, 120, 148
Mobile telephones, 152
Modelldeutschland (Model Germany), 109, 163, 164, 191
Modernisation *Modernisation*, 106, 163–91
Mondadori group, 115
Monopolkommission (West Germany), 133
Montpellier, 173
Motorola, 16, 21, 39
MTV, 17
Multimedia concerns, 98–122, 128, 130
Multimedia-diversification, 5, 98–122, 128, 213
Multinational (companies, conglomerates), 5, 6, 8, 12, 13–14, 18, 24–9, 40–1, 50, 62, 99, 102, 109, 121, 128, 130, 156, 180, 208

Munich, 119, 120
Murdoch, Rupert, 1, 6, 8, 14, 15, 16, 18, 21, 24, 26, 41, 100, 111, 112, 113, 117, 120
Music Box, 3, 50, 118

NAGO, 182
'Narrowcasting', 3, 99
NASA, 108
National Association of Broadcasters (NAB, United States), 138, 139, 141
NAB-code, 138
National Computing Centre (British), 202
National Council for Civil Liberties (Britain), 202
National Investment Bank, 168
Nationalisation(s), 170, 171, 183
National Semiconductors, 21
NATO, 12, 16
NBC, 114
NCR, 39
NEB (National Enterprise Board), 165, 166
Netherlands (Dutch), 3, 15, 29, 30, 107, 112, 113, 148, 150, 154, 175, 200
New media laws (West Germany), 18, 29, 34, 43, 106, 107, 128, 135, 136, 137, 139, 140, 141, 142, 143
'New realism', 180, 183, 188
New Technology Agreements, 180, 181, 182, 188
News International, 100, 112, 113, 117, 120
Newspaper industry (see Press, Publishers), 178–92
Nexos, 165, 166
New Social Forces, 164, 165
New Social Movements, 164, 176, 179
New Technology Enterprise Corporation, 169
NGA (National Graphical Association), 181
Nippon Electric (NEC), 16, 20, 24, 39, 59
Nixdorf, 26, 71, 160
'No-strike deals', 180, 181
Nora/Minc Report, 18, 63, 103, 107, 170, 171, 183, 184
Nordic co-operation, 93–4
Nordic countries (see Sweden, Norway, Finland, Iceland and Denmark), 109
Norsk Data, 149f, 153, 160
Northern Telecom, 20, 59
North-Rhine-Westphalia (*Nordrhein-Westfalen*, West German *Land*), 175
Norway (Norwegian), 109, 149, 153, 160, 204, 208

OECD, 20, 30, 195, 199, 206, 208
Office automation (office systems), 150, 166, 175
Oftel, 33, 35, 39, 42, 44, 58, 60, 62

INDEX

Ohmae, K., 24, 25
Olivetti, 17, 24, 25, 149, 154, 159, 160, 168
Ombudsmen, 207
Optic-fibre (see Fibre-optic)
Optoelectronics (see Fibre-optic), 151, 191
Oracle (ITV), 98
Orwell, George, 196, 190
OSI ('Open standards interconnect' model of standardisation), 152, 153
OTV (West German Public Sector and Insurance Workers' Union), 187, 190

Paris, 100, 122, 171, 173
Parteienstaat, 176
Participation *Participation*, 164, 170, 172, 173, 181, 184
Partnership (i.e. Social Partnership), 169, 170, 176, 179
Peacock Committee, 39, 118, 120
Personal files, 195−211
Philips, 16, 17, 21, 25, 66, 148, 150, 154, 159, 175
Pilot Projects (i.e. Cable and Telematics), 106, 118, 119, 140, 173, 174
Plan Câble, 19, 32, 33−4, 36−8, 44, 64−5, 104, 107, 110, 15, 120, 172, 173, 185
Plan Calcul, 170, 201
Plessey, 24, 26, 58−62, 148, 150, 151, 154, 166
Planning contracts, 170
POEU (Post Office & Engineering Union), 167, 180
Police, the, 200, 201, 205, 207
Population numbering, 196, 200, 202, 206
Population registering, 198, 200, 201
Population Registration Bill (West Germany), 200
Portugal (Portuguese), 15, 149, 159
'Post-materialism', 176
'Post-industrial society', 4−6, 173, 179, 192
Premiere, 118
Press, the (see Publishers, Printing), 98, 99, 100, 104, 114, 115, 117, 118, 119, 128, 174
Prestel, 3, 38, 40, 52 n.12, 98, 115, 168
Printing (industry, sector etc.), 180, 181, 186
Privacy, 195−211, 214
Privatisation, 166, 167, 168, 185
Programme d'Action Filière Électronique (PAFE), 171
Programme Informatique à l'École, 171
Programme Télématique (telematics programme), 63−4, 103, 115, 170, 172, 173
Programm Technische Kommunikation, 174
Public-service broadcasters, 98−124, 125−46, 167

Publishers (see also Bertelsmann, Dupuis, Maxwell, Murdoch, Berlusconi, Hersant, Springer, Mandadori etc.), 14, 100, 106, 111, 113, 114, 115, 118, 120, 126, 135, 213

Quotas (programme), 100, 105
Quotron, 21, 27

Racal, 25, 36, 39, 58, 153
RACE (R & D in Advanced Communications-technologies for Europe), 15, 17, 20, 77, 96, 151, 155, 158, 213
Radio telephone, 148
RAI, 113, 114, 127
Rationalisation, 164, 168, 170, 177, 178, 179, 184, 186, 187, 188, 190
Rau, Johannes, 177
RCA, 14, 18, 20, 41
Reagan, President Ronald, 1, 12, 13
Rechtsstaat, 43, 45
Rediffusion, 25, 36, 37, 41, 103, 117, 120
Reed publishing, 128
Reform Law on Audiovisual Communications of July 1982 (French), 19, 44, 104
Rennes, 173
Research computer network, Europe, 149
Research, joint, 148, 153, 157
Research, pre-competitive, 150, 151
R & D (Research & Development), 148, 150, 151, 153, 154, 160, 161, 168, 169, 171, 176
Research and Technology Minister (France), 149
Research and Technology Ministry (W Germany), 174, 175, 176, 186
Restrictive practices, 181
Rette Quotro, 114−15
Reuters, 3, 6, 13, 18, 27−8
RFFU (West German Broadcasting Workers' Union), 187
Riesenhuber, Heinz, 175
Rigueur, 171
Rocard, Michel, 48, 67
Rolm, 14, 41, 59
Rome, 120
Rousselet, André, 105, 116
Royal Committee on Publicity and Secrecy (Sweden), 201
RPR/UDF, 30, 65, 67
RTL (*Radio Télévision Luxembourgeoise*), 26, 41, 100, 109, 110, 118
RTL-Plus, 3, 26, 109, 137

Saab-Scania, 91
Saatchi and Saatchi, 23, 24
Safari project (France), 201
Santer, Jacques, 110

SAT, 1, 3, 34, 109, 118, 119, 120
3 SAT, 3, 41, 119
Satellite(s) (programmes, systems, television, etc.), 1, 3, 98–125, 125–46, 148, 171, 177, 185, 195, 197, 212
Schmidt, Helmut, 106, 174, 191
School records, 202
Schwarz-Schilling, Christian, 34, 175
SDI (Strategic Defence Initiative), 1, 12, 25, 149, 156
SDP (British Social Democratic Party), 168, 169
Secrecy Act (Sweden), 201
Security (of data, information, etc.), 195–211
Security services, the, 205, 207
SEL (Standard Elektrik Lorenz), 26, 70
Select Committee on Home Affairs (Britain), 204
'Self-managing socialism' (*socialisme autogestionnaire*), 183
Semiconductors, 16, 21, 150, 155
Servan-Schreiber, Jacques, 170
SES (*Société Européenne de Satellites*), 110
Seydoux, Jérôme, 1, 15, 31, 38, 105, 111
'Shareholder-democracy', 167
Sheffield City Council, 168
Sherman, Barrie, 182
Shorter Working Week (see Thirty-five Hour Week), 164, 171, 178, 180, 187, 190
SIC (Standards Implementation Committee), 152
'Skills-gap', 170
Siemens, 17, 20, 25, 26, 66, 68, 70, 74, 75, 85, 147, 148, 150, 151, 153, 154, 159, 160, 168, 175
Sky Channel, 1, 3, 8, 21, 26, 117, 118, 120, 137
SLECs (*Sociétés Locales d'Exploitation Commercielle*), 104, 105
'Smart' electronic card, 148
W H Smith, 128
Social contract, the, 168
Social democrat (General), 101, 199, 201
Socialist Party (see French Socialist)
Social-Liberal government (West German, see SPD/FDP), 174
'Socially-oriented Technology Policy' (West German), 176, 177
Society of Conservative Lawyers (Britain), 202
Société Générale Belgique, 154
Software, 150, 151, 165
SOGAT 82 (Society of Graphical and Allied Trades), 181
SOGT (Senior Officials Group, EC), 151
Soviet Union, 2
Spain (Spanish), 15, 17, 149, 159, 208

Späth, Lothar, 175, 190
SPD (West German Social Democratic Government, Party, etc.), 29, 31, 34, 43, 48–9, 68, 70, 106, 107, 109, 110, 119, 135, 137, 164, 174, 175, 176, 177, 178, 186, 190, 191, 200, 201
Springer Group, 14, 25, 29, 100, 118, 128
Staatsvertrag (Inter-state Treaty, West Germany), 109, 120
Staff associations (replacing trade unions), 180
Standards, technical, 8, 11, 14, 15, 17, 20, 148, 149, 150, 151, 152, 153, 156, 158
Stock exchange reforms (see 'Big Bang'), 13, 18, 25, 27, 28, 181
Stockholm University, 201
STC, 41, 58–62
Stuttgart (in West Germany's 'silicon valley'), 190
Submicron lithography, 153
Superchannel, 41, 118, 120, 122
Supreme Administrative Court (Sweden), 201
Supreme Court (United States), 132
Surveillance, electronic, 176, 197
Sweden (Swedish), 7, 17, 25, 26, 48, 80–97, 109, 149, 150, 154, 159, 166, 176, 199, 200, 201, 203, 204, 205, 206, 208, 209, 212
Swedish Trade union Federation (LO), 80, 88
Switching (Telephone switching equipment, etc.), 2, 3, 7, 8, 11, 15, 16, 19, 20, 26, 148, 154, 166
Switzerland (Swiss), 109, 116, 149, 150
Symphonie satellite, 108
System X, 26, 58, 59–62, 86, 166, 180
Systems network architecture (SNA), 20

TDF *Télédiffusion de France*, 35, 108, 110
TDF 1, 1, 26, 36, 38, 41, 50, 108, 110, 111, 116, 117
Technical workers, 178–92
'Technological culture centres' (France), 171
'Technology gap', 147, 156, 159, 160, 174, 213
Telebanking, 98
Telecommunications, 98, 99, 100, 101, 102, 103, 105, 106, 107, 119, 125, 128, 136, 144, 147–62, 163–89, 212, 213–14
Telecommunications Act (1984), 18, 32, 35, 42, 44, 103, 166
Telecommunications monitoring equipment, 197
Telecom 1, 110
Teleconferencing, 172
Telefonica, 17, 25
Telematics, 2, 7, 11, 63, 108, 115, 170, 172, 173

INDEX   233

Telematics plan, French (see *Programme Télématique*)
Télétel, 3, 38, 98, 115, 119
Teleshopping, 98, 172
Teletext, 98, 119
Teletex, 153
Téleurop (Tve), 115
Televerket, 84–96
Teleworking (see Homeworking)
Tele X, 91–2
Terrorism, 202, 207, 208
Texas Instruments, 21
Thames TV, 17, 118
Thatcher, Margaret (Thatcherite, Thatcher Government, etc.), 30, 101, 102, 103, 166, 167, 170, 189
Thery, 64
Thirty-Five-Hour-Week (see Shorter Working Week)
Thomson, 16, 21, 26, 62–7, 91, 108, 148, 149, 150, 153
Thorn-EMI, 14, 24, 36, 41, 108, 117, 118, 120, 128
Toffler, Alvon, 4, 181
Toshiba, 17, 21
Trade Unions, 6, 7, 135, 142, 158, 164, 165, 169, 175, 176, 177, 178–92, 200, 206, 214
Training *formation* (re-training *reconversion*), 121, 168, 169, 170, 171, 172, 180, 183, 185, 198, 212
Treaty of Establishment of the EEC (see Treaty of Rome)
Treaty of Rome, 130, 131
'Trustee model of broadcasting', 125–46
TUC (British Trade Union Congress), 180, 182
Turkey (Turkish), 149
Turner, Ted, 17
TV 5, 3, 41, 116, 117
TV SAT, 108, 109, 118
Twentieth-Century Fox, 18, 41, 117, 118

UCC-CFDT (French Union of Engineers, Technicians and 'Cadres', see CFDT), 183, 184, 185
UGICA-CFTC (French Union of Engineers, Technicians and 'Cadres', see CFTC), 184
UGICT-CGT (French Union of Engineers, Technicians and 'Cadres', see CGT), 184, 185
'UK Ltd', 167, 182, 189
Unemployment, 163, 164, 169, 179, 181, 183
Unions (see Trade Unions)
UNISAT (United Satellites Limited), 108, 118, 120
United Kingdom (see Britain)
United Nations Covenant on Civil and Political Rights, 196

United States (American, US), 1, 2, 4, 14, 15, 16, 17, 20, 21, 22, 23, 26, 27, 30, 40, 41, 53 n. 28 and n. 34, 56, 62, 73–4, 99, 100, 101, 105, 110, 111, 113, 114, 115, 117, 120, 122, 125–46, 148, 154, 155, 160, 161, 170, 171, 174, 199, 204, 206, 208, 213
Universal Declaration of Human Rights, 196
Universities, 150, 157

Value-added (networks, services, etc.), 3, 8, 11, 39, 58, 59, 67, 98, 103, 167, 172, 208
VCRs (Video Cassette Recorders), 11, 14, 16, 19, 20, 21, 40, 52 n. 11, 98, 99, 164
Vélizy, 173
Videoconferencing, 11, 13
Videophone, 172
Videotex, 3, 8, 11, 14, 26, 38, 89, 98, 103, 104, 115, 119, 170, 172, 173, 174, 177, 178, 187, 208
Viewdata, 166
Virgin Group, 14, 108, 118, 120
Visual telephone signals (see Videophone), 152
VNU (Netherlands), 113

Wang, 148
Walden, Brian, 202
WARC (World Administration Radio Conference), 38, 40, 121
Warner Brothers, 118
Weber, Max, 4
Welfare state, the, 197
West Midlands Enterprise Board, 169
Whitechapel Computers Works, 150
Whitecollar workers (and the 'communications revolutions'), 178–94
White Paper on Data Protection (Britain), 203, 204
Willis, Norman, 182
'Wired society', 2, 102, 167, 170, 172, 174
Witte Commission, 32, 45, 68, 73, 74
Word-processors, 164

Xerox, 148

Younger Committee, 202
Younger Report, 196, 203, 204

ZDF (*Zweites Deutsches Fernsehen*), 22, 127, 119
Zentralverband der Elektrotechnischen Industrie, 69
Zimmermann, Lothar, 186